Chicago
Renaissance

Books by DALE KRAMER

Heywood Broun

Ross and the *New Yorker*

The Heart of O. Henry

Violent Streets

The Wild Jackasses

Chicago

Renaissance

THE LITERARY LIFE
IN THE MIDWEST
1900–1930

by DALE KRAMER

Appleton-Century   New York

6/1967
Senl.

First edition

APPLETON-CENTURY
AFFILIATE OF
MEREDITH PRESS

Library of Congress Catalog Card Number: 66-22240

MANUFACTURED IN THE UNITED STATES OF AMERICA FOR MEREDITH PRESS

VAN REES PRESS • NEW YORK

To my friend Angus Cameron,
who suggested this book

ACKNOWLEDGMENTS

The author wishes to acknowledge with thanks permission to quote from the following works:

From *The Journals of Arnold Bennett*. Copyright 1932, © 1960 by The Viking Press, Inc. Reprinted by permission of The Viking Press, Inc.

From *Homecoming* by Floyd Dell. Copyright 1933, © 1961 by Floyd Dell. Reprinted by permission of Holt, Rinehart and Winston, Inc.

"Docks," "They Will Say," "Blacklisted," "Mamie," "Harrison Street Court" and "To a Contemporary Bunkshooter" from *Chicago Poems* by Carl Sandburg. Copyright 1916 by Holt, Rinehart and Winston, Inc. Copyright 1944 by Carl Sandburg. Reprinted by permission of Holt, Rinehart and Winston, Inc.

From *Always the Young Strangers* by Carl Sandburg, published by Harcourt, Brace & World, Inc., by permission of Harcourt, Brace & World, Inc.

"On the Building of Springfield," "The Illinois Village," and "The Proud Farmer" reprinted with permission of The Macmillan Company from "A Gospel of Beauty" in *General William Booth Enters into Heaven* by Vachel Lindsay. Copyright 1913 The Macmillan Company.

"The Tree of Laughing Bells, or The Wings of the Morning," "General William Booth Enters into Heaven," and "Springfield Magical" reprinted with permission of The Macmillan Company from *General William Booth Enters into Heaven* by Vachel Lindsay. Copyright 1913 The Macmillan Company.

"The Congo" and "The Sante-Fe Trail (Humoresque)" reprinted with the permission of The Macmillan Company from *The Congo and Other Poems* by Vachel Lindsay. Copyright 1914 The Macmillan Company, renewed 1942 by Elizabeth C. Lindsay.

"The Village Improvement Parade" reprinted with permission of The Macmillan Company from *Collected Poems* by Vachel Lindsay. Copyright 1923 The Macmillan Company, renewed 1951 by Elizabeth C. Lindsay.

"The Lame Boy and the Fairy" reprinted with permission of The Macmillan Company from *The Golden Whales of California* by Vachel Lindsay. Copyright 1920 The Macmillan Company, renewed 1948 by Elizabeth C. Lindsay.

Contents

III
BURST OF TRUMPETS

IV
PROPHETS IN THEIR RAGS

I

Six Poor Boys in
Search of Themselves

1

A Time and a Place

> The map on the wall of the railroad station—the map with a picture of iron roads from all over the Middle West centering on a dark blotch.
> "Chicago!" he said to himself.... The rhythm of a word that said itself over and over in his mind: "Chicago! Chicago!"
>
> —from *Moon-Calf,* by Floyd Dell

AT the turn of the century that raucous yet lilting beat— "Chicago! Chicago!"—pulsed in the blood of all the adventurous young of the great United States hinterland. Any farmer who had ridden a hog train caboose to market was a glamorous figure, to be listened to with awe. Quite saga enough was the account of a meal in a stockyard beanery (wisecracks to the waitress and hers back) and a night in a drovers' hotel. If a man spoke knowingly of the sinful Levee, of schooners of beer in Hinky Dink's saloon, a ride in a skyscraper elevator—well, unless he was a liar he was a dangerous liver.

Into the annals of every small town had gone the local banker's account of personally watching the frantic bidding in the "pit" as rumors flew that "Old Hutch" was out to corner wheat. The greenest rube knew that "pit" or "floor" meant the Board of Trade and that "Old Hutch" was Benjamin P. Hutchinson, the legendary speculator. One could believe or not the tales of the wastrel son of a local high-muckety-muck spending a hundred dollars in a single night's carousal in that gorgeous palace for libertines, the Everleigh Club. Most believed.

This was only the tinsel. The deeper lure of Chicago was the money chance for the fellow with hustle. As one of Henry Blake Fuller's characters remarked in his novel, *The Cliff-Dwellers:* "Here is a town full to overflowing with single men. They come from everywhere, for all reasons. They are taken on faith, largely, and are treated pretty well." The facts amply bore him out. Had not the merchant king, Marshall Field, risen from clerk in a Chicago dry-goods store? Wasn't it on record that Gustavus Swift had butchered his own animals and sold them from his peddler's wagon? These and a dozen other glories were told around every Midwestern cracker barrel.

Henry Fuller had another character, this one from *With the Procession,* declare that Chicago was "the only great city in the world to which all its citizens have come for one common, avowed object. ... In this Garden City of ours every man cultivates his own little bed and his neighbor his." The boosters, of course, had invented the Garden City label, as well as the earlier Gem of the Prairies. The term Windy City had sprung up on its own. When one of Fuller's characters used it, another remarked sardonically, "Don't abuse our wind; we should all die like flies without it." Another agrees that "the wind is our only scavenger."

As a man born into the upper crust, Fuller was at his best describing pink teas, footmen in knee breeches, and other affectations of the social leaders. Yet his glimpses under the crust were accurate enough, even though seen as from a distance. In *With the Procession* ("Keep up with the procession is my motto, and head it if you can") a lady and her coachman and a mare named Mabel faced the perils of street traffic:

> The grimy lattice-work of the drawbridge swung to slowly, the steam-tug blackened the dull air and roiled the turbid water as it dragged its schooner on toward the lumberyards of the South Branch, and a long line of waiting vehicles took up their interrupted course through the smoke and the stench. ... A junk-cart ... a bespattered buggy. ... Then some street-carts; then a butcher's cart ... an insolently venturesome landau, with crested panel and top-booted coachman. ...
>
> ... Brazen blare and gaudy placards (disgusting rather than indecent) invited the passerby into cheap museums and music-halls; all the unclassifiable riffraff that is spawned by a great city leered from corners, or slouched along the edge of the gutters, or stood in dark doorways. ...
>
> A big lumpish figure on the crossing had loomed up at the mare's head, a rough hand had seized her bridle, and a raw voice with a rawer brogue had vented a piece of impassioned profanity on both beast and driver.

"Well, I don't thank that policeman for hitting Mabel on the nose, I can tell him. August, did you get his number?"

"No, 'm," answered the coachman. "I got his breath."

Fuller employed the satirist's license in declaring that *all* had come *only* to make money. The heroine of Hamlin Garland's *Rose of Dutcher's Coolly* had left her Wisconsin farm home to seek the exuberant freedom of a poet in tumultuous Chicago. And if she was fictional, the Art Institute in which Garland had placed her—there being no formal school for poets—was not. Even Fuller portrayed a few moneyless artists and writers in his *Under the Skylights*.

Fuller's sensitive-nosed description of the public library in *The Cliff-Dwellers* showed an intellectual ferment at work in the humble masses. The protagonist was in the main room when the windows were shut against the rain. "The downpour seemed but a trifle compared with the confused cataract of conflicting nationalities within, and the fumes of incense that the united throng caused to rise upon the altar of learning stunned him with a sudden and sickening surprise—the bogs of Kilkenny, the dung-heaps of the Black Forest, the miry ways of Transylvania and Little Russia had all contributed to it."

Mighty true-life barons walked the Chicago streets: hotel-owner-financier Potter Palmer, Marshall Field, Gustavus Swift and fellow packer P. D. Armour, railroad magnate George Pullman, and newspaper publisher Joseph Medill. With luck one might glimpse, by day, the stately Mrs. Potter Palmer driving in her brougham, or by night, bedecked with jewels, riding in her carriage. The lowest might look upon the battlements of Palmer Castle, showpiece of the Gold Coast on the lake. The average mind boggled at the newspaper visions: Louis XVI salon, Gothic-pillared hall, Spanish music room, Moorish ballroom, Flemish Renaissance library, English drawing-room. Word had been let out that Mrs. Palmer washed her hands in a basin inlaid with mother-of-pearl, soaked in a sunken tub formed like a swan, and took her repose in a King Louis bed under a silken canopy ten feet high. Where Potter bathed or slept was of little moment. It was enough that the barber shop of his great hotel was paved with silver dollars.

A gangling, open-mouthed young easy-payment collector named Theodore Dreiser had witnessed the great sights, while with equal excitement hearing the noisy strains of a tumultuous orchestra striking harsh but somehow grand notes at a feast where he ate and drank "in a delirium of ecstasy." In the vice districts he had been accustomed to "plump naked girls striding from bed to dresser to get a purse"—after failure to reduce the bill by exchanging certain favors —and had marveled at the regions "crowded with great black factories, stockyards, Pullman yards, where in the midst of Plutonian stress and clang men mixed or forged or joined or prepared those delicacies, pleasures and perfection for which the world buys and sells itself." In the very slums the promise of life had seemed to him glittering. "Raw neighborhoods where in small, unpainted, tumbledown shanties set in grassless, can-strewn yards drunken and lecherous slatterns and brawlers were to be found mooning about in a hell of their own. . . ."

Specters of the anarchists hanged after the Haymarket Square bombing in 1886 walked the city and subtly imbued the air. Seven of the police dispersing a meeting in the square had been killed, others wounded, by the bomb thrown by an unknown hand. Amidst wild hysteria, seven anarchists had been tried for conspiracy and sentenced to death. Four had been hanged, one had been a suicide, the sentence of two had been reduced to life in prison, and an eighth suspect had been given fifteen years. There had been the omen of August Spies crying through his gallows hood: "Our silence will be more powerful than the voice you strangle today." His voice was still heard from the lips of his widow-by-proxy, a socialite who, falling in love with him during a visit to prison, had married him, at least in her own eyes—his brother had stood in at the ceremony. So, too, was heard the voice of beautiful, dark Lucy Parsons, wife of eloquent Albert Parsons, the leader, who had walked from hiding to join his comrades in death.

Did this atmosphere hold the various ingredients necessary for creation of a major new literary movement—the sort of thing critics and historians in due time might call a Renaissance? Surely the country was ready for one. More than half a century had gone by since the massive New England "flowering" of Emerson, Thoreau, Lowell, Whittier, Longfellow, Holmes, and their lesser associates. Other regions had had their great figures—Washington Irving and Whitman and Melville around New York, Joel Chandler Harris and George W. Cable in the South, Bret Harte and Ambrose Bierce in the West—but none had produced a sufficient quantity at a roughly given time to be called a group or movement. So far the Middle West had not raised up giants. Mark Twain might be claimed, of course, but only by ignoring the touch of the South, a good deal of the West, and even some Eastern influences.

Both Henry Fuller and Hamlin Garland belonged to the realistic-naturalistic school which was being given fairly wide attention. In the East, Stephen Crane's frankly sordid *Maggie: A Girl of the Streets* had been a distinct break with the gushing romanticism of the period, and his *Red Badge of Courage* had, although relating the unheroic behavior and feelings of a common soldier, won almost popular success. Frank Norris had openly emulated Zola, founder of the naturalistic school, in his *McTeague,* the tale of a greedy unlicensed dentist who murders his wife for her savings, and in *The Octopus,* wherein farmers are crushed by great railroad powers. The novels of the older William Dean Howells, leader of the native realists, were less stark than Crane's and Norris's, but as an influential critic and editor his advice to write honestly what one knew best was having an impact on younger authors.

The trouble with Fuller and Garland as possible leaders of a peculiarly Midwestern or even Chicago movement was that neither was a wholehearted realist either as an artist or as an individual. Garland had been once. A poor Iowa-Wisconsin farm boy, he had worked his way through Harvard, fallen under the spell of Howells (then editing the *Atlantic Monthly*), called on Walt Whitman, and in 1891 broken new realistic soil with his *Main-Travelled Roads,* grim tales of Midwestern rural existence. For his *Crumbling Idols* a few years later he had prophesied the shift of "literary supremacy" from the East to the Mississippi Valley, and to prove his faith had settled in Chicago. Unhappily, he appeared to have aged beyond his forty years as the century turned. For one thing, he had become a "literary man," if not exactly a lion. He was large, gregarious, aware of making a distinguished figure in his frock coat. Having lost touch with the farmlands without really coming to know the city, he was fonder of talking about writing than of describing, after careful observation, the lives of ordinary people.

Henry Fuller, too, was a comparatively young man, reaching forty-three as the century changed. In repose his finely chiseled bearded face looked patrician, which was fitting since he came of a distinguished "old" wealthy Chicago family. His manner, however, was shy almost to furtiveness. He had never married, and he lived in rooming houses and took his meals in obscure restaurants. Why he had chosen to write two novels in the realistic vein is not clear, unless he wanted to express his dislike for the ugliness of many phases of his native city. The life that appealed to his imagination was the long-ago romance of the Old World, such as he had pictured in *The Chevalier of Pensieri-Vani,* which to some critics had been reminiscent of Stendhal. That book had been published in 1890. *The Cliff-Dwellers* had appeared in 1893, *With the Procession* in 1896. Whether Fuller's realistic period had ended remained to be seen.

As it happened, a Chicago novel with the strength to lead the way, written by a man steeped in the depths of Midwestern rural and urban existence, was published on the very nose of the beginning of the new century. This book was Theodore Dreiser's *Sister Carrie.* For the time being, though, its power was not widely felt since distribution had been small. For one thing, its publisher had belatedly decided that the title figure was not properly chastised for adultery, and he had done little to encourage sales.

Chicago would have to keep on growing, and vigorous young men and women, mostly from the little towns, would have to take up sharp weapons before the region and the city could emerge into literary glory.

At the end of the first decade of the twentieth century, Chicago's population had grown to roughly two millions and a quarter. The last huge immigrant waves had been the Italians and the Jews. No language, not even English, dominated the cacophony of this modern-day Babel. The black factories, stockyards, steelworks had at least quadrupled in belch and stench since the nineties. Traveling notables chose one or more of the epithets from the standard hellbox—raw, ugly, chaotic, turbulent, brutal, frenzied—but granted Chicago's lusty will-to-do. "Chicago hustle," the boosters called it.

The city's position on the western shore of Lake Michigan had been a handicap to area terminology. The business Loop, named for the noose of elevated railroad tracks, was the center semantically but far from geographically. Lake Michigan made an East Side out of the question. The Near North Side began across the narrow Chicago River from the Loop. Where it became the North Side was a matter of opinion. The South Side was yet without a "Near." At first these Sides had been hemmed by river branches running almost parallel with the lake, and they remained so in common thought. This left a gigantic amorphous West Side with its outer borders, said hardy travelers, at Mexico and Alaska and the Pacific Ocean.

The West Side was mostly a working-class section, the Great Fire of 1871 having, by and large, driven out the wealthier classes. On the South Side, Prairie Avenue, the old street of the Marshall Fields and P. D. Armours, was growing unfashionable. The red-light Levee on the South Side was, despite the increasing raids of the police under pressure from the moral element, outlasting Prairie Avenue's gilded castles. The elite of the Near North Side as well as from the West Side and Prairie Avenue had followed or were following the Palmers to the Gold Coast, which might have been called North Side except that it seemed to run all by itself up the lake shore. Naturally the residents of the Gold Coast had not originated the name. The newspaper reporters had—to the secret joy of the Gold Coasters.

The limestone mansions of the Near North Side had survived the Great Fire of 1871. Strolling up from the Loop, with its skyscrapers (of which Chicagoans were so proud), one passed through the aromatic river-bank market with its spice bins and fruit stalls and vegetable wagons, into the region which was now changing to a bohemian colony. Carriage houses and stables were being turned into studios, the manors themselves chiefly into rooming or boarding houses. Another bohemia, one of the more curious of the world, had taken form on the South Side near the lake at Jackson Park. Two rows of one-story shops had been thrown up for concessionaires for the 1893 World's Columbian Exposition, or World's Fair, as it was generally known. These old shops had been taken over as residences by painters, writers, and others in allied fields. Into these bohemias of the Near North and South Sides young men and women of high hearts were moving.

As elsewhere in the land, radicals were lifting voices growing ever stronger. The Socialist Party was growing by leaps and bounds; the number of sympathizers even faster. Not many spoke of "dictatorship of the proletariat" or any other iron power. Socialism was to be a brilliant, lovely, kindly world—a sort of rosy dream. The capitalists, those cruel exploiters, would be voted out of power, after which good things of life would be showered upon all amidst equal rights in a golden democracy.

Even the adventurous young of the upper classes were plunging into social revolt and the havens of bohemia. One example, Joseph Medill Patterson, was a chief heir to the august Chicago *Tribune*. He wore a Socialist badge and was the author of a flaming novel. At least the upper classes thought of it as flaming, and so did he. His new comrades were not quick to disabuse him of the notion.

Some thought that the anarchists were subordinating politics to "kissing games." It was a fact that Emma Goldman, the most famous of the lot, fell into more trouble with the law over her denunciations of "bourgeois" love and marriage than for political agitation. Newspaper editors seeking to titillate readers had but to rail mightily against "Red Emma" and "free love." In Chicago Emma always received notable attention from the police as well as from audiences. A favorite cohort here was huge, leonine, flowing-caped Ben Reitman, her certified ex-lover and now her lecture agent. She called him the master of the first phase, but claimed he was fickle.

Other prophets were demanding that in a great soul-love the personality must be allowed to blossom unhampered, the spirit to soar in freedom. Even a woman's—well, particularly a woman's. In the *Evening Post*'s literary section the Swedish oracle Ellen Key, whose daring *Love and Marriage* was having a great vogue in the United States, carried a description of the Woman of the Future:

> She is chaste, not because she is cold, but because she is passionate. She is noble, not because she is pale, but because she is full-blooded. She is soulful, and therefore sensuous; she is proud and therefore true. She demands a great love because she can give an even greater. Her refined idealism will make the erotic problem very difficult and sometimes insoluble. But, on the other hand, she will be able to feel and give a happiness that is much deeper, richer and most lasting.... She will dedicate her best strength to the difficult art of being a mistress and a mother.... She is many women and yet always one.

The city felt the disconcerting impact of fifty thousand homeless men. Ben Reitman had crowned himself King of the Hoboes. The proud term hobo was often misunderstood. A hobo traveled widely and sought work at least some of the time; a tramp was footloose but would not work; a bum was a stationary tramp. Chicago was the staging area for the great hordes of the Northwest who worked the harvests and the loggings and other seasonal jobs. They, too, gave a subtle charge to the atmosphere.

A more precise title for Ben might have been Minister of Culture. At the moment he was getting up a College of Hoboes with the help of a young angel fallen out of the rich bourgeoisie. Hoboes were smart; tests showed them well above average in intelligence. Tattered books and pamphlets, usually having to do with social rebellion, were common baggage. The ranks were salted with natural philosophers and even ex-professors who felt more at ease outside the pale. Young men forced to the road by hard times or wanderlust were treated to a down-with-the-system education in lumber camps and harvest bivouacs and off-season flophouses. Those who subsequently climbed over the pale—and they were numerous—often carried their rebellion along.

If the hoboes had a king, he was one-eyed Big Bill Haywood, a silver miner at nine and a one-time cowboy. Accounts of the Haymarket trials had launched him on a stormy path, including a famous trial of his own for bomb murder. At thirty-six he had presided over the founding convention of the Industrial Workers of the World—better known as the IWW's or the Wobblies. Naturally the scene had been Chicago. He was the president, the headquarters still were here, and the Wobbly red card was a prized possession of a vast number of hoboes.

It had been no wonder that young Upton Sinclair, the most starry-eyed of the Socialists, had journeyed from the East to Chicago for the material for his sensational novel, *The Jungle*. Several groups might have served to make his point, but only his choice of the slaughterhouse workers for characters and his depiction of the foul conditions under which meat was prepared could have so turned the nation's stomach.

The rich Founders of the city had been satisfied, by and large, with their reputation for shrewd and often ruthless hustle. Their children, especially the daughters, blushed when strangers, usually abroad, spoke of their city as Porkopolis and kept referring to their fortunes as "pork money." These strangers also talked too much of "brazen crime" and "anarchy." The result was lavish expenditures for "culture." The greatest offering had been the magnificent Auditorium of lower Michigan Avenue, designed by the gifted architect Louis Sullivan, aided by youthful Frank Lloyd Wright. Then it was the home of grand opera and contained a grand hotel in the bargain. Next to it up the avenue stood the ornate Fine Arts Building with its theaters, a bookstore designed by Wright, and expansive and gracious studios of sculptors, painters, and musicians.

One of the studios was the meeting place for an oddly named literary group, the Little Room, fostered by novelists Garland and Fuller. On the whole it was in the genteel tradition, although careful not to feature celebrated visiting speakers. Fuller had some years ago been quite funny about "the uplift movement" in the *Atlantic Monthly*, describing his fellow Chicagoans as sitting about open-mouthed waiting to swallow any pearls tossed out by traveling lions.

The Fine Arts Building and the Auditorium, plus the latter's hotel annex, called simply The Annex, on the other side of Congress Street, was a remarkably lovely complex. The Annex was famed for its worldliness, especially its block-long Peacock Alley decorated with nudes and onyx columns, a stunning glass fountain, lush sofas, a fine restaurant, and a gallery of art. A promenade inside and under the three palaces could be a satisfying experience. "One might receive a baptism of intellectual or even spiritual stimulus in the Fine Arts Building," one of its tenants, Ralph Fletcher Seymour, etcher and fine printer, was to say, "move south to the Auditorium bar to fortify the temporarily neglected body with expertly concocted drinks, pass through the marble-lined rabbit burrow to The Annex, there repose on a soft divan and watch a pleasant and not very spiritual segment of life, or sit between classic pillars alongside the finest fountain in the world and eat pompano, then proceed to the Reinhart Galleries and stock up on art."

To this rough yet genteel Chicago came dedicated poets, novelists, and editors who created what would be called the Chicago Literary Renaissance. The sudden meeting of hinterland youth with the boiling city was surely to a large extent responsible for it.

2

Floyd Dell

FEW small-town lads ever had their high-school poems accepted by *Harper's* and *Century* and *McClure's,* as Floyd Dell's were. Nor had many been, like him, a card-carrying Socialist and religious freethinker at fifteen. Dell nevertheless fitted a certain pattern: the dreamy, sensitive boy or girl of impoverished family whose thoughts roamed to conquests of artistic worlds, the kind in whom a teacher or librarian saw the fire and felt the iron and urged, "Go try!"

Some time later Dell grew into the very picture of a gay, brave, poetically handsome city bohemian, indeed the acknowledged Prince of New York's Greenwich Village, lover of the haunting Edna St. Vincent Millay, his name a synonym for uninhibited, reckless love. He would sit nonchalantly in court as the Government sought his life for, so it claimed, treason in the first World War. He was to be, too, a well-known editor, a successful novelist, a Broadway playwright.

Yet his most important work was done in the first blush of young manhood, as a book critic on the one hand and on the other a personal leader among the young men and women of Chicago who were assaulting old traditions on their way to making a literary Renaissance. It was as though he had come fully armed into the world, from the unlikeliest of parents and an environment which would have to be labeled incredible had not others sprung from similar sources.

Dell's first home town was Barry, in Pike County, southwest from Chicago almost to Mark Twain country. Hannibal lies across the Mississippi River a few miles downstream. In those days local citizens took pride in John Hay's famous *Pike County Ballads*, with river pilot Jim Bludso crying out from his burning ship:

> I'll hold her nozzle agin the bank
> Till the last galoot's ashore.

—even if Hay, after marrying money and becoming Secretary of State, wanted to forget the rough idiom of prairie and river which had seemed appropriate while he was Abraham Lincoln's private secretary.

Pike County was old, measured in pioneer time, when butcher boy Anthony Dell rode off to help save the Union. In size Tony was half a pint but his fierce horsemanship was equalizer enough. His flesh tasted the hot rebel steel, but he survived. After the war life was good. Besides a farm trading post, the town had a woolen mill. Tony opened his own butcher shop, prospered, and married school teacher Kate Crone, a gentle Irish girl. They soon had a brood of three: Charles, Harry, and Cora. Tony himself was of Pennsylvania Dutch stock. He enjoyed recounting deeds of war and talked up the Republican party, as befitted a man who had served with President Grant and risen into the moneyed class.

Grant was long out of the White House and Tony out of the moneyed class when the third Dell son, Floyd, arrived on June 28, 1887. The meat market had slipped from Tony's grasp—he just wasn't a good business man for the long haul—and after a time as employee he had been reduced to wage hand in the woolen mill. Floyd was to know only a beaten, although kindly, father. To Kate Dell this son of her forties, with his golden hair and blue eyes and delicate features, was a solace and a refuge. She was frail, more poetic now than when she had fallen in love with the cavalryman. She curled the boy's hair much too long, both in time and length. To shelter a child in a small town is very hard. Later Dell was to wryly describe his mother's effort to help him "help the poor" during the Panic of 1893 when he was six:

> That fall, before it was discovered that the soles of both my shoes were worn clear through, I still went to Sunday school. And one time the Sunday school superintendent made a speech to all the classes. He said that these were hard times, and that many poor children weren't getting enough to eat. It was the first that I had heard about it. He asked everybody to bring some food for the poor next Sunday. I felt very sorry for the poor children.

Also, little envelopes were distributed to all the classes. Each little boy and girl was to bring some money for the poor, next Sunday. The pretty Sunday school teacher explained that we were to write our names, or have our parents write them, up in the left-hand corner of the little envelopes. . . . I told my mother all about it when I came home. And my mother gave me, the next Sunday, a small bag of potatoes to carry to Sunday school. I suppose the poor children's mothers would make potato soup out of them. . . . Potato soup was good. My father, who was quite a joker, would always say, as if he were surprised, "Ah! I see we have some nourishing potato soup today!" It was so good that we had it every day. My father was at home all day long and every day, now; and I liked that, even if he was grumpy as he sat reading Grant's *Memoirs*.

Taking my small bag of potatoes to Sunday school, I looked around for the poor children; I was disappointed not to see them. I had heard about poor children in stories. But I was told just to put my contribution with the others on the big table in the side room.

I had brought with me the little yellow envelope, with some money in it for the poor children. My mother had put the money in it and sealed it up. She wouldn't tell me how much money she had put in it, but it felt like several dimes. Only she wouldn't let me put my name on the envelope. I had learned to write my name, and was proud of being able to do it. But my mother said firmly, no, I must *not* write my name on the envelope; she didn't tell me why. On the way to Sunday school I had pressed the envelope against the coins until I could tell what they were; they weren't dimes but pennies.

When I handed in my envelope, my Sunday school teacher noticed that my name wasn't on it, and she gave me a pencil; I could write my own name, she said. So I did. But I was confused because my mother had said not to; and when I came home, I confessed what I had done. She looked distressed. "I told you not to!" she said. But she didn't explain why. . . .

The lad, driven inward by the family misfortunes, needed to create a better world of his own. Already he had found words leaping out of a page at him. He could read! His mother had been enthralled, and why not? Here was a beautiful golden boy with golden gifts, for to the intelligent poor, education meant hope. Fragile and intro-spective, and discovering the eyes of the pretty little girls on brawny somersaulters, the boy made do with an imaginary girl living in the attic. The public library was a refuge. He lived the simple life with

Robinson Crusoe, soared with Jules Verne to the moon, suffered nobly with Mark Twain's prince who was a pauper, stood with Horatio at the bridge, and scorned pomp with the Count of Monte Cristo.

For the aging Tony, only two havens remained: his war deeds and stout Republicanism. Young Floyd glowed to the battle tales and stood with his father against the wild-eyed Populists and Bryan Democrats seeking to defile the Gold Standard. When a copy of the Socialist paper *Appeal to Reason* came into his hands he renamed it "Appeal to Treason," as the old soldier nodded approvingly. Yet Socialists in Pike County were not pariahs as individuals. One of his father's best friends was white-bearded Jim Houseweart, whose debt-free farm had gas lights in the house and barn, fueled from his own well. Floyd could not help notice the irony when sound—and soundly mortgaged—Republican farmers called Jimmy an impractical visionary because of his Socialists ideas.

There were rebellious roots deep in the native soil. In the seventies Illinois had been at the heart of the Granger revolt against monopolies, especially the railroads. Farmers had marched on the legislature as their fringe-whiskered leader, Steve Smith, muttered darkly of hangings or at least tar-and-featherings of enemies of the common people. A freight-regulatory law had been won, and when a judge ruled it unconstitutional he was beaten at the polls. By capturing one legislative house the Grangers had frightened the old-line politicians into ending the worst abuses. While the eye of the storm had moved west to Kansas, there remained plenty of rebels of all shades. The iconoclast was a part of the frontier. In a good neighbor queer ideas were overlooked. You needed a good neighbor. Who could say what new, even outlandish notion would prove valuable. The most entertaining of the orators were dissenters. God-fearing people would hitch up and drive hours to hear Colonel Robert G. Ingersoll, the Great Infidel, on "The Mistakes of Moses."

The Colonel's stamping ground had been in Peoria, only a hundred miles from Barry, and the churchly had still to counter his influence. A well-meaning soul handed young Floyd a book disputing the Infidel. He read it, turned to Ingersoll's own works, and became a doubter. The enchantment of war instilled by Tony was routed by Floyd's brother Charles. He had come home from the Spanish-American war with his health and spirit too low for carrying out his ambition to go in search of Chicago gold. He settled for

Quincy, a small nearby river city. A little while later the rest of the Dells followed him there.

The Quincy library was larger, and Floyd, about to enter high school, widened his horizons, moving all the way to Russian Nihilism. Goals of respectability and fine manners went out, heroic struggle against tyranny came in. A little red pamphlet depicting Socialism as bringing with it beauty as well as economic freedom came into his hands. The beauty aspect appealed to him, since rather unexpectedly he had begun writing poetry. He listened to a Socialist street orator (the man happened to be a park cleaner but wasn't on duty) and began attending local party meetings in a jewelry store back room. Only half a dozen others came but he was not despondent over the magnitude of the task of overhauling the social order.

After the Dells had been in Quincy for a year or so, Floyd landed a summer's job with a candymaker and enjoyed the delicious sweets of love for a Socialist girl. Bittersweet, which was prophetic. Then, in 1902, the family moved upriver a hundred miles to Davenport.

The tri-cities of Davenport, on the Iowa side, and Rock Island and Moline, on the Illinois side, totaled a population of a hundred thousand. Davenport, the main river port and commercial center, was a mellowing old city (by frontier standards), proud of its wide streets and parks, its stately homes, and its history. Close by, Black Hawk, banished to Iowa, had led his Sacs and Foxes back toward his Illinois village, only to be crushed by U.S. troops. Enough time—seventy years—had elapsed for a younger generation to hail the forest-prairie red men for seeking liberty over virtual slavery.

There was a large German element in Davenport, much of it descended from freedom-loving intellectual refugees from the ill-fated revolution of 1848. Cultural and political activities flowed in the big Turner Hall. The German Jews were well represented and as usual they were influential in the cultural life out of proportion to their numbers. The well-to-do older families, Gentiles and Jews alike, sent their sons to Eastern colleges and often for a few terms abroad. Girls went off to finishing schools and to Europe for the Grand Tour. Davenport's one famous author, Octave Thanet, was proudly claimed, and the works of younger men and women—Susan Glaspell, George Cram Cook, Arthur Davison Ficke—pointed to.

The Dells arrived by river steamer, moved the family goods of three and a half decades into a working-class house, and the three older children found steady jobs. Even with hair and mustache dyed, old cavalryman Tony gained only odd jobs. All agreed that Floyd, now fifteen, must pursue his education, working at the candy trade only during vacations. He did not quite share the family's hope. As he saw it his future lay in a factory job, a wife, a little house—and in that house a night-poet writing verses for his own pleasure—even after the mighty Philistines had been hurled from their Davenport mansions, a fate he anticipated with some glee.

He made a beeline for his tested sanctuaries, the public library and the Socialist Party. The librarian was a goddess—tall and slender, light of step, wide-browed, with soft, dark hair, gray-blue eyes, and a tender whimsical mouth. Worship of this divine spirit in the sacred precincts was, he felt, his proper role. From a distance, of course, as she went serenely in and out of her private office. Even the cocking of his ears to her soft impetuous voice seemed within reason.

What consternation to be suddenly accosted among the book stacks with out-thrust friendly hand, and, "I'm Marilla Freeman. You're Floyd Dell, aren't you?" His own name on the lips of the goddess!

Marilla Freeman was hardly to be censured. Besides a creature of Olympus she was a dedicated librarian, and such individuals, who spend a whole lifetime handing out sentimental novels, guiding reluctant students to Lincolniana, helping club ladies with papers on James Fenimore Cooper, are not to be denied when a talented youth hunts out dusty classics and reads them for pleasure. To this lad, gazelle-handsome, tall for his age, fair (although the yellow hair had darkened), and quite probably lost, she talked of his poem written for a school volume. But it was only an excuse for confrontation. He must be taken in hand, encouraged, taught poetic discipline, readied for greatness in the world of letters.

In the months ahead he fought against her hopelessly. As she saw it, one need was for him to be made acquainted with cultivated adults, which meant taking him into the very houses he had vowed to pull down. One of those belonged to the legal counsel for the Rock Island railroad, Edward Cook. Cook's grandfather, having arrived from the East while Black Hawk was in chains, had eased the way for his son, Edward's father, to be a member of the Territorial Council and of the U.S. Congress as well as a prominent lawyer and financier. The old Cook Bank Building was now the Cook Library. Floyd sipped his tea, disapproving of the talk he heard.

Most of it came from a dark, big, thirtyish man with brooding eyes and a lock of gray hair which he twisted morosely.

This was George Cram Cook, the writer, second son of the house, outlining what he called an ideal society. It was to be drawn from Nietzschean-autocratic concepts with its base on a slavery like that of ancient Greece. The visiting young Socialist was not surprised. The fellow had had all the advantages—education at numerous colleges, leisure enough for writing a novel (a romantic tale of the Maximilian Empire), and to wallow in ancient Greek lore. A truck farmer now, to be sure—but on the Cook River acres with the help of a Cook slave, or at least an old Negro family retainer. It was all Floyd could do to keep a polite tongue in his head.

The Socialist Party, after being oddly elusive, materialized suddenly as he was locked in verbal combat with a street-orating Philistine lackey. A cheerful party member named Fritz Feuchter, who had been listening, invited Floyd to a glass of beer in nearby Turner Hall and afterward to be a member of the Socialist local. He quickly accepted and soon was a leading functionary. As it turned out, the wisdom and courage of big Fritz, a mail carrier, was just what he needed. Father Tony was a good companion, able to defend his stout Republicanism genially over a pail of beer. What he lacked was a worldliness Floyd could admire. As for his mother, she was doting as ever but with little knowledge of his requirements. (Nearly two decades later she was to write to him after reading his autobiographical *Moon-Calf*. "Your novel is very amusing to me and I like it but there are some things that I don't understand. To know if my little boy was really so unhappy when I was sure he was the most contented and happy little boy I had ever seen.")

Others gave stimulus. Rabbi William Fineshriber, young, unorthodox, a searcher, became the boy's friend. An elderly journalist-poet, Charles Eugene Banks, labored with him on his verses. But when *McClure's* offered to buy one if a few changes were accepted, a hammerlock by the librarian-goddess was required to get his consent. (The poem was not used, however, for another couple of years.) A young reporter with literary taste, Harry Hansen, who in time would become a leading critic, got wind of the curious school lad whose poem had been accepted by a national magazine and who at the same time was a Socialist bigwig. Looking him up, he found "a slight, diffident lad, who walked as if he were treading on eggs and who smiled faintly and deferentially at whatever was said, especially when he did not believe it." They walked the streets and parks, endlessly discussing books. Hansen, tall, with a slender face and longish nose, got an introduction to the works of James Huneker and to A. E. Housman's *A Shropshire Lad*, as well as new insights into Ibsen, Frank Norris, Shaw, and an array of others.

Yet Floyd still lacked faith in himself. He quit high school, overriding family protests, and found work in a candy factory. (After all, he had become a candymaker in Quincy.) Laid off, he was gazing through a window at the daily *Times'* new press when it occurred to him that a roller washer might be wanted. Inside he began to apply for work when it was assumed that he was after a cub reporter's job. He landed it, and in the next three years he covered everything from train arrivals—a citizen's visit to Chicago was a fairly big item—down to German language theatricals which he couldn't understand. Off duty, he edited a little crusading paper notable for (1) hurting the feelings of the leading brothel-keeper by implying that he was a white slaver, and (2) winning more space in the library for the children's section. Naturally he fell into sundry affairs of the heart, chiefly memorable, perhaps, for the girl of the upper class who initiated him into carnal love but rejected him as a husband.

At a meeting to launch a freethinker's society he again met the despised Nietzschean-Greek aristocrat, George Cook. Named a committee of two to draft a program, the "St. Bernard and fox terrier," as Cook's mother was to describe them, became inseparable (and would remain so in spirit after both were famous, Cook as the founder and moving force in the Provincetown Players which launched the most famous of American playwrights, Eugene O'Neill, on his career). Dell knocked the Nietzschean-autocracy out of Cook's head and knocked Socialism in. The Greek part he left alone, thinking it not harmful within reason. "In Greece one's eyes can still be glad," Cook had written at fifteen. At nineteen, entering Harvard as a senior from Iowa University, he had continued: "I sit here and dream of Greece. I hear—see—the blue waves of the Aegean beating on the shore."

Long ago Jig Cook (the "Jig" was a holdover from a pet name of his mother's) had decided to live half of each year as a hermit. Now he was doing it most of each year in a family cabin-house at Buffalo, nine miles inland. Except for the free use of the land and a servant's labor, his truck farming would have put him in the hole. He admitted at thirty-five that he was mostly in search of himself, inquiring in his diary: "Who are you, George Cook? Are you the boy of Heidelberg whom Elsa Ritter loved? Did you hear those sweet old fountains splash and tinkle through the fragrant long May nights? Did you fall asleep on the stone bench beneath the tree among the ivy, near the Cyclopean castle wall that holds the mountain back? . . . You loved the beauty you saw, and the deeper beauty you could not see, and from the faintest star, as from the leaf at your foot, the all-pervading spirit flowed back in love upon your heart, and body and soul were in rapture."

Was he the long-ball hitter for the Iowa University baseball team, or the violin player for the English classes he taught there later? Was the real George Cook the drunkard who had verged on lunacy in a San Francisco bohemia? Or the freedom soldier rallying against the might of Spain and hearing the whistle of lead—but only from the gun of a Florida swamp sentry who fired at him as he returned late to camp. Which was the true novelist, the author of the Maximilian romance, or of the bitter *The Faggot and the Flame* which editors had thrown out of their sanctums, presumably with the aid of tongs? What kind of a woman did he need? Evidently not the finishing-school girl of charm and beauty he had married in Chicago. When he shut out the world she left him to his cabin and sour novel and corncob pipe. Now he was awaiting a divorce and the coming of Mollie, the Chicago anarchist girl he had met and loved. It wasn't that he opposed unlawful open cohabitation. Believing that Susan Glaspell, delicate writer of fiction, had engaged in a secret affair or two, he and Dell playfully accused her of "lacking the convictions of your courage." But Cook himself was reluctant when it came to trampling the family's good name in Davenport.

During the panic year of 1907 Dell lost his job. He thought that if conditions looked up in 1908 he would, at almost twenty-one, try Chicago. While hoping that the capitalists would get a steadier grip on themselves, he wintered with Jig Cook at the farm. The house-cabin was spacious—the family used it in summer—with a huge fireplace bastioned with shelves of books. Jig being now a Socialist, he was working on a Socialist novel, to be laid partly in Russia during the 1905 revolution and partly in cozier Moline. To keep him company, Dell wrote a novel, too, and learned to smoke a corncob pipe.

Mollie came in the spring. After the wedding, Dell stayed as a hired hand, living in a shack a little away from the house. Susan Glaspell, visiting, concluded that "in the whole history of Iowa there has probably not been so stimulating a hired man. . . . Spraying the apple trees with arguments about Haeckel and Nietzsche and Marx, weeding potatoes and theories, plowing the earth to its greatest poems!" In honor of the first fruits (muskmelons), the farmer and his hired hand carried them to market in the dawn light, chanting from wagon to wagon Sappho's "Ode to Aphrodite."

Aphrodite in her role as goddess of fertility was one thing, as goddess of love, another. She hung around more than was good for the idyl of the farmer and his wife and hired hand. Mollie was twenty-two, richly endowed with those qualities which sculptors ascribe to Aphrodite. Indeed she had once posed in the nude for a sculptor, a fact suppressed in Davenport. Mollie's nature was guileless and sparkling, but she could be lonely during her middle-aging husband's gloomy spells of wrestling with the novel. Dell, with countless years stretching ahead, dropped his novel the better to enjoy the company of one of his own age. Mollie told him of life in Chicago —predicting his success there—and of New York's Mouquin's, Lafayette, Brevoort, and other famous dining places. At her suggestion he sent a poem to the anarchist periodical *Mother Earth*. Back came acceptance from the editor, Alexander Berkman, who had shot capitalist Henry Frick and become the "dear Sasha" higher in Emma Goldman's esteem than Ben Reitman. Berkman had somehow got the notion that Floyd Dell was "an interesting girl," and as a result his letter was a trifle heady.

As if Aphrodite were not wholly competent in the matter of the farm trio, the god Thor bulled in with thunder and lightning. It was on a night Jig Cook happened to be away. Mollie was fearful of storm. For protection she fled to Dell's shack. He comforted her in quite a stodgy bourgeois fashion. Whether she might have accepted the condolences of more advanced sexual thinkers he was never to be sure. Of one thing he was positive: as a matter of course, since it was the anarchist philosophy to conceal nothing, she would tell Jig all of the events of the night. Dell had to consider the possibility that Jig was not fully emancipated.

Next day, convinced that he was in love with Mollie and fearing the consequences, Dell began leisurely preparations for his Chicago adventure. Returning to Davenport, he sought work but found little of it. He had to be satisfied with putting aside twenty dollars above his train fare, after paying a month's house rent and part of the grocery bill. His older brother Charles, recently ill, would be able to return to work.

On the night before Dell's departure, he and Fritz Freucher were taken by Cook to the genteel Contemporary Club for a lecture by an incredibly handsome lawyer-poet whose father was Davenport's next-to-richest man and whose father-in-law was the richest. This was Arthur Davison Ficke. A book of his verses had been printed— which Dell had snooted at in a review. Ficke's subject for the night, however, was court injunctions in labor disputes. Dell found the presentation lacking in social significance. It seemed to him that the distinguished audience complacently waited for Jig Cook's wild men to supply it. He tried, as did the others, and all, in his view, made fools of themselves.

Later, at Cook's home, the chagrined Dell was introduced to the Davenport High School's new teacher of English, Margery Currey. She had heard of his impending Chicago invasion. Why not come to Thanksgiving dinner at her parents' home in Evanston? She kindly placed it for him as a suburb adjoining Chicago at the north. Accepting the invitation, he quickly prescribed for her intellectual growth Frederick Engels' *Socialism, Utopian and Scientific.*

Next morning he took a last look at the depot's map—"the map with iron roads centering on a dark blotch"—and mounted a train for Chicago, and as it turned out, a pilgrimage to a literary renaissance. His mind was wholly occupied at the time, of course, with his chances for finding a newspaper job of any kind.

3

Theodore Dreiser

OF the six poor Midwestern small-town boys who were to loom vast in the making of the Chicago Renaissance, Floyd Dell was the youngest. Theodore Dreiser was fifteen years older; the second oldest, as Edgar Lee Masters ranked first. But Dreiser had been earliest in Chicago and was the first to be published by a book house gambling its own money. Who was the poorest? Sherwood Anderson might win the nod in a close contest. But the Dreiser family, being very large, could have polished off a Sunday school's food contribution without feeling sated.

Why a man so changeable, with the power to wear a hero's mask at times, and then a monster's mask, emerged from such a family, is not easy to explain. Nearly a century later the critics would still be seeing the monster in him, while those viewing him as a hero rated him as perhaps the greatest novelist in the United States.

In 1908, as Dell was on his way to Chicago, Dreiser was already a resident of New York City. But he would now and again return to Chicago. More important, his *Sister Carrie*, the story of a member of his own family, would be a major force in the Literary Renaissance. It had been reissued in 1907 after the original publication by Doubleday in 1900. The yeast had been working, and Dreiser's future novels would have a mighty impact on the other Renaissance makers.

All the small-town poor boys hurled into Chicago's maelstrom were blown in roughly similar directions. Dreiser's fate had created the rawest elements, setting up almost incredible tensions.

In Germany, young Paul Dreiser, Theodore's father-to-be, had fled his native village near Coblenz to avoid conscription, and even-

24

tually made his way, in 1844, to the United States. By trade he was a weaver. After improving his skills and learning something of management in Eastern mills he moved westward in the hope of establishing his own. In Ohio he fell in love with "a ravishing country belle—lovely as a garden of roses or a field of wheat," as he was to recall. Her name was Sarah. She was sixteen, daughter of a prosperous farmer from Moravia, member of a close-knit Protestant religious sect. The young weaver, besides being a footloose stranger, was a Catholic devout beyond the ordinary. After he had taken a job in a Dayton mill she ran away to him and the parental door was closed forever.

At first Dreiser went rapidly toward wordly success with jobs as woolen mill boss and finally his own mill at Sullivan, Indiana. Tragedies came, too. Three children died in the space of as many years. More babies took their places, many more. The mill burned down, uninsured. During the rebuilding a falling beam incapacitated Dreiser for a time. Trouble with his backers followed and he was squeezed out. Broke, confidence gone, he became a simple weaver, often unemployed and forced from town to town. Sarah tried to follow with the growing band of children, but often the new job was too insecure.

Theodore was born—the twelfth child, the ninth living—during a sojourn in Terre Haute, Indiana, on August 27, 1871. He grew up with a long gloomy face and a cocked right eye. Even the mother took the child, solemn and dreamy, for a bit odd. His impressions were strong and unyielding. In after years he would speak of his father as an unwitting villain at bottom. The thin, bearded man was "dogmatic ... a Catholic and a bigot. I never knew a narrower, more hidebound religionist, nor one more tender and loving in his narrow way. He was a crank, a tenth-rate Saint Simon or Francis of Assisi, and yet a charming person if it had been possible to get his mind off the subject of religion for more than three seconds at a time.... He was so clear an illustration of the beaten or at best psychologically depressed."

But his mother! In her forties now, short, plump, worn by toil and poverty, she was in her own way indomitable.

I certainly had one of the most perfect mothers ever a man had. ...A happy, hopeful, animal mother, with a desire to live, and not much constructive ability wherewith to make real her dreams....

A great poet of a mother, because she loved fables and fairies. . . .
She loved the trees and the flowers and the clouds and the sound of
the wind, and was wont to cry over tales of poverty almost as
readily as over poverty itself. . . .

Whatever his outer mien, Theodore gloried in the world about
him—if only "hanging around listening," as a sister complained.
When he was seven the family moved to Sullivan, also in Indiana,
to a house at the edge of town. Sarah kept boarders, thereby adding
variety to the boy's existence. Sometimes with his younger brother,
Ed, but usually alone except for his little dog Snap, he roamed the
nearby fields and woods.

It was a desire and a custom of mine then to arise as early as
three or four o'clock in the morning in the summertime, and after
looking at the clouds over the fields or watching the sun rise, examine all the wonders of the morning—bejeweled spider webs,
striped and tinted morning glories of ravishing form and color, the
yellow trumpet-flowers which covered our porches, our many
varieties of roses in full bloom, bluebirds, swallows, wrens—and
then stroll away through the clover. . . .

Constant family dramas were there to watch and feel. After a
drummer had bought pretty slippers for one of the older girls she
tried to run away with him but was turned back by the depot agent.
Such news had, of course, to be hidden from the rigidly moralistic
father. One of the older boys, let out of jail, hid in the family out-
house (father being home) and sent Theodore with a message to
their mother, asking for help in getting out of town. This brother,
Paul, was as different from his namesake father as it was possible
to be. He came back as a minstrel end man and song writer. Later
he changed his name to Dresser, and in his fashion became a bulwark
for the family and for Theodore a kind of father substitute. Big,
handsome, outgoing, fun-loving, Paul brought the world into the
Dreiser household, and the household very near to the demiworld.
When Theodore was ten, Paul moved the family to Evansville, where
his sweetheart was the madam of a bordello. It was all delightful
sunshine for Theodore. The lady's hotel resort was "white, with
green lattices, rocking chairs out in front, an airy, restful, summery
look" where Paul loved to disport with the smart idlers. "I can see
him yet, clothed to perfection, happy in his youth, health, and new
found honors, such as they were."

Paul had his faults, one being a rather aggravated inconstancy. Yet the Evansville connection held for almost two years, until "an affectional difference between Paul and his lady rose." A tempest blew Paul to New York and theatrical and song-writing conquests.

By now the three older Dreiser girls were in Chicago, and the matriarch Sarah used her strength to gather two of them and the younger children (two boys had followed Theodore into the world) into a six-room flat on West Madison Street. An installment dealer provided more new furniture than was good for all concerned. For Theodore, now twelve, the old pastoral glories and demiworld excitements palled beside the new raptures. He was "lost in a vapor of something so rich that it was like food to the hungry, odorous and meaningful like flowers to those who love. Life was glorious and sensate, avid and gay, shimmering and tingling."

It was summer. From the flat's windows at night Theodore looked into an open beer garden, hearing the clink of steins and music, watching the dancers. The roller skaters took over in the morning. Flags of all nations on the roofs emphasized the conglomeration below: Poles, Irish, Germans, Swedes, Russian Jews with long beards and coats. With brother Ed he ducked under horses' bridles and wove among huge drays and spring wagons and buggies and hansom cabs to sell penny newspapers on the horse cars, or fought swarms of rats charging from antiquated sewers. A boys' gang leader, angered by Theodore's ogling of his girl, received a wide berth, owing to Theodore's realization that courage is a virtue to be won with diligent effort.

Social workers know that slum dwellers provided with better quarters will often move back, missing the babble and especially the quarreling. Although the Dreiser flat was outside the most noisome slums, it was noisy. What livelier entertainment than the overhead couple adjacent to the air shaft? He a bass player in some mediocre orchestra, short, beefy, of fine voice when in liquor. She rather pretty, also a two-fisted drinker and a tragedian. The loud exchanges: "Brute," "dog," "liar," "bitch." Knives and dishes hurled down the air shaft. Gurglings of one being choked, howls of pain from a kneed groin, screams, curses. Even that killjoy, father Dreiser, visiting while some mill was shut down, only managed to increase the drama by getting the couple thrown in jail, whereupon Sarah had to lead a fund-raising drive to "spring" them.

One of the older girls had not joined the menage because she was living comfortably with a "protector." Naturally father Dreiser was stricken by the arrangement. Sarah accepted it, and Theodore did, too, enjoying his visits to the illegitimate establishment.

The Chicago sojourn lasted only three months, but there was action to the end. The household goods were at the depot ready for shipment to a new home in Warsaw, Indiana. Theodore was helping with the final details when the outraged installment merchant descended. To ship unpaid-for goods to another state was against the law. The confrontation scene was grandly impassioned and to Theodore well worth the trouble of having to aid the merchant in sorting the contraband items from the honorable possessions.

In Warsaw the Dreisers soon settled into the house that was to be the favorite of Theodore's youth. Known as the Thralls' mansion, it had, naturally, come down in the world. Yet the brick walls were firm, the woodwork not much decayed, the numerous rooms spacious (the house had three stories on one side and two on the other). Theodore liked especially the autumn, when under a wide-armed fir he stirred a huge iron pot of bubbling apple butter over a fire of pine cones and twigs. There were pleasant hours in a hammock strung between two trees, where of a summer day the boy lay and read, occasionally "looking up between the branches of the trees to the sky overhead and wondering over and rejoicing in the beauty of life." His favorite books were Mark Twain's *Huckleberry Finn* and *Roughing It*, Harriet Beecher Stowe's *Uncle Tom's Cabin*, Lew Wallace's *Ben Hur*.

For the first time he enjoyed school. Earlier Sarah had bowed to her husband's decree insisting on Catholic schools. In the small towns in Protestant regions, these lacked good facilities and teachers, stressed religion over secular knowledge, and narrowed acquaintanceships. With the loosening of the father's grip, the children were sent to the public schools. Theodore was not a gifted student. Mathematics severely nettled him. Grammar was beyond his comprehension. His skinny, awkward body handicapped him in games, and his poor clothes, lack of confidence, and solemn heaviness of manner put him at the bottom of the social heap. His mind, at least, had a greater range now. And, more eventful for a nature so finely tuned, there was a wider variety of human beings. Especially girls.

For him, adolescence was exquisite joy and deadly pain. In the blooming female there was for him extraordinary beauty, "a toxic something in the form itself," that effected "veritable paroxysms of emotion and desire in me, and that over distances of time and space.... A face piquant in its delicacy, with pink cheeks, light or dark eyes, long lashes—how I tingled at the import of it! Girlhood ravished me. It set my brain and blood aflame." Ability to carry emotions over distances of time and space was essential, for in the actual presence of girls he trembled.

The low status of the Dreisers was now turning his bones to jelly. The next oldest living son, Rome, had become a floater and a boozer. Now and again he would be at home, until some trouble made his absence imperative. The pretty Dreiser girls, all warm-blooded lovers of life, were devoted to their mother, but she could provide little supervision, and none at all during their frequent periods of work in other towns or cities. In small-town eyes the Dreiser girls were at least wild, if not altogether bad. One came home to bear an illegitimate child.

In Warsaw a few people nevertheless recognized Theodore's inner qualities and needs. The most encouraging of these was Mildred Fielding, a tall, fair-haired high-school teacher who had struggled to a kind of serenity from her own unhappy New England youth. As they were going over his lessons after school one day, she turned to him with sympathy in her gray-blue eyes and began talking of the "bad name" of the Dreisers in the town. He was, she said, to consider it of no importance, for he was different from other boys and girls, very sensitive, his mind good in areas where he was interested. "You must study and go on," she concluded, "for your mind will find its way. I know it." Those words and his own feelings were to remain forever in his memory. "The thrill of it! The bracing, encouraging thrill! Instantly and because of this strong, affectionate support, I felt so much better about everything. Pooh! Warsaw and its people!"

He stuck it out for another year, until the way seemed too long, the immediate rewards too scant, the present too oppressive. Besides, Miss Fielding had left for a job in New England. At sixteen he was ready to try his luck in that great Chicago world which had been so marvelous four years ago. With the few dollars his mother could spare he took a cheap furnished room in a West Side neighborhood favored by cult leaders, illicit lovers, and others of the "vast hordes of rovers and loafers and crooks and God knows what—the rakings of the slums of the world." The quickest job was as dishwasher in a cheap Greek restaurant at five dollars a week. The food, at least, ought to be bountiful. It was, but too greasy and unclean, and the long hours over rancid dishwater in the airless kitchen turned his stomach. He had grown to a thin six feet plus, and now he wasted almost to a skeleton.

The Greek, too, had noticed special qualities, and said so when giving him a free week with pay after Theodore took a job at a hardware wholesaler's. The hardware foreman, on the other hand, took an active dislike to him—no doubt owing, Theodore granted, to his low competence. His stomach was still disordered, and his strength was further drained by a long trolley ride to the job. After twelve hours of labor—the usual workday of the time—and the ride home, he had barely the energy to force down a bit of food and crawl into bed. Life sang rarely for him now. Rather, he was on the verge of a breakdown.

Then came one of those miracles worked by dedicated teachers and librarians in behalf of poverty-stricken youths of merit. Theodore was barely seventeen. Mildred Fielding returned from New England to be a principal near Chicago, and mistakingly believing that poverty had caused Theodore to quit high school, had traced him to the hardware bins, her gray-blue eyes "looking at me as of yore in Warsaw."

The miracle? Nothing less than an offer to send him to college! He objected to the waste of her savings, even argued that his chances of advancement in the hardware trade ought not to be passed up, yet plumed himself all the while on the suggestion of his individuality, feeling that "there must be something to me after all." She was not to be resisted. "You are too young, really, to know the importance of finding yourself. A year or two at college, if it doesn't do anything else, will make you think."

And so in the autumn he was transported to Indiana University in the quiet, relaxed little town of Bloomington. The student body numbered only six hundred. Aroused by the opportunities at first, he soon felt inadequate as a scholar and in the group. Self-contempt for ineptness with girls overwhelmed him. By spring, distraught, he was glad to escape. He would not hear of more "squandering" of Mildred Fielding's money. Later he would conclude that the year had been the most vitalizing of his life. For the first time he had met radical youths at odds with the social scheme and dogma, girls who were intellectual as well as attractive, men of advanced learning. But now it was Chicago and search for a job. He got one as an installment collector for a furniture house.

Two thunderous blows, one of his own devising, sent Dreiser into fathoms of despair. First, his mother sickened—the doctor didn't know exactly why—and died in the arms of Theodore who worshipped her most; died prosaically as he was helping her to the toilet. Unrelenting poverty, he believed, had at last sent her to the grave. The family had moved again to Chicago, and now it broke up for the last time.

The second disaster came in a wild and foolish snatch at a bauble of life. The wondrous sights and characters and tales met with in his new job was alleviating his grief, but not enough to stop the hunger for a flashy (to him, classy) wardrobe. In particular, an overcoat with a satin lining. He purchased it with twenty-five dollars withheld from his collections, and was immediately caught. He begged abjectly not to be treated as a criminal, and it was one more agonizing humiliation. His employer did not press charges, but there remained fear that a bad reference would deny him other jobs. Again the employer was charitable, and he got the same kind of a job with another furniture house and continued his "gabby" (his description) rounds.

For a youth who appeared to seek fresh handicaps, the choice of a profession for which he seemed little fitted stood to reason. His worst subjects had been mathematics and grammar, therefore he had two choices for a hard role. He picked that of words. He wanted to be a poet and playwright for the simple reason that for him life was an epic of joy and tragedy. The words themselves—whatever the order and form—would come readily enough. Evidence was to be found almost any day in a wastepaper basket belonging to Eugene Field, the poet-humorist whose "Sharps and Flats" column appeared in the Chicago *Record* and who sometimes used verse and prose sent by readers. If he never found suitable for print the bulging "rhapsodies" mailed by his admirer Dreiser, it could be argued that the competition was stiff.

One quality Dreiser was developing in abundance: dogged persis-

tence. If crushed, he might despair for a long time but he would
come back to try again. Now he badgered newspaper editors for
a job as a cub reporter. After being given a few odd chores he was
taken on by the *Globe*, one of the lesser papers. A few of his Sunday
features, notably one on the malevolent slum between Halstead
Street and the Chicago River, drew attention to him not for style
but for content and feeling. In time he would look back on the
"dreamy cub" of twenty-one:

> Long, spindling, a pair of gold-framed spectacles on his nose, his
> hair combed à la pompadour, a new spring suit consisting of light
> check trousers and bright blue coat and vest, a brown fedora hat,
> new yellow shoes.... I had already attained my full height, six
> feet one-and-one-half inches, and weighed only one hundred and
> thirty-seven pounds. Aside from one eye (the right) which was
> turned slightly outward from the line of vision, and a set of upper
> teeth which because of their exceptional size were crowded and
> so stood out too much, I had no particular blemish except a
> general homeliness of feature. It was a source of worry to me all
> the time, because I imagined that it kept me from being interesting
> to women.

To a young lady who encountered him in somewhat less formal
garb about this time he looked "a big silly," wearing "bicycle pants
and a silly little cap and fancy stockings on his skinny legs."
Whether or not he was too awkward to ride a bicycle was a question
not resolved for her, since he did not own one. As a ladies' man he
was gaining. Once launched in the field of love, his monumental
persistence had to be taken into account. His procedure might have
been taken from Casanova's remark that no woman can resist a man
fully bent on her conquest. Dreiser was no masher. But given a show
of interest, the buck-toothed mouth twisted, the right eye canted a
bit more, the ungainly features radiated a stallion's bold desire—all
combining in a leer that frightened or compelled.

When eight years later Dreiser began his novel *Sister Carrie*,
almost by accident, his writing technique had advanced little beyond
that of his newspaper beginning. His claim of having started without
the vaguest notion of his destination is easy to believe, and it could
be argued with some logic that he might have written it just as well
at twenty-two.

Once having chosen for his central figure a small-town poor girl, attractive and malleable, and having sent her on the way to Chicago and temptation, Dreiser found the rest falling more or less naturally into place. Why "Sister" Carrie? Only a single other member of Carrie's family was ever to appear, and then briefly. He seemed to feel the need of identifying Carrie with one of his own sisters, or a composite. For temptation he had only to recall the satin-lined overcoat. For the city itself, impressions welled up as from an eternal spring. The story opens in late August of 1889, when Carrie is eighteen (as at that very time he had been). The city is to her what it had been to him.

Chicago had the peculiar qualifications of growth which made such adventuresome pilgrimages even on the part of young girls plausible. Its many and growing commercial opportunities gave it widespread fame, which made of it a giant magnet, drawing to itself, from all quarters, the hopeful and hopeless—those who had their fortune yet to make and those whose fortunes and affairs had reached a disastrous climax elsewhere. It was a city of over five hundred thousands, with the ambition, the daring, the activity of a metropolis of a million.

The very city itself is a threat. "A blare of sound, a roar of life, a vast array of human hives, appeal to the astonished senses in equivocal terms. Without a counsellor at hand to whisper cautious interpretation, what falsehoods may not these things breathe into the unguarded ear! Unrecognized for what they are, their beauty, like music, too often relaxes, then weakens, then perverts the simpler human perceptions."

Carrie boards with her sister, whose husband is a laborer, in a cheap West Van Buren Street flat. In a little while she finds a four-and-a-half dollar a week job in a shoe wholesaler's. Her sister is grim from a life of "shift and toil." There is no "light and merriment." Carrie feels shabby in her worn shoes and plain dress with its black cotton tape trimming. One day she takes out the commercial firm's card given to her by a drummer she had met on the train. The name "Chas. A. Drouer" is printed in the upper left corner. In Drouer (a name oddly similar to Dreiser) there is little enough music, but, when he comes in response to her letter, a good deal of blare and even something of the roar of life comes too. And with them admiration for Carrie. "My, but you're a little beauty," he is "wont" to exclaim. And he is generous with banknotes from his wallet. Right away he presses on her two ten dollar bills for buying new clothes. "She could not hold the money in her hand without feeling some relief." They dine and see a show.

Drouer is no sinister mustache-twirler of the dime novels. "A truly deep-dyed villain could have hornswoggled him as rapidly as he would have flattered a pretty show-girl." Drouer's forte is his geniality and a solid place with a good commercial house. Carrie's instincts of self-protection are "aroused feebly, if at all, by the overtures." Before long he rents for her three furnished rooms facing a green park on the West Side. It is a boarding house—she doesn't even have to cook. "In the eyes of the starveling, beaten by every wind and gusty sheet of rain, she was safe in a halcyon harbor."

At this point, regarding the whole thing as asinine, Dreiser quit. For an author without a planned story, this action is understandable. As a character Drouer had performed admirably. But he was shallow—as he needed to be—and where was he to go? If down, the reader wouldn't care; he wasn't villain enough. If up . . . well, he hadn't been pictured as the sort who rises.

After two months Dreiser again took up the story. The real-life "kept" sister had in changing men selected the manager of a saloon patronized by the well-to-do, who not long afterward had absconded with a considerable portion of the receipts, taking also Dreiser's sister, who mistakenly believed that he was free of his wife and willing to marry her. He had escaped prosecution by returning most of the money and the couple had settled in New York.

Into the novel's pages now came the elegant hail-fellow manager of an ornate saloon, G. W. Hurstwood, who liked to array himself in "excellent tailored suits of imported goods, a solitaire ring, a fine blue diamond in his tie. . . ." Drummer Drouer was proud to be familiar with such a one. And being vain of his "little number in the West Side boarding house," he fell into the error of introducing them—even of taking the smooth Beau Brummel to the hideaway. Meanwhile Carrie had seen another aspect of the city during a buggy ride past the great lake shore mansions. Afterward the "glow of the palatial doors was still in her eye, the roll of cushioned carriages still in her ears. What, after all, was Drouer? What was she? At her window, she thought it over, rocking to and fro, and gazing out across the lamp-lit park toward the lamp-lit houses on Warren and Ashland avenues."

Hurstwood lived in a nice three-story house on the North Side, with his wife and children. But he was willing, after alienating such affections as Carrie had for the drummer, to break with his wife, if Carrie would fly with him to the South Side. "It's a big town, dearest. It would be as good as moving to another part of the country to move to the South Side." Carrie agreed, with the provision that "I wouldn't stay with you, though, if you didn't marry me." With Hurstwood, Dreiser had a new character with sufficient range to be dispatched up, down, or sideways into a battle with his wife or Carrie or perhaps both. He decided to follow the real-life script, at least to the point of Hurstwood's theft of the funds and escape with Carrie to New York.

Then suddenly Dreiser again quit writing, unable to figure out a way for the money to be stolen. This wasn't a very good excuse on the part of a writer manipulating a trusted manager who handled large sums. The block lasted for another two months. Again moving, Dreiser achieved high velocity—on an almost brand-new story. Now it was Hurstwood's, especially after his luck as part owner of a New York saloon ran out and he began rolling downhill. (The author knew a great deal about downhill slopes.)

There was a new Carrie, or anyhow there were surprising gifts in the old. Forced by Hurstwood's inability to earn a living, she finds a job as a chorus girl and rises toward stardom. Back in Chicago, true, she had been given a role in an amateur lodge the-atrical, but the incident bears the look of having been interpolated. In the old Carrie there had been few seeds of a stage personality and nothing of the iron will of a conqueror.

Down, down sinks Hurstwood, at last to death by his own hand. As a "slow, black boat setting out from the pier at Twenty-seventh Street upon its weekly errand bore, with many others, his nameless body to the Potter's Field," the lovely Carrie, unaware of his passing, goes to the peak of fame and fortune. It is not enough. She waits as of old "for the halcyon day when she could be led forth among dreams become real."

Dreiser finished with a burst of the compassion which lifted his story above the plot's melodrama.

Oh, Carrie, Carrie! Oh, blind strivings of the human heart! Onward, onward, it saith, and where beauty leads, there it follows. Whether it be the tinkle of a lone sheep bell o'er some quiet land-scape, or the glimmer of beauty in sylvan places, or the show of soul in some passing eye, the heart knows and makes an answer, following. It is when the feet weary and hope seems vain that the heartaches and the longings arise. Know, then, that for you is neither surfeit nor content. In your rocking-chair, by your window dreaming, shall you long, alone. In your rocking-chair, by your window, shall you dream such happiness as you may never feel.

4

Sherwood Anderson

IF the weak-father, strong-mother, raised-in-poverty concept of the literary man is given weight, then Sherwood Anderson must be put down as a favorite of the gods. In weakness his father was without a match. Besides, if any little bit of strength showed in his armor, Sherwood chipped until at least in his own mind it was no longer visible. Rarely has anyone been so corroded by hatred of a parent, or been so relentless in seeking imaginative vengeance.

The mother in reverie was lifted into an iron-willed heroine. Long-suffering she indeed was. That she literally worked herself to death for a brood of six might be forcefully argued. But she slaved with equal zeal for her ne'er-do-well husband. A literary psychologist might assign her a dollop of masochism, yet a like amount would have to go to wives of other poor breadwinners who refused escape into slatternly despair.

Hard as the Anderson poverty was to exaggerate, Sherwood managed to. For example, into one short anecdote he brilliantly got the pathos of his mother and the degradation of his father. The time is Hallowe'en in the Ohio cabbage region where the family lives. Traditionally the young bloods on this night pelt homes with cabbage heads. Father Anderson is off somewhere as usual—probably in a saloon drinking up the food money and telling gargantuan lies—when a rain of the cabbages falls on the porch of the family hovel. Out grimly charges Mother Anderson, crying in simulated anger to the pranksters to desist. She retreats and another shower of the vegetables comes down. Again the charge outside with more cries of pretended anger. And so it goes until a winter's supply of cabbage is heaped on the porch.

As history, a few things are wrong with the anecdote. None of the other Andersons recalled any such incident, nor believed that it had taken place. For one thing, cabbage in the region might be had with no more indignity than asking a grower's permission to harvest a wheelbarrow load or two. What was right about the tale was the satisfaction of the author's inner need and a bright thread for the legend he delighted in weaving.

Had Sherwood Anderson become a financial tycoon, the homily writers would have had little need to work their imaginations. He possessed most of the trappings of the rags-to-riches American hero. Old John D. Rockefeller passing out shiny dimes, Henry Ford the homespun philosopher—these would have been poor players beside Anderson. When only a young man he declaimed:

> One good, clean-minded business man, who gets down to work cheerfully in the morning, who treats the people about him with kindness and consideration, who worries not about world politics, but faces the small ills of his day and the people about him, who tries to understand the janitor with his cap in his hand as well as the corporation manager and who sees the manhood in both, is probably doing more downright good than all of the canting moralistic that ever breathed.

He had also the steelier qualities of the buccaneer—egocentricism, a stomach for hard work, a fierce drive to get rich and bestride a goodly portion of the earth.

Sherwood's father, Irwin McLain Anderson, fought the Civil War and then refought it often enough to become nicknamed The Major. Every Midwestern town had a roughly similar character: droll, laughed with and at, usually liked if not admired. Few thought to see him through the eyes of his family. The Major looked the rank conferred upon him, especially when astride a white horse leading a town parade. He didn't mind doubling in the conspicuous role of bugler. He was tall, slender, broad-shouldered, with a handsome countenance adorned with a rakish mustache—a dashing figure to the ladies of a town in which he was a stranger.

The Andersons were of sturdy Old American rural stock, descended from Scotch-Irish. Sherwood's grandfather had been born in Pennsylvania's Cumberland County, and later had established himself comfortably on southern Ohio land. His second wife was the mother of Irwin, born in 1845. Grandfather Anderson was a pillar of the Presbyterian church, a jovial man but a determined enemy of slavery, forceful enough to be elected a commander of militia.

Irwin joined the Union Army at eighteen, when the war was two years old. As a cavalryman he was entitled to his seat on a white horse in later parades. If he came to exaggerate his feats—well, he was a fine storyteller with a generous attitude toward dramatic license. After the war he studied at a women's college in Ohio which admitted ex-soldiers, but settling down was hard and for several years he roved the West. Along the way he picked up the harness-maker's trade and it was as a master craftsman that he returned to Ohio and set up in the hamlet of Morning Sun.

Sherwood enjoyed declaring that his mother had been a "bound" girl. The indenture system was long out of use but in a sense his term was correct. A William Smith had deserted his wife, Margaret, and their two small children. Margaret found another husband but he was of no account, either. After hiring out as a domestic she placed her children with families who agreed to raise them in exchange for work as soon as old enough. At age nine Emma, who was to be Sherwood's mother, was taken into the home of a farmer who lived near Morning Sun. She was a bright, dark girl, not large but strong enough for household duties. At twenty her obligation had been paid, and besides she had always been treated as family.

It was to be expected that a girl in these circumstances would lose her head, given the chance, over so handsome a young gallant as Irwin Anderson. By now she was a pretty country belle with a mass of dark hair, level dark eyes, a lovely mouth, and a slender figure. As for Irwin, the people looked on him as a comer. He kept soberly at his trade, played alto horn in the band, taught Presbyterian Sunday School. He was twenty-seven, Emma twenty-one, when they were married in the spring of 1873. A year later the first child, Karl, was born. Irwin, seeking greater opportunities, moved his family to larger Camden and set up as "manufacturer and dealer" in harnesses. A daughter, Stella, was followed by a son, Sherwood, on September 13, 1876. He was given Berton as a middle name.

Three more sons were born at longer intervals: Irwin, Raymond, and Earl. The last arrived twelve years after the wedding day; it might have been a century ago in a different world. The family had wandered from town to town until settling—or bogging down—in

Clyde, located in northern Ohio between Cleveland and Toledo. By now Irwin had become The Major and most of the breadwinning was left to his wife, who sewed other people's clothes and sometimes washed them. The Major was no longer a proud manufacturer and dealer, not even the owner of a repair shop. Drink was the trouble —drink and talk, big talk.

Sherwood had been eight when the Andersons moved to Clyde. The home was to be maintained, after a fashion, for another decade, so that his youth was spent in a town of just the right size—population some twenty-five hundred—for all to know almost all about the others. No one gathers impressions better than a boy free to rove the streets and alleys. The Major could hardly be expected to find time for the children, and Emma was too worn from her penny-grubbing to do more than get the meals and look after the younger children, with her daughter's help. By now, too, her zest for life had been sapped. Truly bound at last, she went about her labors mostly in silence.

The family's status in the town was low enough, but doubtless higher than it seemed to the boy. In later memories it deteriorated to his belief that for lack of decent shoes the children never went to Sunday school. Naturally The Major had ceased teaching—although still of some value to the church as an Example. Emma did not find solace in religion, but the daughter Stella became devout to the point of fanaticism. The truth was that Sherwood did not care to attend Sunday School and was not required to do so. The Andersons stood among the "respectable poor," living up Piety Hill from Main Street at the edge of a cattail swamp. Their yellow house, rented, was unpretentious but in good enough repair. Emma kept her children and their garments as clean as anybody's.

Even in The Major a distinction was made between shiftless and ne'er-do-well. He wasn't notoriously lazy. The main trouble was that he could be so easily lured from a job. A grandiose scheme for climbing economic heights would distract him until the will o' the wisp vanished. For a while, after dropping from the owner class, he had worked in other harness shops. Then he had imagined an agreeable future in sign-painting. His talent proved slender. As a wall painter he could pontificate on the best way to "grain" and perform other subtleties. But those with jobs to do saw him more as a barn painter.

For riding white horses and bugling in parades there was no remuneration, and very little for horn-playing in town bands. Theatricals looked more promising. He acted in and directed amateur
shows in his own and neighboring towns. But as a career the stage
didn't work out, either.

Sherwood's attitudes were what might have been expected. As the
third child on a falling economic scale he could not have been
welcome in the first place. He was sorry for his mother but not
really close to her. She had become too withdrawn. As for The Major,
the public's view of him was not required to inform a sensitive boy
that he was an eternal juvenile weakling. The Anderson children
gave warmth to one another but their ages were too close together
for any to generate individual strength, such as Theodore Dreiser's
older brother Paul had been able to do. Although quite alone, Sherwood never appeared to be lonely or a loner. He was gregarious, a
mixer, a doer. He looked the part: thin, small, quick, with an alert,
long-jawed face and glowing black eyes and black hair. Small
townspeople are always sympathetic to a bright, go-getting child of
the respectable poor. Sherwood labored hard at so many different
tasks—newsboy, errand-runner, mower of lawns, livery stable chore
boy—that the nickname "Jobby" was awarded him. As a drunkard's
son often becomes a fanatic teetotaler, the ne'er-do-well's son becomes a penny-watcher. The Major's family-degrading irresponsibility made him a symbol to be emulated in reverse.

The people of Clyde said that Jobby would cut the mustard.
Watch him, he'd be a rich man. Sherwood thought so, too. He was
an apt student, but in high school was too busy for regular attend-
ance. Yet even after he had dropped far behind, the venerable white-
bearded superintendent offered to get him into some academy where
promise would stand in lieu of formal schooling. He wasn't interested. It was money, quick money, that he was after. He meant to
go to the big city, Chicago, and rise spectacularly in some business.

In one respect his image as Jobby was out of focus. When reading
a book he often became immersed. The old schoolmaster's library
was available and he read the classics—Dickens, Thackeray, Balzac
—and was deeply affected by Edward Bellamy's utopian *Looking
Backward* for its depiction of a society free of the abject poverty he
knew too well. This aspect was less noticed by the townspeople because his brother Karl seemed to be the introverted one. Steady,

quiet, an apprentice to a gravestone inscriber, he dreamed of becoming an artist.

Sherwood's mind was always open for impressions of the life around him. He listened to rough and lewd talk among the loafers at the livery stables. No bit of scandal or human interest was ignored, and if stories were warped or invented they had some ring of truth for being partly grounded in events of the past. At the hotel he sold newspapers to the drummers, those flashy, easygoing princes, and listened to their worldly tales. Saturdays the farmers tied their horses to the Main Street hitching rack and were in no hurry to go home, not even when wives had finished their gossip and were waiting patiently in the buggies and wagons. The farmers were customers for a few papers, and anyhow the boy was in no hurry to get home, either. The summer of 1892, when Sherwood was fifteen, was particularly lively because General James B. Weaver, the Iowa Greenbacker, was making a strong bid for president on the People's Party —usually called Populist—ticket.

A great visitor himself, Sherwood took pleasure in drawing people out. This was good for whatever business he happened to be in, and besides the time could be spared inasmuch as he rarely went to school. In those days the town characters—the grotesques—were better known and more talked about than in later times when people moved more and outside interests were greater. To some degree all were beyond society's pale and had much in common with the semi-outlaw boys who roved the streets in summer and found warm loafing nooks in winter. Sherwood could not help knowing that in a way he, too, was a grotesque. At least for him the twisted ones were not objects of derision—always with the exception of his father. Most lonely souls found communication difficult even with each other. Hungry to know about them, the boy was, if not fully comprehending, at least a sympathetic audience.

This facet of Sherwood, too, went largely unheeded by the townspeople. Moreover, growing up under the pressures and freedoms of his environment, he was hardly conscious of it himself. In fact he was a boy's boy, rugged for his size. In baseball, playing the outfield, he hit a long ball. He was a girl's boy, too, except that in this field his handicap was painfully evident. For a town's upper strata to pat a bright poor lad on the head, even to predict for him a great future, is a pleasant and harmless thing to do. In the matter of courting the daughters—well, who can be *sure* he will make it big? One thing was certain—Sherwood was the child of the ludicrous Major and a beaten woman who sewed and washed other people's clothes.

Life in the little yellow house by the cattail swamp grew dimmer. Emma was more than simply exhausted. Her health was rapidly waning. At last, when she was forty, Karl was old enough to escape the emotionally barren nest. He left for Chicago and its burgeoning Art Institute. By now The Major was formally deserting. He would disappear from town for long periods, working as an itinerant painter and paperhanger to support his own needs. Returning, he would be allowed by his long-suffering wife to take his old place. Heavier doses of alcohol were now required to fire up his boasts against the cold disapproval of his children. Stella was a pretty, intelligent girl who wanted to go away and study religion. But to leave her mother and remaining brothers was out of the question.

Sherwood was eighteen when his mother went into a final decline. The bound girl was at last unshackled, and her death seemed hardly a crushing blow, at least to the older children. Later when Sherwood came to write endlessly of his youth he would never directly express his feelings about the loss of his mother. Since all of his memories were colored and distorted, his statement that she had died at thirty may have been his way of saying that in the last dark years her importance to him had nearly vanished. Nor was he ever to write of face-to-face trouble with his father—although he presented a fictional character much like himself who nearly choked to death a character much like his father. In the end the Anderson children were content when The Major drifted out of their lives forever.

At eighteen Sherwood remained small for his age. He had joined the Clyde unit of the National Guard which was socially the thing to do and also brought in a few dollars in pay. He kept uneasy company with the daughter of a "best" family but feared, with cause, the rivalry of a lad of more substantial people. Commercially he was not quite the glowing success of his boyhood, although still called Jobby and still a hard worker. There simply wasn't much chance for advancement in the town unless, say, a banker or merchant were to take him in and mark him as a kind of heir. Since none came forward, he worked for more than a year following his mother's death at various jobs, including one as a hand in a bicycle factory. The summer of 1896 was his last in the town as a full-time resident. He played out the season as right fielder for the Clyde Stars and then, just turned twenty, made the break for Chicago. His immediate aim was a job as grocery clerk. He expected to move up fast.

Karl was still there, and Sherwood moved into a West Side rooming house with him. Grocers were avid for his services, he reported after a day of canvassing; ten had offered posts. But a girl who happened to be visiting the rooming house proprietor's family knew of a job in her father's North Side cold storage warehouse. She landed it for him. The truth was that most girls liked to do things for Sherwood. Beyond his attractive person and pleasing manner, there was his seeming need of a gentle helping hand.

Naturally he started in his job at the bottom, being set to wheeling barrels of apples and sides of meat and other perishables. To his considerable surprise he remained at the bottom even after the passage of a year. One man could wheel produce about as well as the next, and his education was too slight for him to be an appealing candidate for a white-collar job with its avenues into management.

Outside, life was better. The rooming house family's name was Paden and he became a friend of a son, Clifton, a bright lad who in time would, after changing his name to John Emerson, become a prominent writer for the screen. Karl had done well at the Art Institute and was now breaking into the commercial field. He was popular with his fellow artists and able to give his brother entry into circles not open to most warehouse hands. Sherwood never lacked for companionship when he wanted it, especially of girls.

Yet he fell into periodical bouts of desolation, often wandering the streets as he had in Clyde. But here no acquaintances lifted his gloom. In those earlier years his dreams of glory had sustained him. To be Jobby, the champion money-earner, had been quite different from being a low-paid roustabout. In the walks at night he sometimes whiled away the time by falling in love with some beautiful girl or woman from a distance. He fell in love with Chicago, too, gradually and almost reluctantly, since it had treated him shabbily. "No man can escape this city," he would write later, adding:

> When you have been sick of it to the very marrow and accepted it, then at last, walking hopeless, endless streets—hopeless your-

self—you begin to feel its beauty, its half-wild beauty. The beauty of the loose and undisciplined, unfinished and unlimited. Something half wild and very alive in yourself is there, too. The city you have dreaded and feared is like your own soul.

After a year and a half he nevertheless sought escape from both the cold storage warehouse and the city. Oddly, he found it in his father's way. It was not the last time he would go in his father's footsteps. The Major could not have better stage-managed the rally to the colors. The Clyde militia outfit was being called to duty in the war against Spain and Sherwood wired to rejoin it. Then in a letter to a Clyde friend he let drop news of the train on which he would arrive. By allowing enough margin he was able to bum freight rides to nearby Sandusky, buy new clothes, and enter Clyde as a worldly success, as announced. The band had turned out for a hero's greeting —also in tribute, perhaps, to its wandering ex-tooter whose son was fitting the warrior mold. No white horse was led out for Sherwood to mount, but he took for granted that his uppity former girl friend rued her defection to a stay-at-home jewelry clerk.

This was in May 1898. The war was over before the unit was dispatched to Cuba, but Sherwood acquitted himself well. He rose to corporal—a higher rank than ever actually achieved by The Major. As usual Sherwood was liked, and as usual he was both gregarious and solitary. A comrade wrote to his sister: "Corporal Sherwood Anderson ('Jobby' for short) is reading his *With Fire and Sword* here at the table, and you couldn't wake him up with a club."

Sherwood had ample time to consider his future. He was going on twenty-four and plainly quitting school had been a mistake. It was known that ex-soldiers would be given advantages in education and he made up his mind to enter college if possible. Mustered out after just over a year, and warmed by a Clyde homecoming, he hurried to Springfield, Ohio, where Karl was on the staff of the Crowell magazines—*Woman's Home Companion* and *Collier's*—and Stella worked in the office. Earl, now in his early teens, was with them; Irwin had a job in Chicago and Ray was supporting himself in Clyde.

On the side Karl was attending Wittenberg Academy. After his visit, Sherwood returned to Clyde and passed the summer working on farms, then entered Wittenberg for the 1899–1900 term. He did very well in grades and as a debater, and was sufficiently eloquent to be named class orator. Altogether he had become better qualified for a white-collar job. A Crowell executive saw his promise and got him a chance as advertising solicitor in the firm's Chicago office.

At first the new road appeared likely to have a sudden dead end. In one phase of merchandising Anderson had been and always would be very competent—at selling himself. But always he had to go about his image-making in his own way at his own pace, and never altogether consciously. To be a good salesman one had to be persuasive whether or not one felt like it. Anderson could not—or would not—project a bright, sunny facade all the time. He could select molds and labor sincerely to force himself into them, but over the long pull he would either do as he pleased or crack up in the effort. His army life had been typical. He had accommodated himself to its rigidity by escaping when possible into books, and his corporal's rank was proof of his ability to conform to the rules upon demand. Although a failure at selling advertising, it turned out that he could write it. The profession was in its infancy. The ads in the newspapers and magazines were rarely over a quarter of a page and carried little beyond the product's name and slogan. The opportunity to spread one's self came in direct-mail circulars and catalogs and form letters. The seller via his writer liked to be pally with the buyers, and the smaller the entrepreneur the bigger he sought to make himself appear.

Anderson moved to the Frank B. White agency mainly as a copywriter. Any soliciting was for accounts rather than space, and better acquaintanceship with his prospects allowed him to go more nearly at his own pace and in his own manner. His salary varied, being partly figured on commission. But in a year it was in the neighborhood of thirty-five to forty dollars a week. "And so, of a sudden, I am lifted up into a new world of well-dressed young men," as he would describe it a long time afterward. "I strut, I carry a cane. I let my hair grow long." Drinking parties were noted as part of the new scheme of life.

In his reminiscences, Anderson never minded getting time and facts mixed up. Obviously there were new shoes and socks and shirts and the rest. Nearly all white-collar workers above clerks affected a cane. Drinking parties were normal in the social life of the man-on-the-way-up. But his thick black hair was not permitted to grow long. Rather, it was cropped fairly short and was always neatly parted near the middle. With his handsome lean face—the good nose and long chin—he might have posed for a collar ad. By now his full growth had been attained: five feet ten inches, weight a hundred fifty pounds. He was a glorified Jobby, once more the go-getter.

"A man might have the best article on earth, but it will do him very little good unless it is pushed," he wrote for a booster publication issued by the firm. "Without push behind it, it is no better than an idle wheelbarrow. Put your shoulder to the wheel, infuse some of that whole-souled energy you have sticking in that frame of yours, and you will find inanimate things will fairly fly." This kind of homespun wisdom fitted the bill, and it flowed easily from Anderson. He wrote two columns under the title "Rot and Reason" and "Business Types." It was in the latter that he celebrated the business man for his clean mind, good cheer, kindness, and humane treatment of "the janitor with his cap in his hand." The shiniest of the knights were in "the greatest business on earth"—advertising. If they (or himself) needed bucking up, he was the fellow to do it.

> Give me the man who thanks his God when a day begins rather than when it closes, who goes eager to his office, who gets as much fun and knowledge out of today's failure as tomorrow's success. I want to love my work because it supplies me with bread and butter, I want to laugh and sing and fight and win and lose, and I want to get a lot of good fun out of the whole business.

It stood to reason that such a philosopher would be noticed by George Horace Lorimer, who a few years earlier (1899) had become editor of the *Saturday Evening Post* and was bringing it to life with massive doses of "the romance of business." As a young executive at Armour & Company, Lorimer had been infused with the Chicago hustle, and later, having trouble finding the ingredients for his editorial formula, he had written *Letters of a Self-Made Merchant to His Son* as a guide. It was a kind of adult version of the rags-to-riches tales of Horatio Alger, Jr. The public's appetite for the fare having proved ravenous, he was combing the highways and byways for writers who might be able to confect it. Anderson was offered a minor place on the staff where he might learn while doing other chores.

Later he said that he turned it down because the Curtis Publishing Company of Philadelphia, which owned the *Post* and also *Ladies' Home Journal* and *Country Gentleman,* was too big. He did try a success story, but without success. In any case, why change now? Already he was in "the greatest business on earth" and looked on himself as only incidentally a writer. After the White firm merged with the Long-Critchfield agency, in his third year there, he was chosen to speak on "Making Good" at a gala dinner. What better proof that he was?

Meanwhile the rising young man's courtship of a "rich girl" had ended in the fashion of the uppity Clyde damsel, who had settled for the jewelry clerk. But a good match seemed inevitable, taking into account his high personal qualifications and his goal. In his auto-biographical writings there would be acres of soul-searching but few hints of his emotional relations with women. Why did he marry Cornelia Lane? After a decade and the birth of three children his answer would be that he didn't rightly know—it might as well have been another woman. If so, almost certainly she would have been very much like Cornelia Lane. For Cornelia possessed many things he lacked: education, cultivated tastes, a social ease and a well-to-do family.

Cornelia's father, Robert H. Lane, was head of his own prosperous shoes-and-rubbers jobbing firm in Toledo, Ohio. She had taken a degree in 1900 from the College for Women of Western Reserve, where she had been a student leader, a sorority member, editor of the class annual. For a while afterward she had attended the Sorbonne in Paris. Witty and fun-loving, although rather quiet, she was more than pretty with her fair heart-shaped face framed by luxuriant dark hair. They met when Anderson, who traveled occasionally for his firm, called one summer evening at the home of a Lane neighbor and, finding him and his family away, accepted the Lanes' invitation to join them on their porch until his quarry returned.

A courtship of several months ensued and they were married in May 1904, when he was twenty-seven and she twenty-five. The ceremony was held in the Lane home. Karl and Stella were there, along with an advertising friend as best man. After a wedding supper and a short honeymoon they took up residence on Chicago's South Side, at 5654 Roselie Court. Before long the head of the family was wearing a top hat to church. Of the two, Cornelia was the less conventional. Her ideas on social questions and literature were advanced, whereas he was the solid man of business. His income went to seventy-five dollars a week, and then, two years after their marriage, he was ready for something grander. He was thinking in terms of an income of twenty-five thousand dollars a year before very long.

The best opportunity arose with a mail order house in Cleveland called United Factories Company. He had run a promotion campaign for it, using astonishing circulars, form letters folksily phrased, and catalogs. The firm still wasn't doing well but the investors had been impressed with his efforts and believed that his promotion would provide the needed zip. Being of like mind, he accepted the title of president and the task of winning buyers for the assorted merchandise. Riches to him were to flow as a share of the firm's prosperity.

If there was a plague the mail order houses avoided, it was understatement. This was true of pictures as well as words. A favorite trick was to rent minor space in a huge factory building and then run a picture of the whole structure as the firm's quarters. Anderson chose this device. Yet the scheme of United Factories was good up to a point. A group of manufacturers would reap the benefits of joint promotion and sales by the "parent" company, which would take a slice off the top. In theory it was a way to finance competition against the giant mail order houses such as Montgomery Ward and Sears, Roebuck. Unhappily, the manufacturers were given to warring for advantage, and there was no way to enforce quality standards.

Yet at cuddling with unseen prospects, mostly farmers, Anderson continued in top form. Under a clean-cut, long-jawed likeness of himself in the catalog appeared "MY WORD TO YOU": "I promise as a decent man trying to be square that every man, rich or poor, small or large, shall have a square deal with my Company. Every word of the book was written under my supervision, and for it I am responsible to you." Naturally the head man couldn't admit that he had actually done the writing. At executive routine, with its big and little irritations, he was neither experienced nor fitted by temperament, and, besides, the problems were far greater than had been anticipated. Unable to get hold of things, he was ready after a year to seek a pasture that looked greener.

He found it in Elyria, Ohio, fifteen miles west of Cleveland, a small city relying about equally on farm trade and minor industries. Forty miles farther west and a bit south lay Clyde. Granted the difference in size, Elyria being a bit over twice the larger, the two were very much alike. In effect Anderson was going home to psychological pressures which might become dangerous should affairs go badly—especially if a situation developed in which he could identify himself with his father.

But now, vigorous and still confident, he struck out in the grand fashion of George Horace Lorimer's business stories in which a stalwart hero pulls himself to fortune by his bootstraps. Lorimer and his imitators were not concerned, of course, with the untold thousands who tugged mightily at bootstraps and fell over exhausted. Into being came the Anderson Manufacturing Company. It made nothing, unless the stirring of ingredients for paint and roofing compounds might be regarded as manufacture. (The very product did not augur well, for The Major had built his hopes high on paint.) The big factory-facade trick was used again. The firm's incorporation with stock arbitrarily valued at $200,000 was an exaggeration, too. Anderson took an eighth as his share, and some of the rest was parceled out to Elyria business men who wanted to make the town grow. Little cash was ever paid in. Anderson believed that credit from suppliers, built in part by discreet kiting of checks, would serve in lieu of capital.

Promotion was in the worn groove. "Tell me your roof troubles." "We can save you money on paint and I want to tell you why." "No salesmen on the road and a very low selling cost." Going beyond word-mongering to solid, honest products was something else. As money was scarce, the easiest path was to ever cheaper materials and louder boasts. The weakness was common among the bootstrap-pullers. Few realized that the merchandising kings won by holding to a certain level of integrity of product, no matter how honeyed their words or ruthless their other practices.

The Andersons had brought their first child to Elyria, Robert Lane (named after Cornelia's father), born in the autumn of 1907. Two other children were to arrive during their five years there, another son, John, and a daughter, Miriam. The family lived in rented, somewhat rundown houses. Cornelia was seen by Elyrians as dignified, charming, cultured—but not a very good housekeeper. As a member of the Fortnightly Club she got up her share of "papers." She labored with Anderson on his promotion copy—his grammar was shaky—and even gave him lessons in French. They joined a discussion group, were members of the country club, and generally kept up socially.

Inevitably, Anderson presented two sides to the community. He played golf, shot pool at the Elks Club, told a good man's story, smiled pleasantly or laughed heartily, grew just properly merry when drinking, was deferential to the town's big men and gracious to the ladies, kidded the girls at the office. Yet now sometimes he let his hair grow too long and remain tousled. His clothes varied from neat to sloppy. He was often out of sorts with the proper world of the best Elyrians, and showed it. Many came to look on him as not only self-centered but as a religious agnostic and maybe a Socialist.

As the Anderson Manufacturing Company steadily resisted medicines, its founder began seeking relief by losing himself in the writing of fiction. He fixed up a room in the attic of his home for the purpose. Two characters engrossed him: (1) a youth such as Jobby, but who had gone into the world and mastered it; (2) a man very much like The Major, whose character was further splintered with each stroke of the pen.

5

Carl Sandburg

A terrible suspicion of other people's honesty fell over Gus Sandburg in the year 1889. He took to drawing an imaginary knife across his throat. "Sharp," he would say, drawing the knife again, when talking of people adept in business traps. The cloud of suspicion naturally spread over his family, over none more tightly than his oldest son, Charlie, who was only ten when the sky came down. The boy's name was in truth Carl but to him Charles seemed more American and he had adopted it. His parents amiably went along with the deception, but, since old-country Swedes had trouble pronouncing *ch*, they called him Shols or, more generally, Sholly. A changing of first names meant little in a family whose head signed an X, whose last name wasn't Sandburg at all but Johnson or Danielson or maybe Holm, and who never bothered to explain to his children why his rightful surname had been dropped and a new one taken.

Gus would have liked it better had "they"—the sharp ones—come at him with a real knife. Although below medium height and slight, he was hard as nails from swinging a blacksmith's hammer ten hours a day, six days a week. Instead "they" had euchered him out of eight hundred dollars. His smithy's pay in the Chicago, Burlington & Quincy railroad shops in Galesburg, Illinois, being fourteen cents an hour, the loss amounted roughly to two years of hard work. It wasn't as though he had sought to be a capitalist. He was quite satisfied with his job, never got mad at the "Q" over long hours and poor wages. All in the world he had asked was a little bit of America's promise—"a nice piece uh proputty," in Sholly's phonetic rendering of his words. So he had bought one, improved it—and then years later, lo and behold, an old mortgage given by a previous owner had turned up and the court had made him pay the face plus interest.

"Sharp." And with it the knife across the gullet. The gesture sank deep into the boy's mind. For understanding him during the next twenty years while he remained Charlie, and for a long time after the reversion to Carl, the hidden mortgage key was essential. "They" could never be trusted. You went warily, and above all you watched your money pocket.

Concerning the elder Sandburg's first name there was no mystery. It was August, properly shortened to Gus. He was Sandberg before he was Sandburg. The older children, Charlie and Mary and Martin, had lightheartedly substituted the *u* for the *e* because to them it looked better. According to one tale, the last name was really Johnson and Gus had changed it while working on a Johnson-laden railroad track gang to avoid pay mix-ups. By the time Charlie got around to making inquiries, his father was dead. His mother believed that the original name was Danielson. A Swede named Magnus Holm, who had arrived in America ahead of Gus, had beckoned him on to Galesburg by letter. As a boy Charlie was under the impression that Holm, who had extended his name to Holmes, was his father's cousin. Later on, Holm-Holmes's widow told him that Magnus and his father had been brothers. It was all very confusing. One thing seemed sure: Gus's parents had died while he was very young and he had eventually saved enough out of wages as a distillery hand to pay passage to America.

The maiden name of Charlie's mother, born in Sweden also, had been Anderson—Clara Matilda Anderson—and *her* mother, a gooseherd, had died early. Disenchanted with a stepmother, Clara had worked out and eventually put aside enough for passage to America in the company of a girl friend. That was about the size of Charlie's knowledge of her life until he was grown up and happened to inquire about his father's courtship of her. Gus had been working on a track gang when in 1874 he had come to Bushnell, Illinois, where Clara worked in a local hotel. He was twenty-eight, she twenty-four. They had somehow met (but not in the hotel, since the gang lived in box cars and cooked its own meals) and exchanged pleasantries in Swedish. Very soon, knowing that transfer to a job in the Galesburg shop could be arranged, Gus had proposed marriage. "I saw my chance," was the way she explained her part. So there it was, the mating of newcomers to a strange land, a poor young man tired of rootless single life and a poor hired girl looking for her chance. It was in the pattern of immigrant society. The result had been what they could logically have expected: continued hard work and poverty, but also companionship and a steady run of babies.

Gus knew how to read, and favored the practice when not habitual. "Wat good iss dat, Sholly?" he would inquire when finding Charlie at some book. About writing he was of two minds. For himself, he plainly was against it. Why else would a man of fair intelligence never learn to write even his own name? For penmanship in others, though, he had a sneaking admiration. In fact he owned and loved to carry in the upper vest pocket of his Sunday suit an "indebible"—as he called it—pencil that had cost him the equivalent of nearly two hours of toil. His son, Mart, who was a bit more irreverent than Charlie about the Old Man, said he did it in the event someone wanted to do some writing and he could say, "Here iss a pencil."

Such remarks were made out of the Old Man's hearing, just as he was always respectfully addressed as Papa. Gus was a "black Swede," with lank black hair, dark skin, nearly black, deep-set eyes; the cheekbones of his broad face were high, the nose large, the mouth a wide slash. These features were not so much out of kilter as ill adjusted to one another. Gus's smiles had come rarely even before the hidden mortgage. There was plenty of "Sholly, do dis," and "Sholly, do dat," but praise for tasks well done was not forthcoming. A boy's duty was to help out and that was the end of it. Every pay day Gus brought home a bag of candy, the mark of a good father, and never dropped off at saloons as not-so-good fathers often did. For luxury, the pencil aside, he took only a little chewing tobacco and each winter a pint of raw alcohol.

There was no reason to believe that Clara Anderson Sandburg ever regretted having seized her chance when it was offered. She always spoke pridefully of "my man." Her body was strong enough —she was only five feet five, but weighed nearly as much as her husband—for the childbearing and the heavy rounds of household duties. She had skin like fresh linen and light blue eyes and straw-colored hair. In the end there were seven children: Mary, Carl August (Charlie), Martin, Emil, Fred, Esther, Martha.

For the first half dozen years the Sandburgs had lived in small rented houses. Then Gus had purchased—fortunately with no hidden mortgage involved—a big house at 622 East Berrian Street.

They rented several of the rooms out for light housekeeping, but there was a spacious garret in which the older boys slept. A commodious double outside privy near the henhouse served all the families. Gus kept the house in repair with the aid of the boys as they got old enough, and in season tended a large vegetable garden. Although certain that the family would end in the poorhouse, he was resisting stoutly. If some member left a door open in winter, or ruined an umbrella by misjudging the wind, his lapse of good temper was understandable.

In the "pecking order" Charlie had the best of it. His arrival on January 6, 1878, had been two and a half years after that of his sister Mary. Naturally the young parents had been anxious for a man-child. He wasn't any homelier than was to be expected, taking as he did after the father except for lighter coloring—he had brown hair and gray eyes. He grew up skinny but with good bones and showing evidence of growing taller than his father. In manual dexterity, such as tool-handiness, he allowed the Old Man no pride. The Swedish term for dumbhead was often hurled his way. Fortunately he wasn't book-smart enough to worry the Old Man.

It might have been said that he was a red-blooded Swedish-American boy. He could talk some Swedish but was grateful for his ability to pronounce "ch," which a lot of his peers couldn't manage, and proud of his slickness in having changed his name. His mother graduated from "Sholly" to "Sharlie" and finally all the way to Charlie. The Old Man didn't budge in his accent, but he grounded himself sufficiently in the Constitution to be naturalized. In politics he was a devout Republican. At the funeral parade for Ulysses S. Grant he had put little Charlie on his shoulder the better to see, and it had been perhaps the nicest time between them.

As boys Charlie and Mart participated as equals, since Mart, although a year and a half the junior, was quick on the trigger and better looking, with his round, blond pixie face. They were at home in the small-town good-bad boy complex of vacant lots and pastures and swimming holes. Not the gutters, especially, although the usual information to be had in them was dredged up. Charlie took a four-letter-word flyer in a note to a boy classmate, and when it was intercepted by the teacher, and punishment meted out, he was through forever with written-down bad words for passing about in public. He could take work or leave it alone. With the Old Man to take into account, he did his share around the house and by the age of eleven had a paper route and was sweeping out a real estate office every morning for a quarter a week.

He was exposed to the good influence of the Swedish Lutheran church, and it took. He worried over Judgment Day, when his sins would be weighed and a verdict rendered as to his destination (at the Pearly Gates he expected to argue his record of bringing in coal and kindling and picking bugs off the potato plants). Then the old pastor died and a handsome student minister with a curly pompadour and Cupid-bow lips tried out for the post. His name was Carl A. Nyblad. To many his face was spiritual; to others, that of a lady-killer. Before a hiring decision could be reached, a girl from his former town filed a bastardy suit against him. The congregation split over Nyblad's guilt and he led out his faction and established a new church. Gus was one of those finding Nyblad not guilty, as did the trial jury. Charlie had his doubts. It seemed to him that the preacher was mainly interested in his creature comforts. When, puffing a fat cigar, Nyblad castigated some of the boys for smoking, Charlie was through with him. Although his experiences with other men of religion were better, he would always look hard for clay feet.

As a student Charlie was ordinary, neither star nor dunce, liking the teachers, liked by them. That matter of the four-letter words in the note—it could happen to anybody. If none of the teachers was to look on him as particularly gifted, there wasn't much time, after all, for he quit at the end of the eighth grade.

Charlie was against the decision to quit, but it was the Old Man's, and he was overridden or outwitted by Mama only. There was the time she had purchased the *Cyclopedia of the Important Facts of the World* from a canvasser at seventy-five cents. The Old Man had railed, of course, but not dangerously. She had gone recklessly on to *A History of the World and Its Great Events,* at a dollar and a half. When this foolishness drove the Old Man nearly out of his mind, she knew enough to stop. It was the same in education. She might get one child through high school, even another one later. The prospect of Mary and Charlie being there at the same time, and Mart in the offing, would have caused the Old Man to beg admittance to the poorhouse. Mary was a better student than Charlie; she might become a teacher and help the family. Besides, her mother hated the thought of her as a kitchen slavey waiting her "chance." Charlie would have the second-hand advantage of reading her high-school textbooks if he wanted to.

For the next half-dozen years Charlie was an aimless drifter. Not that people said he'd never amount to anything. They simply didn't think he would amount to much. Whenever he left a job it was of his own free will. He was clean, if not dressy or particularly neat, and chary with the few dollars left over from pitching in on family needs. He came to drink intoxicating beverages with the other lads, but sparingly. He didn't "run" girls, and when they failed to set their caps for him he lacked the drive and sweet talk to overcome the disadvantages of his gangly body and homely countenance.

For learning a trade he had the bad luck to enter the labor market just before the Panic of 1893, with its hard times. Even the Old Man's hours (he had never risen above blacksmith's helper) were cut to four a day. Charlie was fortunate to earn twelve dollars a month working a milk route. The death of his young brothers, Fred and Emil, from diptheria, was a shattering blow. In addition, most of his wages were needed for the medical and funeral bills. It was the few dollars he "threw in" for Mary's graduation dress which permitted her to "look as good as any of them." When she found a country school job at thirty dollars a month, Charlie quit his milk route, partly because of a Scrooge-like employer. One fall and winter Charlie worked in a drugstore, sweeping, dusting, running errands, filling prescription bottles down cellar. He rather freely sampled the medicinal wines but limited himself to a daily half-mouthful of rum, and he avoided whiskey, which he feared was stronger, because of a low tolerance for hard liquor. After failing to get a chance to learn the plumbing, carpentering, house-painting, or even boilermaking trade, he settled for barbering. The worldly atmosphere of the Union Barber Shop fascinated him. "You meet the bon ton of Galesburg while you work here, Charlie," the owner told him. Charlie was pleased, too, with the neighboring fancy saloon where he was allowed the run of the free lunch counter.

After a few months he decided that the barber trade was not meant for him. He went back to delivering milk, this time for a likeable fiddler. Charlie himself was a fair hand on the banjo, having come to it by way of a willow whistle, comb-and-paper, kazoo, tin fife, wooden flageolet, ocarina, concertina, and accordion—the last, oddly enough, the property of the Old Man, who could play a solitary tune on it. The banjo had set Charlie back two dollars at a pawnshop, and he had invested four bits for three lessons. He practiced it strictly for pleasure, not with the idea of making money, as with the catching of fly balls, by which he hoped to get into the big leagues.

Reading was among Charlie's diversions, but never enough to upset the Old Man. He liked the dime detective heroes Old Cap Collier and Nick Carter and Macon Moore. The dollar-and-a-half *A History of the World and Its Great Events* was a treasure, particularly for stories of the great battles, and he was a partisan of *Hotstetter's Illustrated United States Almanac,* which, besides noticing the wonders of Hotstetter's Stomach Bitters, gave advice on gracious living, such as how to rid oneself of warts and corns and the like.

Mary's Latin and grammar textbooks he mostly let alone, but he plowed through her literature readers. He wasn't much taken with them. Poetry he didn't waste his time on. The prize for him in Mary's book bag was John Fiske's *Civil Government in the United States,* a mine of basic facts which helped him piece out subjects he was beginning to think and talk about. Whereas the Old Man was merely suspicious of individual sharpies, Charlie had an idea that the slick big bugs were rigging the whole deal against the little fellow.

Gold bugs were probably the worst. These were advocates of the Gold Standard, who had been the targets of Populist ire in the 1892 election. No less a figure than William H. ("Coin") Harvey, the money reformer, had spoken in Galesburg, recruiting Charlie into his secret Patriots of America. When William Jennings Bryan, the Boy Orator of the Platte, stampeded the 1896 Democratic National Convention in Chicago with his Cross of Gold speech he brightened Charlie's morning on the milk wagon. As soon as there was enough light he read it over again. In free time he harangued all who would listen, exhorting them to scorn the Gold Bugs in favor of "free and unlimited coinage of silver." The Old Man, for one, turned a deaf ear.

But Coin Harvey and the Boy Orator were milk-toast compared with a local tailor, a Swede named Sjodin, who impressed Charlie with his "I bow to no master" attitude. "He was the first radical I knew," Charlie would declare later. "In his carriage of head and shoulders as I saw him many a time he seemed to be saying, 'I cringe before no man.' Then on talking with him you would find he wanted a new society, a new world where no man had to cringe before another. He was an anarchist, a Populist, and a Socialist, at home with anyone who was against the government and the plutocrats who rob the poor."

Charlie had been nine when the Haymarket anarchists were executed, and with other children had echoed their parents in denouncing them. But half a dozen years later when Governor John Peter Altgeld, a Democrat, pardoned the three who were imprisoned, Charlie pored over his sixteen thousand words of reasoning and agreed that the jury had been packed for conviction. When the Old Man had refused to side with striking "Q" engineers, Charlie had. Now he listened to the proud tailor Sjodin and the tailor's son, his close friend, and moved to active rebellion against the established order.

Getting only twelve dollars a month from his milk route—the same as from the mean employer years ago—Charlie quit and set up as apprentice to a tinsmith at three dollars a week. The tinsmith, a heavy drinker, was rarely in condition to teach anything. Next was a hitch washing bottles in a pop drink factory. He was allowed all the pop he wanted, which was too much, for he came down with diarrhea. He set out to learn the potter's trade. The pottery burned down. He dished up ice cream at a refreshment stand one summer and harvested ice the following winter. At 115 pounds he was big enough for the one but light for the other.

The way things were panning out in Galesburg, he felt free to see more of the world. After a good deal of badgering, the Old Man landed a pass for him on the "Q" line to Chicago. For food and lodging and the sights he had a dollar and a half, and for luggage a pocketknife, a piece of string, a pipe, tobacco, and two handkerchiefs. The price of a hotel room on South State Street was the worst part: two bits. Pittsburgh Joe's restaurant on Van Buren Street near Clark didn't, on the other hand, hold a fellow up. A stack of flapjacks and coffee were a nickel, a big bowl of meat stew with bread and coffee a dime. After a wild fling of two nights at vaudeville shows—a dime apiece—and a visit to the waxworks Eden Musée—another dime—he had to slow up.

But for plenty of excitement all he had to do was to keep his feet moving in the streets. A nickel purchased a mug of beer which, along with free lunch, brought a racy adventure for regaling the boys at home. He would write of it:

> I walked miles and never got tired of the roar of the streets, the trolley cars, the teamsters, the drays, buggies, surreys, and phaetons, the delivery wagons high with boxes, the brewery wagons piled with barrels, the one-horse and two-horse hacks. . . .
>
> The afternoon of my third day in Chicago I stopped in at a saloon with a free-lunch sign. I helped myself to slices of rye bread and hunks of cheese and baloney, paid a nickel for a glass of beer, and sat down at a table by myself. . . . A woman came and took a chair alongside me. Her face looked young, with hard lines at the mouth and eyes. She smiled a hard smile and said, "What yuh doin'? Lookin' for a good time?" I said, "I'm polishing nail heads for Street and Walker." It was a saying then. If you were out of work and looking for a job you walked the streets where the wooden sidewalks had nail heads sticking up and your shoes polished those nail heads. Her face lighted up and she blazed it at me: "I'm goin' to polish your nail head fer yuh!" . . . I waited a few seconds fumbling around with what to say and then told her, "You're up the wrong alley, sister. I ain't got but two nickels and they wouldn't do you any good." She stood up, said, "All right" cheerily and skipped along toward men at other tables.

Back home again, he was more restless than ever. The shift from boy to young manhood was hard. As usual he was popular with other lads, who nowadays often shortened "Charlie" to "Cully"—but with girls he continued to be tongue-tied. He looked and dressed the proletarian, but finding a niche even among the manual workers was proving difficult. Besides, he wanted something more—he didn't know what. The tested method in his circle for seeing more of the world was to go as a hobo and work the harvests of the West. At nineteen he was big enough—five feet ten and a bit over a hundred and forty pounds—for the project. One cool afternoon in late June 1897 he trotted beside a moving Santa Fe freight and hopped into a box car. He'd had the courtesy, at least, not to steal a ride out of town on the Old Man's line. He was set for the road: "No bag or bundle, wearing a black-sateen shirt, coat, vest, and pants, a slouch hat, good shoes and socks, no underwear." In his pocket "a small bar of soap, a razor, a comb, a pocket mirror, two handkerchiefs, a piece of string, needles and thread, a Waterbury watch, a knife, a pipe and a sack of tobacco, three dollars and twenty-five cents in cash."

In a pinch he might get along without a piece of string, but money he planned not to be without. On the way to Kansas—he was early for the harvest, anyhow—he unloaded kegs of nails from a steamboat, washed dishes, blacked stoves, toiled on a section gang, and by various other jobs replenished his treasury. He was traveling incognito for some reason he never satisfactorily explained to himself. He called himself Gus Sandburg. For that matter, being named Carl August, he had a better right to Gus than to Charlie.

On the money question he tangled with two "shacks" (the hobo term for brakemen) in the coal car of a train running full speed for Kansas. One, plainly the kind who'd work the hidden mortgage trick, ordered him to hand over two bits, or else. He took the position that the shack was not authorized to collect fare. He then took a position, after a right and left to his face, on his back in the coal soot. The shack was bigger and had a reinforcement. He was fair, though, in keeping his "or-else" word. "You can ride," he said, laughing contentedly, "you've earned it." What he didn't realize was that a search of the victim might have occupied a good deal of his time and still not have paid dividends. A fellow who numbered among his friends a master tailor and packed along a neeedle and thread wasn't one to carry bills or even coins where just anybody could easily get at them.

Charlie worked the harvests without strain. After all, since grade school he had been holding up his end in hard labor. To his comrades he was just another young hobo, readier than most to listen to the veterans. Consequently in the jungles he got better than his share of "lumps" (wrapped food handouts) which older brethren had solicited but were too full to eat. He traveled on into Colorado, looked at Pike's Peak, and then rode the freights back home. He had been gone three and a half months. After telling his adventures, he found life was about the same. He was working on a dairy farm milking and delivering it when at last there came a chance to apprentice to a house-and-barn painter. He took it, although not wanting to be a house-and-barn painter.

Succor came from an unexpected quarter: the Spanish-American War. In April 1898 he became a private in Company C, Sixth Infantry Regiment of Illinois Volunteers. Wars being upheavals which turn and toss people in all directions, he was, as it happened, to be turned in a direction he wanted to go.

The role of Company C was tiny. It had been Galesburg's unit of the state militia, and all the members except Charlie and a dozen other fill-ins had had some training. After a month in Springfield they were sent to Virginia, drilled and maneuvered until July, and then dispatched toward Cuba. Instead of landing they were sent to invade Puerto Rico, where for a few minutes they had the mistaken notion they were in a fight. Panicky soldiers a little distance away had fired their guns. The enemy never did appear, but the men of Company C did a lot of marching with heavy packs in sweltering heat, were stung by enormous mosquitoes, fed on by vermin, and had their stomach turned by tinned beef which they called Red Horse but which later became more famous in public inquiries as Embalmed Beef.

Five months after leaving Galesburg they were back. The *Annuals of Knox County* were to describe their ordeal: "Although the Company suffered no loss in killed or wounded, all of them returned emaciated and worn. . . . They arrived amidst the rejoicing and acclamations of thousands of citizens. . . ." At later reunions nothing tickled the veterans more than one of their number sardonically expounding on their mighty heroism. Charlie, though, never forgave Peter Finley Dunne for having his "Mr. Dooley" refer to the invasion as a "gran' picnic and moonlight excursion to Porther Ricky"; nor Richard Harding Davis, the incredibly handsome war reporter, for calling it a "feast of flowers"—in French, to boot. "Dicky Davis lived with the high commanding officers," Charlie would say bitterly.

Galesburg heralded itself as the College City, owing to the presence of two liberal arts institutions, Knox and Lombard, and a business school. All had been outside Charlie's ken. A dozen of his war comrades, however, had been Knox or Lombard students, and from them he gained a notion that he, too, might get in if veterans were given special opportunities. An ex-comrade got him accepted at Lombard with a year's free tuition. Lombard had a few more than three hundred students. Another ex-comrade interceded with the mayor and won him a job as a "call" fireman at ten dollars a month. "Considering where you've been, Charlie," the chief said, "I think you'll make a good fireman." Being a hero didn't hurt a fellow any. When the fire whistle blew he had to dash out of class.

When Charlie was a boy, a familiar sight on Berrian Street had been wiry little Professor Philip Green Wright, his silky brown whiskers flowing as he hurried to his classes at Lombard, only six blocks from the Sandburg home. "All we knew then was that his figure and walk were funny and we liked to watch him," Sandburg would declare later. "We didn't know in the least that he had streaks of laughter in him and in time to come would write one of the funniest musical comedies ever seen on the local Auditorium stage even though he was a mathematician, an astronomer, a historian, an economist, a poet, a printer and a bookbinder, a genius and a marvel."

As a member of that heavenly band of teacher-librarians ordained to guide young writers, Professor Wright had drawn Charlie—rather distressing raw material on the surface. The neophyte almost escaped. One veteran of Company C was to be appointed to West Point, meaning free education. Charlie got it, subject to a battery of tests. Found wanting in mathematics and grammar, he stayed at Lombard. During his nearly four years there he captained the basketball team, was a debater, edited the annual, and was active in other student affairs. But Wright, then in his early forties, was the center of his life. The best hours were on Sunday afternoons when the Poor Writers Club—all poor and hoping to be writers—gathered in the professor's study to read and discuss their compositions.

Wright afterward said that Sandburg had looked decidedly proletarian and unintellectual. Exactly why he now concentrated on writing was a mystery, unless, like his father and the "indebible" pencil, college stood for the written word, and having the college in hand he wanted to see it made use of. No one could have been more surprised by the results than Wright. They were set down—or, more accurately, set up—by Wright himself. He hand-picked the type in his basement print shop and in the autumn of 1904 issued forty copies of a book of verse and prose titled *In Reckless Ecstasy*, by Charles A. Sandburg. The lead poem:

THE IDEAL

A Fantasy to the Unknown Goddess

Every man must have a pole-star.—Old saying.
A man's reach should exceed his grasp.—Browning.

O star! radiant, glowing orb!
Matchless, beautiful, scintillant!
When the brute surged fierce and lust sought hold,
And the minions that drag men down,
Then thou didst shine, O queen! O star!

O star! exquisite, piercing luminary!
Soft, superb, undying iridescence!
Thou fated one of all the hosts
Didst pencil on my brow in living gold,
Indelible as light, that one word, "live!"
O star! O dazzling, splendid gem!

Deep as I go in the pits of muck,
Far as I stray on the roads to hell,
Meshed as I am in the throes of flesh,
Ever your eyes are the eyes I see.
Their light beats in on the pulse of my soul,
To rouse to thought the things to be;
O star! inspiriting, marvelous star!

The little book, exquisitely wrought like its contents, was dedicated to Sandburg's mother and carried a foreword by Wright and an introduction by the author. Robert Browning was given high billing with: "When I rest myself in the sumptuous saddle of 'The Ring and the Book,' and ride its reckless ecstasies, I get more light and truth and wonderment than in listening to any preacher who splits hairs and platitudes for a living."

Thus the old Charlie and his disenchantment with the Reverend Nyblad emerged in the last reference, as Charlie did a few times elsewhere. One was in "To Whom My Hand Goes Out," beginning:

The unapplauded ones who bear
  No badges on their breasts,
Who pass us on the street, with calm,
  Unfearing, patient eyes,
Like dumb cart-horses in the sleet!

In much of the prose he settled for rich ecstasy of words, as: "Evening is the meeting of Day and Night. The sun nears the horizon, salutes in proud, flaring red, and writes his regal homage on a crimson canvas. Soft, loving, gentle, sacrificial, sympathetic, blood red. Hard, cruel, blazing, relentless, unforgiving, fagot-fire fed . . ."

By this time Sandburg was peddling stereoscopic views to Wisconsin farmers. These were picture cards which, placed at the end of a hand viewer, and the lens box held up the eyes, gave three-dimensional vistas, usually of colored scenery; almost every rural parlor had a set. Before taking to canvassing, however, Sandburg had gone out once more as a hobo. This time he had gone East as far as New York, where he held a job as police reporter for six weeks—and in the course of his travels spent a week in a Pittsburgh jail after being hauled off a box car and charged with vagrancy.

For Wright's foreword to *In Reckless Ecstasy*, Sandburg had provided a statement about stereoscopic-slide selling. "When one has the right swing and enthusiasm it is not unlike hunting, a veritable sport. To scare up the game by preliminary talk and to know how long to follow it, to lose your game through poorly directed argument, to hang on to game that finally eludes, to boldly confront, to quietly circle around, to keep on the trail, tireless and keen, till you've bagged some orders, there is some satisfaction in returning at night, tired of the trail, but proud of the day's work." Wright continued on his own: "Then he is free to read, observe men and things, and to think. . . . And so he moves from place to place; reading, reflecting, and growing inwardly from the deep impressions of beauty and grandeur which his soul drinks in from surrounding nature." Favorite authors listed were Boccaccio, Walt Whitman, Emerson, Tolstoy.

After tiring of quietly encircling Wisconsin farmers, Sandburg got a job in Chicago on *The Lyceumite*, writing news of the "platform world," mainly Chautauqua. He got up for himself a lecture on Walt Whitman and secured a few dates. In Chicago he met the state organizer for the Wisconsin Socialist Party and was hired to work in the Milwaukee area recruiting members, selling literature, making speeches, and the like. His wages had to come mostly out of the collections, but the party was influential and he was good at his job.

In the course of the work he met a slim brunette girl named Lillian Steichen, whose Luxemburger family lived at Menominee, near Milwaukee. Her brother Edward was making a name for himself as a painter and photographer, and Lillian herself, besides teaching Latin in a high school, had translated books from the French and German for the Socialist publisher Charles H. Kerr of Chicago. After a somewhat formal courtship—he addressed her in letters as "Miss Steichen" and the enclosed poems were not love poems—they were married, in June 1908. Sandburg was thirty, she a few years younger. When Socialist friends arrived to shivaree them, expecting treats, Charlie—still Charlie the Careful—took up a collection for the Socialist Party. His percentage would come in handy for the new responsibilities of marriage.

6

Edgar Lee Masters

OLDEST of the six small-town boys, and the only one in Chicago during the autumn of 1908, was Edgar Lee Masters. His office phone was listed as Edgar L. Masters, his home phone as E. L. Masters. Usually he was called Lee, and for a pen name he now favored Webster Ford. He was forty, and growing disenchanted with humankind.

During a recent visit to New England he had stood at Ralph Waldo Emerson's grave and admitted that life had "cornered" him. Whether the admission was directed to the shade of Emerson or to himself, and why at Emerson's grave, was neither clear nor pertinent. Masters loved drama. The formal raising of a white flag to the Philistines suited his momentary need. Any smart listening Philistine would have taken his words with salt.

Of the small-town boys, Masters was the only one to have in his youth felt genius. And he did still. He behaved like a genius, so far as he understood the behavior of geniuses, and always subject to environmental inhibitions. The drama at Emerson's grave meant simply that, since genius was often thwarted by fools, he too might end a victim, and just now the fools had the upper hand. As a boy he had differed from the others, too, in admiring the male over the female parent (not that either had won his complete devotion). His family background was the solidest of the lot and he was the best fitted to cope with the established social order.

Hardin Masters was twenty-four and practicing law in Garnett, Kansas, when his girl wife gave birth to their first child, on August 23, 1869. Of the baby's given names, Edgar Lee, they decided to use mainly the second. Before reading law, Hardin Masters had spent a few aimless years in college and as a grocer and a pharmacist, and had received a working knowledge of farming on the Illinois family acres. Now he had staked out a homestead near Garnett to go with his law practice. He failed in both, and returned with his wife and the baby to Illinois. His father established them on a farm near the site of the defunct New Salem, where Abraham Lincoln had read for the law.

Although restless, Hardin was no weakling. In time Lee would describe him, perhaps a bit enviously, as "one of the handsomest of men, athletic and strong, a fast racer, a good swimmer and handler of horses, and much beloved and admired through all his days." The first part was accurate. Hardy (as he generally was called) was the very picture of a sport: a robust manly figure dressed in style (he liked colorful vests), with regular features set off by thick, curly, black hair, a mustache and goatee and straight brows over the fine eyes. But he was a man of controversy who, if believing that fists might not suffice against ruffian enemies, carried a pistol. He stood forthright against the "moral element" who abominated liquor and horseracing and ran the churches.

The portrait is of a willful man. Too willful, in the opinion of his high-keyed wife, Emma. For his good she determined to break that will. In turn he labored to harness, in self defense and for her own good, Emma's mettlesome spirit. She was known for her beauty—high forehead, great dark eyes, shapely lips, soft brown hair—and for her razor wit and flaming temper. In the conflict the husband proved indomitable, the wife unsubduable.

The Masters family were of stern stuff. An ancestor, Knottley Masters, had been driven out of England, or perhaps Wales—the point was never settled by family historians—by his stepmother, who evidently was of even sterner stuff. He had taken up a rude existence on an island off Wales when the captain of a sailing vessel on his way to America picked him up. The further details of the saga became lost in mists, but a great-grandfather of Lee Masters acquired lands in Tennessee, which in 1829 he sold and then moved to Illinois, where he gave his son Davis money to buy a farm near Petersburg, some twenty miles northwest of Springfield. Davis was a patriarchial figure by the time Lee knew him, although not in the brawny, sweatbrowed manner. He engaged in very little tilling, being more at ease in broadcloth than overalls. He was eloquent, a Bible lover, a speaker in the neighborhood church—but inclined to bring his listeners to tears with quoted poetry rather than to outrage against sinners. He had employed Lincoln as legal counsel, yet as a member of the legislature had voted against him for the United States Senate, for he believed that Lincoln's policies would bring war.

Such a grandfather was bound to warm the heart of a lad. But the grandmother!

Her name was Lucinda, her father a footloose Irishman who had early wandered away from her Tennessee mother, who soon died. A grandmother had brought the child to a tavern which she ran near the Masters farm. Growing up, Lucinda had enjoyed the gay revelry of dances which good Methodists like the Masters frowned upon. After falling in love with her, young Davis had prayed strenuously before concluding that God approved of marriage to so worldly a maid.

On Lee's maternal side, the Dexters were better educated and, by and large, tamer. His grandfather, although of violent temper, was a Methodist preacher who got on well with his New Hampshire flocks. His grandmother was pre-Revolutionary stock. Love had deprived their daughter of higher learning when, at seventeen, visiting Illinois, she had met Hardy Masters and been bowled off her feet into marriage.

When the physical assets of the Masters and Dexter families were mingled and passed down, Lee got rather a poor shake. He had his mother's high forehead and a facsimile of his father's straight brows. But instead of the majesty of his grandfather Masters' nose or the flaring jut of his father's, he received a stub—which was proper enough for his broad face. His eyes bugged just a little and his strong mouth was too wide. Instead of his father's virile mass of black hair he got his mother's soft brown locks, which for him came out mousy. Davis Masters had determined to keep Hardy on a farm, and he succeeded for nearly four years, until the son escaped by getting elected State's Attorney for the county with the help of the wet German vote. The job paid little, but a Petersburg courthouse office went with it and he could practice on the side. Lincoln had surveyed the town and had tried many cases there. His old partner, William H. Herndon, was a member of the bar. The population was about two thousand, larger than that of most rural county seats.

The Masters family lived frugally, anyhow poorly, since money was scarce and Emma was not a very good housekeeper. A daughter, Madeline, had followed Lee by a year, and now a second son, Alexander, came along. The nicer moments came for Lee when his grandparents drove up in a closed carriage with oval window and blue silk curtains, Lucinda in a black silk dress and bonnet with silk ribbons, Davis in broadcloth and a silk hat and buckskin gloves. They were gay as well as dignified, neither trying to break the will or put a halter on the other. Even better were the visits to their farm with its big hickory-walnut house, white board fence, pine and maple trees, and, in season, red and yellow roses and tulips and phlox and lilacs. He loved the fragrant kitchen and great fireplace in the living room and the quiet repose of the parlor with its piano and books and bound volumes of *Godey's Lady's Book*, that monthly bible of genteel women. Outside was the barn with its scented hayloft, the smokehouse wafting rich odors of hams and bacon, the brisk martins going about their pole house. Here was peace and abundance—yet there had been thirteen children. Lucinda still milked her kitchen cow and minded a vegetable garden in addition to her flowers.

When Lee was eleven, in 1880, his father pulled up stakes and moved to Lewistown, another county seat, about thirty miles northwest of Petersburg. It was little different, with its dozen lawyers scrambling for a living. But Hardy had thought his law revenues would increase, and they did, but not immediately. Emma cared little either way about the towns, since she hated all the Midwest. The younger son had died, but another, Thomas, was born at this time. Except for Lee, all the children received a share of their parents' good looks, especially Madeline, who was much too aware of them for Lee's comfort. He was strong, a wrestler, precocious and sensitive to the elements about him—especially girls. After the age of ten he was infatuated with a girl most of the time.

A few miles from Lewistown was winding, tumbling Spoon River. Lee enjoyed visiting an idyllic little river hamlet called Bernadotte, where he was the guest of a young doctor and amateur botanist who led him to the beauty places of wood and stream, besides, as they went by buggy to call on patients, regaling him with accounts of Spoon River people.

Lee's particular angel was Mary Fisher, a teacher of rhetoric and literature, who, while visiting the East, had met Louisa M.

Alcott of *Little Women* fame. Lee remembered that "night by night the four or five of us who had taken a fresh start in life under Miss Fisher's ministrations repaired to her rooms where she talked to us of Emerson, Dickens, Scott and Thackeray, of Byron and Shakespeare, of Eugene Field who was a name to conjure with at the time."

Writing verse and stories and essays, Lee secretly determined to be one with the great masters of literature. Unhappily he was not Miss Fisher's pride and joy, for a nervy lad declared straight out that he aimed to be a great author, and, even more important, struck the proper attitudes. When the claque was led into Robert Ingersoll's *Mistakes of Moses*, all turned atheist, but the star went further to a Byronic gloom. Lee's boulder-like face wasn't right for that, and besides he was known as "Giggles." It was taken for granted that no world-weary author ever giggled.

The Masters house was short on books and periodicals. In her girlhood, though, Emma had doted on Wilkie Collins and Trollope and Dickens and Thackeray. She was a friend of Mary Fisher, who declared her to be capable of good writing if she were to put her mind to it. Hardy, a "liver," got all the reading he wanted from his cases and the newspapers and therefore saw no point in a youth cluttering his head with lumber that might get in the way of useful knowledge. At sixteen, unbeknown to his father, Lee got a job as printer's devil on a local newspaper, earmarking his dollar-a-week wages for books. One could get the complete Shakespeare for thirty-nine cents and the translations of Marcus Aurelius, Euripides, Virgil, and the like in the same range.

There never was any question about Lee's admiration for his father and his stand beside him against the Philistines who fought him for drinking his liquor openly and battling for underdogs. But with Lee first things as he saw them came first, too, and he refused to quit the paper when Hardy suggested it. An advantage of being a learning compositor was that one could set up one's own poems and slip them into the type forms, if only under a pen name. Poets were as numerous as the old buffalo and they tracked up all the country weeklies. Lee was prolific for his own paper and sometimes got his work accepted by others, notably the Chicago *Inter-Ocean*, whose Sunday page was a great repository of verse. He signed himself Lee Masters.

As the subject for his high school commencement oration he chose Robert Burns. Although unpromising as a speaker, he was saluted at least by his grandparents as a budding young man of letters. His hope had been to go on with "miscellaneous studies"—as his father called his inquiries into the matters of the ages—during a summer at his grandparents' farm, and then to enter college for a mastery of Latin, Greek, and assorted other matters. Instead he found himself at a telephone switchboard (put at it by his father) shouting toll messages to the next towns. He was a kind of booster station. After a while he was set to drudging in his father's office with the idea—his father's, not his—of preparing him for the law. A tug of war developed. Hardy pulled mightily; Lee was simply dead weight. After a year Hardy, taking a new tack, eased up and permitted Lee to enter a local makeshift academy in exchange for a promise to halt the "miscellaneous studies." The promise got broken. Instead of yanking again on the rope, Hardy gave out more tether. This time he sent Lee to Knox College at Galesburg. Knox was another disappointment. Although older at twenty than most other new arrivals, and surely more filled with miscellaneous knowledge, he lacked credits even for status as a freshman. If given enough time he was confident of getting a foothold. But Hardy, back to yanking, hauled him home after a year and set him to teaching a country school. Resorting to the dead-weight technique, Lee quit before his time was up and returned home. This time he settled, however despairingly, to law studies, and after a few months passed the bar examinations in a fashion that won his father's applause. It didn't last. There was the continued affair of his miscellaneous studies, and other difficulties besides.

Who had gone to Knox for no better reason than a bit of polish in French and drawing? Beautiful sister Madeline. Earlier she had been decked in finery and sent on a visit to the Dexter relatives in New Hampshire. Both expeditions had been arranged at least in part to get her away from unwanted suitors. For years Lee had been irritated as Madeline held court, strumming her guitar and singing to fawning beaux. She was a catch, even he saw that, and he didn't mind his parents wanting to get full measure. But according to his figures a lot more had been spent on her polishing than for his schooling. It appeared also that mother and sister were leagued against him, and he was leagued with no one. His mother had taken up French and was pursuing it along with Madeline, the two of them looking down at his Greek. Worse, they set themselves up as rival authors, favoring the short story. He admitted that his mother's efforts were good, but sessions in which the three read their compositions aloud usually ended in quarrels.

In the office Hardy was satisfied with his son's potentialities as an attorney, but not with his attitude, which was mainly boredom with the profession and the town and its people. A little money was advanced so that he might investigate St. Paul, Minnesota, as a place where practice of law and literature might go together. It turned out there was no opening in either branch and he came back home. The next destination for which he packed his valise was Chicago, after his mother hit him over the head with a window blind amidst literary strife.

To look at the stocky youth lifting a heavy canvas valise aboard a coach of the Narrow Gauge Railroad one hot summer evening, few would have believed that it contained such miscellaneous interests as the works of Homer, Gautier's naughty *Mademoiselle de Maupin,* an Italian grammar, and the manuscripts of an ardent spirit hounded by fools and Philistines. True, the youth's limpish brown hair fell to the nape of his neck. But that was the fashion of normal country boys as well as poets. The flowing tie might have been a sign except for the tall, shiny collar of a type Chinese laundrymen washed and ironed for all village dandies. The collar wilted as the little train wound through the cottonwood bottomlands where the Spoon River poured down from picturesque hills. Puffs of black smoke coming through the open window quickly sooted the traveler's white vest.

It was early July of 1892. Lee, almost twenty-three, was riding on a pass gained through his old newspaper connection, and the twelve dollars in his pocket were all he had in the world. Through the night he sat staring out at the prairies, reflecting on the wrongs done him (he confessed to indulging in self-sorrow) or resolving to make his way in the great city. In the valise were letters to old attorney friends of his father's. He would present them if he had to. A greater prize was a warm letter from William Busbey, managing editor of the Chicago *Inter-Ocean.* Perhaps Mr. Busbey would give him a newspaper job and thereby help send him into the literary skies.

This was Lee's first visit to Chicago. Day had broken when the train passed through outlying truck gardens and into the flat streets of the South Side. He was to be met by his ex-Uncle Henry, who had been married to a dead sister of his mother. As a boy he had always heard him spoken of as a prosperous downstate business man. Henry was at the Polk Street station, now weary-looking and old beyond his sixty years. They rode a trolley through the roiling traffic, turning south on "patrician Michigan Avenue where the jingle of harness and the glockenspiel of the docked horses" impressed Lee as a world's wonder. Henry's place was a three-story brick with a high stoop near Twenty-second Street. Outside appearances were deceptive. It was a boarding house, and Lee discovered that a room and two meals a day would cost him seven dollars a week. No sentiment here.

In remarrying, Henry had won a bonus of his wife's sister and their mother, all remindful to Lee of the Graeae hags of Greek mythology. Poor Henry toweled his head and began sweeping the rooms. There now appeared an array of outlandish boarding house guests: a huge race-track gambler and his fleshy wife, a blowsily amorous French nurse of uncertain age, a niece of the landlady with red sultry eyes and feverish lips, a hard-drinking accountant for the Chicago Edison Company. That night in his tiny room at the back of the house Lee heard from across the alley the off-key rattle of pianos, hoarse singing, and the squalling of women. Two blocks west was the heart of the "sporting" district, the famed Levee, which spilled over to Henry's alley.

Employment rounds started auspiciously. At the towered *Inter-Ocean* building at Madison and Dearborn, Mr. Busbey ushered Lee into his private sanctum. It was exhilarating to sit there as a known author hearing warm praise from the white-bearded editor. The atmosphere changed when Lee asked for a reporter's job. It wasn't that Mr. Busbey could not give it. He simply wouldn't. Journalism in his opinion was slavery. Better to go into the law and become independent. To prove his point, he scratched out a letter to a poet-lawyer who had arrived in the same circumstances and been given like advice. If he didn't admit that he was glad for having followed it, then Lee was to come back and have a job. The poet-lawyer, it soon turned out, was on vacation.

Lee's money ran out. He worked a day as a printer but couldn't stand the heat. At Henry's, the Graeae harassed him for rent in the daytime and the amorous French nurse pursued him at night. The fortunes of the nurse were the better. Although he was frightened and appalled by "bad" women, she got into his room easily. The affair of the country nephew and the woman-of-experience tickled the worldly denizens of the house, as it would have the denizens of the livery stable back home where a good deal of ribald wit had to do with green lads seduced by city wantons.

Nevertheless a high-life incident led to the country nephew's salvation. One Saturday night the roistering accountant for the Edison Company got drunker than usual, concluded that he was dying, and shouted to Lee for help. As it happened, aid was already there in the form of the French nurse, but a certain decorum had to be observed and Lee saw her padding swiftly down the hall as he went to the rescue. After the accountant recovered he helped Lee get a job at the Edison Company as a bill collector and minor lawyer. The pay was a miserable fifty dollars a month and the duties even worse. He was compelled to trudge about the city seeking payment from rude characters. Being unfamiliar with the city, he got lost often enough to earn the office nickname, "Charley Ross," after the kidnapped, never-found boy. When he hauled a delinquent into court a verdict was hard to win because meter readings were not in themselves sufficient evidence.

If Masters did not enjoy the "gabby" bill-collecting, as Theodore Dreiser had his installment runs not many years before, there was the difference of his drop in economic status, whereas Dreiser had gone up a little. The periodic gloom that settled over both was heavier than for most. Yet Masters in lighter times was the gayer of the two. With the raffish characters at Henry's he got along, and afterwards in other boarding houses the pattern was much the same.

When Masters and Mr. Busbey's lawyer-poet finally met, a warm friendship sprang up between them. Ernest McGaffey was a shortish man who at thirty was totally bald and whose teeth, having the appearance of butternuts, seemed ready to go. McGaffey quickly endorsed Busbey's views on journalism compared with the law, remarking that in a partnership he now earned $250 a month, without strain. In the city he affected poetic attire and was forever in and out of love. He knew all the winestubes and other atmospheric haunts for drinking and dining, and even better, was a member of the Press Club where the wit was quick and usually Rabelaisian. As a guest Masters visited with celebrities, notably Opie Read, a novelist-lecturer who had edited the *Arkansas Traveler*. A venison or bear dinner at the club and the convivial aftermath mitigated the ignominies of bill-collecting for two or three days.

Masters wrote most of his verse as a quick emotional outlet. He might, for example, wing over the centuries for a word about a figure large in his imagination. Considering an ancient vase representing in bas-relief the flight of Helen of Troy, he began:

> This is the vase of love
>   Whose feet would ever roam
> O'er land and sea;
> Whose hopes forever seek
> Bright eyes, the vermeiled cheek,
>   And ways made free.

—and ended quite a number of verses later. The poem, entitled simply "Helen of Troy," was one of his favorites.

For the seasons he had but to remember the Spoon River country, as in "Ode to Autumn":

> Season of gusty days and cloudy nights,
> The wind which showers wine apples to the ground
> Blows at midday the long, pale, lunar lights
>   O'er weedy fields with melancholy sound.

He dealt with the conflict of poetry and existence in a world of Philistines:

> For each man's breast
> Hath a bard for a guest
> And ah! 'Tis best
>   The bard should die.
> Who heeds his behest
> Will reap life's jest,
> And the thorn hath pressed
>   Where his heart should lie.

McGaffey celebrated his younger friend around the Press Club, where the writing of verse was not looked down on, and tried to find a publisher for a collected work. It was McGaffey, too, who arranged an escape from bill collecting. On his recommendation Masters was taken into a law firm where he drew the same fifty dollars a month but was allowed his own practice. Unhappily for a quick rise, he lacked a courtroom flair. Just as he was a poor dancer, there was no speaking rhythm in him. But as a paper man, a drafter of pleadings, briefs, contracts, and the like, he was able and diligent.

In spite of the occasional dark moods, he was enjoying the semi-bohemian existence with McGaffey and other friends, even the rather moldy love affairs which for him seemed to go with every boarding house. He was no joyous Casanova delighting in adventure, yet between the fear of, say, Jake, who ran a gambling hall, and dallying with Jake's mistress, he came down on the side of dalliance. From time to time he met a "good" girl and plunged into a state of wonder and reverence. There was, for example, the rich girl with jewels and expensive clothes who, although from Minnesota, was to him like an ancient Persian beauty owing to her tan skin and tiger eyes. She never wearied of listening to him recite his "Helen of Troy," and, of course, the poems addressed to her in the manner of Swinburne. Later on, after studying the matter for some forty years, he concluded that "if I had not been so proud, so diffident and sensitive"—as well as green—"she would have been mine." As it was, he lost her to prizefighter James J. (Gentleman Jim) Corbett, the conqueror of John L. Sullivan, before his very eyes at the Old Vienna restaurant on the Exposition's midway.

Glimpses of a higher strata of Chicago life were provided by, of all people, sister Madeline. An aristocratic Chicagoan named Carl Stone had gone to Lewistown to be with his fiancée, who was visiting there. He had been introduced to Madeline, fallen under her spell, and before long had shifted his allegiance. In Chicago Stone visited Masters and soon had him to the family's Prairie Avenue mansion. The Stones were very old Chicago, and Mrs. Stone, now a widow, had in her day been a society leader. Masters sat grandly at dinner, waited upon by butlers, surrounded by more silver and exquisite China and cut glass than he had ever seen, while Mrs. Stone listened with cordial respect to his literary aspirations. Here, it seemed, was a patron to give intellectual sustenance while prodding him and opening doors to the salons where reputations were to be made. But he did not know how to take advantage of his chances. In time his brother-in-law got him a membership in the exclusive Calumet Club, where he was not at ease among the haughty Philistines, yet he was not adverse to impressing young ladies with notes written on club stationery.

While one facet of his nature welcomed any patronage of the rich, another stoutly resisted. It was the latter which in 1896 thrilled to the voice of William Jennings Bryan crying out, "You shall not crucify mankind upon a cross of gold." Hardy Masters, as a delegate to the national Democratic convention, had gotten him a ticket to the gallery. He was to recall: "As the vast crowd rose in ecstasy and cheered, and as the delegates marched about yelling and rejoicing for the good part of an hour I sat there thinking of what I had read in Milton, in Mill, in More, in Bacon's *New Atlantis,* in Shelley, and resolving that I would throw myself into this new cause. . . ."

He did, getting himself appointed a precinct committeeman, organizing meetings. He read a speech to a meeting at Petersburg. A major Bryan supporter in Illinois was ex-Governor Altgeld, the pardoner of the anarchists. So Masters, too, became an anarchist in the eyes of many of his old home-town friends and relatives—to say nothing of the members of the Calumet Club. The failure of Bryan to sweep the country merely caused his disciple to triple his scorn for the "financial oligarchy." For one thing, he became, like Charlie Sandburg, an authority on the "money question."

As Masters reached his late twenties, the lonely, chaotic nature of his way of life became oppressive. His relations with women continued to alternate between easy victories and tortured crushes on girls in whom he saw lofty, exotic qualities. He was tired of eating meals out and gathering up his laundry. What it came down to was a longing for stability. When thinking of marriage he had, of course, to envision it as somehow changing him into a solid burgher. The time gained from the simpler life would be employed for better literary work. He created an image of himself in this halcyon state.

One night at a charity bazaar he met a girl who struck him as having a "golden aura." Although her hair was ashen-gold and her eyes yellow-gray, these were not mainly responsible for the aura's color. To him a blue aura was cool-brilliant. Golden or yellow was sunny. The young lady, whose name was Helen Jenkins, seemed drawn to him and together they visited booths and ate ice cream. Later, wanting to call on her, he discovered through inquiries that she was the daughter of a prominent attorney who also headed an elevated railway company. That being the situation, he resorted to a note on the Calumet Club stationery. For days he imagined that he had made a social error, but it turned out that the club had lost her reply. As soon as it was put into his hands he made the necessary arrangements to accept her invitation to call.

They sat in the parlor of the Jenkins house—a three-floor stone front on the South Side—getting better acquainted and appraising each other, until her parents came in from a missionary meeting.

Masters had already learned that Mr. Jenkins was a Sunday School superintendent, a foe of alcohol and tobacco, and the kind of Republican who ranked Bryan only a little above Satan. In the recent conversation it had developed that Helen, too, was an ardent church worker and shared her father's views on the evils of alcohol and tobacco.

At least Masters was plunging into the courtship with his eyes open. The girl was indeed beautiful, with the classical features he worshipped and a fine figure besides. He did not conceal his own politics, or that he was a cigar smoker and a tippler in moderation, or an absentee from church. The Jenkins consensus seemed to be that he possessed a fine mind but a weak character, that being a poet was not in itself fatal, and that a Democrat was tolerable unless wild-eyed. It was held, too, that his character was not beyond redemption. In his favor was the connection through his sister with the Stones, who outranked the Jenkins family socially.

The upshot, after some more courtship and his pledge to quit smoking, on no account to take drink unless ill, and do his best to believe in Jesus, was a formal engagement to last for a year while he was being tested. All this folderol galled him, yet it seemed proof that here was a safe and sane realm if he could get into it. He chewed gum to lick the cigar urge, attended church, and turned his back on strong drink. They were married in the spring of 1898, honeymooned at Niagara Falls, and became the parents of a son at the end of the first year. The realm was stable enough. Masters, as might have been expected, wasn't.

He sought escape in hard work, both in his profession and at his home writing desk. McGaffey had arranged for publication of a collection of his poems, called *A Book of Verses,* by a firm which went out of business just as the edition was ready. Its successor refused to take it over. The handsome volume contained 207 thick pages (leading off with "Ode to Autumn") and was bound in gray boards. Masters had signed all three of his names. Inasmuch as he had put up a subsidy, all the copies were given to him. He sent a few to reviewers, whose treatment was not unkind, and stored the rest in the Jenkins basement.

Masters was dismayed but undeterred. After a long day at the office he customarily strove until midnight on a blank-verse play titled *Maximilian* which dealt with Napoleon's imperial escapade in Mexico but was meant also as an attack on the United States' adventure in the Philippines. A Boston publisher issued it in book form (with financial backing from the author) but no producer was willing to stage it. Only a few copies were sold.

All the while Masters was continuing his political activities. He organized and was president of the Jeffersonian Club, which gave dinners to Bryan, who was the Democratic candidate again in 1900, and to Tom Johnson, mayor of Cleveland, and other reformers. General poetry was somewhat neglected. But for the Chicago *Chronicle* he wrote political and constitutional essays. His pen thrust hard. "It goes without saying that President Theodore Roosevelt has never shown any regard for constitutional liberty; and he seems to have little understanding of the real forces of civilization." He attacked John Marshall, hallowed by conservative lawyers as the greatest of Supreme Court justices; Alexander Hamilton; the Philippine "conquest"; imperialism; the federal judiciary.

Ironically, his reputation as a foe of the oligarchy turned him toward law prosperity as a partner of Clarence Darrow, who, some fifteen years the older, was already famous as a labor and criminal lawyer. The backgrounds of the two men were much alike. Raised in an Ohio village, Darrow had come to Chicago in the late eighties to practice and had at first made a name as a social rebel. Then, toning down, he had been counsel for a major railroad until quitting to defend Eugene V. Debs and the railroad workers during the Pullman strike of 1894. Afterward he had gone back to social and moral questions and become a celebrated lecturer and debater, taking the advanced position except in his opposition to women's suffrage. In ex-Governor Altgeld's sad declining years Darrow had taken him into his firm, but even without that connection he would have been labeled atheist, free-lover, anarchist, and worse.

The Darrow firm was nevertheless busy and prosperous. Its office and Masters' were in the same building, the Ashland Block at Clark and Randolph. The two men had been acquainted for some years when Darrow, noticing Masters' work in underdog cases, invited him to join his firm. Masters did, in April of 1903. His forte as usual was paper work. He managed the office and handled civil litigation, having little to do with criminal cases. Darrow and Frank Wilson, the other partner (the firm name was Darrow, Masters, and Wilson) made nearly all the court appearances. Before many years had passed each partner was earning from $25,000 to $35,000 a year.

Obviously Masters was very skillful in the law. But he took no real pleasure in it. His style of living rose, a daughter was born. He knew that his wife would follow him anywhere. Yet he felt more trapped than ever. A book of his poems titled *The Blood of the Prophets,* signed with the pen name Dexter Wallace, gained little attention when it appeared in 1905. There was no sign of advance in craftsmanship, as shown by a verse from a stanza of "The Pioneers":

> For we, thy children,
>   Will not fail
> When we remember thee,
> Thou pioneers, whose trials avail
>   To bring us victory.

A year later he conceived a novel with Spoon River people, but set the idea aside. More money was to be had in the theater. Perhaps this was the way out of the trap. He wrote two more plays, *Althea* and *The Trifler,* both in prose, and had them printed and sent around to producers and stage celebrities. Nothing came of these efforts, although Minnie Maddern Fiske pondered for a while over *The Trifler.*

So things stood in 1908 when at Emerson's grave he lamented that fate had "cornered" him.

7

Vachel Lindsay

ONCE upon a time a lame boy met a fairy. The encounter was in a flowering meadow, and the fairy, kissing him gaily, gave healing and

> Shoes of song and
> Wings of rhyme.

Then—

> Kept him laughing,
> Led him dancing,
> Kept him climbing
> On the hilltops
> Toward the moon.

The adventure was in time duly reported by the lame boy himself, Vachel Lindsay. Although not physically crippled, he was lame in this world, and knew it. He saw fairies plain, but realized that his visions were fantasy. And so in his poem he told only a portion of the story. Of course he had met a fairy and gone dancing and laughing into the heavens. But on earth the shoes of song were often leaden, the laughter either forced or choked into silence.

It is one thing for a poet who is called a town dolt to escape to the beauties within his own head. If he has set up as prophet of the cosmos hardly anyone is alarmed. If he has announced sackcloth and ashes for himself and lives by them he may even be admired in a headshaking way. But if he trumpets that the rest of the citizens are doltish, appoints himself prophet of town uplift—then violates the high-blown creed—his lot can not be a very happy one.

To piece together the fragments of the mold that shaped Vachel Lindsay would be difficult even if all of them could be found. The town—Springfield, Illinois—naturally was a part of the mold. When he was born there in the night of November 10, 1879, it was a typical small prairie city except for its state capitol and the aura of a martyred hero. As it happened, Vachel (his first name, Nicholas, was rarely used until he attached it for rounding out a poetical signature) saw the earth's light first in a house next to the governor's mansion and in a bedroom in which Abraham Lincoln had probably slept. At any rate the house had been the residence of a sister of Lincoln's wife and there was reason to believe that he had stayed in it the night before setting out for his first inauguration.

All Springfieldians felt that some of Lincoln had rubbed off on them, or perhaps that some of Springfield had rubbed off on him. It may be that Vachel, growing up, was nudged toward a prophet-martyr's role by this environment. Since most of his contemporaries were not, his sensitivity would have had to be responsible. In its general pattern the town was go-getting and self-satisfied like others of its time and region. Much of this Vachel rejected, as young rebels, especially rebel poets, do everywhere. Springfield, because it was Springfield, probably shaped Vachel Lindsay no more than he was later able to shape it by his heroic-comic endeavors.

Heredity? The family set great store by it. "My people were not only important but they were self-important," Vachel was to observe. The Lindsays had been three generations in Kentucky, and before that in the Scottish Highlands. Other blood had seeped in through marriage, including some, the family claimed, of Pocahontas. From carpenters and log-cabin farmers the Lindsay branch had risen to become plantation slaveowners, and then had been reduced by the Civil War to proud destitution. The Fazee clan, the maternal side, were Scottish, too, with some English and a touch of Spanish. They had also lived in Kentucky, but Vachel's grandfather had moved across the Ohio River into Indiana. He was a Sunday lay preacher and, in his grandson's view, a fine example of the Proud Farmer.

> That brow without a stain, that fearless eye
> Oft left the passing stranger wondering
> To find such knighthood in the sprawling land,
> To see a democrat well-nigh a king....

These were not forebears likely to produce, it would seem, a glorifier of the beggar, as Vachel was to be. Since plainly he admired them, no revolt against sturdy pioneer traditions is discoverable here. And in religion Grandfather Fazee was lukewarm compared with Vachel, into whose vision the saints and angels often trod.

In Dr. Vachel Thomas and Catherine Lindsay there were personality lineaments that were graven into the one son among their six children. The doctor, short, big-shouldered, black-bearded—(he resembled General Grant)—seemed often wrapped in a shroud of tragedy. For him there had been heartbreak enough to darken the mind of any man. His youth had been spent in heavy labor, getting an education and helping seven brothers and sisters to do the same. After establishing a practice at a crossroads village near Springfield he had returned to Kentucky for his boyhood sweetheart. Communication between them had been strangely poor. He found her wasted from tuberculosis and on the verge of insanity, but they were married and took up residence in a cottage in the Illinois village. In the bride's mind grew the terrible hallucination that he might abandon her. He did, to an asylum. Then, learning that she was refusing medicine and food, he secured her release after a week. She died only two and a half months after the wedding. For years he wore a mourning band around his hat. After finally remarrying, he would see three of his children die of scarlet fever a week apart.

In his profession Dr. Lindsay was always a general practitioner, but his horizons were somewhat broader than most. Four years after his first wife's death he spent a year in Europe, mainly for study in Vienna. Traveling part of the way with him was a younger sister and her friend, Catherine Fazee. "Miss Kate" was twenty-seven. She required only a little time to get the crape band off the doctor's hat. They were engaged by the time he was ready to settle for the winter in Vienna. Kate selected her trousseau in Paris and later had the doctor outfitted by a London tailor. Home again, the doctor moved his practice from the village to Springfield before the wedding.

Kate Fazee Lindsay was no formal women's rights battler. All she sought was domination, which as it happened meant reducing the going idea of male superiority. At an Ohio women's college, forced to be satisfied with defeating members of her own sex, she had dashed ahead of the class with all "perfect" marks. At mathematics she was a whiz. In the arts she was a painter, a getter-up of theatricals, and a reader of the classics—often aloud, since she was fond of elocution. Then at Hocker College (later to be merged into Kentucky University) she taught and was assistant to the president.

Having chosen to join the housewives, she bent her energies toward organizing them. If not the original of the federated woman, as detractors said, at least she gave the role the same kind of drive that had won perfect school marks.

She was no beauty. Her nose was rather large and gourd-shaped, being fleshy at its end. A rather deep trough cut her long upper lip down to her wide (the better for elocution) mouth. High cheekbones and wide-apart eyes and a narrow chin gave her face an angular look. Her coloring was light. The eyes were luminous bluegray; her hair, worn short and frizzled and parted in the middle, was like dark hay. Her skin was milky white. The angularity of the face contrasted with her short, squarish body. As bearer of children she performed full duty. Her first, a girl, arrived when she was twenty-nine; the last when she was forty-one. Although of a nervous temperament—the cause traced by her to a girlhood sunstroke—she managed, usually, a patient smile when dealing with the children and doing a certain amount of housework, aided by a Negro maid.

Vachel was the second child. After him came the three girls who at seven, four, and two were to be swept away by scarlet fever. At that time Vachel was eight and a half. His sister Olive (named by Kate for the doctor's first wife) was two years older; the last of the children, Joy, was born in the year after the tragedy. Vachel had his mother's coloring and features, somewhat exaggerated. He was nearly albino. His mouth was even wider, his upper lip longer, the trough under his nose deeper, and—a condition strictly his own—his forehead slanted outward to a heavily ridged brow.

He grew into a Mama's boy. Once she perched him on a stool, gazed solemnly into her eyes, and appointed him a genius. He didn't care for rough games, his idea of fun being to sit in an apple tree with a girl cousin and make up stories. His older sister easily dominated him. Animals and nature interested him very little. He was scared of Papa. A savage vein in the doctor was expressed mainly in wild buggy driving, usually at night or in storms while on rural calls. He wasn't able to do much driving at home; Kate held the reins. But once, for striking matches around the barn, he gave his son a terrible thrashing, and thus became a secret ogre.

The Lindsay house in its best days had ranked as a mansion of at least the second rank. Now the veranda had been stripped away; yet the wide facade, adorned by shutters at most of its dozen front windows and surmounted by three chimneys, was impressive. The neighborhood was no longer "good" in spite of the governor's mansion next door. The interior of the house clearly showed the ravages of time. The doctor's practice was never among the wealthier people, and the little extra money went for travel (they camped nearly every summer in Colorado) or for Kate's interminable literary and religious meetings.

Among the things the Lindsay and Fazee clans had in common was a religious faith. They were early Campbellites—followers of Alexander Campbell, who in 1812 had established a society formally titled Disciples of Christ. One purpose having been to unite all Christian denominations, any local group establishing a place of worship usually referred to it as the Christian Church. Since theological training for ministers was not required, ordainment was easy or ignored. Kate's father on a Sunday morning, for example, would merely leave off his farmer's straw hat, put on his black stovepipe, and set out for his pulpit. Every preacher interpreted the scripture to his liking, but to hold a Campbellite audience he had better whale demon rum and gambling and the pleasures of the flesh—except for gluttonous feeding. Moreover, each member was free to place his own view of Holy Writ on a level with, or above, the preacher's. An elder or deacon or other influential member of the congregation often rivaled the preacher in thunder and original thought. The Sunday outbursts, capped by sawdust trail evangelistic orgies, had gained for the sect a wide adherence on the frontier. All these conditions resulted in a concept of a very personal God.

Dr. Lindsay was an elder of Springfield's First Christian Church and of good voice. But Kate was nearly omnipotent and surely omnipresent. The adult Sunday School class was under her tutelage. She was regularly president of the Woman's Missionary Society and head of a union of the societies. She organized and taught a study class. "The house was always packed," Vachel was to say later, "with religious committees of which Mama was always chairman, and woe to any one who proposed something else." Besides the power drive, there was in Kate a deep strain of mysticism. Religious visions were not uncommon to her. Family devotions held each morning just before breakfast were never short and when guests were present became elaborate. At the end each knelt beside his chair for a longish prayer.

On his mother's activities in the Sunnyside Literary Club (she also belonged to the Author's Club) Vachel recalled that she had lectured it for two years straight. "By the time she was through with them she had filled them up with what I had before I was thirteen." This was a mixture of the classics and details of her year abroad. To illustrate the latter she had numerous lumps of cinders, bits of rock, and pieces of bric-a-brac from Pompeii, Rome, Dresden, and other points of interest. Nor was she lacking for family copies of the great books to read from. Those handed down from the Fazees and Lindsays filled many shelves. Around the walls were copies of hundreds of art masterpieces. After all, Kate's first creative love had been painting. It was toward that career, in fact, that she guided her son. At least that was what he thought she was doing.

At thirteen, brimming with Mama's lectures, Vachel took a bypath not entirely to her liking. He became a star-struck admirer of the verse of Edgar Allan Poe. Mama could hardly approve of a man who had spinelessly yielded to rum. In addition to Poe's subtle rhythms, Vachel was infatuated with the supernatural atmosphere of much of his work. The disciple's poems in high school nearly always had to do with some drawn picture. After all, Mama had stamped him with the artist's genius. Moreover, she had decreed that his verse lacked promise. In one field Mama fell down: critical judgment. Vachel drew atrociously. His poems were at least superior to his pictures. Whatever kind of genius he was to be, Vachel was anxious to get on with it. He looked much younger than his age, was physically not well coordinated and poor at games. The attractive girls disregarded him—he adored them—and he was beset by nightmares and strange daydreams. Altogether he had suffered quite enough of adolescent boyhood as he knew it.

In the pattern of the out-of-step—lame—child who somewhere in the town finds a champion, Vachel had his in Susan Wilcox, a young teacher of English. He carried his poems to her because, if not predicting an eminence for him beside Poe and John Milton (his second favorite), she accepted them as worthy efforts and encouraged his hope for a life in the arts. No one competed, however, with Mama —not then.

It turned out that Kate merely planned for him to be a sparetime genius. His real career was to be in medicine. Vachel had known that his father wanted him to go in his own footsteps. But when had Papa's word been law in the house? It came down to this: Mama had forsaken him. He did not rebel. Not openly. All he did was to go, as directed, to Hiram College, a small Campbellite institution in Ohio (his sister Olive was there also) and proceed to fail his medical subjects. He was persistent. He failed for two years and into his third before the white flag was raised at home. But he wasn't finished with Mama, or Papa either. For a decade and a half he would seek the goal Mama had prophesied when she was his goddess, still do it while Papa, sick and going blind, and Mama, taking in boarders, groaningly paid the freight.

But his spirits were high when, exactly a year after the turn of the century, he enrolled in the Chicago Art Institute. He was a mighty planner, now that he had seized the bit, and an even mightier keeper of notebooks and diaries. "Behold," he noted in one of the seven he had going at the moment, "I shall be a Caesar in the world of art, conquering every sort, every language and people, and lead their kings captive before the men of Rome." He then added, "(WOW!)," as if to suggest to himself that hyperbole might have a limit. Actually, all he planned for the next five years was to be "the biggest man of my size in Chicago." He meant to become a sought-after illustrator and religious "cartoonist." Fine painting would come later. Poetry, for the time being, was to be only for self-satisfaction. A second five-year plan called for three years in France, two in Japan. After that . . . well, history would in time record it.

As for marriage, he was of two minds. Dedicated bachelorhood appealed to him. So did marriage and the siring of twelve children. In the latter he had chosen Milton for emulation, since Poe would not do. Vachel abhorred strong drink, frowned on the use of tobacco, and revered chastity. All this was sound Campbellite thinking. But in the matter of sex there had been the further benefit of a talking-to on venereal diseases by his father. It had been strong—perhaps not quite up to the session on matches around the barn, yet similar in effect. The girl who married Vachel, if he took that path, would have no cause to worry about his purity. He talked enough about it to seem headed for professional virginity.

It was lucky for Vachel, as his new life was turning out, that the Campbellites did not damn sensuous foods. His taste for sweets was his main relief from grimness. For a quarter he fared a whole day on cream puffs (very good for breakfast), pie, cookies, candy, and the like. At first he saved carfare by bucking the icy lake winds between his West Side Paula Street room and the Art Institute in the Loop. It was an hour each way. Later he moved deep into the South Side near the old World's Fair grounds, which as a boy he had visited only to have the wonders go awry when his stomach became upset. Now he was compelled to lay out a nickel each way for the elevated railroad, except when dire poverty forced him to walk.

As a student he was, of course, a flop. Accurate reproduction of a subject, even a box, was not within his capacities. His line was thin and altogether his work was stilted. He sought refuge in the theory that if only he could master the elementals, greatness would follow owing to the richness of ideas bursting in his imagination. Even so, doubts often assailed him. No one could fool himself quite so monumentally, but he was a long way from being a fool. It occurred to him that his poetic talent might have developed faster than anticipated. He broke his rule and dispatched to *Harper's* a sample of his work called "The Battle," drafted in high school but since overhauled. A nightmare had been its genesis, Poe its stepparent, the warring characters the hags of Plague and Love. The editor, William Dean Howells, who as novelist and critic was leading the tiny realistic movement, considered it, and, badly shaken, dispatched an oddly harsh reply. Vachel summarized it for his diary: "Howells said my work was frantic, frenetic and obscure." Then he added: "Went home to eliminate obscurity." If the editor thought Vachel's offering was frantic and frenetic—well, what could one expect of fogeys? "The man who is too much in harmony with his time," he noted bravely, "is a compromiser."

His mother, for one, was all for compromise. She wrote advising him to cut out the poetry and get on with the art—practical art. For better or worse, the Institute seemed unlikely to throw him out, and he gave himself another two years to reach a higher plane or else dig ditches for a living. At twenty-one, looking no more than eighteen, shabby, a bit ungainly, eyes starry whether from inner beauty or from hunger, Vachel had the appearance of a somewhat off-focus rustic lad braving the city. For companionship he had to rely on a friend or two from Hiram. He went to Sunday School, found the YMCA a small refuge, and spent a nickel now and again for a gallery seat at a theater. Mostly he buried himself in his room and let rhymes and pictures and reflections tumble into his diaries and notebooks.

Much loneliness was inevitable, he realized, for one of his nature. Yet in two essentials he did not fit the shy, ill-at-ease young artist-poet. One was a capacity for self-mockery. A Hiram yearbook had tacked after his name the Shakespearean line, "I am not in the roll of common men." Vachel rather agreed, with an amendment: "A child of destiny with a taste for sweets." The other difference was a boldness in treating with strangers and crowds. To him they seemed faceless, without power to intrude on his inner consciousness. There was, for example, his encounter with the Rough Rider, Teddy Roosevelt, who was Vice-President at the time. Walking alone, Roosevelt was viewing the Institute's gallery of paintings and statuary. Others were awe-struck. To Vachel he was "public"—a representative of the crowd. A letter home about the incident joined together the elements of boldness and self-mockery:

> . . . So I walked up to the man, and since he looked like his picture, I said, "Isn't this the Vice President?"
>
> He said, "I am," and we shook hands with mutual pleasure. Then we had a flow of mutual soulful smiles for several seconds. He wanted to know my line. I told him I was just a student learning to draw. I said, "You don't want somebody to walk around here with you or anything like that, do you?" I was keeping step with him. We walked abreast in sooth.
>
> But the V.P. answered with his blandest tone that he preferred to enjoy the works in solitude.
>
> Then I shook him kindly by the hand and said, "I am pleased to have met you, Governor," and left him to the smiles of the plaster nymphs.

In the Lindsay household this hobnobbing with Teddy was not deplored, although Dr. Lindsay was a fervent Democrat given to horseback-riding in torchlight parades. Vachel was simply pressed to take hold among less exalted mortals. He did, in Marshall Field's toy warehouse at six dollars a week, mostly pushing a handtruck. He lasted three months and quit during the Christmas rush after his hours had been advanced to fifteen a day. It seemed to him that the newspapers ought to want him as a reporter, or the advertising agencies as an illustrator. None did.

For more than two years Vachel's Chicago battle went on in this fashion, with the demands upon his parents rising as painting instruction called for expensive oils and canvases. He never exactly claimed to his parents that he was doing well, unless his stated feeling that with a bit more progress he expected to be taken on the Institute's faculty might have been so construed. In one matter his frankness nearly cost him his remittances. Somehow it had never occurred to his parents that the Institute might ask him to draw the live female nude. But it did, and he foolishly took the results home. Papa received the devil-wrestling assignment. To make the situation worse, Vachel had got himself more or less engaged, by letter, to a former Hiram schoolmate. Thus it was not simply a matter of self-defilement. By gazing in his virgin state upon a nude woman he had dishonored his betrothed.

Stung to the quick, Vachel begged forgiviness. Yet once back in Chicago, he compromised. The instructor in the nude class, examining Vachel's efforts, found the model chastely draped. Vachel did not conceal from home his lapse into the pit, only arguing that he didn't *like* the nude female, much preferred her draped. The gambit was satisfactory; his parents could reason that, as some lewd males undress women with their eyes, Vachel could robe the nudes as he gazed.

At the end of two and a half years Vachel took stock. Half the time allotted for becoming "the biggest man of my size in Chicago" had been used up. All the time earmarked for becoming independent was gone. His final conclusion: what he needed was more and *better* study. The next stops in the original plan, France and Japan, were out of the question. Besides, he had made up his mind to concentrate on American pioneer subjects. A New York art school would be required. He fought the inevitable battle with Mama and Papa and came out on top. In the autumn of 1903, not quite twenty-four, he sallied forth to conquer the nation's first city. Presumably obstinate Chicago would afterward fall into line.

For nearly five years New York was to be one pole of Vachel's existence. The other was, as always, the Lindsay household in Springfield, which in his mind became a mystically hopeful but still flawed city-village. At last in New York an art teacher performed the service of advising him at least to subordinate his art to poetry. This was Robert Henri, an outstanding painter who taught at the New York School of Art, where Vachel had for competition such talented youths as George Bellows, Rockwell Kent, and George Luks.

Vachel had called at Henri's studio to seek a judgment. It being necessary to provide an example of verse, he startled his audience,

which included Henri's wife, by leaping up and declaiming his "The
Tree of Laughing Bells."

> From many morning-glories
> That in an hour will fade,
> From many pansy buds
> Gathered in the shade,
> And dandelion buds
> From fiery poppy-buds
>   Are the Wings of the Morning made.
>
> These, the Wings of the Morning,
> An Indian Maiden wove,
> Interwining subtlely
> Wands from a willow grove
> Beside the Sangamon—
> Rude stream of Dreamland Town.
> She bound them to my shoulder. . . .

The longish poem goes on to tell of the Indian girl's dispatch of the
now-winged poet to a sky Chaos-land in quest of the Laughing Bells.
After a long journey the tree is found.

> The leaves were tangled locks of gray—
> The boughs of the tree were white and gray,
> Shaped like scythes of Death.

Yet it is beautiful.

> The fruit of the tree is a bell, blood-red—
> The seed was the heart of a fairy, dead.
>
> . . . A thousand bells from a thousand boughs
> Each moment bloomed and fell.

It is told how the poet snatched up two of the fallen bells and
hurried back to earth.

> I panted in the grassy wood;
> I kissed the Indian Maid
> As she took my wings from me:
> With all the grace I could
> I gave two throbbing bells to her
> From the foot of the Laughing Tree.
> And one she pressed to her golden breast
> And one, gave back to me.

The meaning? The journey was one of Vachel's many into the heavens, and perhaps suggested that beauty and hope are to be found amidst chaos and even death. A literal interpretation was not important. Henri, usually dour and often caustic, was struck by Vachel's poetic fire and vision which was in such odd contrast to his lifeless drawing. He heartily recommended a shift in emphasis.

This turning point in Vachel's life did not come, however, until more than a year after the initial assault on New York. In between there had been a severe emotional crisis, most of it to do with a visit to Springfield for the marriage of his older sister to a young doctor-missionary he had known at Hiram. Vachel hadn't wanted to return, had pleaded a desire to get a job and continue in New York as best he could. Kate would have none of that. He was ordered to the wedding, obeyed, and in a cutaway served as best man. Then he remained for the summer, mowing the lawn and feeding the cats.

Up to this time Vachel's religious fantasies had been dreamy poetical imaginings. Now they became starkly real. Old Testament prophets in glorious raiment filed through the bedroom. In daylight he saw them parade under a big elm tree. They came in blazing power, not in Biblical roles but in a magical universe he was creating for his own. In New York his one little triumph had been the purchase of two of his short poems by the magazine *Crisis*. One depicted the sun and stars as bubbles which burst each day, sending faith to the angels and love to men; a goddess dispatched fresh supplies. The poem's title was "Queen of the Bubbles." For illustration he had drawn a skein of bubbles emerging from a point in the heavens.

From this beginning he had worked up a map of the Universe which was to engross him all the rest of his life. Its main features were the Jungles of Heaven in which angels hovered over the thrones of the Trinity; the Earth, from which a vine of amaranth (a mythical unfading flower) climbed as a symbol of Beauty to Heaven; a Hell to which Lucifer (not the wicked Satan but the former Morning Star) had been hurled to his death by other angels jealous of his powers of song; a massive flame leaping from Lucifer's stilled harp all the way to Heaven. Boats of the prophets rode in the skies; the Chaos-star of "The Tree of Laughing Bells" was given equal space with the sun. The same attention went to Lucifer's Tomb in the River of Hate, and the Palace of Eve, from which all bright, pretty girls were said to come. The soul of a butterfly was another symbol of Beauty.

A spider depicted Mammon. Hieroglyphics represented boats like those in which ancient Egyptians believed dead souls were transported to the sun.

Although less than a rounded cosmic philosophy, the map showed the new direction in which its maker was going. At last hope of worldly success had expired, or nearly so. Beauty, always important, was expanding to fill the vacuum. As the sojourn at home dragged on, Vachel amplified his universe with poetry and prose and more drawings. These were gathered into a book manuscript, *Where Is Aladdin's Lamp*, which featured three vagabond heroes called Painter, Evangelist, and Counselor. Back in New York after six months, he had begun offering the manuscript to publishers.

Now he took for himself the evangelistic role of his manuscript: the purveyor of beauty. First he had two of his poems printed cheaply on leaflets. Each had a message: "Cup of Paint" denounced burlesque shows; "We Are Playing Tonight" protested the lot of slum children. Then he went forth at precisely 11 P.M., March 23, 1905, to midtown's Tenth Avenue to exchange poetry for bread. Literally he asked cash, but symbolically his first call was at a bakery. List price for a leaflet was two cents; he was ready to come down. No sale. With his usual public boldness he proceeded to various small establishments—laundry, fish market, candy store— and after a while moved over to Ninth Avenue and to Broadway. All told, his haul for the night came to thirteen cents.

The evidence put down in his diary indicated that except for bewilderment and amusement the shopkeepers treated him as they would have any clean beggar. There may have been something else. He wrote: "Those who bought under all disguises could not conceal from me that they had hearts full of dreams, and some of those that refused were dreamers too shy to confess it to themselves."

After a few more night sallies, he quit peddling for the time being. During the next year he earned a little from art appreciation lectures at a YMCA and labored for three months in a gas tube factory. Then, with more printed leaflets, this time of "The Tree of Laughing Bells," he undertook a walking journey in the South, going by boat to Florida and then striking out for home by way of his ancestral Kentucky. Trading rhymes literally for bread—anyhow, food— proved easier than for cash. The next two years were spent either in New York, mostly dependent upon remittances from home, or with his parents, including a trip to Europe. The five years self-granted for reaching a high worldly place had stretched beyond seven. At last Mama and Papa dug in their feet.

Vachel lowered his sights. Chicago and New York having withstood his best onslaughts, he would have to make do with conquering Springfield. In the autumn of 1908 he was preparing to engage the home-town Philistines in a holy crusade for Art and Beauty as well as for Godliness. A formal declaration of war and the issuance of war bulletins were planned. Surely it would be one of the stranger brawls of history.

II

A Hewing in the Jungle

8

Friday Literary Review — Dell and a Brash Young Irishman

FLOYD DELL'S vision of himself as a blue-collar working-man married to a neat wife in a gingham apron, he writing poetry at nights on the kitchen table, had been quite different from what was to be. At twenty-two he was married, all right, but to a gay, worldly "new woman" bound lightly to a kitchen. And he was assistant editor of Chicago's only newspaper literary supplement—one of the very few, as a matter of fact, in the nation. It was called the *Friday Literary Review* and was a part of the distinguished *Evening Post,* which was read mainly by the business class. Margery Dell—Mrs. Floyd Dell—was still Margery Currey on her job as high-school teacher across the city line in her native Evanston.

The high post of assistant literary editor had not fallen as a plum into Dell's lap. Seven whole months had passed after his exodus from Davenport before it was landed. At the very beginning he had been jobless, although welcomed to the city so royally that his low condition was hardly noticed. Not long off the train, he had inquired at the *Evening Post* for one Charles Thomas Hallinan. Among a bundle of letters of introduction was one to this gray-templed, young-ish man. Hallinan was one of the four editorial writers who shared a large room. The introductory letter was from Marilla Freeman, the librarian-goddess who long ago had insisted that the high-school poet must face up to earning a living by his pen. Hallinan, about thirty, had been expecting the youthful city stormer, due to a direct letter from Marilla. The men took to each other at once. Hallinan was erudite, a rebel in sociological matters, and bent on writing, if not the great American novel, at least the great Chicago novel. A second editorial writer was Francis Hackett, also the book critic and a rebel. The others were at peace with themselves, one a liberal-conservative, the other a tamed cynic. No job was open, but Dell was allowed to make the editorial room his search-in-the-city head-quarters. Hackett gave him a book to review. The *Evening Post* was heavy on editorials, usually running three columns of them in a paper that was seldom over ten pages. Dell further paid rent by contributing occasional editorials.

Another of Dell's mentors, the elderly poet Charles Eugene Banks, formerly a Chicago journalist, had provided letters to editorial friends praising the youth's "talent for making the commonplace interesting." Hallinan guided Dell in off hours into the city rooms. But jobs were worse than tight. If the twenty-dollar backlog could only have been magically quadrupled, Dell would not have been concerned at all. A second letter by Marilla Freeman had put him in the care of the director of a settlement house. Mollie Cook had directed him to her father, "Doctor" James Russell Price, a hand-some man with a big glossy mustache and a mane of gray hair. Dell never learned what the "Doctor" stood for; nor, for that matter, the entire panorama of the old gentleman's creeds, except that among them were anarchism, Rosicrucianism, and simplified epicureanism. Dell accepted an invitation to be a member of a bohemia-plan domi-cile consisting of, in addition to Dr. Price, an inventor whose crea-tions never worked and a universe-problem-solver whose crates of notes probably held the answers. Under the bohemian plan the four would rotate as cook for a week each. Dr. Price, leading off, boiled up a peck of potatoes as sole provender. He repeated every time his turn came around.

Dell had arrived in time for the anarchists' memorial for their Haymarket martyrs (November 11). Naturally Dr. Price was going, and he took Dell along. It was the twenty-second anniversary of the hangings, but memories were still fresh and the crowds in Waltheim Cemetery large. In those days the anarchists were often characterized as of The Word (simply philosophical) and The Deed (direct actionists). A leader of The Word faction, Voltairine de Cleyre, was the main orator. The still-beautiful Lucy Parsons, widow of Albert, was there, and for the occasion her animosity to-ward the after-the-fact "widow" of August Spies, also present, was forgotten. Dell was impressed by the ceremony, but except for Dr. Price, a warm and picturesque human being, he was never drawn to the Chicago anarchists. Even their free love looked unappetizingly moldy when seen up close. He attended a Socialist local meeting and was bored by the trivia.

What enthralled him were the city's tall buildings and its hurtling crowds, and his aesthetic pursuits, when the worries of job-hunting could be laid aside. The resources of Marilla Freeman, who had moved to the Cleveland Public Library, seemed inexhaustible. A letter from her took Dell straight to the bookwoman of the Chicago *Tribune*, Mrs. Elia W. Peattie, and, moreover, into her home, where she read to him from the works of the Irish poet and playwright, J. M. Synge. Mrs. Peattie, forty-six, was a tall, dignified, kindly woman whose son, Donald Culross, was at ten already a poet. Although grounded in the romantic tradition, Mrs. Peattie was not bitterly against realism so long as it was passed over fleetingly and, if possible, lyrically. Synge's work was earthy and even violent. But it was clean earth, and in the violence there was little bleeding.

When Margery Currey had arrived from Davenport for the Thanksgiving holidays, Dell, having been in correspondence with her, waited in the massive LaSalle Street depot. She was unrepentant, even gay, over the breaking of the promise made to him on the night before his departure to read Engels' *Socialism, Utopian and Scientific*. Her nature better fitted the satirical fun of the Gilbert and Sullivan light operas. Left to himself, Dell had seen Israel Zangwill's *The Melting Pot* and the darkly emotional Alla Nazimova in *The Comet*. Margery soon had him attending orchestra concerts by means of visits to Walter Damrosch and Chicago's own Theodore Thomas, and even to grand opera in the Auditorium. This last naturally meant a stroll down The Annex's Peacock Alley. A check for a poem taken by a magazine long ago had replenished Dell's purse slightly, and Margery as a "new woman" rather enjoyed paying her share. The weather being warm, they spent much time in Lincoln Park among the late-blooming flowers, and walked along the lake beach. They ate in chop-suey joints or in one-arm restaurants. And naturally they had Thanksgiving dinner at the Currey home in Evanston.

Here was a different Chicago—a suburb, to be sure, but what naked eye could see the boundary line? Evanston with its wide lawns and flowers and shaded streets was the Garden City which booster-dreamers had wanted for all of Chicago. It contained a few rich men, such as banker Charles Gates Dawes with his Romanesque mansion. But it was chiefly well-to-do middle class. Two decades later an old friend of Margery's father would orate at his funeral: "He represented, as does Evanston itself, the old Anglo-Saxon stock, which in these days is being cast into the shade by alien elements." J. Seymour Currey was Anglo-Saxon, and he would have noted any invasion for the reason that he was a historian with several mighty tomes and a mile of newspaper pieces about Chicago and Evanston to his credit. He liked aliens. He liked everybody. Best of all he would have liked an invasion of characters from the world of Dickens' novels. Indeed, he might have stepped from one of them.

The Curreys lived in a tall, gracious frame house set well back in a spacious lawn. Mr. Currey was a frail man in his sixties whose neat white hair and beard contrasted with his dark eyebrows and mustache. He had been an accountant for Swift & Co. before going into his own never successful ventures. His real interests had always lain in the past and its preservation, so that with good reason he was a Founder of the public library and the Evanston Historical Society. Mrs. Currey was a very small, reserved woman who, in spite of a crippled back, had given birth to seven children. Fortunately she had inherited money, although not enough to relieve all of the strain of so large a family. By now most of the children, of whom Margery was the eldest, had gone into the world. Mrs. Currey was extremely proper, even straitlaced, and therefore not appreciative of the outlook of a daughter who was a militant suffragette, advocate, at least in speech, of greater sexual freedom, smoker of cigarettes, and—well, the friend of a penniless Socialist.

Naturally, Mr. Currey was delighted with the visitor. He would get at Engels' *Socialism, Utopian and Scientific* the moment he could possibly spare the time. Meanwhile Dell might enjoy lending a hand on the sixth volume of the Chicago history—perhaps the section on anarchists and Socialists. True, the young guest was not the Dickens enthusiast for whom one might have hoped. From Mr. Currey's fondness for the Victorian era, though, it was not to be inferred that he was archaic. He would be pleased to know of the modern literary trends and indeed to break bread and drink wine with the advanced literati.

Although Margery was twelve years older than Dell, the gap was hardly noticeable. Small and compact, her brown hair worn in a coronal above an open vivid face, she appeared no more than in her early twenties. At twenty-one Dell had been old in his mind for a long time, and he was used to the companionship of his seniors.

Margery's zest was not to be confused with frivolity. In high school she had won and used a scholarship to Vassar. Between sessions she had tutored Greek and Latin. Now, of course, she was teaching English and had mastered stenography. After her return to Davenport they had had more to write about, and in the Christmas holidays their cultural travels had been resumed.

Then suddenly Dell was given a reporter's job on the *Evening Post*. Soon it was discovered that he could manage the tone of urbanity for which the editors strove, and he was allowed to do theatrical criticism and other special writing. For this tone of urbanity he largely credited Margery. Her letters and conversation had—

> a graceful lightness of their own; the image which it had called to my mind was that of the butterfly shimmering in a sunny landscape which has a smoking volcano in the background. The world was, to my mind, the volcano ... a volcano, in my thoughts, merely as a vague general promise of hell to pay; and the butterfly was the way the mind could, in thought and talk, catch and reflect in an idle winged dance the glints of sunshine in the landscape. That was the way her mind worked, and it fascinated me.... Her thoughts went to Gilbert's *Bab Ballad* tunes, taking for granted that the world was a pretty terrible place, and seeking to get some gaiety out of that fact, in the way that Gilbert turned the horrors of cannibalism into the innocent-seeming jingle of "I am the cook, and the captain bold, and the mate of the Nancy brig." She did not really wish, as I did, to find order in the universe; she was at home on her terms of whimsical humor with an essentially chaotic universe....

In late August they were married in the Currey home. The very start was a bit unconventional. Margery, too, had become a friend of Davenport's Rabbi Fineshriber. They wanted him to officiate, and of course it had to be a Jewish ceremony. The Dickensian Mr. Currey was delighted. He personally chose the wine, and, knowing that his elder daughter loved to give parties, got ready for any literary soirees which might develop.

Already Dell had been made assistant to Francis Hackett on the new *Friday Literary Review*.

That a literary young Irish immigrant with a hot temper and a sense of humor should have ignited a Chicago Renaissance was fitting. The Emerald Isle had provided the earliest foreign wave to leaven the thin granite ranks of those dollar-minded Anglo-Saxons from the Eastern states now being hailed as the Builders (as they would be unto eternity). Most of the early Irish temper had been vented, true, on each other in the streets and saloons of old Kilgrub-bin Patch or similar slum neighborhoods. In a mellower frame of mind the Irish offered "Mr. Dooley" via Finley Peter Dunne's by-line in the *Tribune,* plus "Bathhouse John" Coughlan and "Hinky Dink" Kenna, those lighthearted boodle aldermen whose shenani-gans might or might not be worth the price.

Francis Hackett, Dell's boss and literary editor of the *Evening Post,* had served the crass dollar-grubbers by selling wares in Mar-shall Field's basement, but nowadays a subtle wit flowed from his pen. "A farmhouse stood on a plateau, looking out on the soft blue hills. As he (Hackett's father) walked into the yard a girl with golden hair was milking a cow. He was the young doctor, she had gone to school in Dublin, her father was a 'strong farmer,' and in that instant, if you please, I was born. Not, however, until a dozen or so had been born before me. These things take time."

At the age of eight Hackett had "embraced the proletariat and became a member of the Workingman's Club." At eighteen he had sadly departed his beloved Kilkenny for America because of what he felt was lack of proper Irish fervor against the British oppressors.

Counting back from 1908, that had been seven years ago. Around the *Evening Post's* editorial rooms it was taken for granted that the brilliant, personable young critic would settle for the rich bride that Chicago was bound to offer. Not *all* Chicago heiresses, even "pork heiresses," married European royalty. Hackett was of sturdy con-struction, with strong, good features, and he had a quizzically charm-ing manner except when angry.

Francis, educated by the Jesuits at Clongowas Wood College at Kildare, had changed little from his workingman's club days, even though believing his early rebellion had sprung from defense of his farmer's-daughter mother against the pecking of refined in-laws. His newer bias, he felt, was a desire "to be outside all regimentations and standardizations, all totalitarities, all absolutes." He had con-cluded that "we are born to revolt and reshape." One of the worst of youth's agonies "is to fight out the duel between what was given to us as essential and what we are driven to prefer. The primeval slime is nothing to the platitudes we are born into. To clean our-selves of it, our hands caked with custom, is the painful experience of our growing years. We cannot avoid the revolt. We must revolt, if we are worth our salt."

After arriving in New York, the eighteen-year-old rebel had found a prosaic job as law clerk at $3.50 a week and risen steadily for three years until he was bringing home $5 every Saturday night. Yet he threw up the law. As a salesman he was a whiz, it turned out after he had moved on to Chicago, in 1904, and to Marshall Field's basement. After a year and $40 a week—almost to the Philistine class—he switched to "Beauty and Health," the title of a book he had in mind. To write it he lived in an icy rooming house where "a bath, in the cavern that was called a bathroom, brought my land-lady from the basement with a zinc bucket of steaming water." He was glad to escape to the massive Newberry Library (gift of an early Builder) for research among the tomes. The manuscript had no effect on either the beauty or health of the world, as it never saw publication, but it was good training in composition. All these years he had read voraciously, so that, his memory being retentive, he was truly erudite. He won a job as reporter and editorial writer for the *Evening Post*. When literary editor Henry Fuller quit, Hackett was given a trial and succeeded. In fact he was much sought after by hostesses who liked an occasional tangy bouquet of culture at one or another of their multitudinous displays.

Hackett failed to employ his social advantages in a way to make his associates' prediction of a grand alliance come true. He lived at Hull House. To be interested in settlement work was one thing. It was openly known that Mrs. Potter Palmer herself sat down in Hull House with Jane Addams, the founder and mainspring. To serve as city garbage collector, as Jane had done, in order to clean up filthy streets and alleys was amusing and really brave. Aid to the "worthy poor" was a burden that somebody had to carry. Yet a line had to be drawn. It was not forgotten that Jane Addams had sided with the railroad strikers—and plenty of others since—and was forever carp-ing in favor of child labor laws, shorter work hours, higher pay, better working conditions. And probably worse, if all the truth were known. That Hull House was a refuge for agitators and dreamers had been pretty well established by the newspaper defenders of the public's social and political morals. To actually live there en-dangered a young man in the eyes of certain people. But it was exciting. Founded in 1889 on South Halstead Street by Jane Addams and Ellen Starr, Hull House had grown from its original slum-inundated mansion into a community of schools and club rooms, a theater, art and music studios, and housing for three or four score residents of both sexes who gave time to various projects. Two thousand persons of a dozen national origins passed in and out every day. Some got advice or courage or medicine or food. Others studied, painted, sang, fiddled, debated, or acted. It was a sort of cultural melting pot. Hackett contributed to it while savoring the heady brew, and Floyd Dell took over an English class.

The *Evening Post* was a fine springboard for a young man's leap into the upper classes. Heavy stock-market and other financial news made it popular with the gentry. Its reputation for advanced taste in cultural matters pleased their ladies. In all fairness, many of the newer Builders, and the sons of the older, were appreciators or at least backers of the arts. And many Builder wives and widows, in addition to their cultural interests, had shrewd eyes for market news. Rather grandiloquently H. L. Mencken was later to speak of the Chicago of this time: "The elemental curiosity of a simple and somewhat ignorant people—the naïve delight of hog butchers . . . in the grand clash and clatter of ideas. . . . Eagerness to hear and see, to experience and experiment. . . . Colossally rich . . . ever changing . . . it yearns for distinction. . . ."

For a newspaper to strike a balance as champion of the economic status quo and cultural avant-garde was not easy. Writers long on respect for capitalists tended to monumental dullness. The bright and witty authors—at least those available at journalist's pay— generally were iconoclastic, which meant vaguely anticapitalist if not downright socialistic. Also sneaky, descending to underhanded word tricks to get their views into the papers. It became, too, a fun game and they were ever at it. A bit of judicious publisher-currying and Hackett easily would have been a favorite. Instead he was extremely hard to keep under control. To begin with, his articles and reviews were very popular with the readers, who purchased the books he recommended, a state of affairs reflected in the advertising department. Too valuable to be lightly fired, he was the worse for not even being satisfied with underhandedness. He was reckless and brave and could be a demon when aroused.

It was a time of puffery and pedantry in the nation's literary criticism. They went nicely together, for most pedants also puffed. In this world Hackett was a fresh breeze and sometimes a howling gale, as witnessed by a young man, George Soule, just beginning a

distinguished career as an editor and author in New York. At the
moment he was working for the dignified and conservative Frederick
A. Stokes publishing house. The custom of the larger hinterland
dailies was to send their literary editors for rounds of the Eastern
publishers, the cost justified as in lieu of good wages and for advertising solicitation. George Morrow, a top executive at the Stokes
company, received Hackett, with young Soule present. Soule was
to recall:

> Francis Hackett was widely recognized as the leading critic of
> the current journals. Morrow tried, with too obvious an attempt
> to be diplomatic, to put pressure on him to pay more attention to
> Stokes' books. Morrow referred to the fact that Stokes advertised
> its wares generously in the *Evening Post*. Hackett replied with con-
> trolled but eloquent fury.... He wrote the reviews, he said, with-
> out reference to anything but the merit of the books in question.
> He was not for sale, and if Morrow did not like the way he did his
> job, Stokes could damn well stop advertising in the *Post*. But that
> would not make the slightest difference in Hackett's choice of
> books to review or what he wrote about them. If commercial pres-
> sure should by any chance endanger his job, he would rather dig
> ditches than compromise his integrity.

It would have been easy to imagine Hackett in London as a member—along with his fellow Irish expatriate, George Bernard Shaw—
of the Fabian Society which was dedicated to lighting a path to a
Socialist order by means of novels, criticism, plays, and other intellectual endeavors according to the members' various talents. The
new world, thought the society, would come gradually, almost as a
by-product of critical examinations of the manners, morals, preju-
dices, economic conditions, and other elements of modern life.
Hackett saw no hope in the regular American Socialist organs. Although idealistic enough, they had small interest in literary craftsmanship or even in the subtleties of American life. In London he
would have had access to bourgeois publications with audiences
ready for his wit and erudition. Here he was a kind of brave missionary to the heathen.

It was necessary to go warily. For developing a proper climate in
pre-*Friday Literary Review* days, he had invoked the Europeans of
advanced thought whenever an occasion arose: Shaw and Henrik
Ibsen; H. G. Wells, another leading Fabian; John Galsworthy and
Anatole France. In drawing attention to Galsworthy's *A Com-*

mentary, for example, he had prepared his readers for a thesis that fashion is blind, comfort smug, power is harsh, sport likely to be wanton. It was not a point of view likely to set well with most *Evening Post* readers.

H. G. Wells not being among Hackett's literary gods, he had no qualms, when speaking of Wells' *First and Last Things,* in remarking that "the propaganda of Socialists often fails to be persuasive." Yet he nudged his readers toward examination of the book as a "considerate statement of the heretic's present position, the heretic as an idealist and a socialist." Gentle indirection had sometimes been put aside, as when G. K. Chesterton sought to raise a "rebellion against rebellion" by satirizing "the modern doctrine of revolt" in his *The Man Who Was Thursday.* "It is hard to believe," Hackett had declared waspishly, "that Mr. Chesterton is any other than a fat person who never has really known what despair is." Harvard literary professor Barrett Wendell got the back of the hand for his *Privileged Classes,* a "smart but shallow" effort to prove that "the lower classes in the country arrogate to themselves a number of rarely recognized but genuine special privileges." In Boston the professor had seen, for example, a workingman sprawled over two trolley seats. Foolishness or worse was expected by Hackett from literary professors.

Hackett was of two minds about Friedrich Nietzsche, "poet, critic, rhapsodist and man of genius," the mention of whose name gave notice that the ultramodern in literature was up for discussion. Nietzsche's thundering glorifications of the "superman" excited the advanced writers and intrigued most readers. Even many Socialists easily passed over his contempt for the rabble while thrilling to his concept of the great soul and fierce will of the rampant male. Hackett's "man of genius" remark was the heading for his review of an ecstatic volume on Nietzsche by the young Baltimore newspaperman H. L. Mencken. But Hackett was suspicious of Mencken's estimate as too high and he spoke of Nietzsche's "chaotic effusions." Reviewing Jack London's *The Iron Heel,* he raised a warning finger against "a large supply of that Nietzsche masterful quality" and made it plain that in his opinion an author by proclaiming himself a Socialist and creating a Socialist hero could not insure his praise. "The truth is," he said cuttingly, "that Mr. Jack London combines with a contempt for the fixed order of things an effeminate admiration for brute power in the abstract and the bully in the concrete."

Hackett was willing to fudge just a little, though, to promote local talent. There was the special case of young Joseph Medill Patterson, the *Tribune* heir. Joe (as he wanted his Socialist friends to call him) had not been quite thirty when in 1908 his novel *A Little Brother of the Rich* had appeared. "The tricks can be learned," Hackett had said. "The spirit cannot. And Mr. Patterson has the spirit. Like his Sylvia, he knows so little yet, and he must know more! But life, luckily, is not so much shorter than art." Perhaps Hackett had fudged just a bit more than a little. Early in the book Sylvia addresses her fiancé, Paul Potter, captain of the college eleven:

> "Oh, Paul," she exclaimed suddenly after a silence, "I am very proud of you—not because you are tall and strong and straight, not because of your mere envelope, but because you, yourself, the inside of you, is fine and purposeful and inspiring. The body after all is but the hired carriage in which the spirit is transferred across the City of Today from the station Past, to the station Future."

Grand expressions like those do not come often from college girls. But she is wrong. Paul Potter is a mucker, the "little brother" toadying to the rich. Sylvia's village banker father loses his money and of course Paul throws her over. Much later Sylvia, a celebrated actress, has another chance to address him, a stockbroker now. "Her words volleyed forth. 'What is it you mean, but the chance to go to garish, vulgar houses of sure-thing gamblers, to guzzle yourself stupid and talk putrid pseudo-sentiment to their empty-pated doll-women? You are a cheap little tout, Potter, whose business in life is to pull in victims for the operators of gigantic confidence games.' " Whereupon she rings the bell for a servant. "Give Mr. Potter his hat and show him out." But he has the temerity to propose marriage, and hears this: "Oh, you BEAST. GO!" He does, because it is quite plain that the author will have her servants fling him into the street; already a wronged husband had threatened to have *his* servants throw Potter into the street. Outside Sylvia's house, he mutters, "I need whisky, lots of it, and I'm going to get it."

Fine spirit or not, young Patterson would need fast legs, a long life, and all of Hackett's cheers to overtake art.

Another Chicago novelist Hackett had been able to praise more fully. Robert Herrick, an exception to the professorial mossbacks, had been teaching English at Chicago University since its founding in 1893. A New Englander, he was repelled by what he regarded as the crudity and greed of Chicago's Builders and their imitators. This being evident in his work, the attitude of most local newspaper critics ranged from cool to horrified. Reviewing *Together,* about a sensitive girl married to a rich waster, Hackett had felt that the author ought to be proud of his book. "The most eager, the most restless, the most inquisitive and probably the least disciplined of womankind that the world has had the fortune to know," he commented, "have been linked to a race of indulgent, self-centered, simply organized and somewhat tired business men." To the Chicago upper classes in that year 1908 it had seemed that a plague of literary vipers was loose. A third novelist, Arthur Eddy, had held a steady spotlight on the rich in *Ganton & Co.,* dealing harshly with a meat packer ("Nothing irritated John Ganton more than a demand for fewer hours a day") and his social-climbing sons.

As a point of honor Hackett praised the novelists who lambasted Chicago's rulers to the hilt, and then, lest he might seem to be pulling his punches, drove the knife deeper. Yet obliquely he granted that readers might have different interests and opinions and still not dwell in total darkness. Vernon Lee's *Gospels of Anarchy,* for example, was carefully noted as for "the philosophical reader." Maxim Gorky's *The Spy* was offered as "a fine sidelight on the present question of extradition of Russian revolutionists," while Auguste Forel's *The Sexual Question* was treated quite chastely. The reader was warned that a prison novel called *9009,* by James Hopper and Fred R. Bechdolt, would not be light reading, although its "ferocious realism" was justified. Light reading was sometimes praised. John Fox, Jr.'s *The Trail of the Lonesome Pine* was given a kind word, and Zona Gale's *Friendship Village* even a kinder one, although it was full of sweetness. He enjoyed Kenneth Grahame's fantasy *The Wind in the Willows.* On the other hand, the enormously popular romances of Francis Marion Crawford, Winston Churchill, and their fellow confectioners were mostly ignored. He had not yet felt strong enough to tackle them head on.

After Hackett had been named in the spring of 1909 to expand the literary section into the *Friday Literary Review* (available separately at a dollar a year) he had chosen Dell as his assistant for his developing style, willingness to work hard, and his literary and political outlooks. Hackett had explained cheerfully, "You'll wash up the dishes in the kitchen while I sit in the parlor and discourse enlightenment to the suburbs." Yet Hackett was a stern disciplinarian about words on papers—which was what Dell needed. The young men were not intimate off the job. Hackett, as he said, was of a somewhat monastic temperament. Dell enjoyed the theatrical and musical night hours and even more the endless discussion of literature and politics with Hallinan and other dealers in ideas. All this refreshed him, and he worked best in the quiet hours after midnight.

The initial *Friday Literary Review* had appeared March 5, 1909. It was eight tabloid pages—almost half the size of the usual ten regular pages. There had been no advance fanfare, nor was there comment within the paper itself. Not even a masthead. Readers had to wait until the second issue to be quietly told that the supplement would be a regular thing. Standards would be "catholic and scrupulous," the editors wary of quagmires. "The slough of the advertisement seekers on the one hand, and of the academic bore on the other, are always there to engulf the writer of book reviews."

A report on Susan Glaspell's *The Glory of the Conquered* in the third number illustrated the Hackett-Dell cleavage with newspaper standards of the day. In the novel a lovely, talented girl painter marries a brilliant University of Chicago scientist. Her work receives wide acclaim. He is on the threshhold of defeating cancer, but unhappily it has been his custom while peering through the microscope to rest a finger in a corner of one eye; acids have been transferred and he goes blind. Secretly his young wife renounces her ambitions— "conquers" them—and begins studying to be his assistant. Her spirits are lifted by the dedication of other students. Now the husband sickens further, death approaches. He must never, never know of his wife's sacrifice, for he would hate himself. In the end, quite by accident, he learns that she will be able to carry on his work—and forgives.

A photograph of Susan Glaspell in the *Friday Literary Review*— her longish pretty face and big eyes—was bound to please her. A chastisement of *The Glory of the Conquered* was certain not to. Although unsigned, the review was by Hackett; the objectivity of the young assistant who barely a year ago had with Jig Cook listened to the author read parts of it could hardly be trusted. Hackett did not approve of the wife-artist's sacrificial way of proving her love, and found the students too high-minded for validity. Then he "excused" the author by noting her conscious selection of "the romantic rather than the realistic metier."

According to Elia Peattie in the *Tribune* Miss Glaspell could not have selected more wisely. Mrs. Peattie was elated to find the University of Chicago "treated with something akin to idealization" in a tale "sincere in feeling and high in purpose." The story she flatly declared to be "a noble one." These high words were lukewarm compared to those of the bellwether New York *Times,* whose *Saturday Review of Books* was one of the few other supplements. Its heading spoke of a "story of a great love" that "might with equal truth be called a romance of the spirit." Within the covers the anonymous reviewer had found so much beauty and grace and imagination as to wonder if Susan Glaspell was not indeed the pen name of some celebrated romantic author.

The cleavage was shown, too, by the handling of Morris Hillquit's *Socialism in Theory and Practice.* Hackett neither affirmed nor denied the cause of the author, who was a noted New York lawyer and a Socialist Party leader. He merely said that "to understand socialism one must grant first of all that something's rotten in the state of society." He ended by urging all "thinking people" to read the book for a better understanding of the world in which they lived. Meanwhile the New York *Times* faced up to its task of defending the status quo. "The essential fact is that Socialism does seek to overturn the present order of things, and not even so careful and instructed a Socialist as Mr. Morris Hillquit can present the case in a manner as to soften the blow." Fortunately, Hillquit's "erroneous notions" were so laughable to the conversative mind as to cast doubts on the whole.

Mrs. Peattie did not consider Hillquit's book; just now she was thankful for Francis Marion Crawford's *The White Sister,* "a real story" in what for her was becoming a "blatant and flippant age." Hackett did less than reassure her with his remarks on Robert W. Chambers' war novel *Special Messenger.* "His Lady is most charming and most wise, most brave and most sad, all in a perfectly impossible way. His Hero is most faithful, most loving, most handsome and most stupid, in an equally impossible way. And together they quite disprove General Sherman's perfectly horrible remark about War." Moreover, Hackett seized the opportunity to praise, in contrast, Stephen Crane's realistic *The Red Badge of Courage.* And so it went. In a front-page essay Hackett rediscovered Walt Whitman for the uses of a new generation. "In his writings there is the first swelling of a vast social wave on the shoals of literature. And he who wishes to understand democracy, in a revelation always veritable, if sometimes incomplete or discordant, must sit at the feet of Walt Whitman."

To the amazement of the publishing world, the *Friday Literary Review* sold books. Heads of the major book houses sent letters of praise beyond any hope of currying favor. And they sent advertisements—enough, at least, for the *Evening Post*'s executives to continue the experiment. The *FLR* editor and his assistant—their years adding up almost to middle age—nicely complemented one another: Hackett with his European schooling and erudition, Dell with his mid-American background and seemingly born sense of the true and false. Both were rebels and changers, mixing social ideals and aesthetics. They knew, at least dimly, that the response augured a changing taste and a revolution in American letters. They tried to speed it, while hoping the *Evening Post*'s moguls did not realize what they were up to.

9

An Emerging Bohemia

WORRIED lest the editors of the *Friday Literary Review* become high and mighty, George Cook sent barrages from his outpost on the Mississippi. One editor, the younger—Floyd Dell—he saw ripening toward rot at a truly amazing pace for fruit so recently green. A blast of shot: "How the mighty have fallen, and how hath F. Dell degenerated! ... If you wish to remain alive do not cease to be a partisan. F. Dell *was* egocentric. Now he aspires to write like everybody in general, nobody in particular, to be a literary ventriloquist, to have no color in his own soul, to let other men's light shine through unstained, to have no bias, no preconceived opinions. ... "

By this time Cook was acquainted with Hackett and Hallinan, who gave to the *FLR* all the time spared from editorial writing. "You Postians," Cook addressed them. "You modest, humorous, self-critical Postians ... humor turned on from spigot C." He wanted no compromise, no lights and shades in the battle for realism. His temper was less than soothed by his experiences with the novel he had begun when Dell had been his farmhand. Stokes wanted the novel, but there was an "if." Cook wrote to Dell: "I have to conventionalize, bourgeoisify, and respectablize that confounded *Chasm*." He perked up a bit when a Stokes editorial reader sent him glowing praise of the deeper aspects of the manuscript. Dell was asked to find out more about the reader, whose name was Sinclair Lewis.

The publishing connection had been made by Susan Glaspell, who naturally stood high as an incipient female Crawford or Chambers. The executive brass would have turned out to throw a guard around her if they had known what the intractable (and probably unsalable) new author was up to. He was converting Susan to, if not quite harsh realism, at least to Socialism. The two were collaborating on stories. One thing had led to another. By the winter of 1910 Cook was writing to Dell that his and Mollie's little daughter, Nilla, was big enough to call him "Papa Jig." Mollie was pregnant again. But Papa Jig was in love with Susan. In the spring he was on his way to Chicago with a trunk. This time he would wait in the city for the divorce. There being no job on the *Friday Literary Review,* he found one on a dictionary. (A sad little note came to Dell from Mollie: "I find myself growing Puritanical. I have little patience with my former deification of passion. I think the value of sexual love is very much over-estimated, and holds too consuming a place in the scheme of things. The old-fashioned God of Repression has a wise purpose behind him.")

Hackett, too, was restless from a malaise of the spirit contracted in too many years of fending off the owners' minions. Yet his criticism was as free as ever. He drew attention one after another to books which had meaning for the new generation. Of Herbert Croley's *The Promise of American Life,* which was to be the creed of many young men and women, he said, "In a long list of political books he stands out for breadth of vision, sanity of judgment and inspiration. It is with the spirit of Lincoln that the whole book is concerned, and the possibility adumbrated of a true democracy, some time, in these states." Of his friend Jane Addams' *Twenty Years at Hull House:* "To hear a Chicagoan talk, you would imagine that every Chicagoan was still under thirty, a potential millionaire, and a born 'busy booster.' . . . How Chicago shirks its burdens, and sacrifices its citizens, is in reality the story of Miss Addams' life in the Nineteenth Ward."

In midsummer 1911 Hackett bowed out of the *FLR.* Fatigue was the main cause, but he also wanted freedom to get on paper a novel he had in mind. Dell, advanced to editor, brought Jig Cook from the dictionary as his assistant.

Dell, more than Hackett, was a carrier of literary messages into the byways, a café and beerstube talker, a cross-legged debater upon studio floors, even a parlor poet. The café was usually a Greek's under the Rush Street bridge near the *Post,* where he took extended lunches with Hallinan, Cook, and those other budding poets and novelists who chanced to be in the neighborhood. At four o'clock there was an ale break at a nearby stube. The favored studio was Martha

Baker's, on the Near North Side. She was a talented young minia-turist now expanded to larger canvases. After the Dells had oblig-ingly posed for her in the nude she had given them a signed pencil sketch of the result, adding, for convention's sake, "Paris."

The parlor—or roughly its equivalent—was one of the four rooms of the Dell apartment on the North Side. In a new building in the Rogers Park section near the lake, it was handy for Margery to catch the El to her school in Evanston, and for Dell to go the other way to the Loop. They had furnished it conventionally, using Margery's savings and Dell's credit at Marshall Field's, which he was surprised to find he rated. Chicago was no slowpoke in modern trends. Dell had seen at once that purchase of any but twin beds would have made him an old fogey in the clerk's mind. The apart-ment contained, in addition to bedroom, bath, and kitchen, a front room with a fireplace and adjoining dining room—in effect, one very large room—and a smaller room used as a library-study.

To Dell the past seemed very long ago. Here he was, barely twenty-four, boss of his old boss, that scion of a Davenport big house he had vowed to pull down. World-famous authors addressed him on equal terms. A kind of salon was being established for him by a charming, indefatigable wife.

An early habitué of the Dell circle was Eunice Tietjens, warm-hearted and adventurous. At twenty-seven, having just ended a mar-riage with Paul Tietjens, composer, among other things, of the ex-travaganza *The Wizard of Oz*, she wanted to be a writer. Later she would describe the bardic climate of that Rogers Park flat:

> Not many people surely remember with such absorbing accuracy as I can the exact moment of their awakening. . . . I remember the room in which it took place with almost painful distinctness. It was . . . lined on all sides with books which reached to the ceiling. In the space between bookshelves there was room only for a couch, a chair or two, and a few feet of space in which to move about. . . . I had met the Dells through Martha Baker, the miniature painter, and cottoned to Margery at once, she being one of the three most gifted people for friendship whom I have known. Now she had in-vited me to dinner and to meet George Cram Cook.
>
> Jig Cook was just short of forty, with a remnant of the great beauty of his youth; a somber personality much of the time lit at moments with an almost cosmic gaiety; a good male drinker . . . and with a queer ability to cast out shadows. After dinner on this

vital evening we repaired to the little room which was Floyd Dell's study. There Margery and Floyd curled up on the sofa, Jig alternately sat or paced the step or two of free space, with a pipe in his mouth and an inalienable dignity about him, and I sat translated. For the talk ran on poetry. For the first time in the many years of my long sleep I heard what had been like a secret vice with me brought out boldly into the open, with no apology, as though it were indeed one of the great facts of existence.

"Here," said Floyd, "do you remember this?" And he put up a lazy hand without otherwise moving, plucked down Swinburne, and began to read in a rather light but beautiful voice the chorus from "Atalanta" in *Calydon:* "When the hounds of spring are on winter's traces . . ."

"And here," said George Cook, taking a book from a high shelf. And he too read in a deep voice full of shadows, this time the part about death from Whitman's "When Lilacs Last in the Dooryard Bloom'd": "Come, lovely and soothing death."

And Margery added Middleton, whom few now remember, and we had out Richard Hovey and Byron and Shelley and so many others that we could hardly have moved in the tiny room had not Margery, very tiny, risen to put them back in their places. So we sat till two o'clock.

Afterwards I walked home through the dark streets of Evanston. And I walked on air, like one warm with champagne, though I had had no alcohol except of the spirit. Poetry, I cried to myself, is not a dead thing, something that is shut in books to dress library shelves. . . .

In one of Eunice's trial poems a self mocking, half-serious note enchanted Dell, and he memorized it. Addressed to a rake, or at least a "man of considerable experience" (she had Jig Cook in mind), it expressed the high-hearted sadness of liberated love which in the works of Edna St. Vincent Millay and Dorothy Parker were to be on the tongue of a later generation. Eunice sent it to compete for a place in a volume to be called *Lyric Year 1912,* and it was accepted. Such flights of the imagination being taboo for a young lady of the period, it was signed "Eloise Briton."

> Dear vagrant love whose heart is scarred
> By the deep wounds of passion's war;
> Whose every kiss, a blood-red rose,
> From seed of dead desire grows,
> And kisses gone before;

Dear love, whose arms sure magic know
To kindle all the form they hold;
Whose hands are sweet against my breast
Because of others they have pressed;
And love-lore learned of old;

Dear, I have left you, ere the flame
Should cease to leap from lip to lip;
Ere my white limbs should lose their power,
Or into that last pallid hour
Love's waning moon should slip.

Vachel Lindsay came in the summer of 1911 for a visit with the
Dells. Two years earlier he had sent to the *Friday Literary Review* a
pamphlet of his illustrated verses titled *The Tramp's Excuse.* As it
was the sort of thing for the wash-up man in the kitchen, Dell had
reported on it in the October 29 issue: "Nicholas Vachel Lindsay is
something of an artist; after a fashion, a socialist; more certainly, a
religious mystic; and for present purposes it must be added that he
is indubitably a poet!"

Lindsay had been unused to reviews, much less favorable notices.
From Springfield he had written good-humoredly but with a certain
pathos: "If you can assure the dear public that I *have* a system, that
I am not disorganized or irresponsible, that all I require is patience
and a second reading—well, I will be deeply grateful." The booklet
had contained his Map of the Universe, along with "The Tree of
Laughing Bells" and other poems having to do with his "system."
Neither Dell nor the public could have been expected to fully understand it on the second or any other reading. But the correspondence
between the two young downstate Illinois natives had continued, with
Dell cordially invited to send examples of *his* poetry, which he did.
Lindsay rated the poems by drawing hearts—one or more according
to his liking—while advising Dell to study painting at the Art Institute for discipline. "Look upon Art, and double your soul." This
counsel from an older head was on the linen stationery of the
Woman's Missionary Social Union, the listed president of which was,
naturally, his mother. "I consider you," Lindsay went on, referring
to the letters and poems, "one of the fine adventures of my life."

The earlier request for Dell to assure the public that "I am not
disorganized or irresponsible," had been evidence of grievous wounds
suffered in the war against Springfield. As a cunning yet honest

general he had attacked without warning and forthrightly outlined the terms of surrender. *War Bulletin Number One* had been issued July 19, 1909. After offering it to the enemy at five cents, and having all copies refused at the price, he had passed out free copies on the streets. Four pages, nine by twelve inches, it led off:

> I have spent a great part of my few years fighting a soul battle for absolute liberty, for freedom from obligation, ease of conscience, independence from commercialism. I think I am farther from slavery than most men. But I have not complete freedom of speech. In my daily round of work I find myself taking counsel to please the stupid, the bigoted, the conservative, the impatient, the cheap. A good part of the time I can please these people, having a great deal in common with all of them—but—*the things that go into the War Bulletin please me only.*
>
> *To the Devil with you, average reader. To Gehenna with your stupidity, your bigotry, your conservatism, your cheapness and your impatience!*
>
> *In each new Bulletin the war shall go faster and further. War! War! War!*

Thus the terms for the enemy were easy! To halt the cannonade all his neighbors had to do was to make themselves intelligent, broadgauged, progressive, noble, and patient. *War Bulletin Number Two,* a fortnight later, extended the conflict to Morristown, New Jersey, of all places. Once Lindsay had gone into a mission there seeking balm for his soul but had been fumigated, given a down-the-nose sermon, a plate of vile food, and a scabrous bed. His blast was meant to scotch this phase of modern religion.

After nearly a month, *War Bulletin Number Three* spelled out for astonished eyes his "Creed of the Beggar." Taking St. Francis as his master and praying to attain his divine immolation, Lindsay proclaimed Beggary to be "the noblest occupation of man." Followers were exhorted to march with him to the cities and shut down the great marts of commerce without violence. If the bloated spiders— the owners—held fast to their dens, the faithful must go out "carrying neither purse nor scrip, ragged with a beggar's pride." They must cast out "the Devils of money-lust in those we meet. . . . If any man has a dollar in his pocket let him throw it away, lest it transform him into spiritual garbage."

The stung Philistines made ready pots of boiling oil and sent them down upon the head of the invader. Even his partisans (a few Single-

Taxers, YMCA devotees, fanatic Campbellites) deserted. For the next communiqué, in September, he was content to offer his *The Tramp's Excuse,* remarkable for "On the Building of Springfield," which Dell was to praise in the *Friday Literary Review* for its "throbbing, glowing realism."

> Let not our town be large, remembering
> That little Athens was the Muses' home,
> That Oxford rules the heart of London still,
> That Florence gave the Renaissance to Rome. . . .
>
> We should build parks that students from afar
> Would choose to starve in, rather than go home,
> Fair little squares, with Phidian ornament,
> Food for the spirit, milk and honeycomb. . . .

War Bulletin Number Five, handed around just before Thanksgiving, was a humorous tale (with a sobriety message) of a tipsy ice man dancing to a hurdy-gurdy. And in the Christmas season Lindsay offered a "truce" via the *Sangamon County Peace Advocate,* which he thrust into the hands of shoppers. The tone was set by "Springfield Magical," ending:

> In this, the City of my Discontent,
> Down from the sky, up from the smoking deep
> Wild legends new and old burn round my bed
> While trees and grass and men are wrapped in sleep.
> Angels come down, with Christmas in their hearts,
> Gentle, whimsical, laughing, heaven-sent;
> And, for a day, fair Peace have given me
> In this, the City of my Discontent.

Ever since Vachel's return to Springfield conditions in the Lindsay household had been worsening. His father's vision, dimming from cataracts, injured his practice. In an effort to make ends meet his mother was filling the house with roomers. Vachel had reneged on his promise to dig ditches or whatever was necessary to earn a living. He eked out a few dollars by lectures for the Anti-Saloon League in nearby towns and villages. He would charge into some den of iniquity and give Satan's bar helper "what for" and then exhort Satan's victims to reform. These excursions were gratis. For a full-dress lecture his fee was ten dollars. In some periods he was out every Sunday, often filling a pulpit. The income was never sufficient even

to meet his printer's bills. He insisted on good paper and workman-
ship, and, since his illustrations were costly to reproduce, his parents
had to chip in.

Lindsay's main project for 1910 had been a heavy, handsome
volume called *The Village Magazine*. There were seventy-six pages
of thick-coated stock, nine by twelve inches, with a stiff gray cover.
Most of the text was hand-lettered by himself, which added to the
cost since it had to be electroplated. He ordered seven hundred
copies to be run off, with the idea (but no real hope) of selling them
at a dollar apiece. Now Springfield had become for him a village
(although the population was nearly fifty thousand), the inhabitant
a fine specimen of the human race, especially in contrast to a city
dweller. "His *crudity* is plain, but his delicacy is apparent also."
Whole pages were given to celebration of "The Village Improvement
Parade." A poem of the same title accompanied the illustrations:

> Guns salute, and crowds and pigeons fly,
> Bronzed, Homeric bards go striding by,
> Shouting "Glory" amid the cannonade:—
> It is the cross-roads
> Resurrection
> Parade . . .

Most of the copies had been distributed free by Lindsay's own
hand or, when he could get the postage, by mail to editors, artists,
poets, and philosophers whom he admired. This sowing of the winds
was according to his habit, and it was bearing a tiny harvest. He
was in warm correspondence with other young poets: Witter Bynner,
Arthur Davison Ficke, Anna Hempstead Branch, Fannie Stearns
Davis, and of course Floyd Dell. Even William James, the venerable
Harvard psychologist and philosopher, sent a friendly letter, although confessing his inability to fully comprehend the Map of the
Universe. Eastern editors blithely rejected the proffered verse which
Lindsay kept in the mail—a dozen packets at a time—and so he
was the more thunderstruck when *Current Literature* gave two pages
of its March 1911 number to praise for *The Village Magazine*. This
Illinois art evangelist and authentic western poet was a fresh voice,
the editors said, that readers would do well to heed.

One who had (and had sent two dollars for two copies) was
Hamlin Garland, who sought evidence for his thesis that the Mississippi Valley would be the new seat of American literature. After

finding the *Magazine* to his satisfaction, he invited Lindsay to be a luncheon guest speaker—travel expenses to Chicago paid—at the Cliff-Dwellers Club, a semiliterary group which Garland had helped to found. If upon arriving there Lindsay seemed out of place to the city men in their handsome dining room, his hearty greeting to "Brother Garland" and his quite loud message did not show it. After all, he was used to shaming the Devil in his own lairs.

Since Garland was a power in Chicago's cultural affairs, he had easily arranged for the young visitor to address the students of the Art Institute. Lindsay needed all his powers of forgiveness not to be triumphant, for not long ago a former teacher at the Institute, who had been sent a copy of *The Tramp's Excuse,* had written that "many of your poems seem to me so unbalanced, so diseased, so egotistical that I can find no sympathy in them. Your drawing, as I have always said, is all of this—it is bad." True, Lindsay wasn't exactly being greeted as a conquering hero artist—a role he had, of course, expected to play long ago.

On this trip Lindsay had barely had time to meet the Dells, but in the summer he was back to stay with them as long as he chose. The mild flurry over *The Village Magazine*—Dell, too, had given it a favorable notice—had not caused editors (at least those who paid for verse) to be noticeably more receptive to his work. A new poem, "The Eagle That Is Forgotten," in memory of ex-Governor Altgeld, had appeared in the *Illinois State Register* (Springfield) and later in the St. Louis *Post* and other papers, and Dell had found space for "The Wizard in the Street," a celebration of Poe. But these hardly forecast a break in the long years of bad weather. The ebb of his life, Lindsay felt, had reached its lowest point.

At first he was quiet and solemn, his hosts not being "public," or else full of obscure chuckles and quaint ways. He confided to Dell, "It isn't generally known, and don't tell anybody, but my mother owns property in Springfield." Dell took the remark as a kind of defense against probable Springfield charges that he was a leech on his parents. Dell's confidence in him and Margery's quick understanding and tact soon raised his spirits and put him at ease with the group around them. The hot nights were often spent on the near-by lake shore, often with picnic baskets. Dell and Cook and Hallinan had read William Butler Yeats' suggestion that poetry ought to be chanted. They tried it. Lindsay had used short, quick rhythms, as in "The Potatoes Dance," which he had once read-sung for a kindergarten gambol. But he had never tried a powerful beat for an adult topic; a large part of his verse was gentle, especially his "Moon-Poems." The chanting seemed to go deep into his inner ear. He wanted to write of America, folk America, and before long he was noting down old songs—"Nellie Was a Lady," "Put on Your Old Gray Bonnet," etc.—whose rhythms might perhaps be used in poems.

Other talented young people wrote to Dell simply asking to meet him. Among these was "a prim little Englishman," Maurice Browne, who for this purpose used a letterhead of the Progressive Arts League of America. This was his right as Organizing Secretary. He wasn't cutting much of a swath. He was envoy as well for the Poetry Societies of Great Britain, Australia, and South Africa, holding a mandate to annex the United States. The trouble was that someone else had already run up the flag of the Poetry Society of America. At the moment Browne was more or less resting. The author of the "prim little Englishman" phrase was Arnold Bennett, now at the height of his fame as British novelist. Which only showed his ignorance of Browne. Browne was not large and he was English. But prim! At the age of thirty, the number of his dead loves strewn over sundry continents and islands was already impressive.

In his letter, after remarking that the *Friday Literary Review* "is the most stimulating thing in Chicago," Browne suggested that while his name as a writer would probably not be known to Dell, perhaps as a lecturer it was, inasmuch as he had just finished a series at Chicago University on "Poets of the Future." What he didn't say, and didn't need to, was that Dell could hardly have missed a recent story in the *Tribune* blazoned: "Young Britisher Denounces Ten Commandments." A lecture agent had arranged a date for him in Lincoln Center, where his suggestion that the Mosaic Decalogue might not suit the Chicago of 1911 had resulted in the *Tribune* story. The demise of a career of light-bringing to the dark city had been expected, which proved how little he knew of the matter. To say what he had, or anything faintly like it, was a very bad thing to do in a public place. His immediate booking by the agent into a dozen fashionable residences—the plush road of the circuit—was inevitable.

Browne let Dell know that while in London he had written for A. R. Orage's *New Age,* one of the most respected of the advanced journals, had founded the Samurai Press, and was still in touch with the new movements abroad. His stated wish to meet Dell was soon gratified, along with Dell's natural desire to know why so accomplished a young man was lingering in Chicago. A black-eyed girl was at the bottom of it; her name was Ellen Van Volkenburg. The two had first met in Italy and he had followed her across Europe and the United States, pawning family heirlooms, failing to get, or getting and losing, teaching jobs, collecting grandiose but empty titles.

Ellen was an imitator of great stage performers, especially of Maude Adams and Ethel Barrymore and Minnie Maddern Fiske. Yet to describe her as merely an imitator was to give a false idea of her curious and remarkable talent. Uncannily, she added imitations of the whole cast. It was only necessary for her to be at a single performance, preferably a rehearsal, where she would fall into a trance. She always wept, not knowing why, and the players' lines and voices and manners were somehow recorded on her inner consciousness. Then she would awaken, feeling fine, ready to give the play in its entirety.

Ellen wanted to quit imitations for real acting. Maurice burned to bring art to the people. Why the people of Chicago? He didn't know, except that Ellen's home was there, and the very fact of the *Friday Literary Review*'s existence boded well for his ambition.

Lucian Cary wrote to Dell somewhat less out of the blue. Hackett had turned over to him a notebook containing the names of reviewers and remarks on each. Cary was rated "very brilliant, but hard to get anything out of." Cary's letter was the sort to delight an editor except for the evidence confirming Hackett's judgment on his procrastination. Headed *"Tribune* Local Room," it was typed on copy paper.

A year ago last March or April I wrote 400 or 800 words on a book by Clayton Hamilton and sent them to Mr. Hackett. He printed them and sent me a box of books to review.

I left my Indiana address [he had been teaching college English] before the books arrived there and came to Chicago. Mr. Hackett received me with such unreasonable courtesy that I became confidential. He prescribed the *Tribune.*

The point is that the books are still on my hands, not altogether unread but altogether unsung so far as the *Review* and I are concerned.

I appeal to you, as Mr. Hackett's successor, to relieve my conscience of those books. It is not a New England conscience. If it were I would have sold the books long ago and saved the money.

The *Review* is the one feature of Chicago newspapers that I invariably read, even to the clippings from the New York *Sun* and the New York *Sunday Call* that I have read before. I have defended it by word of mouth and by thousand-word letters and by silence, even. But I have not sent it notices of those books.

What am I to do with them?

I am glad that I can still look forward to the *Review*. Your final sentence in your notice of Arthur Schnitzler's dialogues was the subject of one of those thousand-word letters—and I am glad that Mr. Hackett is going to write a novel. I assume he is going to do that.

But in the meantime I shall be glad to learn of some way out of my moral predicament.

Dell quickly dispatched a box of fresher books for review. The two men did not meet, however, until a night when Cary was sent by his editor to see if there might be an item in Martha Baker's birthday party in her largish studio. His wife accompanied him as far as a nearby drugstore. Cary scouted ahead, found no usable item, but was invited—by Dell, everything being informal—to join the party. His wife, too, was summoned when her lurking place became known.

Cary was a few years older than Dell. His eyes twinkled with merriment or mischief. He liked to insult the girls to please them, and his indolent movements and slow speech—with dashes of acid—added to his charm. From his native Kansas he had passed through Wisconsin and Minnesota, working on newspapers. In Madison he had found and wed the golden brown Augusta. Her tousled wavy hair was piled high above a lovely face with expressive blue eyes. Her long-fingered hands were expressive, too, as she spoke. At Martha Baker's and for a while afterward she was quiet and shy, until a river of challenging knowledge and opinions burst out. Then she was "Gus," of splendid energy and high heart. When Cary spoke of the Hackett-sent books as "not altogether unread" he might have been accurate without having cracked a single one. Many of the books he discussed so brilliantly had been read in the family by Gus alone. The Carys liked Bernard Shaw and Arnold Bennett, H. G. Wells and Thomas Hardy, Flaubert and de Maupassant, Ibsen and Arthur Schnitzler—all the modern Europeans. Politically, they were less radical than the Dell-Cook-Hallinan triumvirate. In matters of unfettered soul and body they were far advanced. Until their advent no one in the Dell group had heard much about Sigmund Freud and psychoanalysis—and certainly none of the Freudian talk that in another dozen years would be the rage.

Not many bourgeois standards of behavior were smashed in this incipient bohemia. A beach picnic was a picnic, no more. Bathing suits of the men came to the knee. Those of the ladies had also a skirt. As for Bacchic revelry, the Anti-Saloon portion of Vachel Lindsay's character never impelled him to exhortations. True, the Dells served cocktails. If not daring, at least they were uncommon enough in the lower bourgeoisie that proper vessels were not to be had in the stores. Sherbet glasses were resorted to. Light wines embellished dinner parties. One night when Lucian Cary found himself a sheet to the wind, and Dell was walking him around the block, his major concern was lest his wife might think badly of him for overindulgence.

The Dickensian Mr. Currey was often present and never ill at ease; nor was Margaret Anderson, the literary editor of *The Continent,* a religious journal. She had become a friend of the Dells after judging a book or two for the *Friday Literary Review.* Dell considered her reviews the most ecstatic in the known literary world. He didn't like them. Or, rather, her madly idealistic point of view. He reasoned with her. But her blue eyes—innocent and fresh as the morning dew—stared him down, her unearthly red-gold beauty unnerved him, and her breathless gasps over the volume in hand took away his own breath. To have foreseen, a few years hence, Margaret Anderson in the grip of the constabulary for having published the earliest pages of James Joyce's *Ulysses* was quite impossible.

Margaret was the kind of girl who, if she wrote to the author of a column advising young ladies, would be invited to come at once for a personal chat. And upon whose appearance the author would drop everything and take her to dinner and the theater and ask *her* opinion on whatever problems bother advisers to the lorn. It had happened. After college Margaret had been restless in her Indiana home town. Fifty dollars a month in pin money was no solace. "Mother could fill the house with those vibrations that penetrate every wall, even if you were reading in concentration in the attic."

Especially since Margaret was apt to be reading Ellen Key or Havelock Ellis or her treasured calf-bound volume of Ibsen or the works of Shelley, Keats, or Swinburne. Her pleas for advice on how to leave home had gone to Clara E. Laughlin, whose column of advice appeared in *Good Housekeeping*. Miss Laughlin, who lived in Chicago, had bid her take a train at once. They talked for days. Miss Laughlin begged suggestions for a play she had in progress. Margaret, giving it, missed her homebound train by five dollars worth of hansom-cab waiting fee.

By the time she had caught another, the offer had been made of a job on the religious magazine, *The Continent*, which Miss Laughlin edited. After a bit Margaret returned to Chicago, pin money cut off, and held the job until snatched back home for having charged an oriental rug for her YWCA room. She squandered a nickel every day on a yellow rose, smoked, and taught other Y girls to smoke. Who had blown the whistle? Miss Laughlin herself. But immobilizing Margaret was impossible. Selling the calf-bound Ibsen and two gorgeous negligees, she had escaped again to Chicago and her Y room. Then she had worked in Francis Fisher Browne's remarkable bookshop in the Fine Arts Building and aided him on his magazine, *The Dial*. She had walked the promenade through the Auditorium and The Annex like a slim fair princess imagining herself a poor working girl, quite forgetting that she was a poor working girl at wages of eight dollars a week. If that is involved, or paradoxical, it was Margaret at her simplest. That winter her destination had usually been The Annex's Elizabethan Room, where she had steeped herself in the atmosphere of soft davenports, low lights, and rich hangings while reading or composing letters. Naturally the attendants treated her as royalty. And so she was, even after repairing to her narrow Y room. She and Mr. Browne were probably equal in elegance, but, taken all in all, he probably knew more lyric poetry (they had quoted it to one another). She had had no way of knowing that such wantonness would in the end lead to his endeavor to kiss her. And so she had quit and gone back to a job on Miss Laughlin's magazine.

Margaret came to the beach picnics (Diana in a blue bathing suit) as well as to dinners and parties. So did a more placid but iron-willed girl, Fanny Butcher, a neophyte reviewer. Among the others were Ephra Vogelsang, an aspiring singer; and Susan Glaspell's friend, Lucy Huffaker, another dreamer of a better theater. It was

Lucy who introduced into the group Edna Kenton, writer for the highbrow magazines and a seasoned (although still in her thirties) warrior in social and literary causes. Short and growing fleshy, Edna was a vivid talker and a nonconformist doer. Abominating the whalebone corsets of the time, yet forced to deal with her own bulging contours, she had created flowing outer garments which left her unfettered and were striking besides. Sewn with her own hands from China silk, they hung, or billowed, from a sort of yoke about her neck. A descendant of frontier fighter Simon Kenton, Edna came naturally into the ranks of skirmishers riding ahead. Not only was she an agitator and magazine commentator on feminine rights ("There is a sex war as well as a class war"), she was also something of an authority on the early Jesuit missionaries, geology, and the novels of Henry James.

For Dell and the others seeking to break new literary ground, Edna was especially fascinating for her friendship with Theodore Dreiser. As an early underground fighter for *Sister Carrie* she was a maker of the legend that inspired them all. Long ago, in 1900, she had reviewed the novel, praising it, for the Chicago *Daily News*. The notice, to be sure, had been a mere paragraph. But she had continued to strike blows. As a rumor spread that the publisher was trying to suppress the book, she had discovered and bought ten copies for circulation among advanced readers. Five years after publication she had written a letter of encouragement to Dreiser. This message from a votary—a lady at that, perhaps young and pretty, surely a free soul—had been a flash of light in Dreiser's gloom. He had written back of a "haunting sensation that I have met you before. In 1892 I worked on the Chicago *Globe* and there was an editor there who wrote a book. . . . As the price of my admission to the staff of the *Globe* I was compelled to take that book about. Somewhere on the South Side, in a nice, quiet street I met a young lady who laughed and joked over the thing and gave me the price of the book as well as the kindliest reception I had ever received. She remained and remains in my memory and as I read your letter somehow the feeling came over me that you must be she." It wasn't the same woman. But he invited Edna to visit him when in New York. She did, and they had become good friends.

In the autumn of 1911, Edna was in New York when Dell arrived for his literary editor's due of making a round of the publishing houses. For his first journey East he had raised a mustache and out-fitted himself with a pince-nez, stiff hat, cane, and spats in order to appear older and more worldly. The savings account had been emptied for Margery to come too. By far the greatest adventure—if Edna succeeded in working it out—would be an intimate con-versation with Dreiser, whose first novel in eleven years was about to come off the presses. If it proved an advance beyond its prede-cessor, *Sister Carrie,* the large but shadowy hero perhaps would emerge as a giant able to break the shackles of American fiction.

What was he like nowadays? Dell and Margery were anxious to find out.

10

Dreiser: Masks of the Monster and Hero

D REISER'S luck since his coming of age had been both good and horrible. When he left Chicago in 1892, at the age of twenty-one, for a reporter's job on the St. Louis *Globe-Democrat,* it had been sunny. His editor had arranged the transfer so that he might get training on one of the best of U.S. dailies. He had done very well, being assigned even to minor theatrical openings which he felt would be helpful in his ambition to be a playwright. Then bad luck had pushed in. To review stock company offerings without seeing them was common practice, a few lines from the program being enough. Dreiser, busy on another assignment, wrote notices of three; they went into the paper—and owing to a railroad washout the companies did not appear. Nor did he, at the office. The crime was in being caught.

He found a job on the inferior *Republic* and was sent back to Chicago as Boswell for a group of Missouri schoolma'am winners of a trip to the World's Fair. Among them was a Dresden doll redhead who became his fiancée and much later his wife. This was Sara White (called Sally), whose father was a prosperous farmer at Montgomery City, about seventy miles northwest of St. Louis. Sally was biding her time, teaching school until the proper man came along. She was four years the older, mildly "literary," better at grammar, at least, than he. Newspaper friends warned that she was conventional, set in provincial ways. These things, along with her resolute chastity and his admiration for her father, were for Dreiser her best attractions. Mr. White was a towering patriarch, both headstrong and religious. If a sick neighbor sought his intercession with heaven, he dropped unaffectedly to his knees and prayed, expecting a prompt and favorable response. When out to right a temporal wrong or accomplish a good deed he could be imperious, but usually was of good cheer. A very different man from Dreiser's own father! Sally was to be the anchor, and the White home a safe harbor, in stormy years ahead.

In the spring of 1894, Dreiser had set out for the East. In Toledo he had gotten a few days of work. Cleveland and Buffalo had offered nothing. His luck changed in Pittsburgh, where he worked as a reporter through the summer and fall. Then it was on to New York, which promptly licked him. He was given a trial on the *World* and failed. As Paul had long ago come out of the mists to rescue the Dreiser family, he extended his warm, strong hand to his brother. Now Paul was becoming famous for sentimental songs: "My Gal Sal" (indeed, the lost madam of Evansville), "Just Tell Them That You Saw Me," "On the Bowery," "I Believe It, for My Mother Told Me So," and others that were to be national favorites. Theodore looked down his nose at them as popular mush, but he furnished the idea and several lines for "On the Banks of the Wabash."

The truth was that a part of his nature was every bit as sentimental as Paul's. It was contradicted by a massive gift for estrangement. The "vain and more or less dependent snip"—his later words for himself—managed to fall out with Paul, rejecting his largess, and sank rapidly toward the Bowery's world of homeless men. For one thing, he had trouble drinking alcohol without falling into excess. At last Paul, coming home from a road trip—he was still an occasional performer—snatched him out of the morass and got him a job editing a new trade magazine for a music publishing firm. Dreiser stayed with it for two years, until he was selling enough articles to risk free-lancing. His topics varied from slum conditions (a few) to success stories of the great (very many). For the latter he was admitted to the presence of no less than his old fellow Chicagoans, Marshall Field and P. D. Armour.

Sally White had gone on teaching and waiting, cheered by visits to or from her "Teddy," a departure in nomenclature from that used by most of his girl friends, who called him "Theo" after his manner of signing himself. Once, forseeing eventual pain for Sally, and being at the moment in love with another—a not unusual condition—he sought to break the engagement. Sally reached her hands to his shoulders and declared gently, "No, Teddy. You need me."

The courtship had lasted for nearly six years when they were married in the Christmas season of 1898. Dreiser was twenty-eight, Sally thirty-two.

The following year he was more or less coerced into being a novelist. When he had stopped off in Toledo five years before, he had struck up a friendship with Arthur Henry, the city editor of the *Blade*. Their reaction to one another had been almost violent, which was no great surprise to Dreiser, a strong believer in the "chemistry" of personal relations. Henry, a bit the older, dreamed of being a novelist and poet. Dreiser had tried his hand at enough poetry to question his muse, but the playwright's star beckoned. To him Henry was "the sentimentalist in thought and the realist in action," he "the realist in thought, the sentimentalist in action." Since his gift for friendship matched his capacity for estrangement, over the years the two had seen just enough of each other to "revel in that wonderful possession, intellectual affection."

In the summer of 1899 the newly wed Dreisers had become guests of the Henrys on the River Maumee near Toledo. For a long time Henry had been urging Dreiser to try fiction, and now he insisted. Dreiser politely tossed off a few stories. He was incredibly swift once pen was taken up, never braking to hunt a choice word or nicety of construction. Also he was blessed with the stamina that makes a lumberer a fast racer once the first yards of paper have been covered. Three of the stories had been filtered through a combination of a philosophy of life drawn from childhood experiences and his reading of naturalists Charles Darwin and Thomas Huxley and the philosopher Herbert Spencer. He saw their concept of "survival of the fittest"—including the use of the weak by the strong—as a simple fact of life. Man was "a mechanism, undevised and uncreated, and a badly and carelessly driven one at that."

The first story, "McEwen of the Shining Slave Makers," was remindful of the boy Theodore sprawled on a creek bank speculating on the lives of wild creatures. A newspaper man finds himself turned into an ant, a participant in the ordered yet senseless violence of the ant world. For another story, "Old Rogaum and His Theresa" —a struggle between a German butcher and his boy-fascinated daughter—the author had merely to put his father and one of his sisters on stage. In a third, "Nigger Jeff," a reporter is set to capturing all the insensate cruelty of a lynching. Reading them over, Dreiser had been disgusted. Henry had said they were good. Argument was cut off by Dreiser, who, in need of ready money, turned to articles.

The following autumn, Henry moved to New York and resumed the attack. This time he demanded that his friend begin a novel, if for no better reason than to keep him company on one he had begun. Dreiser obliged. At least, he afterward gave it as the sole reason for beginning *Sister Carrie*. Yet, since he was a devout if intermittent believer in his own genius, and since he had tried short stories and was a fast writer, it seemed inevitable that he would some day try the form. After quitting several times he set down the final words in early April of 1900, bringing the total to some 240,000, or more than twice the size of the average novel. In a working time of roughly four months his daily output had been an amazing two thousand words. Henry assisted in pruning out about a sixth of the words.

The first publisher to whom Dreiser had carried the manuscript, Harper Brothers, fulfilled his expectations by rejecting it. He tried Doubleday, Page and Company, a new firm which might be hospitable to unconventional work. The heavens lighted up. Frank Norris, the novelist, acting as editorial reader, uttered a fervent endorsement. A contract was signed. Norris wrote to Dreiser, calling *Sister Carrie* "the best novel I had read in manuscript since I had been reading for the firm, and it pleased me as well as any novel I have read in any form." Although barely the older, Norris, Chicago-born but reared in the Far West, now had a solid literary name. Only last year he had won the acclaim of vanguard critics and readers for the powerful realism of his novel *McTeague*. Dreiser, far from grounded in current or past literature, had read it almost by chance when his sister-in-law, Ida White, a teacher, had urged him to. The brutal struggle between a lumpish dentist and his miserly wife had been to him the blood and bone of life.

The resounding praise coming from the brilliant novelist and editor naturally raised his hopes. Moreover, he had spoken with one of the Doubleday partners, Walter Hines Page, a former editor of the *Atlantic Monthly*, and come away sure of the house's resolution to promote the book heavily when it came out in the autumn. Being human, he passed the grand news to friends and got ready to push the work with might and main. Although panicky at the thought of speaking to an audience, he readily agreed to "lecture," after the book was out, at the Players, a club frequented by literary as well as theatrical notables. Then with Sally he had departed for her Missouri family home to await the great day. In the meantime he would weave the contents of his research notebooks into magazine articles and, his confidence now as boundless as his energy, begin another novel.

One July night he tossed and turned in his bed, nerves deranged by a psychic "feel" of trouble winging its way toward him. Such was his memory of the night before the shattering letter came. A skeptic of psychic phenomena might have wondered if such tossings had not been common during that summer, if in his subconscious there had not been a lack of faith in Frank Norris' fine hopes. The letter was from Doubleday, who wanted to be released from its contract. Wrote Page: "I think I told you, personally, these kind of people did not interest me, and we find it hard to believe they will interest the great majority of readers." What the diplomatic Page (later he would be U.S. Ambassador to Great Britain) thought he had said did not jibe with the author's recollection. Dreiser fought back, by letter and then personally in New York. The publisher's lawyer declared that the contract must be fulfilled, but only to the technical letter. Dreiser, seeking to be cooperative, removed words and phrases which suddenly had become offensive: "by the Lord," "damn," "by God."

The full history of the conflict (at the time, a publisher's minor skirmish with a minor author) and the facts of the disposal of the one thousand books printed were to be gradually obscured by legend. Two years later one of the best observers, Frank Norris, was dead. In the legend, the entire edition moldered in the basement of a Doubleday warehouse except for copies surreptitiously dispatched by Norris to reviewers. The villain of the piece was a lady author, mostly of bird books, who wrote under the pseudonym, "Neltje Blanchan." She was also the wife of Frank Doubleday, ranking partner in the publishing house. Reading advance proofs of *Sister Carrie*—so ran the legend—and finding it immoral, or at least unworthy of the firm's imprint, she had urged her husband to break the author's contract. Failing that, he had in effect suppressed it.

At least some of the facts were out of agreement with the legend. Review copies had gone in the normal way to a hundred periodicals. Five hundred copies had been sold in trade channels (but without an advertising push). If the rest were in a warehouse basement, the storage place was usual enough. About the low sales it was possible to argue in two directions. If a publisher has small faith in a book, and critics and early readers agree, he seldom risks cash for much promotion. The *Sister Carrie* notices did not add up to enthusiasm and the "discoverers" were too few and tardy to provide momentum. On the other hand, it is accepted in publishing circles that if the decision-makers of a house become irritated with a book's author who has become "difficult," or have decided the work will damage the firm, they can usually cause it to fall dead from the press. A hint to the promotion staff that such a fate is wanted is probably enough. As for the ogre of the legend, no ironclad evidence of Mrs. Doubleday's part—even evidence that she had one—reached the outside world. Dreiser always said that he had had it straight from Norris' lips that she had raised the rumpus, but he never revealed how Norris had arrived at this opinion.

If Mrs. Doubleday did fiercely object to *Sister Carrie,* her mind was only in tune with the times. Yet on the surface there is a contradiction. Dreiser's people were fully clothed when seen by the reader. The highest passion of Drouer's seduction pitch was, "My, but you're a little beauty." Carrie's fate was sorrow to last all her days. And Hurstwood surely got his just deserts. Why, then, was not *Sister Carrie* accepted as a morality tale? The main answer probably was that Mrs. Doubleday and the rest of the hierarchy of the materialistic society could not believe in Carrie's mental sorrows. Had not she won fame and fortune, with desirable men falling at her feet? Carrie had to be deplored as a danger to wives of affluent husbands. The author had capped his mistakes by improper respect for the double standard. Punish the man? Certainly. More than the woman? Never! To do so was a subtle attack on the concept of the gentleman in a male society. Even the women admitted that the men had powerful natural urges to sexual transgressions. The duty of the female, being made of finer stuff, was to help curb these base passions. If she did not, but rather was complaisant, she deserved to be treated as a jungle beast. The author of *Sister Carrie* had grown up, of course, in circles where these things were poorly understood.

That was no excuse. If he lacked the sense to borrow from the mores of his betters, then he had to suffer the consequences.

Dreiser had not been the best witness in the legend-making, for he had sunk into black despair. In the hope of finding a new publisher he trudged to leading houses. Turned away, he came to believe himself ostracized. *Sister Carrie* itself may have been ostracized by the decision-makers, but in some houses it found admirers, generally young editors who raised storms that had to be put down. In England, William Heinemann, seeking permission to issue a shorter version, remarked about its author to the Doubleday firm, "I congratulate you very heartily in having discovered him. You should make a great fuss." The letter was forwarded to Dreiser without comment. He agreed to cut the first two hundred pages by more than half, but in the end Arthur Henry had to do it.

Although English critics and readers gave the book respectful attention, Dreiser hardly stirred in his black morass. A little known American publisher advanced cash on a second novel. Even though a small sum, it ought to have been a thing to hold to. He only sank deeper. A contributing factor—although he didn't know it at the time —was a faulty appendix, which, along with stomach pains, sapped him. In a year all confidence had departed—he couldn't write a single line. For lack of money and because he wanted to fight alone, his wife had gone back to Missouri. Hallucinations gripped him. He was too low in mind, too ashamed, to beg aid from Paul or other relatives. For another year, as it had been with Hurstwood, he went down, down—all the way to homelessness and thoughts of suicide.

Then one day Paul found him in the street, burst into tears at his condition, and packed him off to a health camp run by an ex-wrestler. When somewhat better, Dreiser found a railroad workingman's job. Three years after publication of *Sister Carrie* he at last pulled himself out of the swamp. He raced at once for higher ground as if in deadly fear. Up he went—in four years from assistant feature editor of a small New York daily to editor of popular fiction magazines and then to the rich *Delineator*, owned by the pattern-making Butterick company. Few old acquaintances would have recognized him. The thirty-two staff members addressed him as "Mr. Dreiser," knees often ready to quake. The paneling and massive furniture of his office was of carved walnut. A youth seeking a job found the distance from the door to his desk interminable: the great man was "busily writing, and it was all of five minutes before he took off his pince-nez glasses and looked up." This was William Lengel, a Missourian, who landed a job as private secretary.

To another young man, Sinclair Lewis, who wanted to write for the magazine, the editor looked "more like a wholesale hardware merchant." Not many visitors had the brass of still another youth, this a cherubic one, who lifted one of his jack-dandy yellow shoes to a knee and, as Dreiser said later, "beamed on me with the confidence of a smirking fox about to devour a chicken." To establish order, the great man let go a whiplash of sarcasm: "Well, if it isn't Anheuser's own brightest boy out to see the town!" The visitor replied benignly that the Menckens of Baltimore brewed even finer beer, and he, Henry L., was the brightest lad of the tribe. Dreiser's mask came off, and "we proceeded to palaver and yoo-hoo anent the more general phases and ridiculosities of life." And so began perhaps the most productive friendship in the life of each.

Lengel also became aware of the softer nature behind the raspy exterior. For one thing, he was told by lanky Homer Croy, a young editor also from Missouri, that his job application had been a cinch all the way, that Dreiser never failed to give a Missourian a trial. Lengel felt that Dreiser did not mean to be harsh. "In fact, he tried to be jovial and bantering. But his curiously wandering eye and his twisted mouth made his attempts at lightness seem dictatorial, and what he intended as joviality was often mistaken for sarcasm."

Amid the golden welter of dress patterns and household hints and sentimental uplift, Dreiser did not entirely forget his past. Soon after going to Butterick's he had taken a one-third interest in a small new publishing firm, B. F. Dodge and Company, which had agreed to publish *Sister Carrie* from plates purchased from Doubleday. With the growing legend, and his own strong promotion hand, the new edition, issued in the fall of 1907, received wide critical notice and sold eight thousand copies in the first year—a respectable figure. Grosset and Dunlap then brought out a cheaper edition which sold in about the same quantity. The vindication, if not sensational, was at least a chewy sweet to go with the legend. Word of an incident had already convinced him that Mrs. Doubleday was stung by rumors of her part in the affair. William Heinemann, visiting from London, had told him of being a guest in the Doubleday home when she had argued bitterly—it had seemed defensively—against the book. The two to three thousand dollars earned by the new editions over three years were insufficient, however, to charm back to writing a man in the ten-thousand-a-year class. Even had he been able to divide his mind between uplift and realism, he was not, he found, an effectual spare-time author.

While accepting the inspirational formula, he tried to bring some of the real world into the *Delineator*. A story in which a woman smoked a cigarette ignited one interoffice brawl. The business-side executives demanded that the scene be cut. Dreiser and his aides insisted that it remain. In joint meeting the two sides tore at each others' throats. The scene stayed in, and the editors believed that for the first time a woman had puffed a cigarette in the pages of a general American magazine. The donnybrook was only a little more intense than many others. By temperament Dreiser was incapable of taking orders from above—at least forever. The business executives held final authority, and as the battles grew more fierce he secretly bought control, in 1909, of a shaky magazine called *The Bohemian*. His hope was to flesh it up as a hedge against dismissal.

Away from the office, Dreiser's life was hardly more serene. In ten years of betrothal and marriage to Sally, they had not been together for more than one, until her return after his recovery in 1903. Now, half a dozen years later, at forty, he longed for the youth he had missed. Sally at forty-four called him Honey Bun. He despised being called Honey Bun. Of course, she found less endearing words when catching him in a side romance. Dreiser was a confessed varietist. Sally was a foe of varietism, in Honey Bun's case particularly.

The situation being what it was, good judgment called for Dreiser to shun varietism inside the Butterick establishment. Even more, to avoid as a plague any young girl whose mother was a power there. He met and was overwhelmed by Thelma Cudlipp, seventeen, a girl with a face like a newly opened flower. She had a studious mind and a talent for drawing. Her mother, a spare, gray, domineering widow, headed the Butterick stenographic pool. With two other children to launch into the world, she had been gratified when the august editor had showed a paternal interest in Thelma, for he would be able to get her drawings into the Butterick magazine and perhaps others. Meanwhile he proposed to abet her studies in philosophy.

For a while neither Sally nor Mrs. Cudlipp nor Dreiser's aides suspected that matters had proceeded beyond Hegel and Spinoza.

Then one night the Dreisers were having the Cudlipps, mother and daughter, and the young editor, Homer Croy, to their apartment near Morningside Park for dinner. Croy had been in the kitchen talking with the older women, who were cooking, when he wandered into the living room. In an overstuffed chair sat his boss-host. On the chair's arm reposed Thelma, hands gently mussing and curling her philosophy teacher's hair. Croy admitted to greenness—but what kind of a philosophy class was this? He soon found others noticing things of a like nature.

At this time a young man named Fred Krog was being driven to distraction by the sudden cooling of the girl he had been courting. Feeling the need of an older man's counsel, he went to his employer— a sub rosa one, to be sure, since it was Dreiser in his hedging role with *The Bohemian*. (Krog had been put in as titular editor.) After hearing the problem, Dreiser casually inquired the girl's name. Thelma Cudlipp! Whereupon the consultant, knowing his patient to be highly strung, persuaded him to go to his Midwestern home town for a rest.

Meanwhile Thelma had reported Dreiser's profession of love to her mother. When taxed by the distracted woman, Dreiser readily admitted his emotion to be as described. Besides informing Sally Dreiser, Mrs. Cudlipp raised a hue and cry in the upper Butterick echelons against this editor who had insinuated his way into the heart of an innocent young girl. The condition of Thelma was largely bemusement, although plainly she basked in the drama and was genuinely fond of her admirer. The war swirled hotly on all fronts. At the office Dreiser's old enemies attacked. At home Sally unlimbered her guns, including notice that she would never give him a divorce. The other two Cudlipp offspring were husky young men. Word reached Dreiser that one or both contemplated bodily harm to him—a great deal of it.

At this point Fred Krog arrived back in New York with blood in his eye; the truth about Thelma and Dreiser had reached him. One Sunday morning he called on Homer Croy, displayed a revolver, and announced that he was on his way to settle "man to man" with his rival. He wanted company, and had come to the right place. Croy was temperamentally unfitted to turn down the request of a favor, and he might accomplish two at the same time if he somehow prevented the assassination of his boss. Reaching Morningside Park, Krog, a small, blond German with heavy spectacles, revealed his plan of operation. Telling Croy to go and inform Dreiser that he, Krog, wanted to talk to him down in the park, he concealed himself behind a syringa bush.

Croy sought out Dreiser, who was at an ironing board laid between the kitchen stove and a table, writing with a stylograph fountain pen. This type of pen had a wire end rising out of the top, which, as the hand moved, swayed and caused the wire below to stir the ink into an even flow. The wire end jiggled rapidly. Faced with the loss of his job, Dreiser had gone back to writing. The message when given did not cause him to desist or even look up.

"Tell Krog I'm too busy," he ordered shortly. To Croy it was the executive speaking, ironing board or not.

When the messenger came down, Krog popped from behind the syringa bush. Although disappointed, he was not to be put off. Telling Croy to go back and stress the urgency of the matter, he retired behind his bush.

The wire end still jiggled while Dreiser heard the reinforced message. "What does Krog want?" he asked brusquely.

"Well, Mr. Dreiser," Croy said respectfully, believing he owed a duty to be more specific, "I think he intends to kill you."

The wire end didn't miss a jiggle. "Krog gets crazy notions. Tell him I'm too busy."

Emerging from the cover of his bush, Krog was in no mood to be thrown off by the industry of a man unable to spare the time to be killed. He would go up himself and have it out "man to man." If not back in twenty minutes, Croy was to follow and claim his body. Croy tagged along, and at the elevator the avenger had a change of heart. "I'll let him live," he announced.

Krog's was not the only voice in the matter of whether Dreiser was to go on living. Mrs. Cudlipp and her three children resided in an apartment in Brooklyn. Thelma now having been forbidden the company of her impetuous swain, it was his habit to repair to the apartment roof, where Thelma joined him for brief tête-a-têtes. One night a Cudlipp son somehow learned that he was up there, and Dreiser somehow knew that he knew it and was on his way up to pitch the trespasser to the pavement. Dreiser himself later told of his inglorious clop, clop, clop down the fire escape, until he reached the drawn-up lower floor portion. He leaped it.

Mrs. Cudlipp managed to wall her daughter off, sending her to relatives in North Carolina. Now Dreiser's marriage was in ashes.

During his weakened state his Butterick foes drove him from his job. To Lengel, Croy, and other aides he seemed a broken man. In letters to Thelma he sounded it—and proved that however ludicrously he might put words together, he could still convey deep emotion.

> ...Are you just as sweet as ever? What! Do ju lub me? Had you sweet doe eyes? Or are dey dough eyes? (Oooh what a slam!) And will just always love me? What!...Flower Face, you are so sweet. Dear God how sweet you are & good, but oh the ache—the ache. Don't you feel any of this? Won't you ever say? Why so silent? Why so voiceless? Thelma Sweet! Honey Pot! Little Blue Bird! Divine Fire—I love you, love you, love you....But Honey Pot I NEED you. You are the breath of life to me....I have lost weight & I have no appetite. I just sit and worry.

But not all the time. He sat and wrote. His departure from Butterick's had been in October of 1910. Late in January he was advising Mencken that rumors of his leaving his wife to marry another were false. He and Sally had agreed to try again. The ink had fairly gushed from the stylograph. By the end of April his novel *Jennie Gerhardt* had been accepted by Harper Brothers for autumn publication. The firm would also republish *Sister Carrie*. He was well along with *The Genius* (later quotes would be put around the second word), whose hero was a fellow a good deal like himself, its heroine very much like Thelma. In August he declared to Mencken that "if *Jennie* doesn't sell ... I won't hang onto this writing game very long."

The time might be short, but not the number and size of the books ready for publishing. When Floyd and Margery Dell arrived in October he had *The Genius* "neatly typed on ice" and was twenty chapters deep into *The Financier*, the first of a trilogy of novels, which the Harper editor believed it wiser to publish next.

11

1912: Mostly the Summer

DELL was barely into his New York rounds of the publishing houses when he came onto an omen which made him wonder if Dreiser's trouble with publishing satraps were over. It appeared at a luncheon of the executives and staff members of Harper Brothers, designed mostly, he gathered, to woo Arnold Bennett, the English novelist whose *The Old Wives' Tales* was earning handsome profits for a rival firm. Harper was to publish Bennett's American impressions, perhaps as a way into his profitable graces.

Dell was an admirer of Bennett's literary criticism as well as his sympathetic treatment of the English lower classes. When an opening came, he ventured a tentative inquiry as to whether Bennett was acquainted with the work of Theodore Dreiser? The Englishman, seeming to take him for a member of the Harper staff bent on drawing praise for the soon-to-be-issued *Jennie Gerhardt*, replied that, yes, he knew Dreiser's work. Then in a ringing voice, as if taking care that all should hear, he declared: *"Sister Carrie* is the best realistic novel by an American writer." The words fell into a vacuum. No one begged authority to use them for promotion, and the subject was quickly changed, as when a family outsider mentions the black sheep. Dell was not aware of a story in publishing circles that Harper president George Harvey had refused to meet Dreiser on the ground that he was an "immigrant vulgarian" and a "sex maniac." Harvey was at the table, looking, in Bennett's later words, "accustomed to power."

Naturally Dell repeated Bennett's glowing words to Dreiser at the first opportunity. The young visitors from Chicago had put up at the fairly stylish Hotel Breslin and a meeting had been arranged by Edna Kenton. Now serving as New York correspondent of the *Fri-*

day Literary Review, she was guiding her editor and her friends to noteworthy people and places. Auguries were right for camaraderie with Dreiser. To begin with, he was always extremely susceptible to praise. The Bennett sweet, although modified by "realistic," was tasty, and Dell was good to have extracted and brought it. If the young critic (being properly august) did not fall to his knees, plainly he had been impressed, and doubtless his review of *Jennie* would show it.

By temperament Dreiser might be, as he wrote to William Lengel at this time, "a moody and solitary person." But when a book of his was published he was always quick to descend from his ivory tower. The "solitary" remark, in fact, was part of some biographical material gotten up for Lengel, who, having taken an editorial job in Chicago, was seeking to gain favorable notice for him. Therefore with the editor of the *FLR*—one of the limited number of influential journals likely to be friendly—Dreiser was the suitor. Also, he wanted to know more of this poor young man who had risen so spectacularly and to hear his views on contemporary society and literature. Dell may have seemed a bit aloof, but only from shyness rather than a wish to appear a high critic. Margery was not one to conceal admiration. And as usual with Dreiser, even when no romance was imminent, he found establishment of rapport with an attractive, sympathetic woman easier than with a man.

Even so, the Dells were given a portrait of what Edna had told them to expect—a big awkward man in a rocking chair endlessly folding a linen handkerchief, straining to keep up his end of the conversation, uttering into gaps his eternal "It's a mad world, my masters," or a variation. The handkerchief maneuvers were oddly arresting. His heavy face contrasted with the great sensitivity—the real beauty—of his hands. He folded, or rather pleated, the handkerchief at the edges, using the little stitching motions of a seamstress making a hem. The "stitched" portion was taken into the palm of his hand. If suddenly animated, irritated, say, by mention of a despised person, he would jerk the cloth edge straight and begin over. Usually, though, he turned the corner and kept on going round and round. He did not smoke, and the pleating was like fiddling with a pipe or knocking the ash from a cigar or cigarette.

Not at home in small talk or light repartee, Dreiser's conversation was nevertheless without the lumbering prolixity of his writing. The Dells found him at his best when propounding, say, the conditions and future of American literary realism. In his opinion they were not bright. Still, his outlook was positive. He did not moan loftily that if he wanted to he could grind out romantic best sellers. Rather, he envied the frame of mind and facile skill required for such alchemy. The situation being as it was, he would be content with a frugal living for describing the world as he saw and felt it. The three discussed possibility of a league of realists—writers of all kinds who were "at variance with the modern theory of life"—to gain attention for their own work and to combat the sentimentalists and the puritanical despots.

Margery had endeared herself by asking to read the "on ice" manuscript of *The Genius*. Dreiser liked acquaintances to read his manuscripts, urging them to make suggestions especially for cutting. A woman's opinion of *The Genius* was of great interest because of the passionate love affairs which he thought made of it a "woman's book." In a note he informed Margery that the new issue of *Smart Set* was on the stand with H. L. Mencken's view of *Jennie Gerhardt*. Mencken having appointed himself chief bugler for his old yahooing comrade, Margery would have known the review was favorable even if Dreiser had not warned against calling it to Dell's attention lest it prejudice him. This was in keeping with two facets of Dreiser's nature—his artistic integrity and the pushing of his own works.

The visits between Dreiser and the visitors were, of course, limited. Dell's schedule was heavy, and Dreiser, besides writing steadily on *The Financier*, was preparing to go abroad. The English did seem warmer to him than his own countrymen. Grant Richards, a London publisher, was to conduct him on a European tour, standing the expense against a book of impressions. (In one more try for tranquillity, Dreiser had taken a large apartment far up Broadway for Sally and himself. It wasn't working out.) After he returned from Europe, he completed *The Financier* for autumn publication and began *The Titan*, second of the trilogy which was based on the life of Charles T. Yerkes, the Philadelphia-Chicago-London magnate. Research on the middle phase would take him to Chicago, where he would resume the pleasant relationship with the Dells.

Dell began straining in the Dreiser harness even before getting to his own review. He sent to the *Friday Literary Review* a report on the autumn book lists, seeing the big foreign entries as Joseph Conrad's *Under Western Eyes* and Arnold Bennett's *Hilda Lessways*; the big Americans as Dreiser, Robert Herrick with *The Healer,* and Henry James with a collection of short stories. The choicest words went to Dreiser, and there was even a morsel of the *Sister Carrie* legend:

> It is now several years since that novel was issued, suppressed, and then, to the delectation of the judicious readers, reissued. Meanwhile Mr. Theodore Dreiser has written some three or four novels, all in the same realistic vein and (it is said by some of our more acute critics) with the same tremendous power. The publication of *Jennie Gerhardt,* the first of these novels, by one of the foremost publishing houses in America, seems to signify that the time has passed when a piffling puritanism could dominate our literature; it may signify even greater things, and Mr. Dreiser's book is to be looked forward to with keenest interest.

When Dell came to write his own full front-page *Friday Literary Review* analysis he found the novel even better than *Sister Carrie.* "It is the work of a man some ten years older, who has lost none of the creative vigor of his twenties." This mild astonishment was one of the rare clues that the editor of the *FLR* was a very, very young man. Dell continued: "About the middle of the book there comes the sense of power behind this narrative—the sustained strength, the penetrating vision, the boundless spirit, the nobility of soul. . . . The whole book is the explication of the inevitable defeat of a woman who asks only to give; and of the loneliness of the doomed nature. . . . The author does not blame Jennie's exploiters; nor does he defend them. . . .There is a great sympathy which envelops the history, a sympathy which bathes every incident with tender light and brings out clearly the tragic outline of the whole. . . ."

Unaware of Dreiser's background, he could not have known that Jennie was a composite of his sisters. In a way she was Carrie sent on a different, and more believable, path. Dreiser's own mother was Jennie's mother, seeking, with Jennie in her company, to do the washing of middle-aged Senator Brander. Later the mother chooses to shut her eyes when Jennie becomes the Senator's mistress; he is a bachelor and intends to educate and marry her. Knowledge of the illicit relationship must be kept from Jennie's harsh moralist father— of course, father Dreiser. Then Brander dies suddenly. Jennie is pregnant, and he has not provided for her. After a child is born, Jennie, working as a domestic, is seduced by wealthy Lester Kane, another bachelor well past his youth. They fall truly in love but owing to the difference in their social positions he confines himself to establishing her as his mistress. "One of his favorite pastimes was to engage quarters at the great resorts—Hot Springs, Mt. Clemens, Saratoga—and for a period of a week or two at a stretch enjoy the luxury of living with Jennie as his wife." And he allows her daughter, begot by Senator Brander, to be with her in Chicago, even permits her father (her mother has died) to believe that a lawful marriage has been contracted.

Jennie lacks Carrie's spunk. "If only she had more courage! If she did not always have this haunting fear! If she could only make up her mind to do the right thing! Lester would never marry her. Why should he? She loved him, but she could leave him, and it would be better for him." She doesn't leave him, and he takes a Hyde Park house on Chicago's South Side for her and for himself when not "away on business." Years pass and at last his aristocratic family, finding him out, brings pressure for an end to the relationship. A stronger brother threatens his place in the family business. Thereupon Lester deserts Jennie, after settling money on her, and marries a rich widow. In time, mortally ill in Chicago's Auditorium Hotel, he sends a carriage to the South Side to fetch Jennie. She looks at him "with large, gray, sympathetic eyes" and remains at his side until he dies. Then: "Before her was stretching a vista of lonely years down which she was steadily gazing."

To Dell, Jennie had "an authentic nobility . . . which nothing but utter defeat could bring out." To his colleague of the *Tribune*, Mrs. Peattie, Jennie ought to have no complaint, for she had lived pretty high and ended with a substantial income. If the capable, hardworking Mrs. Peattie spoke from an unconsciously materialistic point of view, denouncing the poverty girl's morals while tacitly accepting the rich man's, she was in the stronger current of the time. Her argument that the fiscal reward of Jennie's sins was rather high was not without persuasiveness. She might have pointed out that Carrie, at least, had earned her way into the big money.

Sales of *Jennie* were brisk, although far below those of popular romances. Even though the new edition of *Sister Carrie* hardly moved, it appeared that the new book was riding on *Sister Carrie*'s reputation—perhaps even more on its legend. The author's hand may have been, as Dell thought, surer, his vision wider, his art more subtle. He was also duller. The milksop Lester Kane was no tragic Hurstwood to lift and carry the story.

Arnold Bennett, who had left New York for a look at other areas, naturally stopped in Chicago. The city's image was big in Europe. And ugly. There could be no denial of the fierceness of odors from the stockyards, which after all were not very far into the South Side—just far enough to have eliminated Prairie Avenue as an elite address. When a south wind blew, the very Gold Coast was inundated. Yet it seemed not quite fair that all ambitious Chicago matrons daring the East and Europe should have to carry the pork stigma—even if at home they contentedly bowed the knee to the Armours and Swifts. Or that any daughter should be called a "pork fortune" simply because she won the heart of an impoverished nobleman.

The "muckrakers" had inevitably found rich mire for their implements in Chicago. With a quite horrible report *McClure's* had helped establish the city as one where murderers and thugs roamed the streets at will. Yet they weren't butchering weaker humans in *all* of the streets *all* of the time. As for municipal corruption—yes, there was plenty. But Hinky Dink and Bathhouse John were florid copy for any journalist happening along. Had not the master fixer, Yerkes, been more or less driven out a dozen years ago? As for the old canard about Chicago being a nest of anarchists—was it forgotten that the pardoner of the Haymarket survivors had been drummed from office and vilified?

The Builders and their offspring were trying, occasionally, to alter the image with culture plasters. The Art Institute's president, banker C. L. Hutchinson, son of "Old Hutch," the grain speculator, was host to Bennett in Chicago. In his journal the novelist wrote that Hutchinson's "idea of hospitality, and of how to look after a sought-for visitor and how to leave him alone, is unequalled by anyone else's in the U.S.A. so far." Hutchinson had personally arranged flowers on the main table for a luncheon at the Cliff-Dwellers' Club honoring the author. The touring British lion set down in his journal certain unflattering items omitted from his subsequent rather dull book of impressions but which unconsciously touched events about to unfold.

Went to Sears Roebuck & Co. in their auto. . . . Most interesting thing was glimpses of real life . . . as seen in ugly common simple stuff. . . . Thousands of cheap violins. In one basket ready for packing, all sort of little cooking utensils and two mugs (fearfully ugly) labeled "Father" and "Mother." 4-cent curling-iron. Most startling realistic glimpses of home life. . . .

Chicago city of superlatives. Biggest bookshop, press club, post. . . . Full of public spirit. . . . Fine twilight effects on magnificent boulevards. . . . Drive out to Evanston. Long gas-lit roads. Very smooth and straight on the whole, but with half-made bumpy intervals. . . . Grey, dirty bituminous region. Can't keep hands or linen clean. . . .

Dinner at C. L. Hutchinson's. Ayer and wife (collector, etc., aged 70), Burnham (architect), Miss Monroe, Mr. and Mrs. Ryerson, President and Mrs. Judson. A crowd of younger ones came in afterwards. General impression of shallowness left after seeing all these people. As if one had come to the end of the time at once.

Hutchinson's dinner guests were not out of the absolutely top social—which meant cash—drawer. The second generation of the colossal builders—Armours, Palmers, McCormicks, Pattersons, Swifts, Fields—did not fete novelists, even English novelists. And certainly not one who sympathized with working people clamoring for preposterously high wages and short hours. Yet the guests were all impeccable citizens whose judgments on cultural affairs opened the purses of the mightiest. Edward Everett Ayer was an industrialist, first president of the Field Museum of Natural History; Martin Ryerson was a business leader, president of the Chicago University board; Harry Pratt Judson was president of the university itself; Daniel Burnham was originator of the current city-beautiful program of parks and boulevards.

As for Harriet Monroe . . . well, Bennett's unawareness of a cultural ferment promising a heady brew may have been owing to his talking too much and listening too little. Harriet Monroe, as it happened, was just then intent on founding a magazine devoted to poetry. None existed in the United States. Yet had Bennett engaged her on the subject, and allowed her to respond at fair length, he probably still would have been unimpressed. The gentle, graying spinster (she was beyond fifty but hated to be specific) did not appear to contain rebel blood, or even very red blood. Neither her background as ode laureate of the World's Fair and the Auditorium nor her current part-time job as art critic for the *Tribune* would have seemed promising.

The others at the table were sure that dear Harriet would have her little magazine. Who could deny her a mite from the funds marked "Charity" and "Good Deeds." She was of an old Chicago family and had made a brave fight after its impoverishment. Moreover, the amazing Hobart Chatfield Chatfield-Taylor, doyen of the genteel arts, had promised to spare time from his biography of Goldoni, the eighteenth-century Italian dramatist, to get behind her. This knowledge would only have depressed Bennett, and, as far as that was concerned, augured poorly for the new and robust in literature. Chatfield-Taylor had expressed himself against the "vulgar realism" of Zola, Tolstoy, even Henry James, and had vented his outrage at the tainting of Chicago by immigrants not of Anglo-Saxon stock.

The day after the Hutchinson dinner Bennett was exposed to the Little Room group, meeting in a studio in the Fine Arts Building. He found no signs of cultural vigor here, either, and regarded only Jane Addams as worthy of a journal note ("a middle-aged benevolent creature"). That night he was allowed into the presence of a McCormick, this one Medill McCormick of an alliance between the *Tribune* and reaper families, and thereby got a look at Builder status. Although young, Medill had retired from business owing to bad nerves and was devoting himself to various studies, including politics. Bennett found him "well up" in the British phases. His wife, Ruth, was interested in politics, too, being the daughter of Mark Hanna, the "maker" of President McKinley. They were all guests at a dinner given by Herbert Kaufman, a backer of Chicago music. At precisely 10:10, McCormick addressed one word, "Ruth," to his wife in a tone of "commanding suggestion." They left and the party broke up at once. Bennett was not sorry. "I was just going to break it up myself."

The plain fact was that, with the exception of Hutchinson, no one was able to impress the British dignitary. Maurice Browne called one morning at his Blackstone Hotel suite. "Prim little professional Englishman," Bennett noted. "Very nice. Gloomy about art in the States." Those well acquainted with the intense young Browne would have assigned Bennett's description of him to a mildly chauvinistic notion that a stranded Englishman *had* to be forlorn amidst the Chicago hustle, especially if a worrier about the state of art. Even the "very nice" may have been a pleasant counter to the image of "professional Englishman" and of ineffectuality. At any rate Bennett got no feeling that Browne had in him the thunder and lightning to shake this rude city.

Dell called, too. Bennett generously encouraged him to be a novelist, remarking that his small-town background would be helpful. There was not enough time for a discussion of Chicago literature. Even if there had been, Dell would not have been very enthusiastic about its past, present, and future—even if the lion had deigned to listen.

A few months later, Dell undertook a series of reports on "Chicago in Fiction." The richest praise went to a man no longer a resident. "The poetry of Chicago has been adequately rendered, so far, by only one writer, and that in only one book." The reference was to *Sister Carrie*. (Dreiser had put Jennie in Chicago some of the time but not much of Chicago into Jennie's story.)

Another essay considered Robert Herrick. Now in his middle forties, Herrick had for two decades been publishing novels at intervals of two to four years. In craftsmanship he was superior to Dreiser, and as a realist he took a gloomier view of the modern world. In seeking to explain him, Dell quoted a comment by H. G. Wells on the "scrambling, ill-mannered, undignified, unintelligent" development of America's material resources. It seemed to Dell that Herrick was out to show this aspect by holding up selected pieces and people of his adopted city for close examination. In *The Memories of an American Citizen* he had drawn a pork packer and politician of crude morals but worldly success. In *The Web of Life* a young architect had been utterly destroyed after revealing that inferior building materials had dishonestly gone into a hotel which burned with great loss of life. In *The Common Lot* a doctor had shed his ideals and become a winner. Dell's complaint was that Herrick had no faith in the future of Chicago life. "He sees it as a muddy pathway down to hell, trampled and bloody in a monstrous and useless conflict."

For Henry Blake Fuller's two Chicago novels, Dell had of course to reach back to the nineties, as for Frank Norris' *The Pit,* although publication had been in 1903. (Hamlin Garland was omitted; the heroine of *Rose of Dutcher's Coolly* in 1895 had studied poetry in Chicago but it might as well have been in any other large city.) In Fuller's *The Cliff-Dwellers* and *With the Procession* Dell saw a

Chicago trying to move from its tight money-making bias toward an aesthetic way of life. Unhappily, raucous Chicago and Fuller's mastery of delicate irony were not compatible. Fuller should have "conceived fiction in such languid and evocative terms as has Anatole France." Norris' *The Pit* had carried his saga of wheat forward from *The Octopus*, laid in California. The "pit" was more celebrated, perhaps, than any other Chicago place. Yet relatively few Chicagoans were actively engaged in its machinations, and the story dealt mainly with a hero winning, losing, and rewinning the heroine, rather than with the grinding lives of small people.

Another novelist considered was Bert Leston Taylor, a favorite columnist in the Eugene Field vein. His "A Line o' Type or Two," signed with his initials, in the *Tribune*, consisted of verse and pithy comments or sketches by himself and a host of contributors. In *The Charlatans*, published half a dozen years ago, Taylor had poked mild fun at Chicago literary and cultural pretension. But said Dell, "Mr. Taylor, like a French duellist, feels that honor is satisfied once he has 'pinked' his subject."

By and large Chicagoans had been hanging on the words of Finley Peter Dunne, creator of "Mr. Dooley," in newspapers and collections since the middle nineties. Just now Dunne had moved on to New York and magazines. But, as Dell said, "Mr. Dooley is a figure which gives us in bold, clear colors the writer and his Chicago." It was the Chicago of the lower middle class and not, as for Herrick, a cruel place. Dell found, however, that Dunne's "charming dialect monologues" also lacked the "spark of reform temperament."

In Dell's "Chicago in Fiction" pieces he was kinder to Joseph Medill Patterson than to anyone except Dreiser. In a foreword to *Rebellion*, published a year earlier, Patterson had thanked Francis Hackett for advice, and Dell had found it a "masterly work." The two Socialist-oriented critics did seem to go out of their way to encourage the young *Tribune* heir found incongruously beside them. Dell now came down a notch or two, celebrating Patterson for his "optimism" and implying a reservation in preferring it over Herrick's defeatism. "Better the journalistic penny whistle of Joseph Medill Patterson, upon which can be played a moving music of love and death and change."

The series was rounded out by George Cook, with articles praising Susan Glaspell and Frank Harris. Readers aware of the circumstances might have taken the first as subjective or even self-congratulatory. Miss Glaspell's recent *The Visioning*, with a Socialist hero for whom Cook might take responsibility, was not, however, an intimate picture of Chicago. European Frank Harris' *The Bomb*, dealing with the Haymarket affair, had been his ticket to the series. It showed, said Cook, "Chicago frenzied, Chicago incapable of reason, incapable of justice, hysterical with fear of the anarchists." All of which had basis in fact, but Harris had made no thorough on-the-ground study.

Chicago's seams in 1912 were not only being menaced by inrushing hordes but were readier than ever to burst with excitement. Population had risen nearly half a million in the 1900–1910 decade, and the pace was increasing. Estimates put the current population at two and a quarter million souls. New York had twice as many, but third-sized Philadelphia a full quarter less. The womenfolk, one way or another, were mostly responsible for the fresh and zestful stimulation, and it was fitting that Dell took up the "woman question" in a series beginning at the end of June.

It did seem that the women were about to reform the Western World. What it would be like afterwards was a matter of opinion. Charlotte Perkins Gilman sought to have women taken out of the drudgery and inefficiency of the home; let there be cooperative kitchens. Olive Schreiner wanted to save women from parasitism by setting them to work in all endeavors. Emmeline Pankhurst would fiercely turn the tables and subjugate the males. Mild Jane Addams sought by neighborliness to bridge the gap between those with cultural advantages and those without. Dancer Isadora Duncan would free the female body, permitting natural movements for good health and beauty. Ellen Key, the most advanced on the sexual relations question (always excepting Emma Goldman), spoke for, as Dell put it, "the conservation of that old custom which persists among peasants and primitive people all over the world and which has been reintroduced to the public . . . under the term of 'trial marriage'; it must be held, she says, as the bulwark against the corruption of prostitution and made a part of the new morality." Of the unwed young, Ellen had declared: "When their soul has found another soul, when the senses of both have met in a common longing, then they consider that they have a right to full unity of love."

Dell seemed to admire most of all the British agitator Dora Marsden, editor of *The Freewoman*, who nerved women "to the effort of emancipation." She "sows in a fertile soil the dragon's teeth which shall spring up as a band of capable females, knowing what they want and taking it, asking no leave of anybody, doing things and enjoying life—Freewomen!" In Chicago the proof of the pudding was found at the convention of the new Progressive Party held in early August. Theodore Roosevelt, teeth flashing, led a mighty parade. But in the line of march was a striding band of women flaunting banners which caused male gnashing of teeth and weeping into beer. The suffragettes were marching boldly in the open! In the convention itself, Teddy roared as perhaps never before, and even Francis Hackett, still in Chicago writing his novel, mounted his chair with other Bull Moosers to bellow cheers. Yet what were these compared with the ecstatic shrieks from suffragette throats as Jane Addams rose, the first woman ever to second the nomination of a U.S. candidate for President—at least a candidate of Roosevelt's stature. Margery Dell gave the sense of drama in a letter to Eunice Tietjens, who was away for the summer:

> ... Do you realize that we have had the first suffrage parade in Chicago! To be sure, it was really an escort for the women delegates to the Progressive convention, and was brought together on twenty-four hours notice; but we *marched*. And we carried yellow banners, and we heard a woman second the nomination for president, and we heard Roosevelt and other convention speakers come out roundly for a definite program of labor legislation, as has never been done before; and "Votes for Women" goes into the platform!
>
> I was never so busy and so exuberant in my life as during this convention week. These have been memorial days—and nights, too—full of wonderful constructive work.... You never felt such a spirit as that which pervaded the convention. Well, you see I am a maniac—but it *was* splendid. My work has been to me a well of mineral water, and a band of music, and a ride on an aeroplane.

A war raging over prostitution was added to the excitement. Since in the profession the customer is almost never wrong—the male rarely being prosecuted for his share in the transaction—it was handled mainly as a women's affair. There were really two wars, or anyhow two sectors. One had to do with the active members of the calling. The other concerned the girls who might go into it or be forced into it. And if compelled, who would do the dragooning or, worse, be responsible for it. The battle lines on the second front were being tautly drawn. On one side were the reformers, largely women, commanded by Jane Addams, with mainly suffragettes as lieutenants. They demanded higher pay, shorter hours, and better conditions for working girls. For women, too, but the "working girl" was the emotional symbol. Facing them, equally determined to "protect the working girl," were employer magnates, especially those from the great department stores and mail order houses.

The argument was very simple. Reformers held that ordinary girls could not live "decently" on wages they were able to command for honest toil. This might be as low as five dollars a week (and this subject to fines and other deductions). However, an average of nine dollars a week was claimed by Marshall Field's and Mandel Brothers', the largest department stores, and the Sears Roebuck mail order house. Even if the figure was accurate, said reformers, many thousands of girls fell into a lower category. And how many at nine dollars a week might in despair choose a path on which primroses seemed to blossom?

As in all civilized warfare, certain weapons were banned by agreement—in this case unwritten. The reformers did not accuse the magnates of plotting to force girls into brothels or to the life of kept paramours. And the magnates, for their part, did not accuse the reformers of consciously wanting the girls to be driven to a fate worse than death. As superior men of affairs they resorted to cold, dignified logic. If required to pay higher wages, naturally they would replace the girls with men, who were, they held, more competent. What, then, would happen to the girls thrown onto the streets? Obviously they would stay right there, or beg admission into brothels, or offer themselves as paramours. All these things on a falling market. It was a hard decision for the average citizen to know which side to pull for.

The war on the other front was easier to comprehend, and a lot more fun. There was a kind of guidebook. To secure it was admittedly a problem, since it was barred from the mails even in plain wrappers, and in the stores was an under-counter item if available at all. The title was *The Social Evil in Chicago*, with a subtitle, "A Study of Existing Conditions with Recommendations by the Vice Commission of Chicago." The commission, appointed by the reform but lackluster mayor, Fred A. Busse, was listed as publisher. The distributor was something called the American Vigilance Association, of 105 Monroe Street. Sales were quite good in spite of the difficulties

put in the way—or because of them. By July 1, the hard-cover
volume, about the size of a novel, was in its fourth edition.

The readers were given quite specific information along with projections. On the police lists were 1,012 prostitutes. Since the law was
behindhand in its records, a round-figure estimate of 5,000, all told,
seemed conservative. Each of these gave "service" fifteen times
daily, according to estimate. The profits of the industry were thought
to be fifteen or sixteen millions a year. The method of breakdown
was not clear, but it seemed that the figure was the middleman's (or
middlewoman's) share, wages of the performers not being included.

There were the case histories. Rosie, from Iowa, cleared $156
in a single month, and this in a fifty-cent house. Her share was thirty
cents, or the going rate of about 60 percent to the girl (out of which
she often paid exorbitant prices to the madam and other overlords
for kimonos and other necessities). In the flats outside the segregated
district the charge was five to ten dollars, and some girls put aside
as much as five hundred dollars a week. The report declared straight
out that a "pervert" method—here the definition stopped—was on
the increase in the elite houses, and that practitioners got two or
three times more cash than "regular" girls.

Thirty "inmates"—a term favored by the compilers—of a superior
house had been questioned in depth. The average age at beginning
of career had been eighteen. Average age at time of interviews had
been twenty-three and a half. Of the thirty, nearly all had tried to
make a living by honest toil. The occupations: domestics, waitresses,
clerks, saleswomen, dressmakers, stenographer, governess, telephone
operator, vaudeville performer, milliner, factory worker. Average
wage: five dollars a week. Department store practices were strongly
criticized. After a twelve-hour day and the low wages perhaps reduced by fines for rule infractions, the girls were vulnerable to the
"cadets," the young professional seducers who hung around employee entrances. Once the cadet's mission had been accomplished
he usually pandered for his victim and continued as her lover. The
young brutes were hard for the law to get at, for the girls were reluctant to give evidence against lovers and protectors.

The report's authors did not approve of the Levee's recent invasion
by evangelist Gypsy Smith. His loud sidewalk praying, they said,
had only succeeded in advertising the district. They were not very
logical in their reasoning. Naming the South Side area at Twenty-

Second Street and Dearborn Avenue, they had declaimed that "the lighted street, the sound of music, the shrill cries and suggestive songs of the inmates and entertainers, all of these features tend to bring the business to the attention of the public and to spread the news to other towns and cities." What nicer puff from the Vice Commission could have been asked by the friendly merchants of any neighborhood?

The vice uproar naturally distressed the aristocracy and made the need for more culture plasters evident. The task of Harriet Monroe in raising funds for her projected little magazine was thereby made easier. And so was that of the "prim little professional Englishman," Maurice Browne, who was on the prowl for money to found a high temple of the arts.

12

Now a Grecian Temple

THE real Maurice Browne was mercurial, untrammeled, erudite, contentious, showy, dictatorial, vain, and entrancing—qualities essential, or at least helpful, to a prophet. He enjoyed Oriental robes and a ring in one ear. These affectations were generally private, and, since he had lived in India, had a certain basis in logic. Usually his neat figure was merely highly groomed, his crisp, slightly curly dark hair well barbered, his face, with its vivid regular features, shaved close. A rich dinner would be traded for the ostentatious comfort of a formal manicure. His linen was all snowy, all garments freshly pressed. Indubitably he had a way with women and prided himself as a mighty lover. But it was in a classical style, far above mere libertinism.

Browne was the son of a minister who had been a school headmaster at Ipswich, England, when he was born there, in 1881. A few years later the elder Browne had died and thereafter his widow had conducted schools in and around London. His adventurous roaming had begun early, when at eighteen he had gone as a soldier against the Boers in Africa. A horse had thrown him and he was invalided home. His mother had packed him off to Cambridge, where he had taken up literature and, with a friend, scientific gambling. The results in three years had been a sheaf of poetry, editorship of a university magazine, and a system for breaking the bank at Monte Carlo. With the friend he had taken ship to give the system a trial. It had done very well until a flaw appeared and their winnings had disappeared. Being scientists rather than gamblers, they had pocketed their reserve and started for home to eliminate the bug. Another appeared: the gambling bug. They had lost their reserve aboard ship, and given up their designs on Monte Carlo.

155

Browne had got together enough money for another fling—this one in literature by publishing his own poems. When the book failed, he had embarked for India with a two-year teaching contract. There he had acquired a taste for mystic ritual, a gorgeous costume, and, as it turned out, a lifelong friend in a "tall, distinguished looking American lawyer," Arthur Davison Ficke, of Davenport, Iowa. By chance thrown together, the young teacher and the two-year-younger lawyer had found a common interest in poetry. Each admired the work of the other.

In London again, Browne had found time to help organize the avant-garde Samurai Press (for poetry, mostly) before going for a year to Capri. An English acquaintance, nodding toward a lovely unspoiled girl, had remarked: "The islanders are an odd folk: Arab blood, with a strong Greek heritage from the great days: observe Margherita's head: unblemished Phidias." Since Browne was nearly as passionate an admirer of the ancients as Cook, he had overcome his fear of vengeance by her protective relatives and become her lover. He might have settled down for good, one way or another, if an English doctor had not obligingly brought about a miscarriage in Margherita.

Then it had been London again, in a Bloomsbury garret, writing poetry, adventuring in love, mingling in the advanced intellectual circles. Then to Florence as a tutor. One day while lunching in the Villa Trollope he had been intrigued by the conversation of four young ladies at a table nearby. One of the voices, light, gay, controlled, had attracted him especially. It belonged to a slender girl with snapping black eyes in her longish, high-cheekboned face. Her quick, incisive gestures were very expressive. An introduction was easy enough for so experienced a man of the world. The girls, in their early twenties, were from Chicago. The high-cheekboned one called Nellie was in fact Ellen—Ellen Van Volkenburg. By now, in 1910, Browne was approaching thirty and weary of leaping from one passion to another. He was hard smitten. Nellie was, too. When she went home they were engaged, with the nuptials predicated on whether he would be able to make a living in the United States.

Browne had pawned the family silver inherited from his father and set forth as an empire builder for the Poetry Societies of Great Britain, Australia, and South Africa. When the American bards stoutly resisted joining, a Victorian urn and a Georgian teapot had followed the silver. It occurred to him that a university, say Harvard, might welcome him as a teacher. Harvard did not, but his fellow Englishman, John Cowper Powys, some ten years older and rising as an American lecturer, got him a job as English instructor in a Pennsylvania college. He was let go at the end of a semester. The title of organizing secretary for the Progressive Arts League of America, with an address at 12 Charles Street in New York's Greenwich Village, proved empty, too. He had founded the League.

And so Browne had settled, a good deal less than a conqueror, in Chicago to be near his Nellie, whose boundless faith in him did not waver. The lectures on "Poets of the Future"—Arthur Davison Ficke, Harold Monro, Wilfrid Wilson Gibson—at Chicago University and in a dozen mansions of the rich had won some attention but little cash. He found a small creative outlet in book reviews for the *Friday Literary Review*. Chicago itself disturbed and excited him. The luxury and squalor recalled Dublin and London except that the contrasts were more violent. India at its hottest had been no match for Chicago summers, when the very pavements boiled with pitch and a blood odor from the Yards lay over the city. Even in the Himalayas he had never encountered winds like those off Lake Michigan in winter.

As for the moral climate, he had seen at once that Dollar was god. Barely visible were the temples of art, empty walls raised to Beauty in guilt-fear. Might he not erect another temple and fill it with the breath of life? Good omens—at least for the raising of the walls—had been encountered in the great houses during his lectures. Besides, some of the occupants were Nellie's friends. The father of Nellie was in the meat trade, but in a relatively minor role as traveler. The Van Volkenburgs lived in a North Side apartment befitting their means. Nellie had made her wealthy friends while giving one-person theatrical performances at social affairs in the great homes. One was the wife of Ogden Armour, old P. D.'s son, now ruler of the clan. Mrs. Armour, an attractive brunette in her forties, very chic, was of the proper Chicago grand manner in often wearing a gown for one occasion only. She had a feeling for the theater. At least Nellie considered the Armour home theatrical, with its central fountain and marble walls and vast staircase, and felt that good judgment had been shown in the choice and placement of furniture. (In the

George Pullman mansion she had been hard put to make her way amidst the forest of potted palms and the heavy Victorian pieces.)

The friend closest to Nellie was Mrs. Chauncey Blair, not quite a social rival of Mrs. Armour but more widely cognizant in the arts. She was slender, like Nellie, with a gay, down-to-earth sense of humor that enabled her to mingle more easily with the creative artists than most society people. Not that the artists were ever completely accepted by their upper-class supporters. Perhaps more exactly, they were accepted as worthy objects of patronage, amusing, but with a touch of the oddball in them.

A third friend of Nellie's, Mrs. Arthur Aldis, came as near as any to bridging the gap. She was an able dramatist and water colorist, and Nellie believed that for her too much wealth had been a handicap—with a discreet amount of poverty she might have better developed her talents. Real estate operator Arthur Aldis was rich enough to keep up an end in the social whirl, and a notable place besides as a patron of the arts. Big, portly, genial, a noted after-dinner speaker, he had just this summer in Paris arranged for a collection of the works of Matisse and Picasso and other ultramodern painters to be sent to Chicago. Mary Aldis, a petite, dark, vivid woman of fifty, was not given to putting on much "side" and her creative life kept her from the singlemindedness of a social leader.

These wealthy friends of Nellie's, admiring her performing talents, and the girl herself for her combination of bright gaiety and serious intellect, were sorry that she had not found expression in the legitimate theater. Not that any, given the talent, would have chosen to be on the public stage. Although Chicago was much too up-to-date for a notion that actresses were fallen women, display of themselves would have meant social disaster unto future generations. This attitude, carried downward, was responsible for Nellie's absence from the commercial stage. At Michigan University she had been a member of the Comedy Club and had wanted to try for a theatrical career. Her mother had objected to the ambition as not genteel. To be an "entertainer," even a paid one, before high-level audiences was not, however, thought to be degrading for nonmembers of the upper classes.

And so Nellie had been allowed to employ her gift of inner recording to entertain university groups, women's clubs, and parties in the big houses. Success at these had increased her desire to play in her own right, to be Ellen Van Volkenburg the actress rather than a puppet automated by a quirk of the psyche. Browne had no technical knowledge of the stage and, though a fair lecturer, had little talent for acting. For the popular theater he had only contempt. Shakespeare and the ancient Greek drama were another matter. He liked the verse plays of William Butler Yeats and the works of a few other moderns: George Bernard Shaw, J. M. Synge, Arthur Schnitzler, Henrik Ibsen, August Strindberg. Dublin's Abbey Theatre, founded by Yeats and Synge and Lady Augusta Gregory, was an inspiration.

The Abbey spirit had boiled over to Chicago during a visit of the group (billed as the Irish Players) in late 1911. There had been advance excitement at news of a New York audience's riot during the performance of Synge's *A Playboy of the Western World*. The main trouble had come from the Irish, who interpreted it as unfair to the Irish character. Browne, an old friend of one of the players, had been asked to raise a kind of militia for defense in notoriously brutal Chicago. Nothing had happened, except for mounting excitement in the advanced set—the Dells, Carys, Cook, Hallinan, Eunice Tietjens, even Harriet Monroe—as the week's repertoire continued. Many socialites had turned out and either were impressed or hesitated to knock anything labeled both European and "ultra."

To Browne it had been the answer to his creative need. He, too, would found a company of players and build a temple of art. The director? Himself, to learn in the blazing crucible of doing. Where? He didn't know. With whose cash? Not his own, surely, for even the heirlooms were all gone. The members of the company? Well, he had Nellie. Beyond her . . . ?

Lady Gregory, one of the leaders of the Irish Renaissance, at sixty an experienced playwright and producer, gave counsel: "By all means start your own theater; but make it in your own image. Don't engage professional players; they have been spoiled for your purpose. Engage and train, as we of the Abbey have done, amateurs: shopgirls, school-teachers, counter-jumpers; cutthroat thieves rather than professionals. And prepare to have your hearts broken." That sounded like just the ticket. All artists must suffer. Many years later Maurice Browne would be a world-famous theatrical mogul operating half a dozen theaters in London's West End, flunkies with "M. B." sewn to their uniforms dancing attention. George Bernard

Shaw, introducing him at a festival, would comment: "None of these things matter a tupenny damn. The work twenty years ago on a four-floor-back in Chicago—that is what matters."

In the summer of 1912, Browne's hope of getting even a fourth-floor-back was not rosy.

The vibrant, emotion-packed chanting of a female Greek chorus filled a Jackson Park store-front studio and wafted through the open doors and back windows.

> Never again
> Shall I sway to the shuttle's song,
> Weaving wool spun from a home-bred fleece!
> Instead, one last, last look at the face of my dead sons,
> Then go to meet yet worse—
> Forced, maybe, to the bed of some lustful Greek—
> Listen, gods, to my curse....

Passersby paid little heed. Not that Greek choruses were ordinary in Chicago, nor that the chanted words of Euripides were familiar to Chicago ears. In a colony of poor artists unconventional behavior was simply taken for granted. When the director interrupted with clipped, frenzied outcries—well, no artist should be denied his temperament.

Maurice Browne was doing first things first, which happened also to be the only things feasible. Having selected for his first production Euripides' *The Trojan Women,* he was organizing his company. The temple would have to wait. Even the rehearsal site had not been his choice—far from it. Lou Wall Moore, sculptress, dancer, and hopeful actress, had offered it free of charge. Lou Wall came with it. She wasn't a very good dancer or actress. Her diction was marred by a harelip and she was overage for a beginning thespian, especially as the virgin Cassandra. Her heart, on the other hand, was pure gold and her spirit indestructible. Wrinkles could be filled with grease, false teeth made to assist her with Cassandra's fairly extensive lines.

The decision to rehearse in the South Side colony, forced or not, was wise. Most of the residents were dedicated painters, writers, sculptors, etchers, photographers, musicians, dancers. How could it be foretold which talents would blossom and endure? The Lou Wall Moores gave courage to others more richly endowed but readier victims of despair.

In a solid colony resident Browne found the master of his stage settings, once they would be needed. He was Brör Nordfeldt, gentle, smiling, a little man with a neat goatee, a painter of note and an Art Institute teacher. Something of a colony pioneer, he and his wife had moved in a dozen years ago when the old World's Fair shop buildings were first being commandeered for studios. Nordfeldt's good friend Thorstein Veblen, then social science professor at Chicago University, had taken a nearby place. In that period the usual term for the little area had been The Corner. Nordfeldt had gone to Paris to study, returning in 1911 as a member of the Post-Impressionist School, after Veblen had moved on to Stanford University.

The Nordfeldt studio, typical but slightly plushier than most, stood at the corner where Fifty-Seventh Street ends against Stony Island Avenue, the park boundary. The little buildings ran a block on both sides of Fifty-Seventh, then turned for half a block on Stony Island. In the hot season relief might be found among the trees of the grassy park, on the lake beach, and in the lake itself. The studios opened on tree-shaded back yards, where tables might be set for meals, with the evening's wine and beer to aid the conversation. The Nordfeldts (she was a practicing psychologist, smaller than he, which made her tiny) had an inside toilet and a coal bin under the floor. These luxuries boosted their rent to fifteen dollars a month, three dollars more than paid by the outhouse-and-coal-pile class. In winter their potbellied stove was ineffective against the cold penetrating the thin walls, and a rag carpet fought weakly against the cold from below. Other items were a gas ring and a big iron sink, and they would have had a water heater except for the longing for an expensive bathtub that would have gone with it.

Nordfeldt solved in part his volunteered stagecraft duties by enlisting one of his students, a husky young Iowan named Raymond Johnson (known to later art connoisseurs as Jonson) who lived in one of the studios. Neither artist knowing anything about the stage, Lady Gregory's admonition to choose only amateurs had been properly adhered to. There were drawbacks to her mentioned categories: cutthroat thieves, shopgirls, teachers, counter-jumpers. The latter callings demanded long and regular hours, too long for Browne, who liked to rehearse his people for nine hours a day, seven days a week. He had to draw mostly on the leisure class. Since even the very rich men expected their sons to learn the family business, the field was narrowed toward daughters and wives. This had led to selection of

The Trojan Women as the initial production, since most of the characters are female.

One of the wives was Margaret Allen (Mrs. Andrews Allen), in her thirties, a patron of and a dabbler in various arts. She was generous, and as the Allens owned a house nearby, she gave the free use of its upstairs to Maurice and Nellie, who had taken a day off to marry. Mrs. Chauncey Blair's wedding present to Nellie of five hundred dollars had to be saved for the temple-raising when the moment came. Nellie had been cast for the lead, old Hecuba, wife of the slain Trojan king and mother of Paris, whose conquest of the fair Helen, wife of the king of Sparta, had brought about the siege of Troy. Browne had found his stage Helen at precisely the moment of finding Nellie. She was Bess Goodrich, one of that party of four Chicago girls who had been at the table in Florence's Villa Trollope. Her beauty was of the classical Greek style. A graduate of Bryn Mawr, she was now a young matron (Mrs. Ernest Reckett) living among the elect of Geneva, west of Chicago.

Excitement over the sublime project had spread rapidly after a few girls had been subjected to Browne's mesmerizing words. Bess Goodrich, shopping in Marshall Field's one day, encountered her friend Alice Gerstenberg. They had been together at Bryn Mawr, where Alice had played leading theatrical roles. Alice must apply to Browne for a place in the cast! (Quite early he had established that membership was an honor for the pure of dedication.) In addition, Alice would be a catch. As the daughter of Erich Gerstenberg, of a grain fortune, she had been a prominent debutante and the family's social affairs in its luxurious house and garden were conspicuous in the society pages. More, a novel by Alice would be published in the fall. (As a playwright she would later invent actor's "aside thoughts" for her *Overtones*, an idea which Eugene O'Neill would borrow for his *Strange Interlude*.)

Always the stern commander, Browne placed Alice in the chorus for seasoning. Its other rank and file members were Genevieve Griffin, Elizabeth Bingham, and Margaret Allen. Browne himself was to be a common soldier. For slightly bigger male parts he had Paul Bartlett and Shelley Neltnor. This left two major roles to be filled: the tragic and beautiful Andromache, wife of Hector, and the leader of the chorus.

To Browne success lay in the ability of the chorus to synchronize mood and movement and speech. As leader he chose Miriam Kiper.

She had come to him from an intellectual Chicago family, along with her sister, Florence, a talented playwright. Browne valued Miriam for her warm "Jewish" voice and natural movements and above all for the intensity of her projections, as if she could dance up the very walls, if need be.

Andromache was the last of the major parts to be filled. But once it was done, the troupe had its own *femme fatale*, its own Helen—minus Helen's scheming nature. Her name was Elaine Hyman and she had barely turned twenty-one. Over her Floyd Dell would lose his head. The head of Theodore Dreiser would follow. Pushing aside those of others in a like condition, they would grapple for her affections. The course of Chicago literature, if not shaped by Elaine Hyman, at any rate would be enlivened.

Advocates of a new and beautiful society were having trouble finding a proper term for their notion of adventurous, unpossessive sex relations. "Free love" didn't really fit, and moreover had been reduced to salacity by the press. "Varietism" had a crude ring. "Pagan love" was nicely abandoned with a high lilt. In those days pagan love meant, in Dell's understanding, "natural, fearless, unashamed, joy-loving." The connotation unhappily was of irresponsibility—as of leering satyrs in pursuit of unhurrying nymphs to whom they had not been introduced. The fault may have been in the vagueness of the ideals. When Dell himself left theory to climb the splendored path of gratified desires, the footing often gave way, hurtling him into abysses of despair. And this in spite of having pondered the contours of the land more than most, and having sat at the feet of that combined evangelist and doer, Jig Cook.

As a Quincy teen-ager, Dell had been astonished to learn from a book he happened to be reading that men loved without necessarily having marriage in mind. Women, too, perhaps, although the author, a male, had written half a century ago when it was assumed that if a girl had loved and was not carried to the altar she quickly dropped to (1) unwanted spinsterhood, (2) a declassed husband, or (3) prostitution. The volume was *Reveries of a Bachelor* by Donald Grant Mitchell, writing under the pseudonym, Ik Marvel. In the book a safely slippered bachelor sits by the fire at midnight happily dreaming of old and rather innocent romances. For Dell the suggestion that love might be sufficient unto itself had been a mildly traumatic experience. At the same time he had made a note that tender memories would be nice for rummaging through during the cold winter evenings of middle age.

A major reaction had been the prompt acquisition of a dream girl who turned up in his sleep. Whatever Sigmund Freud's interpretation, the fantasy was symbolical of hinterland youths about to tear down bourgeois mores. The scene was a barn hayloft (in rural imagination, the place of secret sex). The girl read poetry. Evidently the unconscious censor had stepped in from Sunday school. Some force— probably this same ungenerous one—had also removed the hay. The mow was bare. So there it was: poetry and love and promise of erotic bliss—and no real happiness.

Dell had in fact been made queasy by Jig Cook's break from Mollie and their little children, much as he liked the new bride-to-be, Susan Glaspell. If one were married to the wrong person, said reigning prophetess Ellen Key, he or she ought to ruthlessly break up the union. Well, Jig had. And while waiting for a divorce he was reaching with both hands for between-meal courses. Perhaps Cook was a genius. Surely he was an egotist who had pleasured himself with Nietzsche's concept of the superman.

For himself, Dell repudiated the notion of a genius being entitled to special privileges, and deplored the self-centeredness of egotism. Yet he believed that everyone was entitled to all the rights there were. If one just knew exactly what a man's rights were! What of a girl's rights? He personally could not abide the term "mistress." It meant a poor girl enslaved by a rich man, arousing his Socialist ire. If a married man had a second love, what was she? His No. 2 mate? Or No. 1 mate, without social recognition? What if the lawful wife, although not overly possessive, failed to settle easily into concubinage? It was all very confusing, even before one left the realm of theory for the high road of untrammeled joy.

The companion of Dell's first journey was a girl advanced somewhat beyond him in emancipation. They kissed, and did not stop. Dell explained:

> Suddenly I was in a realm more real to me than the world I had thought of as real—which had become a shadow, a dream, something remote and dim. I was happy and free. . . . All the values in my universe were suddenly transvalued. I felt like a wanderer, long absent in alien lands, who sets eyes again upon his native place. . . . Sex was something too important to be taken that way. And yet I was, and now I knew it, one of those to whom such in-

timacies were beautiful, good in themselves, seemingly a part of
the enchanting intimacy of mutually self-revealing talk; I should
have felt a coward, been ashamed of myself, if that hour's intimacy
of talk had not been made perfect and complete. It belonged to me;
never would I repudiate it, or regret it.

This the flower-strewn portion of the road. Then the nightmarish
stretch. "I did not wish to lose—I wished desperately not to lose—
the peace and order and stability which I had so miraculously
achieved in my marriage." Candor was big in the advanced circles. A
simple incident, perhaps, did not require confession. But this was
more. He had fallen in love. Margery was patiently understanding.
If he so wished, let their marriage be dissolved without recrimina-
tions. He didn't so wish. And Margery had too much pride to settle
easily into concubinage.

He had given up the outside love to save the marriage—and then
fallen in love with another girl. The good and the bad stretches of
road followed each other predictably. The second love was given up,
and then a third, and so it went. "My lost youth shone to me never
so appealingly as out of the eyes of girl poets." Not all the girls were
poets, nor love in every instance carnal. But his feeling of "lost
youth" obviously was a major factor. Perhaps more exactly, he
sought a youth that for him had never existed. The "eyes of girl
poets" were important because he was not satisfied with his own
creative life. "I was being a sensible person, reviewing other people's
books for a regular weekly stipend, instead of starving in a garret."

In the new Freudian jargon, Dell's friends said that, really shy
and tentative behind his sartorial disguise, he needed a "wife-
mother." Margery was, of course, twelve years older, and she created
a social atmosphere in which he was at ease. Moreover, she was his
best hold on reality and he was desperately afraid of retreating into
the fantasy world he had as a boy loved and fought. He believed
that if he went back to that fantasy world, just to spend a night, he
might, like Rip Van Winkle, awaken to find that he had spent a lifetime in the hills of dreams. The shimmering new loves, plunged into
so violently, given up readily if painfully, had to be close to fantasy.
At a distant time they might be the stuff of fireside reveries, but
now, rather than a gay free soul, he felt bewildered and wondered
if in fact his soul was not damaged goods.

Margery's pride was hurt, and, although not believing that his soul was injured beyond repair, worried that it might be eroding. She took a room in a rooming house. Instead he moved into it. Then he came back home to try again. And so it was, this bumpy road of the future. When they talked of renting separate studios in the Jackson Park colony they did not seek, as their friends thought, an advance toward the great freedom, but in fact to retreat and make a new approach to one another.

13

Love and Marriage and Freedom

OF the five marriages of the small-town poor boys, Sherwood Anderson's had been the most conventional. (Vachel Lindsay was, of course, the only bachelor.) That of Lee Masters had rivaled it only on the surface, for Masters had known that he would be under strain in adjusting to a burgher's life. Besides, he lived in a great city with its larger room for freedom. And he did well in that main criteria of the fixed society: the getting of money. Now, three hundred miles east of Chicago, the marriage of the Andersons, like that of the Dells, was floundering. No haze of a dawning new era lightened the misery there in Ohio.

Elyria, although growing, was still a town of less than fifteen thousand. Within the business circle Anderson was as well known as The Major, his father, had been to all of Clyde. That the affairs of the Anderson Manufacturing Company were going from bad to worse in this year of 1912 was something that could not be hidden from the leaders he had sought to emulate and outdistance. He had tried various medicines. To supplement direct mail circulars he was advertising his Roof-Fix in national magazines such as *Collier's* but was rarely able to afford more than an inch of space. A line of paint had been added and a scheme labeled "Commercial Democracy" gotten up to peddle stock to retailers, with the idea that they would afterward feature the company's products. It hadn't worked, although in a little magazine bearing the scheme's title Anderson poured all of his guile.

The Anderson Manufacturing Company had never fulfilled the promise of its name. Goods were bought from various makers already packaged and labeled, or else bulk ingredients were mixed in the space rented in the imposing factory building. The manager, as

Anderson listed himself when not making a pitch as the Roof-Fix Man, spent a good deal of his time corresponding with suppliers in search of cheaper materials. Such cash as arrived was mostly in the mail for direct orders. Lately Anderson had been reduced to advertising his Red Barn Paint in the local paper with an offer to call. So here he was, at thirty-six, after a dozen years in the romance of business, tugging fitfully at ragged bootstraps. At the same age his father had been in Clyde, also in the paint business, going to pieces while harboring ever more foolish dreams. By that time The Major had had four children, the oldest seven. Sherwood had three. Robert was five, John four, Marion one. Cornelia was far too strong and had too much backing from home ever to be overwhelmed as his mother had been. Sympathetic with his problems, she held up her end in the family and community. But he saw her not as a lover or wife or even as an individual. When it came down to it, he had been no better equipped for the maturity of husband than had been The Major. As that windy failure had escaped into tall-tale-telling in saloons, Sherwood fled ever further into story-writing in his attic. And more than ever his prime subjects were that Clyde town fool and the go-getting boy, Jobby. (The Major had, paradoxically, stopped wandering, married again, fathered another son, and become a steady housepainter and paperhanger in an Indiana town. Sherwood either did not know these facts or was not impressed.)

True, escape was more torturous than mere flight into imagination. In the future legend, Anderson would be a secret author, fearful that whispers of his literary yearnings might jeopardize his standing in the business community. Actually, he dictated stories into his office machine. Or he brought handwritten pages from home for his secretary to copy. Manuscripts were sent by her to editors and came back in the office mail. Such variations from Elyria business practices reached the ears of the men who had invested in the company or were prospects for doing so. As a man of the small towns, Anderson knew it had to be so. There was just a chance that the tales would come out better dictated. Yet there was relief, if he were bound to fail, in throwing up the public image of himself as a go-getter. To the solid business men the literary bug would be just one more biting him. Besides, he had now and again toyed with the notion that success in the arts was fairly easy to win; that for him it would be, anyhow. When forced to discard one robe of genius, there was perhaps less strain as a hand were reaching out for another, with other eyes watching.

A part of the future legend, too, would be that Cornelia lacked faith in him as a writer. Anyone has trouble, of course, believing in a self-proclaimed talent without strong evidence, and more so when the claimer has skipped from one field to quite a different one. Cornelia was plagued by the necessity of judging from his oral readings or else by struggling through bad spelling and punctuation and grammar. The purported isolation was of later imagination. Anderson never shied from reading his work, even to guests. Cornelia, if not starry-eyed, at any rate helped set the stage for these performances.

The main escape avenue, of course, was via the lonely flights into imagined (or partly imagined) worlds. Sometimes late at night Cornelia would go to the attic to fetch him and discover him trembling with fatigue. He wrote furiously, almost automatically. The scribbled sheets were piled on his table like leaves, until they had to be raked up and either taken to the office for copying or stored in boxes and bales. His habit was to shift from one project to another, so that around him grew up a barricade of manuscripts.

Anderson's largest and favorite undertaking was a novel which he called *Windy McPherson's Son*. The title was revealing because Windy, although the best drawn of the characters, was given relatively small space, the implication being that his son, Sam, was molded by the father. Windy, of course, was The Major. Sam was Jobby. The rest of the Anderson children were left out, making the narration easier. But Windy's wife, Sam's mother (Emma Anderson) was there, a dim figure as she would be in Anderson's later memoirs. The locale was moved from Ohio to Caxton, a small town in Iowa about the same size as Clyde.

Sam was more of a precocious commercial whiz than Jobby had been, and Windy more ridiculous than The Major. The author mounted Windy on a white horse for a town parade and raised a gleaming bugle to his lips, but denied him the musical skill to blow it, causing humiliation for the boy Sam. The Major, of course, had been a competent player of horns in the Clyde band. One night at supper Windy babbled obnoxiously as his wife lay ill in the next room. Sam, who was bigger than Jobby, throttled him, being careful not to finish him, and then, looking into his face for the first time in many years, carried the inert body out the back door and around the house and rolled it down a grassy bank into the road.

For about two hundred pages of scrawled manuscript Anderson continued with real and imagined events and people of his youth. Sam became a protégé of Freedom Smith, a squat, jovial dealer in butter and eggs; of John Telfer, orator, dandy, philosopher, who had inherited a small income and was married (the only one happily married in town) to a prosperous milliner who never questioned his comings and goings; and of Valmore, a stolid, mountainous old blacksmith. In his attic late at night Anderson poured out memories or imaginations of a small town greatly different from those depicted in the usual sweetness-and-light accounts of the American village. Sam, when no more than fifteen, stood with John Telfer and Valmore, trembling under the blacksmith's great encircling arm, and listened to a crazed assailant of the virtue of several of the town's married women cry out from jail to their husbands:

Are you there, oh dwellers in the cesspool of respectability? ... Do you stand in the mud with cold feet listening? I have been with your wives. Eleven Caxton wives without babes have I been with and it has been fruitless. The twelfth woman I have just left, leaving her man in the road a bleeding sacrifice to thee. I shall call out the names of the eleven. I shall have revenge also upon the husbands of the women, some of whom wait with the others in the mud outside.

And so the crazed man yelled out the names. The author seemed admiring of that demented screamer and a critic of the town society. He was not, however, much concerned with logic. Why should the women have been denounced for not bearing children if the fault was their husbands'? And why should the husbands be denounced if the hero himself, the great man in jail, had also failed to impregnate them?

The story became downright foolish after Sam left Caxton, but for the author the composition must have been great fun. Sam conquered the Chicago business world, married a rich girl, and moved on to supremacy among the nation's capitalists. That should have been enough for even a hero of current fiction. Anderson would not allow it. Sam broke with his wife, an idealist, because of his ruthless ambitions and, in part, their failure to have children. He wandered among the lowly (as Anderson had visions of doing), seeking an understanding of life. But whatever the flophouse he was in, all he had to do was to write a check on his inexhaustible bank account. The nearest Sam (and the author) came to the answers of life was for Sam to adopt the children of a drunken St. Louis plumber's wife and bring them home as an offering to his estranged wife.

From time to time Anderson devoted himself to another novel called *Marching Men*. The protagonist, Beaut McGregor, was not much different from Sam McPherson except that he had grown up in a Pennsylvania coal-mining town. The father was a "right guy," which would have been more of a switch if he hadn't soon been killed off in a mine disaster. The mother was the same dim figure. Beaut—so nicknamed because he was a big, ugly lad—went on to be a successful lawyer, who then, like Sam, turned from wealth to serve the people. What they needed to do, Beaut decided, was to march. Just to march. It would be their release, their satisfaction, the be-all-and-end-all of their existence. In the swing of the limbs, the rhythm of their bodies there was to be, too, a protest against the fixed order. For Anderson it was a way of getting Beaut out of his youth, but it was otherwise perfectly senseless unless for the moment he longed for the submerged oblivion of his army marching days.

And so his brain was a turmoil as he covered sheet after sheet with pen or pencil while barricaded in his attic. For the moment the crushing problems of the following day were obliterated.

The catastrophic morning of November 27, 1912, had no surface difference from the others of that late Ohio autumn, except that in the office of the Anderson Manufacturing Company the mail orders were even lighter than usual. In nearby farmlands the corn was in the shock, the pumpkins taken from the vines, fat turkeys and geese and chickens were strutting in barnyards or already slain for roasting. It was the Wednesday before Thanksgiving. For poor boys the great eating holidays, Thanksgiving and Christmas, are wonderful times of gluttony. But an invisible sadness from the unwonted feasting may cloud those holidays in adult years. Cornelia was at home preparing the festivities of the morrow. When leaving, her husband had seemed no more distraught than usual. At his office his secretary of four years, Frances Shute, watched him open the mail, glance at the low receipts, and then go and stand by the gas heater. He seemed preoccupied. Later she was to think that his behavior that morning had been queer; but that may have been hindsight.

Suddenly he declared, "I feel as though my feet are wet, and getting wetter." At least those were his words in Miss Shute's recollection. Not being of a literary turn of mind she perhaps missed the verbiage as it was to appear in the legend: "My feet are cold and wet and heavy from long wading in a river. Now I shall go walk on dry land." But he did not go at once, as the legend implied. He sat down and wrote a note, folded it, and handed it to his secretary with a request that it be delivered to his wife. Then he went out the door and up a railroad spur and across a bridge, heading away from town. Miss Shute hurried to the telephone and made arrangements for delivering the note. Whatever the message, surely there was nothing to make Cornelia fear that her husband would range for days over the countryside as if under a spell. If there had been, it seems obvious that she would have alerted the authorities. Instead, having sought the advice of friends, she chose to await developments. No word came on Thanksgiving, or Friday, or Saturday. Then on Sunday a friend telephoned that Anderson was a patient in a Cleveland hospital, suffering, the doctors believed, from nervous exhaustion. She hurried to him.

Where had Anderson been those four days and four nights? No one, including himself, would ever know for sure. Later he reported to different persons vague memories of sleeping one night in the back of a lumberyard, of lying in fields, of purchasing a workman's blue shirt and changing to it in a blacksmith shop. He did not remember wandering into the Cleveland drug store where he was identified. An attendant, seeing him dazed and disheveled and feeling that he was desperately seeking help, had gotten him to produce a notebook. In it was the name of one Edwin Baxter, an assistant secretary of Cleveland's Chamber of Commerce. Reached by phone, Baxter proved to be an acquaintance. He came with a doctor and, finding Anderson still incoherent, they had taken him to a hospital where the "nervous exhaustion" diagnosis was made.

Next day the Elyria *Democrat* carried the heading, "Elyria Man Found Dazed In Cleveland." The story told of Anderson being known as the Roof-Fix Man and, on the side, a novelist and short-story writer. The following day the Cleveland *Leader* described him as a "clubman, manufacturer, and author," and said that friends in Elyria were attributing his exhaustion to overwork on a novel that was to be his masterpiece. The secret—as he later claimed it to be—of his writing had indeed been bruited around the town.

In the hospital Anderson was now coming around. To a reporter for the Toledo *Blade* he spoke of days and nights wandering "gypsy-like over the countryside, while in a trance into which he had thrown himself by deep thought." To recapture the sensations of the odyssey he would cast himself back into the spell, he explained, and put them into a book. "It will be dangerous," he was quoted as saying, "but it will be a good story and the money is always welcome." At least it was practice in legend-making.

In time Anderson would believe that his way of bringing about changes in his life was by employing unconscious subterfuges. The obsession with his father was perhaps an unconscious recognition that The Major's subterfuges differed from his own mainly in their transparency. The trance episode, at least, developed into a rever-berating success. The Anderson Manufacturing Company was now a complete shambles which could not possibly harbor him longer. The episode had shaken his marriage beyond repair. An effort was being made to keep up appearances, but the family would never be truly reconstituted. In a short time Anderson would be on his way, alone, to Chicago and a minor job in the advertising agency which had formerly employed him.

On his way, also, to a life of creative writing as dedicated art. In a curious way the legend of Sherwood Anderson turning his back on riches would have an element of truth at bottom. Probably he lacked those special talents of the business giant and fortune-reaping author. But time would show that, once having turned away from the Bitch Goddess Success, he would never swing around for more than a wist-ful look and just a step or two in pursuit.

Lee Masters' dramatic surrender to fate at Emerson's grave, his announcement that he was at last "cornered" by life, proved to be, of course, a sort of inner tactical maneuver. Fate, never hoodwinked for a moment, had been ever ready to thwart him when he tried to break out. If anything it was more alert and struck back harder when he endeavored to burst the bonds of matrimony than in his struggles to escape from the law into literary prominence. His amorous eye had stopped roving only briefly following his marriage, in spite of the vast energies thrown into his office work and politics and writing. He had resumed his nervous prowling, with success poor to middling as usual.

His malaise was intellectual loneliness. Whether his wife might have filled the vacuum was a hypothetical question, since, feeling trapped by the very institution of marriage, he never gave her a chance. Some relief might have been found in literary companionship—for example, with the Chicago University group which included Robert Herrick, or with Hamlin Garland and Henry Fuller and the others of the Little Room. Unable to scrape up acquaintanceships with these, he despised them as dilettantes and snobs. His poet-lawyer friend Ernest McGaffey had left Chicago, and he never had had a warm intimacy of mind with his partner, Clarence Darrow. With old friends of the Press Club he had a certain male semiliterary companionship, mostly of a Rabelaisian nature; he himself produced a goodly supply of ribald ballades, as he preferred to call them. But this companionship was not enough.

Marriage had largely cut him off from "good" girls, whom he had formerly raised to a pedestal and idolized. To a few he made turtle dove advances and even, in the case of a young in-law widow, noticed (or thought he did) a soft wing's tilt in response. After changing roles to that of the mink he found himself denounced as base. He was no longer satisfied with idolizing, and besides, none of the young ladies who came within his limited ken had a really intellectual turn of mind. So it was back to easy conquest with even less satisfaction than before.

Then in 1909, a year after his symbolic kneeling to fate, he met Tennessee Mitchell, who wore the aura of the "new woman" as a proud bright plume. More exactly, he now came to know her—they had met briefly a few years earlier in the home of his sister Madeline, whose children were Tennessee's music students. Tennessee played the violin and piano and was a votary of the free-style dancing which Isadora Duncan was making famous. Tennessee's students were drawn largely from children of the upper class and she was a friend of many society leaders. At this time she was thirty-five but was usually taken for a few years younger. Masters was six years older, and owing to his generally solemn mein, accented by a rimless pince-nez, he seemed in his middle or late forties.

Although not beautiful, Tennessee was striking, especially when in clothing handed on by rich friends. Her taste was impeccable, her slender figure good, and her movements suggested a graceful bird in flight. Her vital presence gave the feeling of a strong, even an iron will. She left, too, an impression of inner aloofness, of a hidden strain of melancholy in spite of her capacity for warm friendship and vivacious conversation. Masters found her "an extremely interesting woman to look at. Her brow was conical, her hair sandy running to reddishness, her nose prominent and strong, her mouth delicate. . . ." This description would be set down more than a quarter century afterward amidst untranquil memories of his crazed desire for her. To most acquaintances she was fiercely honest, independent, bold, a harsh realist and a gifted satirist, but with clear-eyed sympathy for yearning artists.

Tennessee was an eminent figure among the nonediting and nonwriting women (Margery Currey, Nellie Van Volkenburg, etc.) who helped create a Chicago atmosphere in which the Literary Renaissance was possible. Masters himself was to declare that his emotions were greatly deepened by his association with her, and her influence may have gone beyond his admission. Later she would be the fiancée and wife of Sherwood Anderson in his best creative years, and he would credit her for light and warmth in the time of cold and dark—not an easy thing for Anderson to do when speaking of a woman who had been devoted to him, especially a wife. Like nearly all the others, Tennessee had grown up in a small Midwestern community. In her case it was Jackson, Michigan. Otherwise her background was strikingly different, for she alone was the product of a nonconformist home.

In those days anybody reasonably well informed associated the first name "Tennessee" with Tennessee Claflin, the younger of the famous, indeed notorious, Claflin sisters. A further association ranged through free love, equal rights for women, a single moral standard, and other topics having a tinge or worse of scandal. In the case of Tennessee Mitchell there was more to it than the nebulous connection of sharing a given name. She had been named in honor of Tennessee Claflin, who, moreover, had personally conferred her blessing, although slightly prior to the infant's birth.

The Claflin sisters had been at the height of their notoriety when the namesake of the younger was born in 1874. Victoria was thirty-six, Tennessee twenty-eight. Beauty ranked among their assets, but no higher than eloquence, shrewdness, energy, and mettlesome spirit. As young girls they had hobnobbed with the dead at séances to which the public had been sold tickets. Bottles of an elixir of life sold by them while with a medicine show had presumably added joy to the days and nights of yokels. Moving to New York, they had become protégés of Cornelius Vanderbilt, whose tips helped them win a small fortune in the stock market. Next had been their editorship of a weekly that stressed unconventional opinions.

One of their stories, charging intimacy between Henry Ward Beecher, the famous Brooklyn preacher, and the wife of Theodore Tilton, a religious editor, had brought on one of America's most celebrated trials when Tilton sued Beecher for alleged "criminal conversation" with his wife. The six-month-long trial, held in the second year following Tennessee Mitchell's birth, ended in a hung jury, but the nation had been titillated as perhaps never before, and the name "Tennessee" was much on the tongues of the populace. It was bound to cause a namesake a great deal of childhood embarrassment, for the scandal associated with the unusual name would be in the minds of the child's peers as she grew up. This burden was laid on her by her mother, Martha, under the powerful influence of her grandfather. Tennessee's father, Jay Mitchell, a postal clerk, was a simple man with small interest in advanced thought. The old man was an inventor, chiefly of farm machinery, a freethinker, a spiritualist, a devout follower of Huxley and Darwin, a dabbler in many exotic notions and philosophies, including free love. The Clalin sisters had visited when his daughter—living in his home—was pregnant with Tennessee. By having the baby christened after the younger of the sisters, the old man had repaid the honor of the visit and after a fashion raised a banner.

In school Tennessee tried to change her name by writing "Tennis C." or "Tennie C." Naturally the scheme didn't work. Yet all in all she was comfortable enough with other boys and girls, an excellent student, a gifted violinist and pianist. In time she had two sisters: Louisa, half a dozen years younger, and Amber, a dozen. After graduating from high school, Tennessee became a piano tuner and worked for several years at the trade, living at home. Her mother died and Tennessee tried to be a substitute mother to her younger sister. When Jay Mitchell took a new wife, these two sisters were not able to adjust to her; the middle one did. When the strain in the home became unbearable, Tennessee fled, taking little Amber with her to Chicago. Finding work as a piano tuner was hard for a girl, since it called for traveling alone into all sorts of environments, including bawdy houses. Tennessee managed to get a job with one of the large music companies, and once was dispatched to the Everleigh Club to put the Ebony Room's grand piano in tune.

It was a bitter enough struggle for a girl to make her way and support a child sister. Then stark tragedy fell upon the pair when Amber was stricken with meningitis. Tennessee managed to secure medical aid and nursed her as best she could, but at the age of twelve Amber died in her sister's arms. Tennessee's estrangement from her father and sister Louisa continued. After a while she was able to move up from piano tuning to instruction, and gradually she built a clientele among the wealthy. Her private world in 1909 was largely that of musicians, dancers, actors, a few painters and yearning authors. Naturally there had been men in her life. She had been in love with one, a man of fairly high social position, a devotee of the arts, but with distaste and no aptitude for the business in which his family had put him. She confessed a weakness for this type of man—one who, if not altogether weak, was of refined tastes but coped badly with his environment.

The relationship between Lee Masters and Tennessee Mitchell presents thorny biographical problems. Were they lovers? Masters said yes, passionately so. Tennessee said no, it was pure intellectual attraction on her side from start to finish. Both statements were written out many years later, a bit obliquely to be sure, but nevertheless definitely. Each is quite believable. Masters confessed, after all, many failures of conquest, so why invent about this one? Tennessee hardly pretended to be a virgin at thirty-five, and frankly held consummation of love outside marriage to be in some instances good and proper. As for Masters' wedded state, he believed that adultery on a husband's part ought to be accepted within reason by a wife. On this he was a conventional double-standard man unaffected by the freedom-from-possession ideal in which the female, too, was unshackled. Tennessee understood that his marriage had already gone to pieces, and argued to herself that, besides, conventions had done nothing for her.

Perhaps the question whether they were lovers is not vital, since the impact on Masters' life and work is evident without exact knowledge of the condition of their intimacy. Yet the nature of his account makes bypassing difficult. In his memoirs, published when he was sixty-eight, he was brutal to himself owing to a conviction that a writer—especially one who might be accepted by future generations as a genius—ought to reveal all about himself for history. His characterization of Tennessee was poisonous. It is true that she was dead and he did not use her name, calling her instead Deirdre. Later, however, he affirmed that Deirdre stood for Tennessee Mitchell. His thesis in retrospect was that a witch had put a fever on him. A certain ambivalency crept in, for, while picturing himself as a domineering male, he told of asking his wife to release him so that he might marry Tennessee—even though he claimed to have penetrated her scheming mind by that time. The roaring fires of their passion, he decided, had consumed her vitals and she had died a suicide—twenty years later. All this, however, was for ink and paper. Privately, he spoke affectionately of his "Dear Tennis." Tennessee's end was to be surrounded by drama, but he and others were in error in believing her a suicide. A passion that may well have been destructive had burned in her— but for Sherwood Anderson. Not long before her death she had begun an autobiography, never published and probably never seen by Masters nor reported to him in detail. She, too, omitted the name of the party of the second part, and substituted "my poet." The description of Masters was too accurate, however, not to have been meant to identify him. She had found irony in the different situations of "my poet" and the disoriented art-loving business man with whom she had been involved. To the latter she had offered consummation of their love when it was apparent that they could not or would not marry. He had cried out in horror that it would ruin her life. "My poet," on the other hand, had demanded total fulfillment of what he insisted was reciprocated love, arguing that otherwise her life would be ruined.

Another strengthener for Tennessee's version is that, although a yearner in the arts, Masters was far from a non-coper in his unwanted profession. Thus he hardly needed the mothering which, in spite of her worldly air, Tennessee wanted to give a man.

Masters was in what he called a "half-torpid state of life" when he met Tennessee for the second time in the spring of 1909. Losses in bank stock and other investments had further diminished his hope of devoting all of his efforts to literature. Worse, his practice was growing more burdensome. Darrow had procured most of the firm's business, but recently he had spent almost two years in Idaho winning acquittal of Big Bill Haywood on the charge of having murdered an ex-governor of that state. Having returned broken in health, Darrow now spent much of his time lecturing, mostly against the rising tide for prohibiting the sale of alcohol. Masters had to carry the greater load of the practice. Each morning he restored his vigor with a cold bath and exercises and then drove himself through the day. He asked himself what he was getting out of life for "this endless bowing of my back?" Very little, he answered.

One day he had been seeking a respite in the public library when he looked up and saw at another table a woman whom he had known as a lovely girl, an heiress into the bargain. She had been for him one of those girls raised to a pedestal. Later she had married and been divorced. Now they spoke together and he learned that she was living in an expensive North Side apartment hotel. She was quite attractive still and he was delighted to be asked to call for renewing old acquaintances. Having eventual designs, he was not pleased when Tennessee Mitchell, who shared the apartment, came in from a journey out of town and joined the conversation. After two or three similar encounters—and the divorcee proving unresponsive—Masters invited Tennessee to lunch. He had in mind no more than "one of those light-hearted adulteries that do no harm, and involve nothing but a technical breach of conjugal fidelity, which not being known are as innocuous as a walk or a talk."

But he had never conversed at any length with a woman such as Tennessee. Her talk was of Shaw and the Abbey Players and others of the European drama. She was active in settlement work and, like himself, a radical in politics. Her acquaintanceship in Chicago at various levels was far superior to his. While his social and political knowledge and opinions came mostly from reading, she was familiar with the contrasting elements of the population from experience and observation. He was refreshed by the irony which spiced her comments. Neither could have guessed that one day her keen observation and irony expressed in clay figures would bring her a notable reputation as a sculptress.

For Tennessee's part, she was excited to be for the first time with a published author. That his books had been issued at his own cost made little difference to one who realized that all artists must struggle one way or another for recognition. The important thing was that he was serious, had kept going. She was an audience for Masters' fine talking gift. To his anger at literary neglect she was responsive, to his obvious frustration, sympathetic. Naturally she would be delighted to be made a present of his books. That she had not read them could not be held against her; almost no one had. The long years of "miscellaneous studies" had given him, of course, a far wider literary range than hers. She would be further delighted to receive other books which he offered to send, and to accept guidance in her reading. He had a disciple. The literary gods had been indulgent, if belatedly, in sending one in the form of a desirable woman.

Tennessee read his poetry and did not like it much. Her interest, she reported to him, was slight in "fairy tales"—celebrations of Helen of Troy and odes to autumn and syrupy inner joys and bittersweet sorrows. Rather than being angered, he welcomed her attitude as all to the good, calling her a member of the realistic school. A year or two earlier he had read Dreiser's *Sister Carrie* and been moved to write a letter of admiration to the author, leading to a correspondence between them. As the meeting with Tennessee continued, he praised her imagination and credited her insights and inspiration for urging him to new efforts. She was fascinated by his talk, especially of his ambitions, and spoke well of his work when she could. "Mine were new and eager ears for his poetry, his bitterness and his hopes. He took me into a new world of thought and I was flattered that an impetus for writing was coming in the wake of our relationship." She added, "My need was great for stimulating companionship and sex was to me a part of an Entireness which I knew did not exist in this relationship."

Masters saw it differently. All summer—his family was away much of that time—they strolled by the lake and talked and laughed and then dined in good restaurants and talked some more in the apartment where Tennessee was alone for the season. But she "fled my grasp with the skill of a Daphne." To him nothing else seemed to matter. An affair would be "a cure for all my ills, as proper payment to the genius of misfortune that had descended upon my industry and my concentration of mind." Yet "we went on until I was half mad about her, and still she eluded me." At this point, of course, the memoirs take different paths. In his, Tennessee, knowing his home life to be in disrepair, had always intended to force a complete break and then marry him. And so as he was about to quit the race she cunningly submitted to his embraces, whereupon his ardor rose to an even wilder pitch until he was hopelessly entrapped—but she, too, was caught in the fiery furnace of his passion. Paradoxically, she remained a cold schemer while burning to a cinder.

At any rate, he begged his wife to release him, frankly stating his desire to marry Tennessee. The request was turned down, whereupon (in his version) Tennessee demanded that he run away with her to another city or to Europe. In Tennessee's, he insisted that she run away with him. A year had passed when finally he resolved upon a mighty struggle to "use my mind and my will to exorcise this demon that had entered into me." It was responsible for "nausea in the seat of the solar plexus, and had caused the great nerves of that center to writhe and constrict like entangled snakes." When parted from Tennessee he felt "a sensation of sinking" and "a pulsing despair, a grief without words all up and around my heart until my breath seemed to be going out of me." It could be "allayed in a minute by seeing her."

They broke it off, but tortured years were to pass before he was able to pronounce himself cured and assess the impact. On the one hand, he had learned "the secrets and agonies of all the world's lovers, of all the Antonys, the Abelards, the Troiluses. My emotional powers were enormously deepened." On the other, he discovered that "nothing can be more suicidal to the spirit than to fight fire with fire, to destroy beauty with acid and knives, to do terrible surgeries to the heart when it is most tender, to take poison as an antidote to poison, to get back self-mastery by coarsening one's nature, by dulling one's sensitivity, by increasing one's resistance and spiritual muscle by the heavy food of obscene and satirical associations, by drabby contacts in which memories of ecstasies can be mocked until their beauty can no longer be recalled to mind." He had "solaced myself with Grace, Adele, Marie and Virginia" along with excursions into printed erotica. "I had to do this, or I had to turn monk or Hindu, and seek Nirvana by crushing out my restless vitality."

Tennessee merely reported that "when it ended and ended miserably I was desolated." But, writing earlier than he, she offered proof of the inner turmoil he later described. "His hatred became so intense that for years to see him casually on the street affected me like a physical danger. I trembled and ran into buildings to avoid a meeting."

Masters found some relief, perhaps, in writing a three-act play called *Eileen*, which was published in June 1910 by the Rooks Press, Chicago, at the author's expense, and signed Edgar Lee Masters. In it, Carl, the hero, is ready to throw all "to the winds" and go to Wyoming with Eileen; yet he almost knifes her. Eileen declares: "Dear, listen to me. I have always been afraid of you. In the first place I never wanted anyone to have the power over me that you have. I never wanted to love as you have made me love you. I know

now that I have never loved anybody but you." The reader of *Eileen*
and the Masters autobiography and Tennessee's bit of memoirs can
make of this wish-fulfillment or not, as he chooses.

Masters followed in the autumn with a book of poems, *Songs and
Sonnets,* also issued by the Rooks Press, but for it he again became
pseudonymous, this time under the name Webster Ford. The work
showed no advance in technique—but surely many of the poems
were more deeply felt than others of the past. Late in December
another subsidized three-act play, *The Locket,* came out of Rooks
Press, signed with Masters' three names and dealing further with the
travails of the characters Eileen and Carl.

In the marriage stakes, the oldest of these six writers to make his
choice—Sandburg—had laid his money on a sure-footed partner.
True, he was not as complex as the others. "Varietism" in women
had never been a problem for him, as for Dreiser and Masters and
Dell—and for Anderson, too, although the tight boundaries of Elyria
had hemmed him in. Sandburg may have been fortunate in his relative unattractiveness to women. Too, he had come nearer a road
where a wife could better know how to push and haul and guide him.
Lillian Steichen had, like his mother, seen "my chance" and taken
it, not in the same peasant way, but by falling in love with the kind
of man she wanted: an idealist with a literary talent yet to be fully
shaped.

Lillian's Phi Beta Kappa from Chicago University was fairly
minor among her accomplishments. Besides a speaking and writing
proficiency in French and German, in addition to English, she was
grounded in the literary classics and mathematics and economics.
Thorstein Veblen had been her favorite teacher, and it was to study
under him that she had switched from Illinois University to Chicago.
She had been past her mid-twenties in late 1907 when she had met
Sandburg. They had dropped the "obey" from the wedding ceremony
six months later and agreed that either might end the union by a
simple declaration.

Knowing that her husband's Socialist organizing job would take
him from home much of the time, she had, as a loyal party member,
found this condition acceptable. Assigned to a district around Osh-
kosh and Appleton some hundred miles northwest of Milwaukee, they
had begun housekeeping in Appleton in three rooms of a house belonging to a Socialist carpenter. Lillian noticed that her husband

liked to spend an extra day or two visiting in a favorite Socialist home while on his rounds, and to while away time arguing, gossiping, or singing with male companions. His habits had been long unfixed and he showed no wish to fix them. So Lillian did what all of the "new women" wanted to do but rarely managed: let her man go his own way. It was not labyrinthine; she usually knew where he was. One does not guide a monolith, she realized, by waving or shouting.

The Socialist movement in Wisconsin was more powerful than in any other state. The elements in Milwaukee which had carried Socialism with them from Germany and Austria were partly responsible. The party was growing fast, too, in the farm regions and mining camps and small industrial cities. The number of Socialists had doubled since 1904, when Debs had won 400,000 votes. Then in 1908 the Wisconsin Socialists had hit on the sensational notion of hiring a special train to carry Debs to the people. When the famed Red Special arrived at the borders of Sandburg's district he had clambered pridefully aboard and, as was his due, harangued whistle-stop crowds as warm-ups for the star attraction.

But the maintenance of a home was an economic strain, and in 1909 the Sandburgs had taken up residence in Milwaukee. They were determined that he should now make a living by writing. A tentative foot was lifted to a bourgeois ladder when he got a job writing advertising for a department store. The foot quickly slipped off. It was the wrong ladder for his abilities. He applied to various newspapers for work as a reporter or editorial writer and after filling in here and there finally landed as city hall reporter for the *Journal*. He occasionally wrote an article for *LaFollette's Magazine* or some other publication. But in verse he had made little public advance since the promising *In Reckless Ecstasy* of half a dozen years ago. He wasn't "Charlie" any more except to old acquaintances. Lillian had preferred his real given name, and for his 1908 Socialist card he had been plain Carl Sandburg. As if to strike a balance, he didn't care for the name Lillian, and so she became Paula (stemming from her childhood nickname, "Paus'l").

The Milwaukee Socialists were making their greatest push in city politics by running Emil Seidel, a carpenter, for mayor in the 1910 election. Seidel won—the first Socialist to be elected mayor of an important U.S. city—and he chose for his secretary Carl Sandburg, who had drudged mightily in the campaign. Although the new office worker combed back his thick hair and wore a stiff collar and a necktie, he was not at his best as a man for details. At any rate Seidel agreed before his two-year term was up to spare him for promotion of a new Socialist daily, the Milwaukee *Leader*. After it began publication in 1911, Sandburg worked on it as a reporter and feature writer.

14

Dreiser, Masters, Reedy, Garland, Fuller, and Browne

THEODORE DREISER arrived in Chicago just before Christmas of 1912 for research on *The Titan*. His European journey had been stimulating enough to make a tome (he was hard put not to make a tome of any subject), which would appear next year as *A Traveler at Forty*. His one failure in Europe had turned out a blessing: Return passage had been booked for the great new liner *Titanic;* by missing it he had escaped the disaster of its sinking.

Early in November *The Financier* had been published by Harper. Prospects were fairly encouraging, if the response to *Jennie* was taken as a guide. Some fourteen thousand copies of it at $1.40 each had been sold. His share—some $3,000—was not large for a man who had enjoyed a salary of $10,000 or more. He rather expected *The Financier* to do better. At the moment he was strapped, having turned over most of his worldly goods to Sally on their final parting. He was obligated to support her, and was under the impression that she had agreed to a divorce.

Even had his budget been less tight he would have remained hardly more briefly at the expensive Sherman House, where he stopped first. Life had conditioned him to watch dollars and nickels, too. In a day or two he joined his old secretary, Bill Lengel, now an editor for a real estate magazine, in a rooming house that once had been the Frederick Dent Grant mansion. Lengel had a second-floor back; Dreiser took a commodious third-floor front. The mansion was on Lincoln Parkway (later a part of Michigan Avenue) within easy walking distance of the Newberry Library, where Dreiser would pore over newspaper files, old city reports, and other documents for

The Titan, the second novel of his trilogy based on the career of Yerkes. For relaxation he could, if the weather happened to be mild, step out of the library's south door across a narrow pavement into little "Bughouse Square"—Chicago's equivalent of London's Hyde Park and New York's Union Square.

Although not a splendid conqueror returning to his old haunts, Dreiser had the air of a man who has made his mark. His six feet, one and a half inches, with its hundred and ninety pounds well distributed except for a slight bulge at the middle, was commanding when clad in his long, fur-collared overcoat. Lengel, who thought he knew all of his hero's facets, was amazed at the sudden emergence of Dreiser the pugilist. They came home late one night in a heavy snowstorm. Climbing out of the taxicab, they were apprised by the driver, a large man himself, of a sudden hike in fare. The man got down, too, as if to head off flight. Calmly, almost majestically, Dreiser laid his fur-collared overcoat on his companion's arm and assumed the prizefighter's stance. It was a fine portrait of a slugger-killer, there in the swirling storm, yet Lengel was relieved when the bully cringed and pleaded to be let off without a beating. He was, and humbly accepted a reasonable fare.

Plunging into his work, Dreiser at first avoided social affairs. On New Year's Eve, however, he joined Lengel and his girl friend for dinner-dancing at the Great Northern Hotel. Lengel had never learned to dance. An argument might have been sustained that Dreiser had not either. Yet he leaped bravely into the gap and with the young lady assayed the Grizzly Bear and the Bunny Hug and the Two-Step. This until well after the year 1913 had been rung in. Lengel, watching, reflected on one of the master's favorite maxims, "Never take a girl away from an old friend."

Another of Dreiser's maxims was more strictly a guide for the behavior of authors. "Never take a girl away from a critic." But a man wasn't always able to stick to his good rules, as events would prove before his departure from Chicago.

Lee Masters was one of the first Chicagoans visited by Dreiser, once his plans of work had been laid out. The visitor had been, of course, assured of a warm welcome, owing to their correspondence after Masters' praise of *Sister Carrie.* Dreiser's call had another purpose. Masters had been in Chicago during the last half dozen years of Yerkes' power. He had felt some of the buccaneer's impact

and could open doors to men who had known him well. The partnership of Masters and Darrow had broken up over a year ago. The
older man's frequent absences for lectures had caused a strain, and
then he had settled in Los Angeles to defend the McNamara brothers,
accused of blowing up a newspaper plant and killing twenty men.
Months had passed and, besides the added burden, Masters was
not satisfied with the division of fees. The lawyers had not parted
as friends, yet when Darrow himself was on trial charged with jury
bribing, Masters responded heartily and ably by securing depositions
of good character from prominent Chicago citizens.

When Dreiser called, he found, of course, the gregarious Masters,
eyes twinkling and dimples showing, full of Rabelaisian tales and
commentaries on the plight of American literature, society, and
politics. Out came a bottle of liquor from a drawer (a gun was kept
there, too), and feet went up on the desk. Masters found his visitor's
eyes "full of friendliness and a kind of merriment," his conversation
humorous and clear—"not like his writing." Masters noticed also his
"buck teeth," very white, and "his long white fingers when he took
off his gloves."

Inevitably the conversation turned to a mutual friend and hero,
William Marion Reedy, the gargantuan editor of *Reedy's Mirror*.
This weekly, of undistinguished format, was published in St. Louis,
but its thousands of readers in Chicago's advanced circles regarded
it as almost their own. Contributors were paid little or nothing yet
sought avidly to place their poems or stories or articles in it. Acceptance was a guarantee of notice in Eastern editorial sanctums where
Reedy's opinion was respected. Best of all was Reedy's magnificent
personal gift for inspiration, guidance, and consolation. There had
been Dreiser's own case. Back in 1900, learning of his publisher's
wish to abandon *Sister Carrie*, he had found relief while in Missouri
by talking over his burdens with Reedy.

The editor had been thirty-eight at that time, the delicate facial
lines of his youth already lost in a great moon of flesh. Damp black
hair spilled over a low forehead to heavily-ridged brows. Below a
straight nose, which had escaped blemish, a deep fleshy trough
emphasized the sensuality of Reedy's Cupid's bow mouth. Most
striking feature were his eyes—sometimes only great dark mirrors,
but again laughing or scorning. As a brawler in the murky nether-
lands of St. Louis politics and hard-knuckled journalism Reedy was
used to the give and take of character mayhem. If you were knocked

down but wanted to go on fighting, in his experience somebody would help you up, never if you lay prostrate in self-sorrow. This he had conveyed helpfully to Dreiser.

Reedy's own hand was large in the making of the *Sister Carrie* legend. He had begun with an account by a New York correspondent dealing with the book's publishing troubles. For the first time Mrs. Doubleday appeared in the role of villainess. The article had appeared a whole year after the publication of the book, showing Reedy's (and likely Dreiser's) persistence.

Masters and Reedy were boon companions in spite of the jaundice which came into the editor's eyes whenever he read any of his friend's poetry. A dozen years ago he had been prevailed upon by their mutual friend Ernest McGaffey to use a few dribbles of Masters' verse, and from time to time had reluctantly permitted others to seep into his pages. But his advice was to "for God's sake lay off the poetry." The two had gotten acquainted in 1907 when Masters, in St. Louis on a legal matter, had gone to Reedy's office. They had struck it off from the beginning. "It was the outstanding friendship of my life, as it was his," Masters declared later. "No man was so close to him as I was, nor any so close to me as he was." Reedy valued Masters' articles on political and labor affairs, and Masters valued his friend's erudition and literary vision (except in the case of a certain poet's work).

The main basis of their relationship, however, was camaraderie. When together, they talked for hours at a stretch, and when apart exchanged many letters. Above all they shared a gusto for wanton male joys, the difference being Reedy's public lack of inhibitions and Masters' outward conformity. Reedy had married not one bordello madam, but two. Great pleasures and releases for Masters were weekends with Reedy in St. Louis, which began with helping him put the *Mirror* to press and continued with sundry adventures. One of the more bizarre became a favorite story of his, and naturally he told it to Dreiser, who, as a connoisseur of the editor's Falstaffian ways, was appreciative. For some years Reedy had lived with a madam in her plush establishment. One night the last of the page proofs had been corrected just before midnight—it was Saturday— and Reedy had felt entitled to a party. He guided Masters to a delicatessen, where they filled a large basket with caviar, pig's knuckles, pumpernickel, sweet butter, exotic cheeses, and other items striking their fancy. Next, with the basket following in a cab, they called at a winery and filled another basket with choice beverages. Then it was to the bordello, which was to be the final stop for the weekend. The madam complied with Reedy's wish that the house be emptied of guests as rapidly as convenient and the door barred for a private party.

The revelry was not destined to continue in the manner planned. A girl died, whether from a surfeit of rich foods and liquors or from a heart attack. For some reason there was an urgent need to bury her on Sunday—perhaps Reedy's urge to deliver a memorial oration. A death certificate was procured, burial permission gained, and other arrangements attended to. A driving rain threatened to mar the graveyard ceremony, but a numerous throng arrived in hired carriages, mainly to hear Reedy, a splendid orator. After the casket had been lowered into its pit, Reedy took up a ponderous stance on the graveside mound of fresh red clay. Rain was still falling. He was in full voice and gesture when his footing in the clay proved unreliable, and the massive figure catapulted into the grave. He was much too heavy, and the sides of the grave too slick, for the mourners to haul him out. The fire department was summoned and a block and tackle was used to lift him up.

Dreiser was invited to be a guest in one setting in which Masters achieved at least the outer trappings of genius. It was in his home, a large hillside dwelling, a bit short of mansion proportions, on the South Side's Kenwood Avenue in the Hyde Park area. Masters had bought the house for his wife during the period of his infatuation with Tennessee Mitchell, to please her and perhaps also as a sop for his conscience. Now he thought of his wife as a cat full of cream, never considering that she might be doing her best as an intellectual companion.

In the household Masters was treated as a kind of hearth god. At dinner he customarily read aloud his fresh-minted verses for the appreciation of his wife, who regularly applauded. The three children, the boy, thirteen, and the two girls, nine and six, were on notice that a giggle meant instant banishment. After dinner Masters often repaired to his study on the second floor to compose more verse. Below, his wife played mood music on the piano. Strauss waltzes were best, he felt, for inspiration. The children must be silent. When the youngest girl whiled the time by dancing, she had to watch out lest her father come down the stairs. He thought dancing bad for children.

Always one to push a friend, Dreiser called Masters' poetry to Dell's attention while in Chicago. But for Dell, as for Reedy, it was too fragile and derivative. To feel promise in Masters was especially hard because of his obvious lack of discipline. If he was in a mood for Shelley-like beauty, out gushed the lines and rested as they fell. Although painstaking in the law he rejected the notion that literary genius included a capacity for taking pains.

Dell had not himself reviewed *The Financier*, but Dreiser had no cause for complaint about the *Friday Literary Review*'s treatment of it. Associate editor Lucian Cary (Jig Cook had moved with his new wife, Susan Glaspell, to Provincetown, Massachusetts) had given it the whole front page, saying that Dreiser "looks upon life and tells us what he sees. . . . He makes no attempt to lure the reader with words. And so the reader is lured by what he has to say." Cary was ready to begin volume two, and Dreiser, as it happened, had brought a suitcase full of manuscript, including the early chapters of *The Titan*, which he passed out to those willing to read and offer advice.

In one issue Dell commented on a clerk's remark that he had found *The Financier* erotic. Dell considered it "as erotic as Bryce's *The American Commonwealth*." To him the love affair of Frank Cowperwood (the leading character, based on Yerkes) with the daughter of a powerful contractor-politician had been described without "purple passages." Yet it was illicit, Cowperwood being a married man, and that made it erotic. The truth was that the minutely detailed story of Cowperwood's (Yerkes') rise to financial heights in Philadelphia and his fall and imprisonment was not capturing wide reader interest. The author's high hopes seemed unwarranted, for sales were only about half as good as *Jennie*'s had been.

Yet Chicago had groups to honor a pioneer realist and commiserate with wounded veterans. Hamlin Garland arranged that the courtesies of the Cliff-Dwellers' Club be extended to Dreiser and conveyed an invitation to address the members—who were drawn from prosperous male authors, artists, musicians, journalists, and a few other callings. The quarters at the top of Orchestra Hall were at the heart of a downtown Michigan Avenue cultural complex made up of the Art Institute, Fine Arts Building, Auditorium, and Orchestra Hall itself. Dreiser's shyness in public made him reject the invitation to speak but he visited the clubrooms for a talk with Garland and Fuller. A somewhat bossy man, Garland ran the club with an iron hand. Since he abominated liquor it was forbidden on the premises. (Elsewhere when wine was served he ostentatiously turned his glass down.) There had been a crisis when lady guests, members of the Irish Players, had openly puffed cigarettes. The forces of evil had prevailed, partly owing to Garland's weakened condition. At fifty-two he was in poor health and suffering from malaise of the spirit.

Garland and Fuller and their guest filled a corner of the big lounge room with curses against the Romanticists and dire forebodings. Garland was a stocky, round-faced man with traces of his pioneer homesteading youth still on him. He sorrowed over the long-ago reception of his *Main-Traveled Roads* because (as Dreiser remembered the sense of his words) "the reality of the coarse phases of the daily life of the world which he observed" had threatened him with social ostracization. It had stuck in Garland's mind that his *Rose of Dutcher's Coolly* had been called vulgar owing to its heroine's rather strong emotions. The realist's task in those days had been too hard, Garland said, for his "social courage and connections" after he had married a sister of Lorado Taft, the fashionable sculptor whose massive studio on the old World's Fair Midway was a Chicago showplace. Garland ignored the fact that *Main-Traveled Roads* was the foundation of his reputation. More recent romantic novels had won neither a large income nor discriminating readers. Just now he was about to go East for one of his rare lecture dates, carrying with him the manuscript of his autobiographical *A Son of the Middle Border*. (He was to put it later: "Humbly, sadly, unwillingly I left my home that cold, bleak, dirty day, staggering under the weight of my valises, for I was not in good health and my mood was irresolute.") He could not know that Mark Sullivan, the liberal young editor of *Collier's*, hunting fresh material of America's past, would buy and serialize the manuscript (after one more, the seventh, revision) and that with the publication of the book itself he would be reestablished. The Cliff Dwellers' talk, however, gave evidence that in the future he would turn his back on realism, revert to the pathos of self-sorrows, and incidentally call Dreiser a sex maniac.

Fuller, being small and shy and reticent, deferred to the lion of the Cliff-Dwellers. The gray in his dark beard and brushed hair made him appear older than his three years of seniority warranted. Dreiser, in his usual probing way, tried to ascertain the impact on Fuller of the reaction to his *The Cliff-Dwellers* and *With the Procession*. As Dreiser later remembered the reply, he had met not only personal disapproval but contumely. "Sensitive to as well as fond of the society of which he was a part . . . and finding himself facing social as well as literary ostracism, he desisted." Fuller was being agreeable— and perhaps gently pulling the leg of his companions.

There was no question of Fuller's high place in Chicago's past. Henry's grandfather had settled in the city as early as 1840, ahead of the Armours and Palmers, and although away for a while to be a judge in Michigan, had come back in 1849 to amass a fortune in railroad-building. His son, Henry's father, had been a railroad executive and a banker. Although the fortune was now largely gone, Henry not being an accumulator or even a protector, he surely would have hated exclusion from genteel society—and been terribly ill at ease with proletarian or radical agitators. Yet he had exposed himself to the worst contumely by violently opposing the United States' role in the Spanish-American War. When publishers had rejected his blazing verses he had issued them in a lurid pirate cover. A clue to the real cause of Fuller's turn from realistic novels may have been given to young Mary Hastings Bradley, a member of the Little Room group and an African big game hunter. She had shown him a manuscript dealing with shop girls for his advice, and she had noticed how distressed and appalled he was by the near-violence of their lives.

As for Dreiser, he had in Garland and Fuller a perfect audience for his strain of martyrdom: Garland because he wanted to believe cruel forces had done him in, Fuller because of his disposition to be agreeable. A mild persecution complex was doubtless helpful to Dreiser in his role of trailblazer. Unlike Fuller, he knew the harsh lives of ordinary people and never turned his eyes away. Unlike Garland, he was not impelled to win acceptance among the high-placed. Martyrdom toughened his hide into an armor of righteousness.

Dreiser was invited to be honored at Maurice Browne's newly finished temple of art. In a sense the raw and proletarian fighter would be out of place, for it was a little jewel of a temple, built with funds donated by worshippers of the great god Dollar. After newspaper stories of the Jackson Park colony rehearsals, the Fine Arts

Building's manager had insisted that only his edifice was a fitting milieu for so grand a project. True, the facade of its seven stories was more or less in the classic Greek style. On the other hand, rental for its various auditoriums was out of the question. A storage fourth-floor back, after alterations, would cost $3,000 a year. Browne had taken it. His own pleas for cash had been rather humble. For $100 a patron could be a life member, for $10 a year on the honor roll (both entitled to half-price tickets). The opening roll of life members was august: Mrs. J. Ogden Armour, Mrs. Julius Rosenwald, Mrs. Chauncey Blair, Mrs. Erich Gerstenberg, Mrs. Albert Loeb, Arthur Aldis.

The name, Chicago Little Theatre, was apt. There were ninety-one seats, comfortably upholstered in beige cloth. The stage was fourteen by twenty feet, less a structural column in the right wing. The ceiling was eight feet high except for a beam at left. Browne didn't care for flood or spot or footlights, but he indulged in a switchboard with eight dimmers. After watching light bounce off Michigan Avenue into the faces of pedestrians, he had hit upon front-of-house and backstage lights, which were new conceptions. The tiny dressing rooms and toilets were on the floor above.

A unique feature was a tearoom which was entered through a gap in the balustrade which ran down a theater edge. Merely as a tearoom its importance would have been slight; as a gathering place for artists of all kinds, indeed a salon, it was to rival the group's dedication as a major influence in the making of the Renaissance. Trappings were fairly elegant: small round tables and straw-bottom chairs with twisted metal backs in the ice cream parlor mode, a samovar, and food brought in from the famous catering establishment of Mrs. William Vaughn Moody, widow of the poet and dramatist.

Browne himself lectured Wednesday nights (admission a dollar) when there was no performance, and he held a discussion circle each Tuesday afternoon. Simple tea at a quarter was served to members and guests between four and six every weekday. The most influential event was Sunday's Open House between five and seven, unless the performance should happen to be scheduled for earlier. Some visiting dignitary was the guest of honor and, if willing, the speaker. Hawklike John Cowper Powys had been among the first to lecture. Out of this tearoom, Powys would bear acclaim of Chicago writers to great audiences all over the United States and England. Others on the Open House schedule were, besides Dreiser, Sara All-good of the Irish Players and two Englishmen, Granville Barker and Gordon Craig, whose advanced theatrical ideas were much admired.

The Little Theatre's socialite backing and its seeming artiness may have driven away some ordinary drama lovers. Yet at Open House and other functions the creative talents could not have been more revered—and Ben Reitman was given as much deference as Mrs. Armour. (When Nellie Browne praised Ben's gaudy necktie he whipped it off as a present for Maurice.)

The opening play had not been, after all, the endlessly rehearsed *The Trojan Women,* Browne having ruled that his players were still below his exacting demands. So the first program (November 12, 1912) had contained two short dramas by English poets, Wilfred Wilson Gibson's *Womenkind* and William Butler Yeats' *On Baile's Strand.* The fare in the Chicago popular theater being *Mutt and Jeff, Way Down East,* and *Ben Hur,* the critics had responded predictably. Percy Hammond of the *Tribune,* for example, found Yeats' play like "the second degree in the introductory rites of the Knights of Pythias or the Modern Woodmen of the World." The lone, and also predictable, stout defender had been Dell, writing in the *Post* of the play's "sheer beauty of scene and gesture and voice." Each program was to be on for two weeks, with a total of six night and two matinee performances. Arthur Schnitzler's *Anatol,* the second program, was not generally well received, either.

Then Browne had gone to his strength, *The Trojan Women,* and it was almost unanimously acclaimed. Dreiser attended one of the early performances with Dell and Masters and Lengel. Spiritually he was more akin to Chicago's Hull House Theatre, whose amateur players were nearer to Lady Gregory's "counter-jumper" ideal, and whose plays were more likely to have a modern sociological content. Founded in 1900, it perhaps had a better right than Browne's to be called the first "little theater" in the United States (which in later years Browne was always ready to point out when the accolade was given to him). In that particular time and among certain kinds of people, however, Browne's mixture of flamboyance and dedication was essential for an atmosphere in which arts could flourish.

Brör Nordfeldt had painted a simple background for *The Trojan Women* which nevertheless gave enormous breadth and depth to the tiny stage. The background was a shattered wall of Troy. All action was before it on what had been a field of battle. Through a breach could be seen flames and smoke as the city burned. Once the Greek army, marching up from the city, showed itself on the wall—a vanguard of three soldiers (one of them Browne) in ascending order. The dawn to dusk time span was illustrated by subtle changes of light.

As for Dreiser, the most vivid impression received by him was of Elaine Hyman, playing Andromache. From the program (on soft Japanese rice paper to prevent rustling) he could not, however, learn her name. Browne had decreed that the names of performers be listed alphabetically rather than alongside their roles. This was a way of subordinating ego to the glory of art; but there was a limit, and his name stood out boldly as the director. Dreiser's task of identification, however, was easily accomplished. Dell knew. By this time he was infatuated with Elaine, and she with him. Later Dreiser wrote into *The Titan* a girl called Stephanie Platow, who his Chicago friends took to be largely based on Elaine. He described Stephanie as a Russian Jewess on one side and Southern American on the other. She was "tall, graceful, brilliant, young . . . generous, nebulous, passionate, emotional, inexperienced, voiceless, and vainly curious without any sense of the meums and teums that govern society. . . ." In addition there was in her a combination of "optimism and strange fatalism."

Stephanie was depicted as a member of an amateur group performing Greek drama at a little theater—with attached tearoom—in the New Arts Building. Even powerful, magnetic Frank Cowperwood was unable to best all rivals. She was in love with a "young, smug, handsome" drama critic whose "neatly trousered legs" were often "whipped with a little cane." The critic's appearance in the tearoom always irritated Cowperwood. Another threat was the troupe's director, a "smooth-faced, pasty-souled artist, a rake at heart, a subtle seducer of women." A third menace was an aspiring journalist—"tall, fair, passionate"—who at the moment was earning his living as a furniture installment collector. The initiated would, after the book appeared, sort them out as Dreiser (Cowperwood), Dell (critic), Browne (director), Dreiser again (installment collector and journalist). When Stephanie was unfaithful to her love, Cowperwood, with the installment collector it was no blow to the author's ego; one facet of character had merely betrayed another facet. A real-life person, however, could be partly read into the installment collector—

red-bearded Michael Carmichael Carr, who in his wide black hat and flowing cape, with its huge wrought silver buckle, was formidable in the train of Elaine's admirers.

Most of the speculation would be only a literary game, for Dreiser had required numerous lovely females for Cowperwood's eclectic appetite. Yet in shifting and embroidering his story fabric he had, perhaps, allowed dark, jealous fantasies to creep in. Browne was indeed smooth-faced and artistic and to some might have appeared a rake. But hardly to Dreiser. Nor pasty-souled. The two got on well. Browne, moreover, was not among Elaine's suitors. On the other hand, Dreiser may with some reason have blamed Dell for a hard blow to his ego when first he met Elaine. It was at a Sunday night Open House, where Dreiser was receiving deference as a visiting lion. After listening briefly to his "whiny, irritating voice"— Elaine's later description of how it had struck her—she had swept gaily out of the tearoom escorted by stick-flourishing Dell and silver-buckled Michael Carmichael Carr. Dell, aside from being young and handsome, may have looked smug to the aging stranded lion. Carr was also young and slender and romantically handsome, and with his satyr's pointed red beard, he may well have looked dangerously passionate.

A man who had prowled Brooklyn rooftops in hope of fleeting tête-à-têtes with a sweetheart, and shrugged off warnings of an armed rival's advance, was not one to passively nurse his wounds. At the Little Theatre he "hung around"—as it seemed to Dell—and when he managed to hold Elaine in private discourse, his situation improved. Outwardly the girl appeared languid. Her dark cast of features and coal-black hair seemed Egyptian. Her tall, shapely figure was mature, as was necessary for her role of Andromache. And into her bell-like voice she was able to put Andromache's tragic despair over the murder of her child.

When later Dreiser made his Stephanie "brilliant" he failed to do justice to the range of Elaine's talents. Her instructors at the Art Institute had seen promise in her painting. Among the girl poets out of whose eyes Dell liked to see, he regarded her verse as superior. She sang beautifully, especially folk songs. Her reading in both classical and modern literature had been wide, and she was at ease in all the ideas then stimulating the new generation to its growing restlessness. Yet, like Stephanie, she was nebulous and inexperienced, lacking a sense of "the meums and teums that govern society." This was due at least in part to a confusion stemming from heredity. She had joined Browne's rehearsing cast upon returning from the East after making, as she put it, "my half-baked, since I am half Jewish and half New England, entry into Jewish society." As her parents had met the train, her mother (the New England side) had whispered news of arrangements for a tryout with the group, adding, "Don't say a word to your father, he's still angry."

The cause of his ire was the interference with his own ambitions for his daughter. For a long time he had dreamed—fantastic as it seemed to her—of Elaine gracing the chair of literature at Wellesley College in Massachusetts. She hadn't been to college, had not even finished high school, due to her boredom with Latin and mathematics. But he still hoped. Pride in her Little Theatre performances had melted him. Her mother was less enthralled, since, in Elaine's sardonic opinion, she "never approved of my interpretation of any role." It was the daughter's conviction that the mother had helped her into the troupe (Browne had already seen her in a pageant at the Art Institute) to hamstring a growing-up rival in the house.

And so Elaine was in the pattern of rebel girls in conflict with their mothers—although in reverse, since usually the mothers battled to keep their daughters at home or at least within the standard guidelines. As a rival, Elaine had been formidable even before she was almost a grown-up. Her father, aside from the hours given to his prosperous jewelry business, was an appreciator of literature and a student of philosophy and psychology and social questions. In all he aligned himself with the advanced forces. Long ago he had set up as Elaine's teacher, shaping her as his alter ego. She was a happy pupil, striving to please. On her first evening in Dell's company she had taken him straight to her father's study, as if to be applauded for having caught a real live man of letters.

Elaine had not been able, of course, to assimilate all of the facts and theories poured into her, much less to adjust them to the "meums and teums" of life. Between the conflicts of her Jewish-New England heritages and the strain of mother-daughter rivalry her childhood had been unhappy. Now, groping in a haze, she was pulled toward Dreiser. Was he not experienced in life, positive (not to say dogmatic) in his views—except for a few cosmic phenomena? Surely he was a certified (by her father, Dell, Mencken) literary genius ahead of his times. Perhaps a larger factor in the quickening relationship was the other side of the Dreiser coin, his intuitiveness and quick sympathy. He was genuinely concerned with her problems and knew how to analyze them for her better understanding and reassurance.

For Dreiser, Elaine was more than a substitute for the lost Thelma Cudlipp. Baby talk for such as Elaine was out of the question. To the discerning eye of Nellie Browne, Elaine was remindful of one of the big cats, perhaps a leopardess, poised lazily but ready to spring away or else attack savagely. Mrs. Brör Nordfeldt as a psychologist enjoyed watching Dreiser's antics with his handkerchief when speaking of Elaine. The long fingers would be pleating comfortably along an edge, the cloth gathering into his palm, until he struck upon a point of difference that had arisen between them. Suddenly—jerk—the handkerchief would be snapped rigid, accompanied by an exclamation of "What temperament!" or something like it.

Yet Elaine, in spite of her own artistic and intellectual concerns and her flashes of temperament and temper, was able to wrap herself up in a man and his goals. Both Nellie and Mrs. Nordfeldt saw in her the complete female, the man's woman—devoted, willing to slave for the man of her choice. They were reminded—and Dell was, too—of the character Olenka in Chekhov's story "The Darling." In remarking on the story, Tolstoy had suggested that Chekhov's aim had been to make fun of Olenka as a "contrast to the new woman; of her equality with man; of a woman mentally developed, learned, working independently for the good of society as, if not better than, a man; of the woman who has raised and upholds the woman's question." But, being a great artist, Chekhov had made "The Darling, with her faculty of devoting herself with her whole being to any one she loves," quite the opposite—"not absurd, but marvelous and holy." These remarks by Tolstoy were in fact to be a shrewd commentary on the irony of the emancipated woman of the grand new era in the United States. In her idealism she would so often bind herself to a man of genius (as he announced and she so believed). Whereupon "The Darling" in her would emerge, with sacrifices willingly made, until her lover's "genius" demanded a new soul mate and she was cast off.

Now Elaine talked of the abuse heaped on novelists who told the truth about modern society, of the need to go on, whatever the sacrifice. Dreiser's need of her—as he had needed Thelma—was of course a powerful influence. Meanwhile Dell could not help noticing that she remarked less on the plight of young authors who longed to devote all energy to their own poems and stories and novels and books on social questions but were bound to a job reviewing other people's work. Although competing gamely, he found himself steadily distanced by the heavy-footed starter now moving with the juggernaught power and the speed of a bull elephant. Michael Carmichael Carr was out of the race, as he had returned after the holidays to his teaching of art at Missouri University.

Dreiser's always monumental capacity for work and play was at his life's highest. Besides digging at the Newberry Library and interviewing people, he had written dozens of new pages of *The Titan* manuscript at each sitting. His handwriting was strong but neatly rounded. He composed on a stack of loose paper, often allowing unnumbered pages to drift to the floor, so that he was at pains to return them to sequence. Besides his visits with Masters and Garland and Fuller and to the Little Theatre, he found time for parties. At these he indulged in drinks and unbent more than usual. At one given by Margery Dell he became hilarious, it seemed to her. And, incredibly, he courted another girl than Elaine. As it happened Dell was his rival on this field, too. But Elaine was the prize. When Dreiser left Chicago in middle February, Lengel, seeing him to the train, was struck by Elaine's dramatic flinging of herself into his arms. Already she had promised to join him in New York as soon as arrangements could be made.

For literary Chicago the nearly two months of Dreiser's stay had been perhaps the most invigorating time it would ever know. Dreiser himself had given Masters new courage and inspired younger people to whom he was already a legend. The Little Theatre with its production of *The Trojan Women* had been coming into its own as a shrine of the arts. Others of the later famed Renaissance makers were at work, if in obscurity. And one of them, Nicholas Vachel Lindsay, was about to be catapulted into the literary heavens by Harriet Monroe and her "spinster's hobby."

15

Harriet Monroe:
Poetry's Muse

THE Chicago patrons who felt they were indulging Harriet Monroe's whim in supporting her little magazine did not realize that her whim, like that of Oliver Herford's celebrated aunt, was of iron. Nor was Hobart Chatfield Chatfield-Taylor, lover of the old and mellow, aware that, as he aided her in haltering the elite, she was falling under the spell of a cantankerous, bearded young poet-critic who dressed in velvet jackets and billiard-green pants and hated the smug bourgeoisie. His name was Ezra Pound. Harriet and Ezra had never met, but from self-exile in Europe he was issuing terribly avant-garde dictums to her, and she admired them.

But that was Harriet: a mixture of Old Chicago and New World, prim maiden and warring Amazon. Her memories went all the way back to the Great Fire of 1871, when she was eleven. The impact was perhaps the greater because her family slept through the first night of the holocaust and in the morning raised the blinds to find south Michigan Avenue a chaos of refugee wagons piled with household goods. The windows had been shut for the autumn night; opened, they let in the roar of fire consuming the North Side. The downtown office of Harriet's father, Henry Stanton Monroe, a young attorney with a clientele among the Builders, had already gone up in flames. But he demonstrated his faith in the city, himself, and the family's social prospects by ordering the unscathed home expanded to include a library and a double drawing room. The latter had ornate columns, crystal chandeliers, massive furniture, and a velvet rug. Harriet, growing up, preferred the library for its classic busts and walnut bookshelves filled with great literature.

She had been a nice-looking young girl, fragile, with cameo features and pools of eyes behind pince-nez glasses. Something, though, had gone wrong. Later, when it became the thing to probe one's psyche, she concluded that she had been repressed sexually, was afraid of men. The home environment may have been responsible. Her parents struggled between themselves. Monroe spent too much, his wife held, on rare books. He was driven to distraction by her extravagance with household money and her exotic tastes in hats and food (for months she had a wild passion for lemon peel). Toward the children he was indulgent, she rather strict. Neither was very intuitive about them, for a beautiful, aggressive older sister was allowed to drive Harriet into a protective shell.

Harriet was in her twenties when the adored father started downhill. Poor investments; the big cases stopped coming. Harriet worshipped her older sister's husband, John Wellborn Root, a brilliant architect; he died young. Her younger sister, after a few years as a book publisher's editor, married and went to China. Her brother was wrapped up in his engineering. And so in the end Harriet's emotional attachments were to the arts and to countries and to mountains. Not that she lacked friends. Henry Fuller, three years older, was a good comrade. Eugene Field took a fond interest in her and her literary hopes. Harriet dedicated herself to a poet's life. She put it modestly:

> Although my arrow miss its goal,
>   And all my song be lost in air,
> Yet I have aimed the shaft; my soul
>   Has known of song and sweet despair.

Yet if ambition were equated with industry, she had it in rich supply. As Fuller had done in his first novel *The Chevalier of Pensieri-Vani*, she had gone for subject matter to old Italy—all the way to the fourteenth century. In blank verse she had composed a play in five rather long acts with a prologue. She titled it *Valeria* and added: *A Tragedy*.

> If the king doth scorn my empty hands
> And meagre lineage, I repay his scorn.
> Great is he in the empire of the sword—
> In the realm of art my ancestors
> Were kings when his were bandits. On my soul

> I will not wed on sufferance. Give me back
> The wild free life you stole me from, my lord.
> Then I was empress of the world. My mind
> Was sister to great poets, and my soul
> Sang like the harp of God, and was at peace.

And so on and on, with many a one, including hero and heroine, falling dead. If Harriet did not live to entirely regret her plunge into a sea of bathos, she tried to forget the worst of it. She was willing, too, that her earliest paean to Chicago be left to yellowing paper and old echoes in the dome of the Auditorium which had rung to a great chorus of her words. Entitled simply "Cantata," it had been rendered when she was twenty-nine, at the dedication of the awesome civic monument in December 1889. A sample:

> Hail to thee, fair Chicago! On thy brow
> America, thy mother, lays a crown.
> Bravest among her daughters brave art thou,
> Most strong of all her heirs of high renown.

Eugene Field, declining the ode assignment for himself, recommended Harriet, and she, avid for it, had been a little bit unfaithful to the Bright Muse. The flamboyant chief promoter had insisted that the Auditorium be at least named in the poem. Although despising its meter she had knuckled under and the chorus had sung, "The Auditorium of Liberty." Afterward she had quickly begged the Muse's pardon by changing the line to "The temple of our liberty."

Harriet had battled ferociously to be commissioned for the World's Fair ode, largely because of what she regarded as an insult to the Muse. Cash was being flung to architects, painters, sculptors, musicians; not a cent to poets. She had visited no less than Charles T. Yerkes, sitting on the Committee on Ceremonies. Although a power in Chicago for a decade, he had not yet been identified with public boodle. Harriet, acquainted with him through visits to his mansion-gallery as art critic for the *Tribune*, liked him. If anyone could be depended on to emphasize the female in this maiden now past thirty, it was the man whom Dreiser would choose to portray the ruthless American financial titan. Yet with eyes—in Dreiser's words—"as fine as those of a Newfoundland or a Collie and as innocent and winsome." Harriet would describe him later: "A strange combination of guile and glamor, thrilling with power like a steel spring, loving beauty as a Mazda lamp loves the switch that lights it."

In their interview Harriet was forthright. Would the committee raise up "the neglected art of poetry" by including a poem in the dedication exercises? And, even more to the point, ask her to compose it? Yerkes' reply lifted her to ecstasy. "I shall never forget the gallant courage of his answer," she would declare later. It was: "I don't know what the other members of the committee may think about it, but I will make the motion. I hope we can give you the commission, because we shall want a poem that will live." Naturally Harriet had left the office as if on wings.

Perhaps guile had been in his words. More likely, intuition being one of his high qualities, he had felt the iron in the prim little caller. He did put the motion and it carried. But there were foes. The leader of the opposition, industrialist and art collector James W. Ellsworth, was not adventurous in his collecting, as she regarded Yerkes to be, but "more aware of the expediency of using it as a side issue, a precious ornament, in the all-around career of a modern industrialist leader." Ellsworth sought, if there was to be any poem at all, to withdraw the commission from her in favor of a famous name, say John Greenleaf Whittier. At first he moved indirectly, as if to make her quit. She had been incapacitated by a nervous breakdown, largely due to the enormity of her self-set task: no less than two thousand words to pass muster in the eyes and ears of the whole world. The Ellsworth forces spread doubts of her ability to deliver. But she kept working and gradually recovered.

After seeing a first draft, the opposition asked her to cut out four lines honoring (although not using his name) her recently dead brother-in-law, who had done much of the architectural planning. She gave a heated "no." Then she counterattacked, demanding the guarantee of one thousand dollars for the right to use her ode. The enemy agreed, not wishing to appear to insult the Poetic Muse while generously rewarding others, and perhaps feeling that cash would make her amenable to changes, even the striking of the ode from the ceremonies. The formal argument had now shifted to a "need to shorten the program." Finally the matter was put to the Fair's highest command. The foe hired a lawyer to argue its case. He went up against Harriet in person, and lost.

And so on October 12, 1892, the four hundredth anniversary of Columbus' discovery of America, she sat on the platform with Vice President Levi Morton (President Benjamin Harrison was unable to attend owing to his wife's illness), Mrs. Potter Palmer, and other dignitaries while a stalwart actress boomed to the massed scores of thousands:

> Columbia, on thy brow are dewy flowers
> > Plucked from wide prairies and from mighty hills.
> > > To this proud day have led the steadfast hours;
> > > Now to the hope the world its beaker fills.
> > > The old earth hears a song, sees rainbow gleams,
> > > And lifts her head from a deep couch of dreams.

Parts had been set to music. A mighty chorus of five thousand voices welled up:

> > Lo, clan on clan,
> > The embattled nations gather to be one,
> > Clasp hands as brothers on Columbia's shield,
> > Upraise her banner to the shining sun.
> > > Along her sacred shore
> > > > One heart, one song, one dream—
> > > Men shall be free forevermore,
> > > > And love shall be law supreme.

Harriet was to acknowledge that her optimism had bubbled rather high. And right away "love shall be law supreme" had to be ignored while she grappled with the husky New York *World*. A whole page in Joseph Pulitzer's aggressive newspaper had been filled with the "Columbian Ode," plus a large portrait of its author. In the view of the editors she ought to have been content. She charged infringement of copyright. In the payment receipt she had noted that "the author expressly reserves her copyright therein," yet had granted permission to distribute copies to the press. The *World's* editors had jumped the deadline, convinced that she had sold all her rights to the Fair, whose officials would not make a fuss. In addition they were prepared to argue that the ode was legitimate news.

They had underestimated Harriet. What she had was a "textbook case" dealing with the right of authors to control their unpublished works whether copyrighted or not. To have stepped on Harriet was bad enough. To have trampled on poets as a class was for her an outrage to be harshly avenged. She went to New York and won a verdict for five thousand dollars in mostly exemplary damages. The

World appealed all the way to the U.S. Supreme Court, but to no avail. Harriet won also a valuable legal precedent for authors.

For twenty years after that October day when she had listened to thousands of voices trolling her verses to a mighty host, the way for Harriet was stony. She had believed the ode's fame would open pages of Eastern magazines. It made no jot of difference—and besides they paid little or nothing for verse. For a time she had written a weekly article for the Chicago *Times-Herald* at a few dollars each. Her memoir of John Wellborn Root, her brother-in-law, turned out to have been a labor of love. And so when at long last the *World* check arrived, in early 1897, she used most of what was left after lawyer's fees to indulge a cherished ambition to go abroad. Living frugally (two dollars a day except for travel fare) she had stayed for a year and a half in England, France, Italy, Belgium, and Switzerland. Her main interests were art galleries and theaters, historical places and the beauties of landscapes, the peoples and their ways of life. She climbed mountains, met a number of celebrities (Thomas Hardy impressed her the most) and besides her creative work did journalism for *Leslie's Weekly* and the New York *Sun*. Romance approached once in the guise of an eloquent Frenchman who—as was rather to be expected of a Frenchman—engaged her aboard ship on the subject of life and love. "When I insisted that love must be flawless like a diamond or I would have none of it," she remembered, "he launched into a fine rhapsody about youth budding into love adventurously, like a flower that trembles in the wind—nothing in life was flawless; the imperfect was beautiful; one should open one's heart to it, accept the flawed jewel, the stricken joy." His words shook her up. After all, she had had suitors—mostly formal ones, to be sure; perhaps she had sought too hard for the ideal. Alas, the Frenchman was fat, and besides never appeared again.

Not long after her return from Europe, sickness, this time pleuro-pneumonia, again struck Harriet down. To finally conquer it the doctors ordered her to the hot sunshine of Arizona. It was her first journey to the American West. She loved it, both her sojourn in the desert and, when in better health, her travels in the Rocky Mountains. Out of her experiences she worked up a few essays for the *Atlantic Monthly* and other periodicals. Then it was back home and more struggle for a living. Her aging father's fortunes had gone from bad to worse, her mother was dead, her brother married. But her widowed sister had some income, and with her younger sister, not yet married, they all established themselves and the three Root children in a pleasant home on Astor Street.

The early years of the twentieth century, beginning when she was forty, were the most trying. Harriet got a meager income from journalistic odd jobs, lectures, readings, the occasional sale of a poem, by teaching a few English classes in a girl's school; she hated teaching. Now her main literary hopes had turned to drama, this time in prose as well as verse. Her manuscripts were given warm attention by theatrical figures but the commercial managers stopped short of production. Harriet did the best she could with local opportunities. A few of her shorter dramas were given in a little summer playhouse built by Arthur and Mary Aldis on their Lake Forest estate. One was staged at Hull House (where Harriet lived for a few months). A by-product was given at the Art Institute, scene of varied cultural affairs. A symphonic ode to the four seasons was read by Harriet as Lou Wall Moore danced interpretations. From time to time one of her poems was taken by *Century* or another quality magazine, and a second collection of her verse was published. These events together with former achievements made a place for her in the Little Room along with her friends Garland and Fuller and Chatfield-Taylor.

The Monroe-Root house on Astor Street was itself an oasis where artists of all sorts gathered, especially for informal Sunday evening suppers. Old Stanton Monroe had died in 1903, at seventy-seven, and a year afterward Lucy, the youngest sister, had married a Chicago attorney and gone on a diplomatic mission. Young Stanton Monroe and his wife took their places and the home was maintained. As a matter of fact, Stanton, rising as an engineer, was, along with his charming wife, regaining some of the family's old social place in Chicago, and Harriet herself wasn't above putting on a few airs in the social whirl, as long as funds of her own were not required. Her income seldom reached a thousand dollars a year. Yet excursions were managed both east and west. She loved all of nature's beauties— none more than sunrise and sunset on Lake Michigan. But sedate viewing was not enough. The mountain-climbing fever grew on her and she joined the California Sierra Club and scrambled up peaks.

By 1910, her half-century mark, Harriet felt the need for a deeper revitalization. She would go around the world, taking the better part of a year. After almost two decades she was again the *Tribune's* art critic, a fairly satisfying, if not very remunerative post. The theater had at last been given up. The publishers had by and large quit on the poets. Nineteenth-century magazines had given prime space to verse because their small audiences were among the most highly literate; now the era of the popular magazine was at hand with *Saturday Evening Post, Collier's Delineator, Women's Home Companion, Ladies' Home Journal,* and a few others growing rapidly. The editors (Theodore Dreiser of the *Delineator,* for one) had found readers little interested in poetry. The quality magazines were following suit by using verse mostly as page-end fillers.

Harriet bought an inexpensive Cook's Tour ticket for her journey and even so had to borrow and rake and scrape. Beyond this she was no ordinary tourist. For one thing, a rather long visit was scheduled for Peking, where her sister Lucy's husband, William S. Calhoun, was the U.S. Minister to China. And her connections elsewhere were good. In London she was put up at the Lyceum Club, a focal point of the suffragettes. Several old Chicago friends had married and lived or worked abroad. She struck up a friendship with another quiet little spinster, May Sinclair, the English poet and novelist. They called one day at the shop of bookseller-publisher Elkin Mathews, whose tastes ran to the new in literature, especially poetry. As it happened, he had just then been excited by the work of Ezra Pound, who at twenty-four had already renounced his native land as one of Philistines. Mathews had issued two slender books of Pound's verses: *Personae* and *Exultations.* Enough of the bookseller's enthusiasm rubbed off on Harriet to cause her to buy them. Later, on her way across Siberia (after halts in Paris, Berlin, Moscow) she read them and was beguiled with the "strange and beautiful rhythms."

In her own poetry she had come a long way since the odes. Although her rhythms were not classifiable as strange, she had experimented with free verse and was quite out of sympathy with traditional mannerisms. Pound's name was not entirely new to her. She had read a few of his poems in the little magazines published abroad, and the impact of his volumes had already been felt in the U.S. In her hands now was evidence that small books and little magazines could be influential, no matter how obscurely published.

After eight months Harriet arrived back in Chicago (January 1911) ready to make a fight for poetry. The more she thought about its low condition, and especially its shoddy treatment by her own city, the angrier she became. The Art Institute, glory of Chicago's rich patrons, was suddenly an affront. She was irritated by its dozens of cash prizes—up to five hundred dollars apiece—given for minor work. The indignation was seared deep into her memory: "Why this difference between the respectable attitude of donors and press and public toward painting and sculpture, also to a certain degree music and architecture, and the general contemptuous indifference of all these powers toward the poet and the beautiful art he practices or aims at, the art which, more than any other, has passed the 'tale of the tribe' to succeeding generations? . . ."

In all of America there was no magazine devoted solely to poetry. Two hard conclusions formed in Harriet's mind: (1) there must be one, and (2) it was up to her to found it. Where to get funds? "Any man rich enough to back it with cash would probably laugh at such a harebrained project—my grievances would sound ridiculous to the typical hard-boiled business man of my Middle Western metropolis." Arthur Aldis wasn't a typical business man. His head, though, was as hard as any. He might be able to predict the attitudes of his more single-minded commercial associates. The Aldises had summer cottages on their Lake Forest estate which they made available to friends. The allotment to Harriet of one for the month of June gave her an opportunity to talk over her dream at some length with them. The few others with whom she had discussed it had been skeptical. The Aldises regarded the project as quite reasonable. Her spirits rising, Harriet promptly carried the dream to her good friend Chatfield-Taylor, who also lived in Lake Forest. Even more enthusiastic, he was ready to sit down with her and lay out a plan of action.

Hobart Chatfield Chatfield-Taylor was by some a misunderstood man, owing partly to his British-looking name. In fact it had been adopted for a simple reason: cash. Born Taylor, he had been given a "Chatfield" in honor of another branch of the family. But if he wished to inherit from it he would be obliged to legally assume Chatfield as a last name. By means of the hyphen he had effected a compromise, bringing in its wake his friends' tolling designation of him as "Hobart Chatfield Come-Again Taylor." He was for fun and always had been. Once he had let his name be put up for mayor by the high-jinks Whitechapel Club (it had begged the use of his name "in full or any part thereof") with all political donations going into the club's coffers, or, more exactly, the coffin which was its most striking piece of furniture. But as a man of fun, appearances were again deceptive. He was big, clumsy, unathletic, and usually silent. In a group of cronies the talk might seem to be going over his blond, now balding head. But then if he entered the conversation his remarks were discerning and probably witty. As a toastmaster he was perhaps the most entertaining in Chicago.

If Chatfield-Taylor's amiability failed to embrace all humans, he was a true son of the native-born, white, Protestant, aspiring-to-be-gentry society of his Chicago rearing. Now just under fifty, he had lived on the West Side while it was still fashionable and had known South Michigan and Prairie Avenues when they were among the world's great promenades. He had watched family rockaways replaced by victorias and broughams "with rosette head-stalls for the horses and pole chains to clank pretentiously" as, wearing high white hats, the aristocrats had driven highsteppers to Washington Park races. To him the old Palmer House and the Grand Pacific Hotel and the Tremont House had been places of grandeur. "Who did not cherish a nod of recognition from Potter Palmer?" Among these, how many had despised the noisy, dirty hordes of foreigners who, instead of being thankful for jobs at a dollar or two a day, yammered for more—and a hand in running things besides? The anarchists had been executed when Chatfield-Taylor was twenty-one. After college, drawn to literature more than to the law or business, he had cofounded the magazine *America* which sought to limit immigration, restrict the vote, and hamstring the Catholic Church because so many immigrants were members. Animosity toward literary realism had followed, since it gave dignity to, even celebrated, the common man. The magazine had long since gone down the drain.

Generally the newspapers referred to Chatfield-Taylor as a "socialite lawyer" even when his novels (*The Crimson Wing*, etc.) and other works were being considered. His striking wife, Rose, although operator of a book bindery in the Fine Arts Building, was thought to be more concerned with high society. Their friends noticed that when an event was purely social, Rose led the way in; if literary, Chatfield-Taylor kept a pace or two in front. It was plain that the leisured aristocracy for which he had hoped was not going to flower; the accumulators and their sons were firmly in charge. And so he gave lip service to Chicago hustle. "No sooner does one sniff the air of Chicago than life becomes a turmoil of duty." With Garland he had been a founder of the Cliff-Dwellers' Club, where the future was given almost equal status with the past. He no longer went out of his way to denounce realism in the arts. Still, he was not ashamed, like Harriet, of certain old attitudes like fear of "anarchist bombs." What they had together was comradeship of a score of years in the Little Room and various other cultural activities, plus a strong loyalty to their native city. Chatfield-Taylor, at least, would not admit New York's superiority in the arts.

Now he put his mind to her unformed scheme. The answer: each of one hundred individuals must be induced to guarantee fifty dollars a year for five years. That would cover office and production costs. Subscription money would pay for contributions. By the end of five years, he thought, the magazine would either be self-supporting or have proved its inadequacy. There was a major proviso: Harriet must win the pledges by direct solicitation. To lead off the roll of donors he put down his own name and that of his architect friend, Howard Shaw, and promised to break the ground with others. Arthur Aldis was readily signed. Then on Harriet's "successful" list went banker Charles L. Hutchinson, Harriet's brother and her brother-in-law, her childhood friend Mrs. Frank Lowden (of the Pullman family), Mrs. Potter Palmer, architect Daniel H. Burnham, lawyer Edgar A. Bancroft, banker Charles Gates Dawes, Mrs. William Vaughn Moody, Anna Morgan. And so on up to thirty.

Here was the sticking point. The time had come for assaulting the real hard-heads. Julius Rosenwald of Sears, Roebuck turned Harriet down flat. Like a fallen high-wire performer who must go up at once or lose courage, she marched straight to the office of his partner, Albert H. Loeb, who put down his name for a double contribution. She made a rule never to take offense if rejected—but woe to the man who sought to elude her. The haughtiest secretaries were powerless, for she organized telephone calls from the boss's friends. In a bit under a year she was over the top.

Now came the grandest hour of all little magazine editors: issuance of the brave manifesto. Poets were offered "their own place" for finding a public ready to support poetry as an art. All kinds of verse were to be considered—narrative, dramatic, lyric—with quality alone the test. The rate of pay would rise with any increase in receipts, since no profit was sought. In addition, cash prizes would be given when donors could be found. "We promise to refuse nothing because it is too good, whatever be the nature of its excellence. We shall read with special interest poems of modern significance, but the most classic subject will not be declined if it reaches a high standard of quality."

Harriet spent much of the summer of 1912 in the public library, hunting for poets. A few were inside book covers but most were to be found only in the despised page-end magazine fillers. Thousands of pages in diverse publications from the *Atlantic Monthly* to *Farm and Fireside* had to be turned. Upon discovering a bit of promising verse, Harriet would tap out a personal note to the author and send it along with one of her manifesto circulars. Of the poets in the Chicago region, Floyd Dell and Nicholas Vachel Lindsay and Arthur Davison Ficke received invitations; Lee Masters and Carl Sandburg and Maurice Browne did not. Other U.S. poets honored with special notice were Amy Lowell, Edwin Arlington Robinson, Percy MacKaye, Edwin Markham, Ezra Pound, Louis Untermeyer, George Sylvester Viereck, Madison Cawein, John A. Lomax, William Carlos Williams, Ridgely Torrence, and George Sterling. Among the British were William Butler Yeats, John Masefield, Wilfrid Wilson Gibson, and Alfred Noyes. Nearly all replied with encouraging words, and many sent poems.

Far and away the most exciting reply came from Pound. In London he was at the center, Harriet knew, of a bright young literary group, and also close to Yeats and other established poets. She was aware, too, of his acerbic talents and his dim view of his native land. It had seemed likely that if he answered a do-good Chicago spinster in cahoots with the Philistines that his message would be as near to a kick in the teeth as he could manage from the distance. Instead, he expressed great interest in her "scheme," while wondering if she could teach "the American poet that poetry is an *art*." Being open-minded, he offered his aid while she tried. To start off he would allow her magazine to be the sole outlet for his verse in the U.S. (except in books). Then: "If I can be of any use in keeping you or your magazine in touch with whatever is most dynamic in artistic thought, either here or in Paris—as much of it comes to me—and I *do* see nearly everyone that matters—I shall be glad to do so."

In a prompt reply Harriet asked him to be the magazine's foreign correspondent. He was agreeable, and his commanding letters kept roaring in. Harriet was dismayed by the way he "stamped" on poets whom she admired—Masefield and Noyes, for example. But she was delighted by the work of younger poets he sent and by his grim determination to "get something out of" Yeats and to land for her the Bengali poet Rabindranath Tagore, unknown to English readers but guaranteed by Pound to become a sensation. Harriet's trust was not misplaced—although a certain thorniness in her own nature was essential for avoiding his complete domination. Pound was generous to the point of selflessness toward those he admired. More exactly, toward their work if he thought it good or promising—his kindness to the person was incidental. But he was quick and free with cuffs to those who failed to hew to the line which he laid down.

And undeniably he was flamboyant. These characteristics made him seem an odd blend of righteous prophet and wily poseur. When he walked forth with the light step of the dancer, a scowl on his Mephistophelian face beneath a wide black hat, with a cape over his shoulders, making sword passes with his gold-headed cane at imaginary foes, he might have been taken for Beelzebub come up for a prowl. Or perhaps a taller and more robust Edgar Allan Poe. Ford Maddox Ford described him in somewhat gayer dress: "Trousers made of green billiard cloth, a pink coat, a blue shirt, a tie hand-painted by a Japanese friend, an immense sombrero, a flaming beard cut to a point, and a single large blue ear-ring." The color of the beard was somewhat enhanced in this account. Pound's rich, high crown of wavy hair and his whiskers (he nearly always wore a luxuriant mustache but sometimes the beard was reduced to a goatee or the semipointed chin was bare) were as often taken for burnished blond.

The term "sombrero" was misleading, especially if coupled with the knowledge that Pound had been born in Idaho. The hat was more the flat-crowned Spanish style than the ten-gallon hat of the cowboy West. And his Idaho residence had lasted only a year and a half. He was Wisconsin on the Pound side, New York on his mother's. His father had been in charge of the Government land office at Hailey in Idaho when Ezra was born there in 1885. The silver mines were being staked out and Ezra's grandfather, an operator in many fields, had placed his son in the job as a lookout. The Pound fortune, such at it was, neither increased nor was maintained, and Ezra's father had wound up as assistant assayer of the Philadelphia mint. The family lived at nearby Wyncote.

As an only child, Ezra grew up to be learned, opinionated, and vain of appearance. A fellow student at Pennsylvania University, William Carlos Williams, who was studying medicine but wanted to be a poet, was struck by Ezra's hair and his pride in it. As a tennis player, he rated him "good"; as a fencer, "bum." After a switch to Hamilton College in New York State, Ezra came back to finish at Pennsylvania, then got a job teaching at a little Indiana college. The arrangement was a mistake. The official bigwigs regarded him as a showman and maybe a charlatan. He saw them as dolts. At the end of the first semester the balance of his year's contract was paid in a lump with the understanding that he would go away. He used the money to trade Indiana for Italy. In Venice a tiny edition of a tiny book of his verse was published before he had moved to London, where were issued the little volumes which had accompanied Harriet across Siberia.

Quite early in their correspondence Pound advised Harriet: "I don't love my fellow men, and I don't propose to pretend to." As if applying the acid test, his first verses submitted to her, "To Whistler—American," contained these lines:

> You and Abe Lincoln from that mass of dolts
> Show us there's a chance at least of winning through.

If Harriet trembled, or cast agonized looks at her guarantors, the fact was never recorded. She marked the poem as copy.

An advisory committee, a staff, an office, and a printer were being arranged for. Harriet's first selection for the committee was Henry Fuller. He could be absolutely relied on, despite his—as she put it—"uncanny penetration into one's vanities and weaknesses." Conceivably he might fend off the Old Guard in the person of Chatfield-Taylor, who had to be included. The third member was Edith Wyatt, a notable Little Room figure, novelist and poet. A trusted friend, she was regarded by Harriet as possessing a modern mind. For associate editor, Alice Corbin Henderson was selected because Harriet thought her verse and criticism perhaps the best being written in Chicago. At wages of forty dollars a month she would work half time; her husband, William P. Henderson, was a painter. Harriet's own salary was zero. For an office, one of the guarantors let her have the former library of a done-over Near North Side mansion at 543 Cass Street and a few old books. She put a marble French clock, an heirloom, on the white fireplace mantel, and borrowed a rug and comfortable wicker chairs.

For the printing, Chatfield-Taylor advised begging a major firm to do it at cost. To Harriet the notion called up visions of mail order catalogs, and she went instead to her friend Ralph Fletcher Seymour, etcher, fine book designer, and publisher. Looking hard into his face, she put a hand on his arm and exclaimed, "Oh, Ralph, you will do your best for our magazine! There is no reason why it shouldn't stand for the best thing of the sort in the world." Although touched, Seymour had difficulty imagining a little old maid striking poetical fires over the world. His office was a portion of his Fine Arts Building studio, where he never forbade lovely models to dance nude for relaxation. This free and easy atmosphere was somewhat less than enlivened, in his view, by the "pussyfooting in" of Henry Fuller to wait for proofs and eventually to read them, aided by others of the poetry coterie.

For a name Harriet had chosen *Poetry: A Magazine of Verse*. The first issue appeared in late September 1912, dated October. The press run was a thousand copies. The gray cover, with a Pegasus emblem in black and red, was mostly of deckle-edge handmade stock, but a few score were of Japanese vellum. The inside pages, thirty-two of them, were uncoated book stock. Harriet had pushed up the starting date from the announced November owing to fear that another group—this one in Boston—had stolen the "poetry only" idea from her circulars and was intent on beating her to the market. Need for hurry had caused her to use some material she considered not the very best.

Among the poems she did like were Pound's "Middle-Aged" as well as "To Whistler"; Arthur Davison Ficke's "Poetry," a double sonnet; Grace Hazard Conkling's "Symphony in a Mexican Garden"; Helen Dudley's "To One Unknown." Harriet also liked "Fish of the Flood," by Emilia Stuart Lorimer, a young English poet recommended by Harold Monro but not, alas, cleared with "the authority in London." Pound quickly "stamped" on Emilia and trampled the editor a bit. It had been necessary to round out with a longish work, "I Am a Woman," by William Vaughn Moody, whose widow had generously allowed its use in the crisis. In addition to being a caterer of marvelous foods, Mrs. Moody was an eager patron of poets and therefore something of a rival of the editor's. Longish editorial prose—mostly a reworking of the manifesto—helped to pad out the number.

Response from the Chicago newspapers was generous. The *Tribune* extended its best wishes editorially, Floyd Dell in the *Friday Literary Review* was encouraging, and news stories were friendly even when written for mild amusement. Some out-of-town papers were kind but others found the juxtaposition of "Poetry" and "Porkopolis" a side-splitter. The New York *World,* its appetite for verse diminished since the old days when Harriet's ode had been pirated, divined that "the highways need no longer bruise the heel, as, fingering lyres, the slender wooers of the muse wend their way Chicagoward...." The outcries over Pound's "mass of dolts" phrase bothered Harriet only a little.

For the coming numbers "the authority in London" had delivered quality goods, as promised. Included would be five lyrics by Yeats and Tagore's translations of his "Gitanjali." From twenty-year-old Richard Aldington, Pound had secured "Choricos," which Harriet would consider perhaps the most beautiful death poem in the English language. In the November issue, describing Aldington as "one of the Imagistes, a group of ardent Hellenists who are pursuing interesting experiments in vers libre," she drew attention to, and became spokesman for, the little band (later called Imagists) that was to rock the poetry world.

One of the manifesto-circulars had brought in a poem that both excited and worried the editor. It was Vachel Lindsay's "General William Booth Enters into Heaven." Now ready, in the fourth number, to give it to the world, she braced himself for what might be a howling tide of ridicule.

III

Burst of Trumpets

16

Preaching the Gospel of Beauty

On a spring morning in 1912 a mendicant paused at the edge of Springfield, Illinois. He was in many respects a curious figure. A bundle on a stick over his shoulder was in the approved mode of tramps, at least cartoon tramps. Yet he wore a derby hat—plainly no castoff—and a well-fitting dark suit and good shoes. The almost colorless skin of his big-boned face—he looked to be somewhere in his middle twenties—was unstained by the grime of travel, and his long-fingered hands were soft. He extended one hand to a companion, then turned and struck out westward. His loose-knit body swayed with a kind of buoyant zeal as he planted each foot hard and swung well forward on its ball.

Vachel Lindsay had taken the troubador's way again. He was, of course, older than he looked, almost thirty-three. The recent companion had been George Lee, a Springfield union leader who, with his wife, Maydie, was at the center of the little band of political radicals who had backed Lindsay in the stormy time of the War Bulletins, except for a temporary defection after the third. Now Lee had walked out with Lindsay as a kind of delegate to bid the traveler a pleasant and safe journey. Dr. Lindsay, not amazingly, had called the expedition another of his son's "foolish tramps," but Kate Lindsay still had faith that her long-ago-appointed genius would "come up sometime, in some way, somewhere. . . ."

The wayfarer's pockets contained not one penny. The bundle on the stick held documents telling why. These were booklets (sixteen pages, nine by six inches) titled *Rhymes to Be Traded for Bread* and "printed expressly as a substitute for money." Each booklet said in part:

This book is to be used in exchange for the necessities of life on a tramp-journey from the author's home town, through the west and back, during which he will observe the following rules: (1) Keep away from the cities. (2) Keep away from the railroads. (3) Have nothing to do with money. Carry no baggage. (4) Ask for dinner about quarter after eleven. (5) Ask for supper, lodging and breakfast about quarter of five. (6) Travel alone. (7) Be neat, truthful, civil and on the square. (8) Preach the Gospel of Beauty.

In order to carry out the last rule there will be three exceptions to the rule about baggage. (1) The author will carry a brief printed statement, called "The Gospel of Beauty." (2) He will carry this book of rhymes for distribution. (3) Also he will carry a small portfolio with pictures, etc., chosen to give an outline of his view of the history of art, especially as it applies to America.

Most of the forty-four poems in the booklet had been written since *The Tramp's Excuse* and *The Village Magazine*. One, "Upon Returning to the Country Road," was a supplication to the natives of the land he would pass through.

> Even the shrewd and bitter,
> Gnarled by the old world's greed,
> Cherished the stranger softly
> Seeing his utter need.
> Shelter and patient hearing,
> These were their gifts to him,
> To the minstrel, grimly begging
> As the sunset-fire grew dim.

A single printed page held "The Gospel of Beauty," being, as it said, "the new creed of a beggar" by the "vain and foolish mendicant, Nicholas Vachel Lindsay," whose intention was to "carry this gospel across the country, beginning in June, 1912, and returning in due time." The message was divided into two parts. The first explained a "new religious idea," which was not, however, in conflict with any existing creed, only emphasizing beauty. The second part dealt with homes and neighborhoods. "The children now growing up should become devout gardeners or architects or park architects or teachers of dancing in the Greek spirit or musicians or novelists or poets or story-writers or craftsmen or wood-carvers or dramatists or actors or singers." The portfolio, designed to give a "view of the history of art, especially as it applies to America," was a kind of scrapbook bound in black boards. Among the illustrations cut from various sources were Christ leading a flock of sheep, a figure of Buddha, a bust of Ruskin, an Egyptian temple, the Taj Mahal. Lindsay had fashioned a waterproof case of black oilcloth to hold the portfolio and a supply of the other two items and some writing materials. It was the bundle on the stick.

The venturing forth of the earlier Don Quixote had been only a fraction as noble, since he had concerned himself with temporal injustices. In Lindsay's crusade these were to be struck down, too—or made to fade away as neighborhood democracy and beauty came to full flower. The new Quixote's weapons were of finer material, but whether they would prove stouter than the older knight's remained to be seen. Philistines met on the road would be more hazardous, to the spirit at least, than the windmills which had stood athwart the original's path. Yet for Lindsay simply to be on the move was exhilarating after four baleful years at home. One thing the two Quixotes had in common was a warm appeal if viewed from the perspective of a little distance. A note of amused indulgence appeared even in Springfield after Lindsay had dispatched a postcard, in his second day out, to the *State Register*. It was made into an item headed: "Nicholas Lindsay Will Enter Missouri Today, Is Being Well Received Along The Road." And in time this journey originating in black despair would be a major component of a blithe vagabondage legend.

Lindsay had reason to be content with his first day and night of troubadouring. After ten miles—he walked a mile every quarter hour—he asked for dinner at a substantial farm house and was given an excellent meal in exchange for his booklet and recitation of some of the verses. He gave "The Proud Farmer" and "On the Building of Springfield" and "The Illinois Village." These he believed to be the most effective of his repertoire for present purposes. Farmers were close enough to the towns to relish the last two with the first. The hamlet people would like especially "The Illinois Village," beginning:

> O you who lose the art of hope,
> Whose temples seem to shrine a lie,
> Whose sidewalks are but stones of fear,
> Who weep that Liberty must die,

> Turn to the little prairie towns,
> Your higher hope shall yet begin.
> On every side awaits you there
> Some gate where glory enters in.

The next day he sent back, besides the postcard, a tale of his adventure of the previous night. As Don Quixote had had his waiting Dulcinea, Lindsay addressed his Penelope—one Octavia Roberts, a literary lady (two published stories) a bit older than he, whom he had been worshipping and courting. For the journey he had become Ulysses, for whom Penelope had waited out the odyssey, fending off suitors until the hero returned and slew them all. Previously Octavia had been pressed by Lindsay into poetic service as Brünn-hilde and "a daughter of Babylon." She quite enjoyed the roles, while regarding him not too secretly as a foolish wild-eyed faun, a sap who had to cadge a nickel from his father to go to a movie.

The account which Lindsay sent back was obviously written with the hope of eventual publication, and for this very reason it showed the innocent exuberance tempered by self-deprecating humor which all but the pariahs failed to fathom and enjoy. It was like him to adopt the role of Ulysses as a joke on himself while raising Octavia to Penelope's estate.

In the blue grass by the side of the road. Somewhere west of Jacksonville, Illinois. Hot sun. Cool wind. Rabbits in the distance. Bumblebees near.

At five last evening I sighted my lodging for the night. It was the other side of a high worm fence. It was down in the hollow of a grove. It was the box of an old box-car, brought there somehow, without its wheels. It was far from a railroad. I said in my heart, "Here is the appointed shelter." I was not mistaken.

As was subsequently revealed, it belonged to the old gentleman I spied through the window stemming gooseberries and singing: "John Brown's Body." He puts the car top on wagon wheels and hauls it from grove to grove between Jacksonville and the east bank of the Mississippi. He carries a saw mill equipment along. He is clearing this wood for the owner, of all but its walnut trees. He lives in the box with his son and two assistants. He is cook, washer-woman and saw-mill boss. His wife died many years ago.

The old gentleman let me in with alacrity. He allowed me to stem gooseberries while he made a great supper for the boys. I was meanwhile assured that my name was going into the pot. My host looked like his old general, McClellan. He was eloquent on the sins of preachers, dry voters and pension reformers. He was full of reminiscences of the string band at Sherman's headquarters, in which he learned to perfect himself on his wonderful fiddle. He said, "I can't play slow music. I've got to play dance tunes or die." He did not die. His son took a banjo from an old trunk and the two of them gave us every worth while tune on earth: *Money Musk, Hell's Broke Loose in Georgia, The Year of Jubilee, Sailor's Horn-pipe, Baby on the Black, Lady on the Lake,* and *The Irish Washer-woman,* while I stemmed gooseberries, which they protested I did not need to do. Then I read my own unworthy verses to the ro-mantic and violin-stirred company. And there was room for all of us to sleep in that one repentant and converted box-car.

Lindsay had been further pleased to hear old tunes because of his hope of incorporating folk or near-folk music into his poetry. Not long ago he had put down the titles "There'll Be a Hot Time in the Old Town Tonight," "After the Ball Is Over," and "Massa's in the Cold, Cold Ground" on the list of possibilities.

In the next days he walked through rolling, grove-filled Pike County and begged his way across the toll bridge over the Mississippi to Hannibal, Missouri. Some distance beyond he was fascinated by a "wild rose bird"—he didn't know its name—possessed of "twenty different systems of sound." The bird was to be in his memory especially pleasing because of the circumstances in which he identi-fied it. The following night, soaked by a hard rain, and turned down for lodging at a rich stock farm, he applied at a Negro's cabin and was taken in. The Negro was a very old man, remindful of Uncle Remus but with more dignity, whose wife insisted that the wayfarer dry out before the oven in her spotless kitchen. At a laden supper board Lindsay said the grace. Afterward he showed the Lincoln photographs and they spoke of the Emancipator. As the conversa-tion moved on, Lindsay described the wild rose bird and learned that it was called the Rachel Jane. To its music he would later, in "The Sante Fe Trail," set the words:

> Love of life,
> Eternal youth,
> Sweet, sweet, sweet, sweet.
> Dew and glory,
> Love and truth.
> Sweet, sweet, sweet, sweet.

The old couple treated him to their most comfortable bed, warm water for a morning bath, and a huge breakfast. He went on his way rejoicing. As usual he was being received best by the pariahs. In Sedalia, a largish town, a man to whom he applied for alms on the street guided him to his saloon-restaurant off an alley. It was crowded with red-neck ditch diggers, teamsters, politicians, and "daughters of pleasure" (Lindsay's term). The troubadour began with "The Eagle That Is Forgotten" and then blasted with "The Trap," which denounced just such hell-holes as this one. The delighted saloonkeeper called him the goods, ordered a fine meal to be laid, and offered to take up a collection. Lindsay declined the latter, but into his mind crept a thought that a young Negro girl surely "a daughter of pleasure"—who had been quietly listening would have been among the contributors.

The Philistines met along the way were tougher, especially after his derby hat had been stained by dust and rain and his suit had a thousand wrinkles. If one gave him a slice of bread it was usually without butter. For only a little more he would be set to scything weeds or chopping kindling or hoeing in the garden. None invited him to rest for the night in a bed or even a woodshed. By more experienced knights of the road he was told that a livery stable always gave a night's shelter in its haymow. He discovered, too, that a hotel proprietor sometimes exchanged a bed for the entertainment of his dining-room guests. In one hotel Lindsay found how thorny could be the road to beauty. Words came over his lobby transom:

First Voice (sarcastically): That was a hot entertainment that young bum gave us last night.

Second Voice: He ought to get to work, the lazy loafer.

Third Voice: A big fraud. Real poets are highly paid these days.

The last came, Lindsay knew, from the town's schoolmaster. The hotel proprietor chipped in with his decision to refuse the "bum" a promised breakfast. Thus forewarned, Lindsay marched out and thanked the landlord grandly, although inwardly boiling. He had a mind to send the schoolmaster a marked copy of a magazine containing one of his poems.

Already he had sinned against his creed as stated in *Rhymes to Be Traded for Bread.* To cross a toll bridge at Jefferson City, Missouri, he had deposited his bundle for security and gone to the post office, where he knew that letters containing a wealth of stamps awaited him. After returning and settling the toll with stamps, he cashed in twenty-five cents worth and rented a hotel room. Now he had touched money. As for keeping away from railroads, he had walked on tracks and moreover had accepted a ride on a handcar. And now, entering Kansas, he stood ready to plunge into an even deeper sink of iniquity. He would labor for money. All along the way he had been plagued by the question: "Goin' west harvestin'?" After first giving a flat "no," he gradually hedged to save explanations. Then, a month away from home, he was shocking wheat at $1.75 for a twelve-hour day. For three weeks he worked fairly steadily at one job or another —he had bought a wide felt hat to replace the derby, and a pair of corduroy trousers, and he had his shoes repaired—before moving by foot and assorted vehicles through Denver and to a rendezvous with his parents at their annual summer camp.

It was August 7. His Penelope-Octavia, a great friend of his mother's, had come, too, and was sharing a tent with his younger sister and a friend of hers. The wayfarer spent ten days recuperating and walking with Penelope. The August *American* was out, carrying a write-up about him in its "Interesting People" department. It had been composed by Penelope-Octavia, and signed with her initials. After receiving some of Lindsay's poems and other materials, the editors, knowing Octavia's work and that she lived in the same town, had asked her to do a short sketch of him. "A quaint young man, a young poet-artist ... who might have stepped out of a novel of Locke's or Hewlett's," she had written, knowing what the editor wanted but also with an eye to Kate Lindsay's sensibilities. Now on their walks Lindsay enjoyed shouting or singing into the canyons. Among his favorites for the purpose was a snatch of a hymn in which he had often joined the Salvation Army's singers in the courthouse square back home:

> Have you been to Jesus for the cleansing power?
> Are you washed in the blood of the Lamb?

In London, General William Booth, the Salvation Army's blind old commander, lay near death. Thoughts of him led to conversation about the Army and its work and songs.

Three weeks after arriving at the camp, with Penelope-Octavia gone and his family ready to depart, Lindsay took up the road again for California. Twenty days later he walked into the depot of the Santa Fe Railroad at Wagon Mound, New Mexico, and wired to his father asking train fare for the remaining thousand-odd miles to Los Angeles. Dr. Lindsay telegraphed forty dollars. Vachel caught a Pullman.

When Lindsay gathered his diary entries and letters into a book called *Adventures While Preaching the Gospel of Beauty,* he left off the narrative prior to reaching his parents' camp and therefore did not include his Pullman ride to Los Angeles. Those who knew the facts had one more laugh on Vachel. In his diary he argued:

> My reasons for losing my nerve were as follows; (1) In northern New Mexico I outlined a dozen poems on the sun. I was impatient to write them out at leisure at my next stopping place. Los Angeles was the next stopping place. (2) The country was very much like that in which I had been walking for a month and a half, only poorer. (3) Was thinking about home a good deal. (4) The stations were growing poorer and farther apart. Walking lost most of its taste of adventure, was too much routine. (5) The same things were happening every day. (6) Ahead of me was one thousand miles, mainly desert. To cross it afoot would be merely a stunt like walking on one's hands for a wager. I was not out to do a stunt, and I allow myself to lose my nerve whenever I please, knowing I shall get it again in good time. My business is writing and preaching the Gospel of Beauty each day as I see fit, and not doing the thing that bores me, merely to be consistent.

He was also a publicist, as he sadly admitted. What better for himself can a poet-publicist do than create a legend? Lindsay had gone out on the highways and byways to see and hear and give a message, and if he was imperfect as a messiah, he had nevertheless gone a long, long way and experienced much hardship. Who can weigh the impact as at last he sat down to capture the subtle impressions of his journey?

Dr. Johnson Lindsay, a younger brother of Vachel's father, had been practicing in Los Angeles for more than two decades, and it was to his modest two-story home near Pershing Park that Vachel went. Vachel's sudden appearance far ahead of schedule was of no moment. The Lindsay family was close knit and, besides, the older brother had helped the younger at medical school and they had been in Springfield practice together for many years. The guest was made welcome without fuss and it went without saying that he was to remain as long as he chose. Since he often composed late and read aloud (which meant quite loud) to any listener, he was given the parlor as a workroom.

The Johnson Lindsays were parents of Vachel's favorite childhood playmate, Ruby, who bore the middle name Vachel so common in the family. Ruby, now a schoolteacher, was living at home, and naturally the cousins talked of old times. In Springfield Ruby had lived next door to Lincoln's home, already a museum. The two children had spent many hours wandering through the house. They spoke, too, of the wonderful night of pageantry when their fathers had donned broad sashes and tall Democrat hats and ridden horseback in a grand torchlight parade celebrating Grover Cleveland's victory in 1884. General Booth had recently died and the story of his life was running in a local paper. They recalled being fascinated —Vachel especially—by the drumming, tooting, tambourine-jingling and preaching of the Salvation Army zealots in the courthouse square.

Lindsay felt that he knew the Army "from the inside." On earlier journeys in the East and South he had found hospitality in its shelters. "The Army was struggling with what General Booth called the submerged tenth of the population," he declared later. "I was among the submerged." Booth was equated in his mind with St. Francis, a leader of a fanatical army which in the beginning had been "a scandal to respectable religion" and to a large degree still was. Lindsay had just emerged from the dankest of the "submerged tenth" and as a receiver of alms most of his adult life had always been a part of it. He had endeavored also to emulate General Booth. At home he had taken a vow to "preach till I drop" for the redemption of coal miners of nearby Ridgely, who often fell into sin, usually alcoholic. He had preached, but never dropped, and his guilt was unrelieved. The wounds recently inflicted by the scorning Philistines on a humble preacher of a better life still bled. Few were in as good a position to realize and admire the indomitable courage and energy and power of the blind leader.

One night while walking alone, Lindsay's mind was filled with thoughts of Booth. The Army's battle hymn ("Are you washed in the blood of the Lamb?"), which he had heard and sung-shouted a thousand times, pounded in his blood. To him it was less a hymn than an exhortation set to music. In thinking of well-known tunes to use in his poetry he had on this journey written "The Flute of the Lonely" to the music of "Gaily the Troubadour." Now he was blocking out the long "Santa Fe Trail," which was to include, besides the Rachel Jane song, the insistent cries of automobile horns ("Hark to the *calm*-horn, the *balm*-horn, *psalm*-horn") which lent themselves to chanting.

If anyone had recently been welcomed into heaven surely it was General Booth. In Lindsay's mind heaven had always taken various forms, and, having first known the Salvation Army around the Springfield courthouse, it was not surprising that he now gave it a courthouse square into which notables were received. As Lindsay walked that night, a poem "miles long" thundered and sang and whispered in his brain. The task of getting it on paper and cutting and polishing required the better part of a week. To illustrate the deeds of the old hero, the poet sent hordes of the submerged into heaven with him. For various parts instrumental music would be assigned. The bass drum had become a symbol of the Army's street meetings and so it was fitting that the first stanza was to be spoken as the big drum was beaten loudly:

> Booth led boldly with his big bass drum—
> (Are you washed in the blood of the Lamb?)
> The Saints smiled gravely and they said: "He's come."
> (Are you washed in the blood of the Lamb?)
> Walking lepers followed, rank on rank.
> Lurching bravos from the ditches dank,
> Drabs from the alleyways and drug fiends pale—
> Minds still passion-ridden, soul-powers frail:—
> Vermin-eaten saints with moldy breath,
> Unwashed legions with the ways of Death—
> (Are you washed in the blood of the Lamb?)

Then to the banjos:

> . . .
> Every banner that the wide world flies
> Bloomed with glory and transcendent dyes.
> Big-voiced lasses made their banjos bang,
> Tranced, fanatical, they shrieked and sang:—
> "Are you washed in the blood of the Lamb?". . .

Sweet flute music:

> Jesus came from out the court-house door,
> Stretched his hands above the passing poor.
> Booth saw not, but led his queer ones there
> Round and round the mighty court-house square. . . .

And finally reverent song without instruments:

> And when Booth halted by the curb for prayer
> He saw the Master thro' the flag-filled air.
> Christ came gently with a robe and crown
> For Booth the soldier, while the throng knelt down.
> He saw King Jesus. They were face to face,
> And he knelt a-weeping in that holy place.
> Are you washed in the blood of the Lamb?

Lindsay trimmed the poem to fifty-six lines. When late one night he was satisfied with them, he called upstairs to Ruby, not yet in bed. She came down in curling papers and made him cambric tea, then listened to him read it. The full title was "General William Booth Enters into Heaven." Ruby was responsive, but no more than to other poems he had tried out on her. Nor did Lindsay himself have an inkling that he, like Booth and his horde, was being born again—that during all the rest of his days he would place the year 1912 as the real beginning of his life.

Lindsay wrestled mightily with himself to gain the spirit of Booth for resuming his own preaching. In early September he took to the road again, heading north toward San Francisco. Not far out of Los Angeles he doubled back to the comforts of the Johnson Lindsay home. He pulled his weight by helping with the housework while another money request went off to Springfield.

When the money came, Vachel rode the cushions to San Francisco and then crossed the bay to Oakland for nearly a month's stay at the home of English Professor E. Olan James of Mills College, one of his friends by correspondence. At this time Lindsay was too dispirited to keep his diary. His clothes were in such bad repair that James lent him trousers for making a presentable appearance at an art show. He might have bought a pair except for his pleasure in now and again splurging a bit. When the money had come from home he had spent part of it to take Ruby to the theater. The begging of hotel rooms and occasional renting of one had been more than a desire for a good bed. He loved hotels. Their luxury and isolation were for him escape from the hard realities of the world.

Dr. Lindsay in Sprngfield received a third message from his son, this one asking for fare home. The doctor sent it. He had also paid the printer for *Rhymes to Be Traded for Bread* and "The Gospel of Beauty." When the patient doctor remarked that a round-trip ticket would have been a whole lot cheaper, he was speaking from the viewpoint, of course, of a Philistine. Vachel himself felt persecuted by his family for being a poet and artist. For the doctor there had been no choice about sending the money. His wife with her roomers was earning part of the income and besides could never allow her child-genius, a stand-in for her own ego, to be deprived.

Harriet Monroe, leafing through magazines in the Chicago public library, had read Lindsay's "The Proud Farmer" in the September *American*. One of her circulars had caught up with him on the way, and he had answered, promising to submit poems when he got the chance. From Springfield, after reaching home in middle October, he dispatched an envelope filled with short moon-poems and others including "General Booth." She accepted the last and a few of the moon-poems. Since the original draft of "Booth" had not contained the orchestration suggestions, Lindsay now tried them on her. She decided to include them, while wondering if their novelty would not increase the strangeness to a point of absurdity which would bring ridicule down upon her and *Poetry*.

Meanwhile Lindsay was engaged as usual in bitter soul-searching, but also as usual was hard at work. Late in October he began a long poem titled "The Congo." The germ of it had been in a sermon at the First Christian Church, when the pastor had spoken of the recent drowning of a missionary friend in the Congo River. Lindsay subtitled the poem "A study of the Negro Race" and divided it into parts: the Congo Negro's basic savagery, his irrepressible high spirits, the hope for him as a Christian after the primitive gods of Mumbo-Jumbo were overthrown. For the poem Lindsay went to a full chant:

> Then I saw the Congo, creeping through the black,
> Cutting through the forest with a golden track.
> Then along that riverbank
> A thousand miles
> Tattooed cannibals danced in files;
> Then I heard the boom of the blood-lust song
> And a thigh-bone beating on a tin-pan gong.
> And "BLOOD" screamed the whistles and the fifes of the warriors,
> "BLOOD" screamed the skull-faced, lean witch-doctors.

At the beginning of December, Lindsay wrote Dell of a contemplated project to go out among the farmers to commune with them about nature and beauty. "I wish I could talk it over with you," he said. "Come and see me, you and Mrs. Dell, and help me save my soul. I need spiritual backers more than publicity backers." He did not mention "The Congo" and if he had high expectations for "Booth," due for appearance in *Poetry*'s January number, he did not say so. Rather, he was enthusiastic that *Farm and Fireside* had taken six prose "proclamations" of the Gospel of Beauty. He noted its circulation of half a million as proof that he was getting his message to a large public. Occasionally there was a flash of the old humor. "I serve no woman but the Virgin Mary, reverence no knight but Galahad, pray to no god but the Christ-Apollo (despite much contrary advice in your publication)."

Much was changed by "Booth." The circulation of *Poetry* being what it was, he did not, of course, spring to fame overnight. But high praise was not long in coming. "Glorious and touching," said the influential *Review of Reviews*. "Both poignant in conception and expression, and the despair of imitation." William Dean Howells of *Harper's*, who long ago had sent Lindsay home to "eliminate obscurity" from a rejected poem, had no complaint this time. He spoke of "that fine brave poem" which "makes the heart leap." So went the responses by the score. A New York publisher, Mitchell Kennerley, contracted to issue the next autumn *General William Booth Enters into Heaven and Other Poems*, and also the collection of reports from the road under the title *Adventures While Preaching the Gospel of Beauty*.

A writer for *Collier's* put wings on the vagabond legend:

> His face is frank, open, and humocky. Over the hills and hollows whimsical expressions play. The general color scheme is paper white with sorrel hair. The brow bulges forward with animal intensity and then retires in uplifting irregular slopes and swells that suggest an eccentric mind of great vitality. The rear half of the brain seems heaviest and is always tipping the head back till Lindsay gazes at one from under large, smooth lids which overhang the windows of his soul like awnings. The poet has a ready smile and a voice that is high and clarion like, made for the open road and echoing almost harshly in the confines of the ordinary room.
>
> And so Lindsay will fare on, not in little straggling trips, but in great, sweeping cruises over the face of the land.

Lindsay's cruises would be the lecture trail, and, for better or for worse, he would never walk the road again.

17

Anderson Comes to Chicago and Dell Leaves

In the spring of 1913 Karl Anderson was in Chicago, and in a roundabout way he brought his brother Sherwood into the Jackson Park colony, partly through his friend Brör Nordfeldt. Karl, too, was in a cultural brawl over "modern" art that inevitably had an impact on literature. The trouble rose out of the Armory Show (so called because of its initial appearance in New York City's Sixty-ninth Regiment Armory). Karl was a member of the sponsoring committee along with John Sloan, Jo Davidson, George Bellows, William Glackens, and a score of other avant-garde painters and sculptors. Arthur Aldis had been introduced in Paris to the committee's secretary, Walt Kuhn, who was putting together European contributions. Worrying over the show's reception, Kuhn had been bucked up when Aldis offered to arrange for it to be brought to Chicago by that stronghold of traditionalism, the Art Institute.

The Armory Show opened in New York in mid-February 1913. Crowds surged through the armory debating, often angrily, the merits of Cézanne, Van Gogh, Manet, Picasso,Gauguin, Matisse, Duchamp, and other controversial figures. Because of the exhibition's imminent arrival in Chicago, the *Tribune* asked Harriet Monroe, its art critic, to render an account. She liked it, on the whole. "Even the cubists seem to be playing interesting games with kaleidoscopic polygons of color; even Matisse is dancing a wild tango on some weird barbarous shore. We cannot always tell what they mean, but at least they are having a good time." She was careful to note for the benefit of Chicago Philistines certain overheard remarks to the effect that the producers of some of the works were fit subjects for alienists. Although not quite half the show had been brought to Chicago, all the shockers were in it.

As high society turned out for a preview the night before the March 24 opening, word got around that Arthur Jerome Eddy, perhaps the most knowledgeable and surely the most daring of the city's big art collectors, had already purchased heavily. His plunge, along with the acceptance of the moderns by Europe's elite, resulted in dignified, if mildly wall-eyed, viewing by the aristocrats. The painting everybody wanted to see was Duchamp's sensational *Nude Descending a Staircase.* No one had yet discerned a staircase, much less a nude. But each wanted to do his own peering in the hope that the cubes would somehow fall into the title's promise. The second most celebrated exhibit was a real nude, *September Morn,* by Chabas.

The show was indeed made to order for the gamier newspapers, especially Hearst's *American* and *Examiner.* They assigned critics and feature writers who knew what they liked, and it wasn't what they saw. A large body of instructors and students joined the guffawing element of the press, and if anything, they were more outraged. Some instructors had to be forbidden the taking of classes on hooting tours, and students found an outlet in a "futuristic party" with scorning placards like "Stewed Descending a Staircase."

Agents of the Chicago Vice Commission knew better, of course, than to invade the premises of the Founder-backed Art Institute to seize *September Morn.* But when a dealer put in his window a life-size color reproduction the law promptly snatched him up. The censors could make out an unclothed human figure bent over at water's edge exploring the temperature. The figure seemed to be that of a girl a year or two beyond adolescence. The authorities were being pushed by moral elements a few cuts below the Builders. A Mrs. Cornelia Baker of the rising Women's Club had found herself quaking with rage while reading the new crop of novels. Even Robert Chambers, she found, had fallen into the sex snare; even his "good" women puffed cigarettes or drank cocktails, and one, depraved beyond the average, had soaked perfume into sugar lumps and eaten the dangerous concoction. Yet in the affair of *September Morn* virtue was trampled in the dust. Harriet Monroe was perhaps responsible. The jury heard her opinion that the paintings would not corrupt the city's morals, and accepted it as its own verdict.

The creative impact of the Armory Show naturally was on the few. Writers as well as painters realized that audiences could be reached by a subtle indirection of mood—even the grotesque. Sherwood Anderson, not long from Elyria, visited the exhibition with his brother. The interest of Carl Sandburg in painting had been furthered by his brother-in-law, Edward Steichen. The presence of Lee Masters was guaranteed by the attacks of the Philistines. Harriet Monroe was directly involved, of course, and Maurice Browne and Floyd Dell and Margaret Anderson responded, as they did to all matters having to do with the expression of life through beauty. Hundreds of others, all to be players—obscure or not—in the upsweep of the Renaissance, passed through the exhibition.

It was Margery Dell, the seeker for and encourager of all talents, who came upon the fallen business giant, Sherwood Anderson, and led him into a warm shelter. The encounter was not at first direct. She had been talking with Karl Anderson at the Armory Show. Brör Nordfeldt, introducing them, had remarked that Margery's husband was editor of the *Friday Literary Review*. And Karl, having his brother on his mind, and to some extent on his hands, had brought into the conversation Sherwood's manuscripts and his broken career and his ambitions to be a writer. When it came down to it, Karl, more than Sherwood, looked the business man. He dressed conservatively and was of even temperament. His own painting was rather traditional and he made a living from magazine illustrations and other commercial work. But he was emotionally drawn to the avant-garde.

Margery offered Dell as a reader of Sherwood's manuscripts. She was sure of her ground, for Dell read all of the original work put in his way. The transfer of one of the Anderson novels, *Windy McPherson's Son,* was arranged: the author to Karl to Margery to Dell. Sherwood was now back in advertising with a job in the Critchfield agency, but as a time-server rather than a bright man on the way up. His cubbyhole was a kind of cell in which, after turning out the minimum work demanded, he lost himself in his fiction tales. Although yearning for literary company he was too low in spirits to carry his work directly to the editor of a leading newspaper's book section.

Dell read the manuscript, liked it, and in the *FLR* found space to remark on it as an example of Chicago's unpublished talent. Anderson, as he later remembered it, "pranced excitedly up and down my room." His family was with his wife's parents and he was living in a South Side boarding house not far from the Jackson Park colony. In spite of a ready introduction to the colony people, through Karl via Nordfeldt, he did not seek it. Even when the Dells took up separate residences in the colony during the spring of 1913, Sherwood lacked the self-confidence to accept their invitation, by word of mouth through Karl, to drop in for a visit or to be a guest at one of their weekend parties.

Then one night, more lonely than usual, he wandered to the corner of Fifty-seventh Street and Stony Island Avenue. Dell's studio was on Fifty-seventh, Margery's on Stony Island—each close enough to the corner for the back doors to open near each other. A party, Anderson found, was being held in Margery's studio. He was still gaunt from his ordeal, his face bony, his black hair long and tousled. He walked up and down before the curtained windows. Away from the office he wore bright colors to emphasize, for himself, the break with his past, and so he might have been taken for a real gypsy and certainly for a bohemian artist.

He didn't feel an artist—not for sure. The gay, assured people in the studio, as it seemed from the voices, would surely regard him as a fake. "My novel may have impressed them but they will immediately be on to me," he told himself. Now and again a streetcar rattled by. There were enough strollers in the warm evening to keep his loitering from being obtrusive. Peering through a curtain crack he saw a graceful little woman darting among the twenty-odd celebrants, serving drinks, exchanging banter, laughing. This must be the hostess, Margery. He guessed Dell to be the intense youth, remindful to him of Poe, engaged in some heated discussion. In the cacophony of voices it was impossible to distinguish words. After a while the party suddenly broke toward the front door. He moved quickly away, but watched the revelers cross into Jackson Park. He followed—but dared not intrude lest he be taken as a "too slick" advertising man. "I hid myself that evening in the bushes."

A few evenings later, following a stroll in the park, he came out on Stony Island Avenue in time to glimpse, on the other side, Margery entering her studio. He crossed over, meditating whether to knock and introduce himself. It would be easier to face one person—and especially Margery, now that he had observed her friendliness. She popped out again on some errand and they were face to face. A wave of courage stiffened him. Humbly he gave his name. Margery knew something of his troubles and his desperate urge to write. Her errand was forgotten. They walked for a long time in the park. Margery, like Dell, had seen promise in the *Windy* manuscript. She talked intimately of the story and its people—the greatest ego-booster a new author might receive. His doubts of acceptance by her friends were quickly exploded. In some indefinable way Margery transferred her own high spirits, faith, and courage. Anderson would always remember their conversation as a vital turning point. "I could not sleep and spent the rest of the night walking through the streets and in the park and building a new life for myself."

Margery was pretty, a devoted supporter of his goals—and unhappy. He was handsome and a fascinating companion, especially as a teller of tales about himself to a sympathetic listener. They began seeing a good deal of one another.

With the arrival of the Dells in Jackson Park, Chicago bohemia had come into its own. Dell's wide interests and Margery's hospitality drew into it, at least for social gatherings, people of artistic bent from all over the city. Sharp observers like Mrs. Nordfeldt realized that something had gone wrong in the Dells' marriage. But since they never spoke of it to others, the different residences were a kind of titillation for advanced thinkers in sex relations.

Margery's studio was the more luxurious. It had a bathtub and a telephone. For Dell to come to the back door for calls was not much more trouble than in a fairly large house or apartment. For bathing he had to be satisfied, like most of the colony residents, with an iron sink and cold water and a sponge—unless he borrowed Margery's tub. Since Margery would be doing most of the entertaining, the nicest pieces of furniture were in her studio, including her own small piano. For dinners his establishment had the advantage of a great round model's table, left by some artist, at which a score or more could eat. All had to serve themselves from a pot of chop suey or another inexpensive dish cooked on the gas ring.

Some of the colony residents were known to the Dells from the Little Theatre: the Brör Nordfeldts, Raymond Johnson, Lou Wall Moore, Margaret Allen. Others with whom they joined in a communal social life were Ralph Pearson, an etcher using, as it happened, an ancient printing press that had belonged to Margery's father; Kathleen Wheeler, a sprite of a girl who did portrait busts but liked better to sculpt horses; Marjorie Jones, a dark-haired young photographer who wanted to be a dancer; Ernestine Evans, called by the others the "nut-brown maid," a Chicago University student bent on a writing career; another university student, Mary Elizabeth Titzel, with ironic wide-apart eyes, who was secretary for the Little Theatre and wanted to be an archaeologist.

Another Davenport native, Arthur Davison Ficke, often took Jig Cook's place in the Dell circle. Dell had never formally met the wealthy and handsome lawyer-poet until one night when he was having coffee in a restaurant, and Maurice Browne had entered with Ficke and introduced them. It had been a long way around: Browne had met Ficke in Indiana half a dozen years ago and was now bringing the two young Davenport men together. Ficke was still practicing law in his home town, but, trying to break away, spent days or even weeks in Chicago. He and the Dells became fast friends, and his visits meant feasts away from the gas ring in some good restaurant.

Except for Cook and Martha Baker (she had died of pneumonia) the old Dell circle was intact. Charles Hallinan was still writing editorials for the *Post*, and Lucian Cary, Dell's assistant on the *Friday Literary Review*, and his wife Augusta came to the parties. So did the Brownes and Eunice Tietjens and Margaret Anderson, and, less often, Harriet Monroe. Eunice was doing chores at *Poetry* by way of getting on the staff. Margaret was now good and bored with her job as editor of *The Continent*. Michael Carmichael Carr had turned up, once his classes at Missouri University were over for the year. Of the new people coming into the group, one of the most striking was Tennessee Mitchell, who to Dell "carried the aura of the new era." To Margaret Anderson, she represented the sophisticated woman, meaning one of brains and individuality. Tennessee and Margery Dell had met during the preparations for the suffragette march and had been drawn to one another, and Tennessee's invitation to the parties had followed as a matter of course. A somewhat unlikely newcomer was a young matron with three children and no artistic ambitions, Cornelia Anderson. She had come to Chicago not exactly for a reconciliation with her husband, but to seek a way into his self-declared new life. Sherwood brought her to this portion of it, and, far from being treated as an outsider, she developed friendships, especially with Tennessee and Margery. Dell found her a warm and understanding person, slender, delicate, self-contained, wearing a Dante wreath as her "sole recognition of evening dress."

For Dell much of the enchantment of Chicago had gone with Elaine Hyman, who had taken the stage name Kirah Markham and departed for New York in search of theatrical roles. But also—and Dell knew it too well—she had gone to be near Dreiser. After his departure she came back to Dell and he saw victory, failing to reckon with the persuasive pen of his rival. Dreiser importuned, citing his dreadful need of her; wrote glowingly of prospects for the stage aided by his tireless backing; and showed great insight and compassion into her discontent at home. But while she was gone, Dell was forced to marvel at the power of his foe in still another enterprise. He had written Elaine letter after letter. They all came back unopened but sealed in a larger envelope addressed in her own handwriting. Dell thought he knew where the wily Theodore had got *that* caper—from Anatole France's *The Red Lily*.

Elaine was a strong magnet pulling Dell away from Chicago. But there were other factors causing him unrest. Like Hackett, he wearied of laboring to outwit the high command at the *Post*. Except in the Christmas season the book advertising had not come up to its early promise, and the *Friday Literary Review* was dropped as an independent section and made a part of the regular pages. Passing his twenty-sixth birthday, Dell realized that for half of his adult life he had been doing more or less the same thing and over. The fun and sense of creativity had vanished.

And underneath the gay surface of life in the Dell back-to-back studios the acid was eating. Margery knew of her husband's infatuation with Elaine and his courtship of others. He was sick of himself and told her so. But he was not able to fit himself into the mold of conventional marriage any longer, and did not want to. Margery's pride was wounded almost beyond her capacity to bear, and yet she sorrowed about what she felt this rootless emotional life was doing to him. A major portion of the blame she laid on herself, convinced that as a woman she was not adequate for him, whereas in another he might be fulfilled. One night, after a futile discussion of their predicament, including talk of parting and his suggestion that he might go away, she sat down and in her strong, flowing hand wrote to him a poignant letter:

I guess I mean what I said, Floyd. There seems no other way but to drag it up by the roots. I'd rather do that than let it do the poetic *trash* flowers are accustomed to—such as withering slowly, becoming distorted, breaking, being choked by weeds, etc. etc.

I don't know much about the techniques of morality—but I do feel that one should not continue to annoy a man when he doesn't care and never will. I'd like to be in your presence—I found the whole of you so delicious—but it wouldn't be fair to you to let me love you when you knew you couldn't.

I rather resented your saying you are spiritually sick—you're not a bit. You're in fine health. Spiritually, I think. To know one-self—to admit it—that's good digestion; oh it's so much better than hoodwinking your own wisdom. You just didn't hit the right woman (confound my meagerness!) but that's not saying you haven't the sagacity to find her and the capacity to feel her sufficient. I think you have.

I shall probably go on caring for a while with a token now and then for expression's sake. You might encourage the outlet by telling me what you won't throw under the sink. I don't want to get a set of Balzac for instance!

But please don't encourage the *flus*trations of my struggle by throwing brushwood on the fire.

I wish you all the joy and completeness you'll one day know and which I'll dream of for you.

And so the marriage of the youngest of the six men was broken, as was Dreiser's, and those of Anderson and Masters, too, though the fact was not admitted. In spite of the different ages of the four, all the marriages had gone to pieces within a span of roughly three years.

The outer arrangements of the Dell studios were not, however, immediately disturbed. Margery enjoyed the Jackson Colony life. In a way she had found herself through aiding the creative growth of others, and now she determined to quit teaching and seek a newspaper job. Dell had his sense of freedom and both knew that his days in Chicago were numbered. They cleared the air by letting intimates know of the situation, Margery's pride being shored up and Dell cleansed of a portion of his feelings of guilt. And so they acted out the idealistic code of the new era, removing their own bonds as noiselessly as possible in order for each to go on his own with best wishes for the other.

As it happened, Brör Nordfeldt now painted a full-length portrait of Dell which might have stood for the bohemia unfolding in Chicago. It was no accident that in Greenwich Village not long hence Dell would become a kind of symbol of the revolution in love and literature; Jig Cook a moving force with his Provincetown Players; Dreiser and Elaine Hyman-Kirah Markham great rallying figures; Francis Hackett, although somewhat aloof as always from the bohemian life, a continuing shaper of American letters. It was a sort of life-in-capsule that would break out into the twenties—with Sherwood Anderson as a major prophet—and be adopted by the postwar younger generation.

Nordfeldt granted that the portrait, some four by five feet, mostly in browns and greens, was a bit "wicked." The weight of Dell's willowy figure rested on a stick in his right hand, which also held gloves; a wide, soft hat was pressed under the arm. The left hand toyed with a cigarette. A Windsor tie and thick longish fair hair emphasized the slender narrow-mustached face. Dell was caught as if poised for flight or ready to smile deprecatingly at himself. The overall impression was a mingling of tentativeness and flamboyance, of an egotist about to dare but unsure of the consequences.

Sherwood Anderson was always to call Dell his "literary father," and, perhaps not strangely, he had a photograph taken in a pose similar to that of Nordfeldt's painting. The chin of Anderson's gaunt face rested on the head of a stick (he was sitting) and his pile of hair looked carefully tousled. Dell had been guiding Anderson into the uncharted ways of bohemia. Once when he came to use Dell's typewriter he was mildly shocked when its owner, having lent it to Ernestine Evans and finding her absent from her locked studio, pinned to her door a note reading, "God damn your soul, Ernestine, bring back my typewriter." People in manufacturing or even advertising didn't post messages of this nature.

Both the men were late sitters and often later workers. If Anderson came by, Dell would put down the book he was reading or turn from his typewriter—he did much of his *Friday Literary Review* work at home—for an hour or more of talk. They had in common their small-town backgrounds, and for a while there was the fascinating topic of Anderson's days and nights of wandering in Ohio. The victim's own diagnosis was that he had suffered from amnesia.

Dell, as an amateur student of psychology, was happy to have a live case into which to probe. Anderson dredged up the memory of buying a workman's blue shirt and changing into it, but generally he stood apart from himself as victim and they explored the realm of theory together.

Dell was fascinated, too, by the motivations of someone who had turned from business to literature. Anderson talked well on the shallowness of the rewards to be had in commerce, but without the portentous note that would in time mark his utterances on the subject. Except for having read *Windy McPherson's Son*, Dell would have taken Anderson for a slumming businessman with a fine gift for the spoken anecdote and a better listener than most. How to account for *Windy*? When Anderson spoke of fiction he decried the lorn and sad and grotesque. He had not read widely—none of Dreiser nor the Russians and little of the modern Europeans. His favorite author was George Borrow. In Elyria, Borrow's work had fitted Anderson's "trapped" mood, for Borrow had left the dull routine of a clerk to wander over much of Europe as a Bible salesman and journalist. His books—among them *Lavengro* and *The Romany Rye*—were a formless medley of character sketches and personal adventures, often among the gypsies. His examples may have caused Anderson to make Sam McPherson wander in the lower depths, or have made the device seem plausible to an inexperienced writer.

But this portion of *Windy*, aside from the vague quest for a better understanding of life, was the least consequential of the story. The new and different was, of course, the early portion dealing with young Sam and his worthless father and other small town characters and doings. Even the early plot, a garbled success story, was overshadowed by these characters, which were the more remarkable because created by a businessman whose spoken anecdotes were mostly humorous. In other words, the strengths of the novel seemed not to have been premeditated. The best phase—Sam's relationship with Windy—rose naturally from Anderson's compulsive portrayal of his relationship with his own father, as he saw it. The other powerful episodes—Sam's feeling for the town and its people and their doings—had seemingly emerged from the peculiar situation of Anderson's mind. Since he was against the fictional lorn and grotesque it followed that he did not see his really effective characters as one or the other. By this time of his life he viewed most of the human race as lonely, crippled, stumbling. If a character was meant to be good and saintly —like Sam's mother—the author did not go below the surface. The reader might have confidently expected, had he done so, to have been shown gnarls and blemishes. Anderson's mind was somehow better focused to explore the dark than the light. When he described what he saw the clearest—and since ugly demons torment all—he made his fiction realistic in spite of the absurdity of the plot.

Anderson's reason for adopting Dell as his "literary father" was never plain, and Dell rejected the role. The younger man's value was mainly his recognition of merit and promise in the older man's work. To Anderson it was the more appreciated since it came from a literary critic with a growing national reputation who was admired by the Chicago avant-garde. Dell was more than a simple believer. He tirelessly celebrated Anderson as a budding major talent and labored to find a publisher for *Windy*—collecting only rejection slips. True, he acted as a sounding board when Anderson made revisions, and cut out, with the author's permission, four of the six waifs whom Sam was taking to his estranged wife.

Dell was responsible for an event which was another factor in launching Anderson as Chicago's "great unpublished author" or "unrecognized genius." The terms were interchangable and Anderson was to play the role masterfully for many years. He enjoyed reading aloud to audiences, as he had even to guests in his Elyria home. The circuit of private mansions was out of the question and even Maurice Browne insisted on notables for his open houses. The solution hit upon by Dell was to book his man into a "reading party" which he induced Ernestine Evans and Mary Elizabeth Titzel to promote in the Colony studio they shared.

The girls neither knew nor cared whether their attraction was a "great unpublished author." They simply liked the idea of giving a party, and if it advanced the cause of literature, so much the better. They spread the word, made cookies and lemonade, got in some folding chairs, and rewarded the author with twenty or thirty listeners—mostly young ladies, since it was an afternoon meeting, but also Robert Morss Lovett, professor of English at Chicago University, and of course Dell. Anderson, dressed in a working housepainter's clothes, read from *Windy*. The audience could not have been expected to pass full judgment on manuscript excerpts. But they had Dell's word that the novel was good, and the author's literary stance and cadenced soft baritone were persuasive. When he finished, Anderson, nibbling cookies and sipping lemonade, basked in the acclaim normally given a performer at such gatherings.

The literary niche carved in a few months, if not large, was warm and comforting.

One night Carl Sandburg came to Dell's studio bringing a sheaf of poetry. The meeting, the first between them, was not considered significant by either; just two poets, in this case two Socialists, discussing a favorite topic. At the suggestion of a mutual friend, Sandburg had telephoned Dell at his office and they had worked out a time for the visit. One poem which Dell enjoyed was a little word picture of fog coming into the city as if on cat's feet. The rest which Sandburg had brought were precise, the words well chosen for beauty rather than for story content or power—the sort of thing other Chicago poets were doing. Nothing in them caused Dell to expect that his deliberate-spoken visitor was a man likely to capture the raw spirit of Chicago in poetry.

The two doubtless would have become friends except that Dell's time in Chicago was running out. In September he went East for the autumn publishing rounds. While there he learned that the heads of many *Post* departments were rolling; that the managing editor and his friend Hallinan had quit. So he wired his own resignation. He returned, however, to pack and for a farewell dinner. At it Margery revealed that she had found a job as a reporter for the *Daily News*. Lucian Cary would be the new editor of the *Friday Literary Review*, his wife assistant editor.

Then Dell, after not quite five years in Chicago, took a train for New York. Later he was to write of his going:

> I had been happy in Chicago; never would it seem to me a gray and ugly city. . . . I had seen beauty there, enough to fill my heart; there had been days and nights of talk and laughter; the years had passed in a golden glow of friendship. . . . It had been a generous city to a young man. I would be grateful for what it had given me.

18

Margaret Anderson and the *Little Review*

NOW was to be the time of Margaret Anderson. With the *Little Review* she would build a temple, as Hackett and Dell had with the *Friday Literary Review*, Maurice and Nellie Browne with the Little Theatre, and Harriet Monroe with *Poetry*. Margaret's temple would be even less bound to earth, would ride turbulently in the skies. It was to be the time also, a bit later, of Lee Masters, Carl Sandburg, and Sherwood Anderson. In the Chicago eruption, 1914 would be a scintillating year.

Margaret Anderson's double quality of unreality continued, one part outward, the other within. People stared at her as at a living cover girl of one of the rising popular magazines or some theatrical star. In a sumptuous restaurant with an escort having only a dollar or two to spend, waiters nevertheless danced attention upon her and the orchestra vied for her praise. Golden hair and unearthly blue eyes and classic Norse features and athletic tall bearing were factors. At the same time she was fastidious. If evening apparel had declined to a single skirt and blouse, she washed and ironed them and went proudly out—unless a sleeve, perhaps, did not hang just right, whereupon she would not go out at all. There was an indefinable something else. The heavens had cast the royal purple over her. Moreover, she knew it. A princess or queen comes to expect, and will insist on, deference to her person and opinions. Margaret did. But she hated the times when it was necessary to insist. Later she would put it this way:

I wasn't born to be a fighter. I was born with a gentle nature, a flexible character and an organism as equilibrated as it is judged hysterical. I shouldn't have been forced to fight constantly and ferociously. The causes I have fought for have invariably been causes that should have been gained by a delicate suggestion. Since they never were, I made myself into a fighter. Once you start such an idea you find that it creeps up on you. I remember periods when I have been so besieged that I had to determine on a victory a day in order to be sure of surviving.

History records that queens divinely appointed had to rap heads to get their way. And they always blamed the opposition for ignorance and bad temper. Margaret simply hated to have reality intrude on her visions. These might shift and change, but, like Vachel Lindsay's, were always part of a Gospel of Beauty. Unlike Lindsay, she gave no concern to preaching to the masses. For her Whitman's line, "To have great poets, there must be great audiences, too"—taken by Harriet Monroe as a slogan for *Poetry*—was ridiculous. Let the artist do his best; let the audience appear or not. It may seem a contradiction, but in the next year or two Margaret's name was to become well known to Chicagoans because her adventures filled the newspapers as she collided with social barriers she hadn't noticed.

Margaret was impulsive. She admitted it and was skilled in reading her inner tremors. Awakening one night in her narrow bed in the YWCA and realizing that a new journal of the arts had to be founded, she went peacefully back to sleep. It would be done. She would do it. To concern oneself with the obstacles was a waste of time. If there had to be a miracle, a miracle there would be.

During the last few years Margaret had changed, without at first noticing. For one thing, she had been amazed at the trouble arising from her praise of Dreiser's *Sister Carrie* in the religious paper she edited. The higher powers, quite agreeing with the Philistine assessment of the novel, in a kindly way had ordered her to ignore immoral books. In reply they had received Margaret's wide-blue-eyed inquiry: "How am I to know what is immoral?" It was a poser. Now Margaret had come round to art for art's sake and life as a hard, gemlike flame. She talked, as always, in gasps, gaps, and gestures, letting the hearer fill in as best he might, and was herself an imperfect audience. (Dell had been her one conversational idol.) Although a reader of lyric poets and Ruskin and Pater and Ibsen and Nietzsche and the current Europeans, her main love and inspiration was music. When in distress and fancying suicide she was always put off by recollecting that it would be the end of opera and recitals. The piano was her glory and release, and, her loyalties being wildly passionate, she worshipped the Mason and Hamlin; no other make would do. As a practicer she was indefatigable.

Now that the magazine had to be, where to get the funds? Her father, a street railway consultant, was well-to-do and sympathetic to her aims and whims, but there was her mother. The Andersons moved gypsylike from one Midwestern city to another, always into lovely houses with perfectly new furniture. The change of scene was her mother's passion, along with a determination to force Margaret to toe a conformist line. Her tight grip on the purse strings allowed only dribbles for Margaret. One sister had married; another, with Margaret now, could help with the magazine. An angel appeared, as was to be expected. He was Margaret's friend-suitor, large and handsome DeWitt C. Wing. They had met in the Dell circle. In bourgeois day life, Wing was an agricultural journalist, an editor of the *Breeder's Gazette*. She was pleased to find him "one of those civilized men" more interested in an idea than a woman. She had not time for beau-type foolishness.

In her gasps, gaps, and gestures, Margaret explained the magazine to Wing (she called him Dick rather than DeWitt) as they dined in the white and gold room of The Annex. "Dick understood the code and could supply all the words I never had time to stop for. When I hurriedly told him that I was going to publish the best art magazine in the world, he saw the idea perfectly. I was most grateful. People were always telling me that I 'saw' their ideas without necessity for formulation on their part. I felt I deserved one friend who could perform this function for me. Dick was the only person who really 'saw' the *Little Review*." He offered to put up enough from his salary for the printing and office rent. Another who gave out of his wages was George Soule, working, as when he had watched Hackett send up fireworks, for the conservative Frederick L. Stokes firm of New York publishers. He and Margaret had become acquainted during one of her publisher rounds for *The Continent*. He remembered:

I was bowled over by her vitality, her beauty, and her voluble enthusiasms. On a winter Saturday I took her to Long Beach, Long Island, not yet spoiled as an overcrowded public resort, and we had a long walk on the hard sand, refreshed by the clean winter air.

Western breezes blew spume back from the tips of charging breakers, while seagulls wove their patterns of flight not far above the sea and beach. We talked about the sorry state of American letters, and the trashy bestsellers which publishers promoted in their competition for profit. We agreed that something new and adventurous must be done to encourage writers of integrity and talent.

Another who donated a hundred dollars was: Vachel Lindsay. It was inevitable, once he knew of the project. The sum was a prize for "Booth" given by *Poetry*. Royalties from his two books had been small and his long poem "The Congo" had brought only fifty dollars from the *Metropolitan* magazine. But at Margery Currey's studio (she had gone back to her maiden name), listening to Margaret's ambitions to preach a Gospel of Beauty in her own way, he had emptied his purse. To Wing's suggestion that a group or groups be involved in support of the new journal, Margaret had said "no." She distrusted groups. The one exception had been the informal one around Dell; and so it was fitting that at Margery Currey's studio one party night she formally announced the *Little Review*. That she hadn't the vaguest notion of what would go into the magazine was, to her, immaterial. Something would. It would be important.

Of the small-town boys, only two, Anderson and Dreiser, were present at Margery's that night. Dreiser had come from New York recently on business. Elaine Hyman was with him. Dreiser was unhappy. He was suffering jointly from neck carbuncles and the publishing trade. Harper had put *The Titan* into proofs and then had backed away, refusing to issue the book. He may have felt old, for as he stitched his handkerchief a woman sitting beside him inquired if he knew the langorous beauty across the room. "Yes," he said, "it's my daughter." It was Elaine.

The first number of the *Little Review* (March 1914) could hardly be simply blank pages, as a later one would be. Margaret had fallen back on her friends in the old Dell circle—except, of course, for the usual brave manifesto. In this case it was a two-page "Announcement." It declared: "Life is a glorious performance. . . . And close to Life—so close, from our point of view, that it keeps treading on Life's heels—is this eager, panting Art who shows us the wonder of the way as we rush along." She stated admiration for the man or woman who "lives," but a vastly greater feeling for one who produces works of art, who has made life better permanently. "The *Little Review* means to reflect this attitude toward life and art. Its ambitious aim is to produce criticism of books, music, art, drama, and life that shall be fresh and constructive, and intelligent from the artist's point of view . . . untrammeled liberty . . ."

In the final paragraph, Margaret left the earth behind and climbed unashamed into the heavens, bidding other blithe spirits follow:

> If you've ever read poetry with a feeling that it was your religion, your very life; if you've ever come suddenly upon the whiteness of a Venus in a dim, deep room; if you've ever felt music replacing your shabby soul with a new one of shining gold; if, in the early morning, you've watched a bird with great white wings fly from the edge of the sea straight up into the rose-colored sun— if these things have happened to you and continue to happen till you're left speechless with the wonder of it all, then you'll understand our hope to bring them near to the common experience of the people who read us.

Margaret had sought a word of encouragement from but one world celebrity, John Galsworthy. It had seemed to her that in his recent *The Dark Flower* he had proved himself "a man with the soul of the old gods," and had told "with inexpressible beauty the truth about an artist." Her own emotions had been described to her perfect satisfaction. Wonder of wonders, Galsworthy had replied with a gracious letter. One portion distressed her. He feared that instead of living under the stars the editor might prefer the hothouse air of a temple.

Margaret was to declare later:

> When I read "temple" I was disconcerted. A temple was what I wanted. Not the *petite chapelle* of the aesthetes but a temple of the great, the permanent, versus the transient; the exquisite, the special versus the typical; not the discriminations of the connoisseur but those of the creator; not taste nor the standards of taste, but the perception of the masters. For me there was to be (there always has been) one criterion: the "marked" human being, the consequent "marked" quality of his work. Instead of avoiding all temples because of the risk of finding myself in the wrong one, I knew there was no risk involved—I was in the right one. I hesitated about printing Galsworthy's letter. The career of the *Little Review* as I planned it would be a definite betrayal of his gentle hopes.

If on looking back at the first number she would find more of her own adolescence than words to be graven in a temple—well, at least it was a beginning. Nietzsche was heavily leaned on. DeWitt Wing appeared with a review of Arthur Davison Ficke's blank verse *Mr. Faust*, calling it a "remarkable Nietzschean drama," adding that Nietzsche's "marvelously courageous God" Zarathustra had caused Ficke to "leap to manhood out of the corn belt." The simile wasn't very apt, since Ficke was anything but typical of the corn belt. Another rhapsody of Nietzsche, titled "The Prophet of a New Culture," was the first of a series by George Burman Foster, a Baptist theologian and professor at Chicago University. "A man is coming to be leader—a man who as no other, embodies in himself all the pain and all the pleasures, all the sickness and all the convalescence, all the age and all the youth, of our tremulous and tortured times: Friedrich Nietzsche."

For striking a "new note" in American literature, Margaret had backed her foresight by calling on never-published Sherwood Anderson. "In the trade of writing the so-called new note," he began, "is as old as the world. Simply stated, it is a cry for reinjection of truth and honesty into the craft; it is an appeal from the standards set up by money-making magazine and book publishers in Europe and America to the older, sweeter standards of the craft itself; it is the voice of the new man, come into a new world, proclaiming his right to speak out of the body and soul of youth, rather than through the bodies and souls of the master craftsmen who are gone." He had caught a new spirit of youth in the ardent cubists and futurists at the Armory Show, who, together with the anarchists, socialists, and feminists, gave promise "of a perpetual sweet new birth of the world; it is a strong wind come out of the virgin forest." The message closed with an exhortation: "Be ready to accept hardship for the sake of your craft in America—that is craft love."

The final words about sacrifice had a bearing on Anderson. He had gone with Cornelia and the children to the Ozarks for a few weeks in search of a basis for renewal of family life. As none had been found, Cornelia would fall back on schoolteaching in order to bring up the children. One remnant of the effort to join her husband in the literary world appeared in the first number of the *Little Review*. It was only a short article supplementing one by Margery Currey about Rahel Varnhagen, a feminist of a hundred years earlier. Cornelia's article was mostly selections from Rahel Varnhagen's writings. One comment by Margery seemed directed at reassuring herself: "The woman who has been filled with joyful new amazement on finding that her only reliance is on herself—that she may not depend on this person or that convention to preserve happiness—will know how to value Rahel Varnhagen."

From New York, Dell contributed a review of Olive Schreiner's *Woman and Labor* (and a warm send-off for the new journal in the *Friday Literary Review*). Vachel Lindsay appeared with a poem, "How the Little Girl Danced"; George Soule with a poem, an article on "Tagore as a Dynamic," and an unsigned New York letter remarking on the "cubist" writing of Gertrude Stein; Llewellyn Jones, a young Chicago journalist, with "The Meaning of Bergsonism"; Eunice Tietjens, Ethel Sidgwick, and Ficke with poems; Margaret herself with various literary and music comments, including a puff for the Mason and Hamlin piano. In addition there were selections from Emerson's journals and the letters of William Vaughn Moody. The whole added up to sixty-four pages, seven inches by nine, besides the gray-green cover with a white sticker carrying the title, the name of the editor, and the words "Literature, Drama, Music, Art." Book advertising was in fair supply. On a selling expedition Margaret had been well received in Eastern houses. For the magazine's quarters she had rented Room 917 in the Fine Arts Building.

At first her sister helped out and then came a more permanent staff: Vassar graduate Harriet Dean, a friend from Indianapolis, short-haired, radiating enthusiasm, beaming a Teddy Roosevelt smile; and Charles Zwaska, a husky seventeen-year-old, who, having fallen violently in love with the first issue, had quit as office boy in the *American*'s art department to serve at little or no pay as all-chore boy. (He had been renamed Caesar by Margaret because of his Old Roman cast of features.) Margaret, although a hard worker (she still gave two days a week to review books for *The Continent*), functioned very well amidst confusion. Room 917 was often near to bursting at the seams. By now the Little Room was on its last legs. The arrived or arriving poets frequented the *Poetry* office or the salon of Mrs. William Vaughn Moody, who, as she had a crippled ankle and was quite overweight, reigned from a luxurious bed-swing hung from the ceiling of her drawing room. As a port of call for the undiscovered, the untrammeled, even the wild of eye, Margaret's Room 917 had taken a place with the Open House of the Little

Theatre and Margery Currey's Jackson Park studio. At all of these the hungry of stomach and soul found sustenance.

Margaret hadn't the good fortune to publish works that would be famous (later she would have Sherwood Anderson's early tales and portions of James Joyce's *Ulysses* and Ernest Hemingway's first notable work). In the second number, true, appeared more on the "new note" by Anderson, pointing toward his future. "It is the most delicate and the most unbelievably difficult task to catch, understand, and record your own mood. The thing must be done simply and without pretense or windiness. . . . I myself believe that when a man can stand aside from himself, recording simply and truthfully the inner workings of his own mind, he will be prepared to record truthfully the workings of other minds. In every man or woman dwell dozens of men and women, and the highly imaginative individual will lead fifty lives." As Chicago's "great unpublished author" he had not hesitated to pass along a final word that the method had been "such a help and such a delight to me."

Margaret's one "discovery" of the early issues was a hoax. She didn't know it, not would she know it for fifty years, but she would have stood by her judgment of the work, hoax or not. The culprit made the first approach in a letter signed "Sade Iverson" which Margaret printed in the second number:

> What an insouciant little pagan paper you flourish before our bewildered eyes! Please accept the congratulations of a stranger. But you must not scoff at age, little bright eyes, for some day you, too, will know old age; and you should not jeer at robustness of form, slim one, for the time may come when you, too, will find the burdens of flesh upon you. Above all, do not proclaim too loudly the substitution of Nietzsche for Jesus of the Little Town in the niche of your invisible temple, for when you are broken and forgotten there is no comfort in the Overman. One thing more: restraint is sometimes better than expression. One who has learned this lesson cannot refrain from saying this apropos of the first paragraphs in the criticism of *The Dark Flower*. Do not give folk a chance to misunderstand you. Being a woman, you have to pay too high a price for moments of high intellectual orgy. Forgive all this and go on valiantly.

Yes, accept the congratulations of the stranger! Go on valiantly! But the words in between? In the *Little Review* there had been, after all, no scoffing at middle or old age, or jeers at robust human figures; merely an impression that here was a time of youth's freshness. The correspondent plainly was one who, having accepted the subordinate role of the female, was raising the specter of the appalling wages a woman must pay for "high intellectual orgy"—while expressing a hidden fear that "little bright eyes" might escape them. The deadly message was surely from one who either knew Margaret well or knew much about her. A close reader might have presumed that for the letter-writer to have addressed the editor as "little bright eyes," she herself must have been quite tall.

Two months later a typed poem arrived from "Sade Iverson," accompanied by a modest little typed note (signature typed also) asking that the poem simply be thrown into the wastebasket if not deemed worthy of publication. Thus was explained the absence of a self-addressed envelope. Margaret, liking the poem very much, ran it in the July number. The title was "The Milliner."

> All the day long I have been sitting in my shop
> Sewing straw on hat-shapes according to the fashion,
> Putting lace and ribbon on according to the fashion,
> Setting out the faces of customers according to fashion.
> Whatever they asked for I tried to give them;
> Over their worldly faces I put mimic flowers
> From out my silk and velvet garden; I bade Spring come
> To those who had seen Autumn; I coaxed faded eyes
> To look bright and hard brows to soften.

The poet-"milliner" then told of sometimes peeping into the looking glass at a woman turned gray in the service of other women. And of how one night, long ago, she had in her living quarters behind the shop bedizened herself as a dancing girl and danced until she dropped, then had got to her knees and promised her dead mother never to do it again. The poem concluded:

> As long as I live I shall be adorning other women,
> I shall be decking them for their lovers
> And sending them upon women's adventures.
> But none of them shall see behind this curtain
> Where I have my little home, where I weep
> When I please, and beat upon the table with my fists.

"Sade Iverson" had changed her tack since the letter, or else had been converted to the "new note." Margaret simply waited for the author to come forward. Although not yet widely experienced in such matters, she doubted that any poet who had won acclaim ("The Milliner" had been roundly praised in the avant-garde circles) would remain anonymous. But "Sade" did not come forward. Perhaps she wanted to be coaxed. In the September number Margaret begged her to reveal her identity. As an added inducement she published a tribute by a lad named Maxwell Bodenheim who had recently appeared in Chicago. It was called simply "To Sade Iverson."

> I wonder if you scooped out your entire melted soul
> With shaking hands, and spilled it in this
> Slim-necked but bulging-bodied flagon—
> So slim-necked that my sticking lips
> Must fight for wonderful drops.

The subject couldn't have known it, but these words were perhaps the highest praise that Max Bodenheim would ever lavish on another poet. For a biographical note he had given his age as twenty-two (three years more than a figure he settled on later) and his place of birth as Natchez, Mississippi (shifted by him from Hermanville of the same state), and declared that he had just concluded a hitch in the regular army (he had received a dishonorable discharge before his enlistment was over). The note went on to relate that he was now studying law and art in Chicago—the law part being thrown to the ground with his further announcement that "I am not concerned with life, but with that which lies behind life." Bodenheim was fairly tall, slight, blondish, with blue eyes, red eyebrows, and a monumental nose. The gap of a missing front tooth was often occupied by the stem of a pipe; he often put a blue ribbon tied in a bow on the pipe's stem. His conversation was apt to be waspish, and a lisp added to the effect. A month earlier Harriet Monroe had used one of his verses, so that, with his appearance in the *Little Review*, he had become a young poet to watch.

As for "Sade Iverson," she dispatched more verse but failed to appear. Nothing ranked with "The Milliner," but the mystery of her identity continued to be intriguing. For Margaret the symbol of the old, bad, genteel literature was, as for Dreiser, Mrs. Elia W. Peattie, who was quite tall enough to address Margaret as "little bright eyes." Elia was "Sade Iverson." The avant-garde would have been chagrined to think of Mrs. Peattie holding her sides and rocking with laughter. Why did she maintain public silence? Perhaps, satisfied with the joke in itself, she felt no desire to hold up the new generation to ridicule. Another reason may have been stronger. By the time "The Milliner" reached print, the *Little Review* had gone whole-hog anarchist. Had "Sade Iverson" revealed herself, the *Tribune* employers and readers might have disapproved, and besides she would have become a part of the joke.

Margaret went anarchist just before closing time of the third issue. Emma Goldman led her from the fetid bourgeois swamps into the high, clean air of freedom. Dell's judgment that the anarchists were nowadays merely playing kissing games was passed off by Margaret, as was Lucian Cary's view of Emma as "a nice woman with ideas less radical than Emerson's and certainly less interesting." Red Emma was forty-five, heavy, shapeless, with nose-glasses which made her broad face look like a domineering school principal's. Yet Margaret had found her a "practical Nietzschean," a Zarathrustra in female guise, when Emma let herself go before the tieless radicals at the International Labor Hall. "She pushes through the network of complicated society as if it were a cobweb instead of a steel structure; she brushes cobwebs from her eyes and hair and calls back to the less daring ones that the air is more pure up there and 'sunrise sometimes visible.' "

The repercussions to turning anarchist had, of course, been given no thought. When they came, Margaret, though undismayed, was distressed for others. DeWitt Wing regretfully withdrew his association. To have continued would have meant the loss of his job. George Soule was dismissed from the Stokes company partly as a result of his contributions to the *Little Review* (and soon joined the staff, along with Hackett, of the just-formed *New Republic*). Although most book publishers dropped their *Little Review* advertising, the small circulation (around two thousand) was a factor. Well-wishers partly made up the losses. Some, like Eunice Tietjens, who sold a diamond ring and turned over the proceeds, and architect Frank Lloyd Wright, who gave a hundred dollars, acted to support the new in art. Others, not taking Margaret's anarchy seriously, gave to her as a flaming cause—whatever it happened to be.

Emma Goldman, meeting her disciple, saw her as a "desert wanderer who unexpectedly discovers a stream of fresh water." Yet she was unable to take Margaret's revolutionary outpourings at face value. "Before long I saw that the girls [Harriet Dean, also turned anarchist, was included] were not actuated by any sense of social injustice, like the young Russian intelligentsia, for instance. Strongly individualized, they had broken the shackles of their middle-class homes to find release from family bondage and bourgeoisie traditions. I regretted their lack of social consciousness. . . ." Margaret was just breaking the last of the shackles. Her father and mother had taken a lake-front apartment on Ainsley Street and she had moved in, using the money she thus saved on living expenses for the magazine. Then her father had died, leaving the purse strings in the hands of her mother. The ultimatum: give up the foolish magazine or never expect another family penny. The ultimatum was rejected and her mother packed the furniture and left the city. Margaret got in some cots and kitchen chairs and her Mason and Hamlin piano (on free loan from a dealer who enjoyed her eulogies in the *Little Review*) and the barren apartment became the first of the odd living quarters for which she would become celebrated.

Except for the dearth of furniture, Margaret probably could not have induced Emma Goldman to be a house guest. Margaret won her with a glowing account of the hardships, and then was on the point of losing her when they got to Margaret's waiting taxicab. As it happened, a drayman just then fell off his wagon. Emma crawled between the horses' legs and dragged him to safety. Whether at the man for his awkwardness or the cruel bosses for not having provided a safer seat, Emma was upset, and therefore fairly easily managed into the cab. In Margaret's memory the vehicle became a streetcar, but the strong proletarian mood upon her at the time may have transformed it; Emma held firmly that it was a taxi but in her memoirs left out the drayman, perhaps feeling the incident too small in the thick catalog of her adventures.

After she was satisfied that there really was little furniture, Emma telephoned to Big Bill Haywood, Ben Reitman, and other comrades to hurry to the apartment and be gay. To Margaret even Ben "wasn't so bad if you could hastily drop all your ideas as to how human beings should look and act." And she particularly liked Ben's good friend Mary Gallagher, who resembled a czarina and, having lived dangerously all over the world, was a trifle bored with the anarchists and IWWs. She had in mind no precise tortures for the bourgeoisie, but Margaret was sure they would be ghastly. There were rebel

girls, among whom lithe, full-bodied Eulalie Burke was the acknowledged queen. The male comrades, by and large, were hardly worth
attention. Margaret later claimed to have grown tolerant of the bad
smell of her anarchist friends. But she was never to go among their
more secret haunts—for example, the "free love flats" where the
glories of unpossessiveness were never restrained. Haywood (he
avoided the anarchists in time of trouble but had mingled with them
socially) brooded on a window ledge, talking, when he did, of rich
women's lapdogs which deprived children of food. Margaret noticed
a tear in his eye when someone recited Whitman's "Come lovely and
smiling death." Emma sang Russian folk songs, which moved Margaret deeply, and then Margaret was put at the piano and held there
by Emma for an hour's concert. Her playing stirred "a peculiar
effect, like the sight of the sea, which always made me uneasy and
restless."

Margaret irritated Haywood when a bit later she erupted in the
Little Review over the conviction in Utah of Joe Hill, the Wobbly
poet, for the murder of a storekeeper in a holdup. On Thanksgiving
Day of 1915 five thousand paraded in Chicago against the scheduled
death of Hill before a firing squad. Probably it was the form of
execution that led Margaret to call for shooting the governor of
Utah. Then, feeling the suggestion inadequate, she had demanded
impetuously, "For God's sake, why doesn't some one start the
Revolution?" Haywood replied testily when next they met that the
revolution *had* been started. Margaret did not agree. At least it was
too slow for her taste. Now she was calling the *Little Review* a
magazine of "Art and Revolution." Either because he was miffed
or thought the *Little Review* too frivolous, Bill did not give her for
publication two telegrams from Joe Hill, one guaranteed to send her
into fierce ecstasies, the other into wry shouts of laughter. The one:
"Goodbye, Bill. I die like a true-blue rebel. Don't waste any time
on mourning. Organize." The other: "It is only a hundred miles from
here to Wyoming. Can you arrange to have my body hauled to the
state line to be buried? I don't want to be found dead in Utah."

Because of the anarchy, Margaret had to give up Room 917 and
move to the less expensive Room 814. Being a smaller temple, it was
even more crowded. Among the new zealots who caught Margaret's
fancy were Alexander Kaun, called Sasha, a dark, intense political

exile from czarist Russia, reputedly a great lover and surely a passionate devotee of literature; a young Pole, Stanislaus Szuchalski, a painter and sculptor, whose beautifully chiseled strong features were framed by dark hair; Ben Hecht, a newspaper reporter, who had volubly dedicated his life to fine writing with the fond expectation of starving to death in an attic beside a pile of tattered manuscripts which would render his name magic to posterity.

Hecht was perhaps Margaret's favorite. She saw in his "pale green face" a configuration of genius. Marie Armstrong, the newspaper woman he married about this time, was to declare later that although Hecht never admitted Margaret's influence, "he would not be the genius he is today but for the straining, unearthly, hectic fires of her enthusiasm for him. She was the nurse of his earliest talents." By the time Marie Armstrong wrote of Hecht she was his ex-wife and may have touched up her portrait both with high colors and acids. She had found him "brilliant, superb company, highly sentimental, overemotional, like quicksilver in his reactions. He was also hysterical, egotistical, sadistic, unreliable, with no sincerity of belief or convictions. He pretended to scorn all social conventions as a justification for bad manners; in order to tell a good story for the press, or in private, he became a bewildering and bewitching liar. . . ."

Hecht, barely twenty when falling in with the *Little Review* group, was already a name in local journalism. Born of Russian-Jewish immigrants in the garment industry, he had grown up in Racine, Wisconsin. After finishing high school he had been taken on as a cub reporter by the Chicago *Journal* at the behest of an uncle who was a friend of the publisher. The *Journal* spiced its copy heavily with fancy, and at this Hecht was adept. He had, too, the brassy energy needed by the sensational press. Then he had moved to the *Daily News,* a better paper but given to a throbby style and imagination in feature stories.

Hecht worshipped the older journalists who wore cynicism as a proud garment or coat of mail. But he worshipped serious artists, too. Once he had looked to the violin for a career, until his talent proved too slight. He read widely, preferring the esoteric symbolism of Huysmans, Verlain, Baudelaire, and Gautier, and the novels of the darker Russians. The American realists drew him less, but he had enjoyed interviewing Dreiser during his 1912–1913 stay and recent visit. He admired Hackett and Dell as critics, and Dell by reputation as the heart of a bohemian circle. Margery Currey, falling under young Hecht's spell after joining the *Daily News* staff, had invited him to her studio parties, where he won Margaret Anderson's attention. Eager beneath his cynicism, Hecht treasured the belief of these two opinion-makers in a great future for him.

Hecht and Max Bodenheim soon fell into a kind of alliance for mocking conventions. Hecht was a vivid talker with flourishes of adjectives, adept at phrasemaking. "You can't possibly be as valiant as you look," he told Margaret as she paced an imaginary barricade proclaiming insurrection in the arts. Bodenheim was more the counterpuncher, but with a deeper hatred of the fixed order (any order) and a gift for the searing thrust. Not wanting to adjust to society—perhaps not able to—he acted out the Baudelaire role of starving dissipated poet, eating mightily when food came before him, drinking to excess, often homeless and seldom with more than a cheap room. Since Hecht and Bodenheim were a team—some said a vaudeville act—part of the aura of the carefree bohemian Bodenheim fell over his partner, who was really a steady worker, comfortable liver, and an abstainer from too much alcohol. Bodenheim was regarded by his peers as more sensitive and a better craftsman; Hecht as an unharnessed talent of nobody knew what enormous powers.

Szuchalski also lived as a poor bohemian who refused to compromise his art, was less given to posturing than Bodenheim, and had a truer pride. When ordered to remove an anti-British painting from an Art Institute exhibit of his work, he had said nothing at all but had quietly packed his canvases and sculptures and carted them away. Once in the *Little Review* office he fainted from hunger. A story grew up that he had been too proud to accept the tea and cookies which Caesar brought. This was not true; he did drink the tea and eat the cookies. Yet only his collapse had let his friends know that he was in desperate straits. He had no family. After the death of his blacksmith father (his mother had died before they came from Poland) in a street accident, he had permitted the body to be sold (to get burial funds) to a medical laboratory on condition that he be present when it was dissected. In this ghastly manner, as he was sure his father would have desired, he had furthered his knowledge of anatomy.

His studio, whether at a given time in a cheap loft or in the Jackson Park colony, became the gathering place of an informal group calling themselves the Vagabonds. The main figures were Bodenheim,

Hecht, Kaun, Sherwood Anderson, and always the girls who were their appreciators. One of the girls, a slender, quiet poet named Fedya Ramsey, achieved a certain immortality by voluntarily going to her death by riding a horse over a cliff during a western tour of the Little Theatre. A story went around that it had been for the love of a young poet; and that earlier consummation had been enough, she had felt, for her lifetime. The young poet was assumed to be Bodenheim. That he did not claim the honor was no surprise to his wiser friends, who realized that under the surface his emotions were strong and deep.

There were, of course, hundreds of others caught up in the artistic fever of Chicago in the time of the Literary Renaissance. And other gathering places were scattered through the city: the home of Mitchell Dawson, a young lawyer-poet, where Sherwood Anderson was often to be seen arranging manuscripts on a grand piano for one of his readings; Tennessee Mitchell's studio-apartment; the studio of dashing Jerome Blum, as emphatic in his opinions as were the colors in his paintings; the odorous quarters near the fruit and vegetable market of William Saphier, a poet-philosopher who called himself "the machinist"; a barnlike radical workingman's hangout called the Dill Pickle Club, which was beginning to have an influx of bohemians.

Margaret rarely went to gatherings, except for Margery Currey's parties. There was enough conversation in the *Little Review* office, and if that of the locals was insufficient, there were numerous visitors from afar. The guardians of the new temples guided famous callers to one another. Maurice Browne had appeared at the *Little Review* with Rupert Brooke, the young English poet whose fair male beauty caused passersby on Michigan Avenue to turn and stare, as they did at Margaret. William Butler Yeats, reigning poet of the English language, arrived, too, and by setting Vachel Lindsay among the world's great modern poets startled and pleased those who believed in Chicago and the Middle West as a seat of new literature.

One day Harriet Monroe ushered into Margaret's office a very large woman who, although youngish, was dressed in the old style of *Godey's Lady's Book*. This was Amy Lowell. She had a particular interest in Margaret and the *Little Review*. Amy was at war with Ezra Pound, which meant that *Poetry* was in the line of fire. She was out to capture the Imagist movement. Margaret liked the

Imagists, as did, of course, Harriet Monroe. But Pound had the movement as well as Harriet in hand. Amy needed an organ; the *Little Review* would do. Amy had funds in supply; Margaret was worse than broke.

The important guest from afar looked over her Roman nose and asked in her masterful contralto if the *Little Review* would accept a subsidy of one hundred and fifty dollars a month? No strings, only that Amy would edit the poetry section, dictate nothing else. The Roman Emperor was up against the Cold Queen of the North. Certainly not. Why not? Margaret explained that she did not care for associates. This was not of course precisely true; she merely wanted them on her own terms. Amy was furious, naturally, but concealed her feeling reasonably well and invited Margaret to lunch the next day in her suite at The Annex.

Amy Lowell was a match for any of the Chicago peacocks. Margaret found her resting in an enormous armchair, smoking a magnificent cigar. Luncheon was served in the hotel apartment and Amy had brought a retinue of servants. After lunch she ordered a minion to call a cab, and invited Margaret to go with her to the Fine Arts Building where her photograph was to be taken. Margaret pointed out that the Fine Arts Building was hardly more than across the street, and besides could be reached through the underground passageways. Much, much too far to walk. And so they went by taxi.

Before leaving Chicago, Amy proved, if Margaret had any doubts, that she could be dictatorial. Maurice Browne had invited her to be the honored speaker at a Little Theatre Open House. Inasmuch as a full crowd was expected, he limited her to a single guest. She appeared with several, and stood at the rear of the house baying until the embarrassed occupants of a row vacated. The mortified Browne soon had even a worse moment. He introduced Amy as she waited in the wings. The aperture to the stage, as it turned out, was too narrow for her to get through. As she went around and came down the aisle and mounted the platform by its front steps, the onlookers were notably silent.

Margaret chose the magazine's poetry, like everything else, by the sound it made in her inner ear. A good example of the editor at work was her handling of a verse by a high-school lad, Mark Turbyfill. A copy of the *Little Review* had fallen into his hands, and, like young Zwaska, he had fallen in love with it. He brought a poem to

Margaret on the excuse of ordering a book, as she had pleaded with readers to contribute their book trade for its profit margin. The memory of the experience of Margaret—the unearthly blue eyes, the crown of golden hair, the regal presence filling the tiny room— was to be startlingly vivid to him after fifty years. The book order taken, she looked through the poem and handed down judgment. "Work hard for three more years and you'll be ready for the *Little Review*."

Only three weeks later Turbyfill braved the office with another poem, "Amber Monochrome." Margaret read quickly.

> I pass
> Outside into the amber night.
>
> A lamp within
> Prints shadow-flowers
> On the stiffness of an amber screen.
>
> My dream is like that—
> An amber scheme
> Straining through cold, stiff screens.

"This is it," Margaret announced. "I was crazy to say three years and here it is three weeks." Then, finding the boy puzzled by the works of one of her favorite contributors, "H. D.," Margaret resorted to gasps to explain that it all came down to beauty. Without having much idea of what had been said, Turbyfill suddenly appreciated "H. D." fully.

Outside the office, Margaret went on clashing with bourgeois notions, often landing herself in the press. During the summer of 1915 she pitched a tent camp on the wooded shore of Lake Michigan north of the city at Lake Bluff. With her sister and her sister's two children and her maid and Harriet Dean and Caesar Zwaska she lived happily, delighted especially by early morning swimming. Of course the retreat was denounced by the area's stuffier dwellers as outlandish, and maybe illegal (for squatting on public land). Margaret found herself at odds with the police, who finally burned the camp as news photographers snapped pictures. The residents, who had already left, moved into a nearby house for the winter and all might have gone well except that a nostalgic Christmas mood settled on Margaret and she went out and chopped down an evergreen tree. It was on a neighbor's estate. Later on he forgave her and they became friends, but not until after her arrest—with attendant press notices.

A thorn for Margaret was the residence in the neighborhood of Bert Leston Taylor, the B. L. T. of the *Tribune's* "Line o' Type" column. He admiringly nicknamed her "The Colonel" and made her a public character even when she was out of the news.

19

Poems Written Half in Jest

FOR Lee Masters the year 1914 had started inauspiciously and worse, if his mood were taken into account. With Woodrow Wilson in the White House he had allowed himself to entertain hopes of a federal judgeship. Life tenure at a good salary would bring him ease of mind and the leisure, he thought, for a writing program. One handicap was that, never a Wilson admirer, he had not been active in the campaign. Most of his political connections, in fact, went back to Bryan and older times. He would feel the appointment within his grasp, be put off, then have to start wrangling again. Meanwhile he strained at the law, his back bowed at the moment for a waitresses' union hamstrung by an injunction forbidding picketing.

An indirect gain from the litigation was the visit to his office of a poet, and he would trade a hundred lawyers for a poet, especially a talkative one. Carl Sandburg arrived as a reporter for the Chicago *Day-Book*, a small tabloid with labor sympathies, to inquire about progress. Sandburg was an avid visitor, and from pockets stuffed with clippings was usually able to produce an interesting topic. One day he had with him a poem signed Webster Ford, torn from a copy of *Reedy's Mirror*. He, too, was a reader and contributor to the paper, and somehow knew that Webster Ford was the pen name of Masters, who readily confessed to the authorship. His camouflage was only against those who might believe a poet a fumbler in the law. The poem was one of those few used by Reedy for friendship's sake.

Sandburg always had a bundle of his own verse about his person. He handed a wad over, and Masters was amazed to find some describing the most common people and sights and sounds of the city. He was nonplussed. They did not fit his idea of proper subject matter for poetry. In others aimed at beauty and such traditional poetic feelings Masters saw much to admire. It was enough that two poets had come together. The result was talk, much talk, each being a good listener. In common they had political insurgency, memories of a deep emotional response to Bryan's Cross of Gold speech and the martyrdom of Altgeld. They took long walks together, and if Masters shared little of Sandburg's interest in the proletarian aspects of the city, at least he became aware of the artists and writers who in ever-growing numbers were frequenting the little restaurants and saloons in which the two stopped for coffee or beer. It was borne in upon Masters, accustomed, at forty-five, to other men of large affairs in staider atmospheres, that the air of Chicago was being stirred by fresh breezes.

When Dreiser came in the spring, Masters arranged an expedition by train to visit one of the older natives of the Sangamon-Spoon River country. Eight years had passed since his conception of a novel about that land and people. It had grown bigger in his mind as the sad thought bore in that he would be lucky to produce one good book. Dreiser was not, however, being consciously guided to this past for his opinion as a novelist. Masters only wanted to treat him to the flavor of the old neighborhoods and people. Dreiser had been intrigued especially by the prospect of talking with the son of the Jack and Hannah Armstrong in whose New Salem home Lincoln had boarded. The Armstrongs ran all through the Lincoln story. As a youth he had wrestled Jack, later had gotten a son, Duff, acquitted in a trial for murder by showing in an almanac that the moon was not as bright on the night of the crime as a witness had said, and as Civil War President had expedited the return of still another son, a soldier who was ill, after a letter of appeal from Hannah.

As it happened, the surviving son, also named Jack, had moved from the New Salem region a hundred miles to the village of Oakland east of Springfield. Thus Dreiser missed a view of the Sangamon-Spoon River country. But in Armstrong the promise of the journey was fulfilled. Jack was an old-time fiddler, like Hannah's brother, Fiddler Jones, a folk hero of Masters' boyhood. In the Armstrong cottage the men sat around the tall, nickel-trimmed, isinglassed base burner with its sumptuous heap of glowing coals as Jack's wife served coffee and doughnuts and he told stories or fiddled "I've Fetched Your Wagon Home" and others. Dreiser smiled and stitched his handkerchief and plied the old man with questions and requests for more.

At home in Chicago, the Masters couple were living in a state of neutrality. Helen participated in the Hyde Park social life and was a gracious hostess for dinners and parties. As a wife he could not really fault her; it was only that the state of matrimony was not exciting enough for him. He enjoyed the children and they were devoted to him—the more so because of his air of Olympian preoccupation. To the outsider his feeling of being put upon would never have been suspected. Rather, he looked and acted the benevolent patriarch of an earlier time. And gradually he was adjusting to the role, if only from resignation. While age crept upon him, Fate kept him cornered without strain. Word arrived that he would not receive the federal judgeship. And so the road to another attack on the citadels of literature was blocked. For several years he had seen no gain in laying out cash for publication of his works, only to have them ignored.

This was the situation in May of 1914 when his mother came for a visit. The old conflicts between them had been forgotten. They could laugh over the literary rivalry of a quarter of a century ago. She was full of tales of Petersburg and Lewistown people, relating them with the spice he had not before wholly appreciated. He admired, and envied, his father's male dominance and flair, but his mother's insights were deeper, and her wit—as he knew from old scars—the more cutting. Then, too, he was at an age for reminiscence.

These forces were at work when, after putting his mother on a train for home, he went to his bedroom-study and sat down at his mahogany table-desk. (It was the afternoon of Saturday, May 20.) Other forces were busy. Reedy had often exhorted him to write about the things he knew. Tennessee Mitchell had downgraded his "fairy tales," while expressing realistic, often caustic, views of people and events. Reedy often directed him to books and once had caused him to buy—or perhaps had given him—a copy of *The Greek Anthology*. At any rate he had owned the book for five or six years. The songs, poems, epigrams, gravestone inscriptions, and epitaphs had intrigued him. Only a month ago in a letter to Dreiser he had recommended it as a "good book for spring days—for the mood when one watches a craw-fish." In their conversations Dreiser had told of his youthful nature enthrallment, and Masters had enclosed a little poem in free verse which had "Theodore the Poet" sitting on the bank of the "turbid Spoon" waiting for a crawfish to emerge from its burrow. In his letter he had added that in *The Greek Anthology* Dreiser would see the original "of which the enclosed is my imitation."

He had been influenced also by the free verse of the Imagists appearing in *Poetry*—in spite of his scorn of the magazine for the failure of its editors to ask him to contribute. Too, Sandburg's unrhymed verses about Chicago may have impressed him more than he had admitted to himself. The free verse form was of course familiar in Whitman, the choruses of Greek tragedies, and portions of Shakespeare and Goethe. As a kind of joke on Reedy he inked a title: *Spoon River Anthology*. Then he continued in a vein serious enough to him, but which he realized might be taken as ludicrous. In any except very flat country all graveyards are built on slopes, and he titled his poem "The Hill." In the course of lamenting the deaths of a dozen-odd individuals he inserted the occasional refrain, "All, all, are sleeping on the hill," or a variation. After twenty lines he ended with Old Fiddler Jones, who babbled of ancient fish frys and horse races at Clary's Grove.

Of all the people named, only Fiddler Jones was heard speaking from the grave, and his actual words were not reported. The prospect of the dead rising to speak for themselves, while not a new literary device, was too fascinating to pass up. (The poem "Theodore the Poet" had been *to* him; the subject had neither been dead nor did he speak.) Now the ghost of one Cassius (much later amended to Cassius Hueffer) was summoned to address the living. He told of the words on his tombstone describing him as a gentle spirit with mixed elements in him. He confessed that in truth he had warred on life and been slain; that it was just his luck to have an epitaph written by a fool.

Who was the model for Cassius? Plainly the author himself, after Fate, weary of toying with him in the corner, had laid him under the sod. Who, after all, felt more put upon than Masters? Whose solar plexus writhed in greater pain as the elements warred within him, and he warred on life? And who presented to the world a facade of more placid rectitude, if not gentleness? It would be just like some fool to engrave such an epitaph on the tombstone of a slain lawyer-poet.

Of the characters leaping to mind, he selected that day and the

next, six more for epitaphs of from eight to sixteen lines. In the longest—and on the same theme—an "Unknown" told from an unmarked
grave of having in boyhood caged a broken-winged hawk, and of now
searching Hades for its soul to offer the friendship of one whom
life had also wounded and caged. Hod Putt spoke wryly of having
sought to emulate Old Bill Piersol, grown rich from trading with the
Indians and richer by taking the bankrupt law, by robbing a traveler
near Proctor's Grove; the victim had been inadvertently killed and
Hod hanged, which he said had been his way of taking the bankrupt
law; now he and Old Bill slept peacefully side by side. (Proctor's
Grove, like Clary's Grove of "The Hill," was a real place known to
young Masters.) Chase Henry, the town drunkard, given his chance
to speak, found a comforting irony in lying close to the grave of
the banker, Nicholas. Serepta the Scold (changed afterward to
Serepta Mason) lamented a bitter wind that had stunted her life's
petals, concealing from all her flowering side. Amanda (later Amanda
Barker) swore that her husband, knowing childbirth would be fatal,
had got her with child to gratify his hatred. Ollie McGee testified
to the long, cold horror of an unhappy marriage. She told of her
husband walking with haggard countenance through the village due
to the secret cruelty heaped upon her until, broken, she had gone to
the grave.

Here was the beginning of a story. What of the husband's side of
the argument? Surely he must have one. For the time being Masters
did nothing about it, but had the eight poems typed at his office and
sent them to Reedy, signed Webster Ford. Having found pleasure in
the composition, he was prepared to go on no matter if his friend
sent back the customary, or even more raucous, jibes. It occurred
to him that, developed into a longish series—the range of characters
appeared to him nearly limitless—they might stand for his long-
projected novel. No matter. After thirty years of pouring his genius
into reams of verse and drama only to have it received in silence or
worse by idiots and fools, he was not apt to be deterred by a friend
who was plagued with a blind spot.

Reedy fired back a letter so hot with praise that Masters read into
it the worst: the editor was guying him. Then came the *Mirror* itself
(May 29, 1914), with the verses given two-thirds of a page. The
magazine had only twenty 15 x 18-inch pages, the usual number,
and roughly a quarter of the space was filled with advertisements.
On each week's cover—of the same stock as the inner pages—was a

large drawing of a red clown gazing into a mirror, along with the title and a slogan, "The Mid-West Weekly" and the "5¢" price. Reedy's own "Reflections" always filled a page and sometimes two or more at the beginning of the text, and in the back were theatrical and book reviews scattered among the advertisements. Between were a few stories and poems and sketches, many of them clipped from U.S. and British journals and books or translated from those in foreign languages.

Masters' series began on page six under a single-column heading, "Spoon River Anthology." This was halfway down the third and last column, and the series ran a column and a half on page seven. Hod Putt led off, followed in order by Ollie McGee, The Unknown, Cassius, Serepta the Scold, Amanda, and Chase Henry, each with a Roman numeral. Then came "The Hill," unnumbered. Masters had intended the last to be first, but Reedy had either made the switch because none of the six speakers were named in "The Hill," or had inadvertently sent them to the printer in reverse order and hadn't seen the proofs.

It occurred to Masters that Reedy might still be indulging a grandiose whim, or had gone crazy. Why argue? If more were wanted, and Reedy had said he wanted them, then let him get ready for an avalanche. The verses were great fun to write, the characters tumbling as happily to the backs of old envelopes during odd moments in court as to manuscript paper at his study desk. At bedside he kept a pencil and pad for jotting down notes of sequences that leaped into his mind unsummoned.*

Reedy demonstrated his faith by running all of the poems sent, often a whole page of them. The letters of praise raining in were forwarded to Masters, who, beginning to take the affair seriously, proposed to change the overall title. He was drawing many subjects from the Sangamon as well as the Spoon River country, and others were based at least partly on people known in Chicago and elsewhere. The geography, however, had little to do with his feeling about the title. He simply considered it frivolous. Spoon River was an odd name—and who ever heard of it? If the "anthology" theme was to be continued, he liked better "Pleasant Plains Anthology" or some-

---

* No one more than Edgar Lee Masters ever wanted to be a figure in the annals of literature. It is therefore with regret that I am unable to provide excerpts from *Spoon River* and must direct the reader, for gaining a fuller impact of this chronicle, to the work itself. It seems to me to be one of the final ironies of Masters' life and history.

thing else with a rural or prairie tone. But Reedy objected thunderously to any change, and Masters dropped the argument.

Perhaps the most striking of the epitaphs were uttered by wastrels. Many were thus defined by the solid citizens resting in the cemetery, others by the author from his inside knowledge and point of view. Spoon River gradually took shape as a county seat town like Petersburg or Lewistown, with its persuasive weekly newspaper editor (persuasive for his own gain), powerful banker (the bank inwardly shaky), morals-bossing preachers and deacons and others of the "better element" who in life had scourged the weak and less fortunate and now lay under the ground with them. The author's viewpoint was expressed by contrasting the selfish "high-muckety-mucks" with Daisy Fraser, the town prostitute, who contributed ten dollars to the school fund every time she was haled into court.

He was scornful of Editor Whedon, who wore a Greek mask while perverting truth in his eight-page paper; Deacon Taylor, thought to have succumbed from eating watermelon but in truth from cirrhosis of the liver; the unnamed Circuit Judge, deaf in his life to justice but at last knowing that his soul was less clean than murderer Hod Putt's; John M. Church, the wire-pulling lawyer from the "Q" railroad who beat the claims of the crippled and the widows; Anthony Findlay, born in poverty, risen to wealth by grinding the faces of the working people, who from the grave still insisted that the strong must have power over the weak; Banker Rhodes, whose cashier, acting as his instrument, went to prison for gambling with the bank's money on wheat; Henry Phipps, Sunday school superintendent and dummy for Banker Rhodes in various schemes; A. D. Blood, eternal haler of Daisy Fraser before Justice Arnett, who now found his grave the pillow of unholy lovers.

Even more effective were the poignant ironies arising from the author's interwoven stories of the lives of the dwellers on The Hill. There was Knolt (later Knowlt) Hoheimer, who, as a bullet entered his heart at Missionary Ridge, wished he had remained at home and gone to jail for stealing hogs; but Lydia Puckett knew that Knolt had stolen the hogs after catching her "running" with Lucius Atherton, the lady killer (who ended in the cemetery a pitiful superannuated Don Juan). George Trimble had talked bravely from the Court House steps for the single tax and free silver, but his wife, insisting that he must prove himself a moral man before the town, had driven him to advocate Prohibition, whereupon he was distrusted by the radicals and not accepted by the conservatives. Adam Weirauch, the butcher, had fought for Altgeld while Editor Whedon slandered him, but nevertheless the editor had been given a state job both had sought; then Weirauch, trying to recoup his losses, was elected to the legislature and sold his vote to Yerkes on the streetcar franchise, and was caught.

Masters had cut wide open the U.S. small town—in particular the Midwestern town—to show base deeds and secret heartbreaks. He knew such aspects of the towns, of course. His father knew them. His mother knew them. So did tens of thousands of others who had lived or still lived in them. But use of the knowledge—especially in a mordant, even racy, fashion—was outside the American literary tradition. Thirty years ago a Kansas editor, E. W. Howe, had shown the grim side of the village in his novel *The Story of a Country Town,* and Hamlin Garland had dealt with harsh facts of rural life. But neither had gone directly to psychological conflicts, least of all to frankly sexual conflicts. Masters was in a sense free of traditions and pressures. After all, he had begun the verses for his own pleasure and release without worry about publication. And he wrote under the cover of a pseudonym. Let Reedy, that uninhibited soul with surely the toughest hide in the literary world, take the brunt if he wanted to.

In the early "garlands"—as each group after the first was labeled —the positive and good were largely ignored. The strong characters had misused their powers, the idealists had come to grief. The only exception was Lucinda Matlock, who, driving home one June moonlit night, changed partners and found Davis; they had married and lived happily together for seventy years, raising twelve children undaunted by hardships.

Lucinda was based on his grandmother, who had indeed found Davis Masters by exchanging partners, although it was during a winter's sleighride. Since she was the person he admired over all others, he could not present her as different from the way he knew her.

Spring had given way to summer and Masters wrote on. Reedy was abroad but had left word that all the Spoon River material provided should be used. At the end of July the *Mirror* noted that "cognoscente everywhere" were proclaiming the verses. Indeed, they were being widely reprinted. In August, Edward J. Wheeler, president of the Poetry Society of America, lauded the work in *Current*

Opinion, of which he was editor. And in October Masters had the satisfaction of reading a tribute by Harriet Monroe in *Poetry.* "Mr. Webster Ford unites something of the feeling and method of the *Greek Anthology* with a trace of the spirit of Villon." True, she entered a qualification, a mildly snobbish one deriving perhaps from her Chicago birth and world travels. "But the 'tradition' has only served to lead him to a little cemetery in a small town—it might be any small town—in the United States, where death reveals life in a series of brief tragic epitaphs." She reprinted "The Hill," "Doc Hill," and "Ollie McGee." This did not satisfy "the authority in London," Pound, who was excited by Spoon River and demanded that she "get some of Webster Ford's stuff."

For Masters the hiding of his light under a bushel was not an easy thing. Aside from his family and his secretary, a young man named Jacob Prassel, who waited with glowing eyes to type each new draft, only Sandburg had intimately followed the writing. He dropped in from time to time for news of the waitresses' union litigation (Masters lost the case, owing, he decided, to the animosity of a Presbyterian—and Philistine—judge, which didn't brighten his outlook on the religious money-grubbers of the town he was creating), or simply to trade poetry manuscripts. The mordant vein and the psychological probing were out of Sandburg's general sphere of composition. But he said that the Spoon River characters and events were true to life of the small towns and that the poetry was finely wrought.

Masters allowed his identity as the author to be made known to Harriet Monroe, and she, apologizing for never having heard of his early poetry, took his longish "Silence," not in the Spoon River manner, for the December issue, to be signed not Webster Ford but Edgar Lee Masters. To emerge from behind the pseudonym and acknowledge *Spoon River* was a different matter. Already it was being denounced as cynical and sexy and agnostic, and surely there was a certain disrespect for organized religion and the fixed society. Not that unpopular attitudes were necessarily bad for his career. With Darrow he had done very well in grappling from below. And he was still in the tradition—better off in a way, since Darrow had lost the confidence of the labor unions in the McNamara case and was not in this field of litigation. Yet—who could trust a poet in a rough-and-tumble fight? A benign set of verses in *Poetry* was one thing. By now it was apparent that the author of *Spoon River,* if ever revealed, would become famous—and probably notorious.

By late autumn Macmillan was offering, in letters to the hidden author passed through the *Mirror,* to issue the verses as a book. Many firms were importuning Reedy, who had returned from Europe, to flush his poet into the open. Masters had no objection, of course, to the wider audience and the money that a book would provide. The question was simply that of camouflage. The Macmillan editors felt that the book's success would be far greater under the author's real name, whatever it was. Reedy did, too, and he hated to lose the full benefit of what looked to be his one major literary find. He came from St. Louis to argue the matter. They debated for most of a night. Surely Masters was not concerned with more than the question of the worth of *Spoon River* as literature, or acceptance by critics and the discriminating public of it as literature. His mind had been torn to painful shreds all his life by a desire for acceptance as an author. Others may have struggled more valiantly for recognition without gaining it, but, owing to the rawness of his nerves, few had suffered more.

Reedy had no trouble marshaling arguments that literature, even of a controversial nature, does not of itself destroy a man in another field. Brand Whitlock had written novels attacked as too realistic and yet had been mayor of Toledo and now was U.S. minister to Belgium. Although Morris Hillquit's books on socialism were reviled, he had a rich New York law practice. Darrow had waxed on iconoclasm, published a novel, and now without modifying his views was rebuilding his practice—with corporations as his clients. Take even Dreiser —had *Sister Carrie* barred him from the editorship of a big popular magazine? True, not many poets had been equipped for other fields. Yet William Cullen Bryant had been a famous poet and co-owner and editor of a New York daily newspaper. All such arguments were really beside the point. Masters was convinced of what he wanted to be convinced of: that *Spoon River* might have the power to toss Fate aside and let him out of the corner. He gave in.

Reedy announced the true author with a mighty grandiloquence in the issue of November 20. One sentence gave both the gist of the long article and the measure of his style. "Literary folk in this country and Europe have almost shown anger that the author of such a work, splendid in observation, marvelous in the artistry of exclusion, yet of democratic inclusiveness, piercingly analytic of character, of plastic fictility of handling, sympathetic yet universal— such as *Comédie Humaine*—such a creation of a whole community

of personalities, as distinct from, let us say, the 'characters' of
Theophrastus or Sir Thomas Overbury—should be kept concealed
under a pseudonym." The "garland" in that issue nevertheless was
signed Webster Ford.

The following week there was no *Spoon River,* but Reedy printed
Carl Sandburg's "Tribute to Webster Ford":

> A man wrote two books.
>
> One held in its covers the outside man,
>   whose name was on a Knox College diploma,
>   who bought his clothes at Marshall Field's,
>   had his name done by a sign painter in gilt
>   and never did any damage to the code of morals
>   set forth by the Chicago *Tribune.*
>
> The other book held a naked man,
>   the sheer brute under the clothes
>   as he will be stripped at the Last Day,
>   and inside man with red heartbeats
>   that go on ticking off life
>   against the ribs.
>
> Scratched into portraits here are the
>   villagers, all those who walked on
>   Main Street, the folks he knew down on the
>   Illinois prairies where his grandmother
>   raised eleven boys and life was a
>   repetition of corn and hogs.
>
> The shadow of his soul touched the shadows
>   of their souls as he loved them and his
>   fingers knew something about the fine
>   dust of their blood after they are dead
>   and the strangeness of dreams that haunt
>   their graves.

The poet was to be forgiven awarding his friend a college diploma
and somewhat confusing the number of children his grandmother
bore with those actually raised.

For a new garland in the December 4 issue the name Edgar Lee
Masters was substituted for Webster Ford without fanfare. After
realizing that in one way or another the poems would go into a book,
and especially after deciding to use his own name, Masters turned

more and more to characters whose lives had been admirable, even beautiful, and whose philosophy was deep or at least not laced with irony. For writing these he had gone back to mood music, provided either by his wife at the piano or by a phonograph. For the profounder themes he usually put on Beethoven's Fifth Symphony. Among the characters were Seth Compton, who had built a circulating library on the premise that one must know evil to know good and the false to know the truth; John Hancock Otis, born rich, who had devoted himself to the cause of liberty while Anthony Findlay, born poor, had ground the faces of labor; Isaiah Beethoven, who, dying, had crept to Bernadotte and allowed the soul of Spoon River to enter his own soul; Aaron Hatfield, based on his grandfather, speaking in Concord Church.

They would help balance the work, but also they were his favorites. The wide acceptance of the poems as literature had allowed him to go to what he felt was deeper music.

Masters broke into the epitaphs (he had earlier tossed in "Theodore the Poet," the only nonspeaker) with a long poem of some three hundred lines titled "The Spooniad," which was supposed to be a fragment of an epic by Jonathan Swift Somers, the town laureate, describing a battle between the forces of light and darkness. Then, on January 15, eight and a half months after the series had begun, the end came fittingly with the epitaph of "Webster Ford." It gave a veiled yet precise explanation for the author's sudden dash into the hazardous open ground. In "Webster Ford's" boyhood the Delphic Apollo had called him to a life of song, and the call had gone unanswered out of fear. Apollo had been silent until "Webster Ford" the man had been numbed by life, then had called once more. This time he had answered, and now in lamenting the wasted years he told the living young that to fly the call of Apollo was vain. It was better to leap into the fire and die with a song of spring rather than to expire after dull years of sorrow.

Thus for Masters, to answer the Delphic Apollo's call at forty-six and chance a fiery death while seeking a crown of laurels was preferable to death from atrophy.

A few months later, as Macmillan was about to publish the book, Masters received an accolade unprecedented for a new author. The New York *Times* had sent its Chicago correspondent to interview him, and the result appeared not in the book review but in the magazine section, as if ranked above ordinary literary matter. In a way it was the most flattering attention given to any of the six writers. The few long paeans to Dreiser had been in *Smart Set* and the *Friday Literary Review* and other organs usually considered avant-garde. (Dreiser had found a publisher for *The Titan* in the John Lane Company, an English firm with a branch in the U.S.; but the public reaction had not been up to that for *The Financier*.) The article about Lindsay in *Collier's* had celebrated him more as a curiosity than as a major poet. (Now Macmillan had taken Lindsay's book *The Congo and Other Poems,* induced him to drop the somewhat awkward "Nicholas" from his signature, and was ready to promote him as the troubadour reciting his poetry to women's clubs, college literary societies, and other groups on the lecture circuit.)

The *Times* article was in the issue of April 4 (eleven days before release of the book). Across a page of the magazine section was blazoned: "Spoon River Poet Called Great." Just below ran the lines: "Famous English Critic Lifts Edgar Lee Masters from Chicago Obscurity to the High Peak of Parnassus." The critic was John Cowper Powys, who had known the lusty spirit of Chicago's artistic bohemia in the Little Theatre tearoom. Dreiser had sent him the page proofs of *Spoon River* and he had used them as the basis for a New York lecture. Ranking Masters and Edwin Arlington Robinson and Arthur Davison Ficke as the three major U.S. poets, he had described Masters as "the natural child of Walt Whitman" and the "aboriginal American poet." The comments served as an excellent takeoff for the *Times'* Chicago man—who didn't get a byline. For illustration he had accepted an old photograph of Masters in which, with the rimless spectacles and brushed hair and earnest expression, he seemed a likelier candidate for a Ph.D. than for an aboriginal poet of the prairies.

The reporter had come upon his subject in what he described as Masters' library (actually the parlor), sitting before a blazing log; he was recovering from a bout with pneumonia. Duly noted were the broad shoulders which gave Masters an unpoetical look. "He is a modest and unassuming man," the reporter said, "very much wrapped up in his home and his family, who writes poetry as a diversion at such times as he can tear himself away from a busy and successful law practice." A reporter usually gets and writes a story the way he is expected to, and a certain amount of dissembling by the subject is acceptable. Masters was plainly out to protect his lawyer image from too much encroachment by the poet. He got into the reporter's account his reputation as an underdog lawyer (no enemy of Socialists but finding something lacking in their program) and a defender of labor unions—indeed he had gained inspiration for *Spoon River* in his fight for waitresses arrested for picketing Loop restaurants. If indeed a worthy poet, as Mr. Powys insisted, it was, he declared, a somewhat accidental by-product, for he was primarily a lawyer quite able to rough it up for his deprived clients.

On April 15, *Spoon River* exploded in the marketplace as no book of poetry had ever done. The first printing seemed to vanish into the air. Macmillan hurried the book back to press in May, July, twice in August, in September, twice in October, three times in December —and the end was not in sight. Masters now added two score new epitaphs and an epilogue for a new edition with illustrations by Oliver Herford, including the statue of a nude woman in a fountain and a voluptuous Daisy Fraser stepping off with the undertaker. By March 1916 the *Literary Digest* was able to report, in a page-and-a-half article, that a British edition was rocking England, with the London *Nation* calling it "the most remarkable product of America since Walt Whitman first published *Leaves of Grass.*" Translators were busy getting it ready in a dozen foreign languages.

The critics warred mightily. Dell, writing in the *New Republic* immediately after publication, touched both sides of the conflict. "It is a book which whether one likes it or not, one must respect. Whether the art of this book has any relation to the art of poetry is a delicate question. In reading the Spoon River 'anthology' one feels that its author's high ironic attitude toward life cuts him off from appreciation of what is perhaps the most fundamental and characteristic thing in America—a humorous faith, a comedic courage, a gay and religious confidence in the goodness of things." A writer in Chicago's *Dial* lambasted Masters for having "crept like a reptile through slime and evil"—which might exist but oughtn't to be the subject of literature. Another disagreed, holding that "glossing over the black horrors of a chaotic universe" only turned the perceptive from literature. In the *Forum*, Willard Huntington Wright, a protégé of H. L. Mencken and an imitator of his style, was perhaps the harshest critic. Irritated by the "babble set in motion," he found the verses unrealistic—too few details, not lyrical, unvital and cutaneous, psychologically superficial . . ." In the same number William

Stanley Braithwaite, a leading critic of poetry, hailed Masters for his accurate vision and his irony and pathos.

So the battle went, with the fame of Masters growing with every blow struck. When Powys lectured on *Spoon River* at the Little Theatre, the author, who so short a time before had ached for glory, sat in a curtained box lest the knowledge of his presence distract the audience. Now he was welcomed into the *Poetry* circle of Harriet Monroe, Eunice Tietjens, Alice Corbin Henderson, Helen Hoyt, Agnes Lee—the last two being poets recently added to the staff. Mrs. William Vaughn Moody gave him a place of honor in her swing-hung drawing room, although he was not poetic enough in looks and manner for her taste and she was too domineering for his. Margaret Anderson found him a great cutup and called him "Thackeray" because of a certain physical resemblance to the English novelist.

Masters had waited until the winter after *Spoon River*'s publication before acceding to demands to visit New York and "let the people see me." True, he had been convalescing and then had been occupied with the new verses and epilogue for the "definitive" edition of his book. Also, a rich legal plum had come within his reach, and by a mustering of will he had forced himself to pluck it. For a month he was at the bright center of the burgeoning Greenwich Village literary world. Now Dreiser cordially danced attention upon *him,* as did Elaine Hyman-Kirah Markham. At last he met Hackett, increasing his reputation as a critic on the *New Republic,* and Dell, who had joined the staff of the *Masses.* There were, as Masters said later, "Pretty women all about me, all in a mood of light-hearted sportiveness, all interested in me as the new man of the hour." He had gone to New York alone. But the emotional drain of writing *Spoon River* plus that of his bout with pneumonia and his legal struggles was greater than he had realized. "I was taken for a cold man, for a sexless man, for a woman hater, and all the while I was just an ill man."

20

For Sandburg, a Taste of Glory

CARL SANDBURG'S "Chicago Poems," starting in the March 1914 number of *Poetry*, had encouraged Masters to persist in Spoon River's unorthodox form. But for Sandburg the morsel of fame was to be all for the moment, and it contained some ashes and grit. Traditionalists had been appalled by what they called plain ugliness, not to mention lack of beat or measure. Among the scoffers was Chatfield-Taylor, wagging his head over the magazine he had helped found.

To understand the genesis of the "Chicago Poems" it is necessary to go back to Sandburg's migration in 1912 from Milwaukee, planned for years but hurried by the offer of a job on a Socialist daily when a lockout closed the regular press, and then to follow him for a year or two. Into account must be taken Sandburg's ambivalent proletarian habits and his urge to get up in the world. Much of Sandburg's youth had been spent, after all, in a desperate effort simply to establish himself in a muscle-labor trade. Deep-ingrained patterns are not easily shaken off. And how could he be sure that, barely out of the sweat-of-the-brow ranks, he would stay up? No wonder he thought he had married above himself—or that his wife's family thought so, too.

The getting-up-in-the-world portion of Sandburg's nature was expressed in his admiration for Elbert Hubbard, who had been a wealthy soap manufacturer before retiring at thirty-five to devote himself to art and spiritual uplift. Hubbard's paean to stick-to-it-iveness, *A Message to Garcia*, had been flung by employers to their underlings by the hundreds of thousands and put into school readers. True, highbrows regarded the little man as a pseudo-intellectual. *The Philistine*, his magazine, nevertheless circulated widely and his inspirational *Little Journeys* to the homes of the great sold in the millions. He professed to be a follower of William Morris, the English socialist-poet-romanticist, and thus by inference a crusader for the plain people.

As long ago as 1905, Sandburg, angered by the refusal of the intellectuals to take his hero seriously, had lashed back with "The Subjugation of Elbert Hubbard" in a Chicago magazine called *Tomorrow*. "Under the dome back of his forehead," Sandburg had written of his idol, "he chased out the bats, the night moths, chickens, pigeons and ambitions for millions. He let in eagles." Sandburg then inquired: "Why revert to history and follow the styles of Voltaire or of Hugo? Why revivify the suppression of Emile Zola? Why not watch the subjugation of Elbert Hubbard?"

Total emulation of the soapmaker-sage of East Aurora was out of the question, naturally. At thirty-five Sandburg had no business, let alone a profitable one, to retire from. Ironically, his efforts to climb the bourgeoisie ladder—as a stereoscopic-slide peddler, advertising man, arts lecturer on Whitman—had failed; only as a radical had he made a living, poor as it was, and won a bit of status as secretary to Milwaukee's Socialist mayor. Yet it was logical. He could not separate the different elements in himself for a sustained drive for money. The elements were seen even in his appearance. With slickum holding his thick, dark straw hair in a pompadour, and in a freshly pressed suit with celluloid collar and a necktie, he might have been taken for a businessman—the enterprising owner, say, of a machine shop. But the trousers would soon bag around the legs, as if the knees were sprung from heavy lifting or from years of walking behind a plow. His longish spare body was bent at the waist (he liked to say from capitalists standing on his shoulders) and he moved with a deliberation suggesting an old middleweight who had absorbed too many punches. Since bright light hurt his eyes, he wore a visored cap much like a trolley motorman's, wore it at his desk as well as in the sunshine. His tugging at the visor made it broken or otherwise misshapen.

He rarely slicked down his hair, or, for that matter, bothered to comb it. When left alone it fell from a part right of center to the sides and a little forward. Combing was handled nicely by the fingers. He wore roomy shoes—brogans—because he was a great walker, partly to save carfare, more because he liked to tramp the streets.

When not dressed up he moved easily in the byways of the masses, seeing, feeling, eavesdropping, trading opinions, sucking up the emotions of the vast submerged population. There was no "rubbing shoulders." He was a proletarian who could be partly smothered but never eliminated.

When the Socialist *World,* for which he worked, went out of business, Sandburg nevertheless planted his feet again on the bourgeois ladder. While in Milwaukee he had written two articles on prevention of industrial accidents. These helped get him a job on *System,* which had a large audience of prosperous business men. The wages of thirty-five dollars a week were his top earnings to date and he was given the title of associate editor. The same company issued *Factory* and other publications.

Here was opportunity. The old ailment began to act up. He couldn't isolate and harness his commercial drive. The radical proletarian kept striding in and making him, in the opinion of the higher editors, overdefensive of the working man and critical of the businessman. The result was a good deal of office hassling, and after a few months Sandburg quit. Yet he wasn't quite ready to let go of the ladder. He got a job editing a hardware trade journal. Neither he nor the bosses were happy for long. In the midst of these tribulations he had visited Floyd Dell at his Jackson Park studio in the autumn of 1913 and read from his still nebulous poems. Dell had taken a few to the editors of *Poetry,* who pronounced them not worthy, nor even showing much promise.

Discontent often sharpens the perceptions, and as it became obvious that Sandburg was not able to get real drive into the money-ladder climbing, an odd thing happened. The proletarian—the realist —began to seize all power. His verses took on muscle. The layers thickened after he had gone as a reporter to the book-size, adless, penny-a-copy newspaper *Day-Book,* owned by the chain publishing giant E. W. Scripps but fighting the battles of the lower economic orders. For Sandburg the drop in wages to twenty-five dollars a week was offset by the increased quiet of warring elements as the striver was compelled, at least for the time being, to shut up.

Long ago, when Sandburg had been informally Charlie and formally Charles A., he had sought to capture the mood of places. In "Departure," which ran in the July 1906 *Tomorrow,* he had made

a vague trial run in a manner that would bring him fame. He changed
the title to "Docks" later, but nothing else.

> Strolling along
> By the teeming docks,
> I watch the ships put out.
> Black ships that heave and lunge
> And move like mastodons
> Arising from lethargic sleep.
>
> The fathomed harbor
> Calls them not nor dares
> Them to a strain of action,
> But outward, on and outward,
> Sounding low-reverberating calls,
> Shaggy in the half-lit distance,
> They pass the pointed headland,
> View the wide-far-lifting wilderness
> And leap with cumulative speed
> To test the challenge of the sea.
>
> Plunging,
> Doggedly onward plunging,
> Into salt and mist and foam and sun.

The editors of *Poetry,* having only a little earlier read Sandburg's
muzzy verses of this sort, were startled by the clarity and power of
a group of manuscripts which came early in 1914. The magazine led
off the March number with "Chicago," the hog-butchering, brawling,
big-shouldered paean familiar to every new generation. More powerful realistic hammer blows were left to other poems, for example,
"They Will Say":

> Of my city—the worst that men will ever say is this:
> You took little children away from the sun and dew,
> And the glimmers that played in the grass under the great sky,
> And the reckless rain; you put them between walls
> To work, broken and smothered, for bread and wages,
> To eat dust in their throats and die empty-hearted
> For a little handful of pay on a few Saturday nights.

In those days the militant workers who sought higher wages and
shorter hours were called "trouble makers" and "agitators" and

"reds" by employers, and their names put on a dreaded "black list" to keep them jobless. A desperate man about to give up his identity was made to speak in 'Blacklisted":

Why shall I keep the old name?
What is a name anywhere anyway?
A name is a cheap thing all fathers and mothers leave each child;
A job is a job and I want to live, so
Why does God Almighty or anybody else care whether I take a
    new name to go by?

In "Mamie," Sandburg caught the small town girl trying to escape to the great city:

Mamie beat her head against the bars of a little Indiana town and
    dreamed of romance and big things off somewhere the way the
    railroad trains all ran.
She could see the smoke of the engines get lost down where the
    streaks of steel flashed in the sun and when the newspapers
    came in on the morning mail she knew there was a big Chicago
    far off, where all the trains ran.
She got tired of the barber shop boys and the post office chatter
    and the church gossip and the old pieces the band played on the
    Fourth of July and Decoration Day
And sobbed at her fate and beat her head against the bars and was
    going to kill herself
When the thought came to her that if she was going to die she
    might as well die struggling for a clutch of romance among the
    streets of Chicago.
She has a job now at six dollars a week in the basement of the
    Boston Store
And even now she beats her head against the bars in the same old
    way and wonders if there is a bigger place the railroads run to
    from Chicago where maybe there is
            romance
            and big things
            and real dreams
            that never go smash.

An older Mamie, perhaps, was to be encountered in "Harrison Street Court":

            I heard a woman's lips
            Speaking to a companion
            Say these words:

"A woman what hustles
Never keeps nothin'
For all her hustlin'.
Somebody always gets
What she goes on the street for.
If it ain't a pimp
It's a bull what gets it.
I been hustlin' now
Till I ain't much good any more.
I got nothin' to show for it.
Some man got it all,
Every night's hustlin' I ever did."

Sandburg's angriest—and longest—poem was strong meat, perhaps too strong for *Poetry*. It ran in the *Masses*, titled "Billy Sunday." (Most later readers would know it as "To a Contemporary Bunkshooter," with no mention of the evangelist.) Sandburg's opinion of the preacher class had been low, of course, ever since rich-feeding, cigar-puffing Rev. Carl A. Nyblad had wrecked the family church in Galesburg. Billy Sunday hoisted his crowds to a frenzy by, Sandburg declared, squirting frothy, slobbering words. This "slimy bunkshooter," the poet went on, was lined up with the very kind who had nailed Jesus to the cross.

Sandburg never got any angrier than that, at least in print.

The remuneration from *Poetry* being tiny, and from the *Masses* zero, Sandburg trudged along as a reporter for the *Day-Book*, which had only a few small pages. The staff, including the managing and city editors, numbered only a half dozen, squeezed into a dim basement room at 500 South Peoria Street on the proletarian West Side across the river from the Loop. The crime stories, particularly if there was a sex angle, often overwhelmed the humdrum news. But Sandburg was a meat-and-potatoes reporter concentrating on the efforts of working people to win a better life.

In the nation's literary circles, Sandburg's "Chicago Poems" received praise along with reproach—yet the breeze was a whisper compared with the gale blown up by *Spoon River*. No book publisher rushed to Sandburg. Masters tried to correct this situation. Armed with his astonishing fame, he hunted a publisher for Sandburg, offering to provide the mightiest blurb at his command—having to some degree changed his mind about his friend's realistic poetry.

He enlisted, of course, the aid of Dreiser, who in turn set H. L. Mencken to beating the bushes. Harriet Monroe also fought dauntlessly for her new find—the harder, perhaps, because Masters had escaped her notice. She arranged for the 1914 *Poetry* prize, with its $200 honorarium, to go to Sandburg. It took some doing, including the laying of a trap for Chatfield-Taylor, one of the judges. He had privately declared Sandburg a worthy case and regretted his ineligibility for any poet's award owing to the fact that his work was prose. As the judges sat down to cogitate, Harriet offhandedly noted a dictionary ruling that poetry is "usually though not necessarily arranged in the form of measured verse or numbers." Chatfield-Taylor, not being a man to fight a dictionary, shifted ground and cast the decisive vote for Sandburg.

Masters, sinking one day into Harriet's wicker Poet's Chair, assumed a thunderstruck expression and advised the lady editors of Sandburg's intended use of the prize money: for a second child— and this at the age of thirty-seven, hair showing a bit of gray, vision dimming, shoulders bent, wages twenty-five dollars a week. (Masters himself had fathered a child when past forty, but he always felt young and besides had been earning twenty times Sandburg's income.) Harriet and Eunice Tietjens pronounced Sandburg's aim a fine thing, being happy that at least one of their poets seemed emotionally secure. They had recently been at cross purposes in Vachel Lindsay's courtship of the fragile poet Sara Teasdale, raised in the hothouse environment of a wealthy St. Louis home. Harriet's position had been simple: any woman ought to be thankful for the chance to wed a fine poet. Eunice had come down for another man, a rich rival—indeed had connived with him—on the ground that Vachel lacked the stability to be a married man, at least to ethereal Sara. (Vachel had been ditched.)

The paradox of Sandburg the home-lover on the one hand and roamer on the other bothered his wife no more than it did him. Their apartment in a tall two-story frame house on Hermitage Avenue was half a dozen miles north and west of the *Day-Book* office. Set among elms and cottonwoods, it might have been in his home town of Galesburg or the Milwaukee suburb in which Paula had lived. She liked the semiopen country for herself and their little daughter, Margaret, besides having no desire to mingle in the bohemian life of the intelligentsia. A reporter's hours on the *Day-Book* were irregular but always long, and the trolley ride, with a two-mile walk beyond, was hardly conducive to a fixed schedule. It wasn't a case where the husband was expected home when he got there. Sandburg was a fairly conscientious telephoner and meant to be a better one. The trouble was that when he got interested in a thing —likely as not a conversation—he was apt to forget something else.

Paula made allowances. One thing for sure: he wouldn't be squandering the grocery money. His awesome frugality was a by-word among acquaintances. If he searched in his huge compart-mented purse until the tab for nickel beers had been paid by another, there was the reward of seeing him restore the purse to his hip pocket. Thrusting in deep with one hand, he fiercely clutched and choked the bulge with the other; no chance of the purse being accidentally drawn out. He was not really a drinking man, nor capable of holding much liquor even if he had wanted to. As an eating man he was a wonder, and his friends believed that saloon free lunches never stood anybody in better stead. In a hole-in-the-wall eatery he could dawdle over a cup of coffee for hours while expounding to a listener, and if he ordered food it would be pork chops or something else that would stick to his ribs.

In the end, Sandburg's manuscript was padded with oddments such as the eight-line, twenty-one-word "Fog"—taking up a page— and older poems like "Departure" (now "Docks") and others from *Reedy's Mirror*. The manuscript was accepted by Henry Holt & Company, an old-line firm. The author obligingly skirted trouble by changing "Billy Sunday" to "To a Contemporary Bunkshooter" and leaving mention of Billy out altogether (as well as thanks to the *Masses* for the reprinting of it, although bows were made to *Poetry* and *Reedy's Mirror*). In April 1916 the book was issued under the title *Chicago Poems,* bearing on the front dust jacket an exhortation from Masters:

> It is with high explosives that Carl Sandburg blasts from the mass of Chicago life these autochthonous masks and figures of modern circumstance. Poetry here prophesies of Industrial America, Business America, and its consummations. He is an observer with sympathy but without fear; compassionate but with an epic restraint, thoughtful without a synthetic purpose, philo-sophical and therefore without a solution, and comprehensive of a vast spectacle of restlessness, aspiration and pain. He puts words to the use of bronze. His music at times is of clearest sweetness like the tinkling of blue chisels, at other times it has the appro-

priate harshness of resisting metal. He derives from no one, sees with his own eyes, touches with his own hands, is hearty, zestful, in love with life, full of wonder, fundamentally naïve. . . .

And so on. The makers of the Renaissance were lending a hand to one another.

Although not a thundering popular success, *Chicago Poems* received wide critical attention, most of it favorable. The nays were in the vein of the Boston *Transcription*'s "It is a book of ill-regulated speech and has neither verse nor prose rhythm." The yeas rang to the skies. The New York *Times*: "In a line or two you are given the measure of immense contrasts. It is all alive, stirring, human." Amy Lowell in *Poetry*: "One of the most original books the age has produced." *Review of Reviews*: "He has shaped poetry that is like a statue of Rodin."

Had Sandburg wished to change his way of life, too little money came in to make it possible. Then, too, the proletarian side of him had won what glory there was, and as a people's poet the humble life was the more suitable. He stayed on the *Day-Book*. For Paula, the touch of renown had not urged her to a grand social life (although she had accompanied her husband to the home of a wealthy *Poetry* backer, where at dinner Sandburg was mightily awed by the exotic dipping of artichoke leaves in hot butter) and after the birth of a new baby, Janet, she was tied even closer to home.

On the other hand, the modest fame broadened the pattern of Sandburg's unorthodox convivial habits, so that he became more than ever a kind of in-city hobo. One of his favorite hangouts was a new gathering place for literary and political rebels, the Radical Book Store, with hospitable back room, at 826 North Clark Street. It had been founded in the spring of 1914 by the Reverend Howard Udell, a Unitarian, head of Detroit's Associated Charities until disillusioned with social work as a remedy for the ills of poverty. His wife, Lillian, now blind, a former lecturer in literature, assisted in the store. The Udells stocked a great variety of books and pamphlets and newspapers, a fact that kept down profits for reasons peculiar to the radical movements. The more rigid-minded of one group were alienated by the presence of the literature of another. To make ends meet, the Udells had a laundry agency.

In the back room Sandburg might be found knee to knee over

a chess or checkerboard with Bill Haywood or Eugene Debs (the two disagreed on tactics but were comradely in the store) or scholarly, goateed Charles H. Kerr, the publisher, or towering Jim Larkin of the Irish revolutionaries, who was unable to go home to Ireland because of a British price on his head. At Saturday night open house Sandburg was usually on hand with the guitar, which he had mastered as better accompaniment than the banjo for folk-singing. The teen-age Udell daughters, Phyllis and Geraldine, looked on him with special favor, both for his singing and his pleasant way with young people—just as they loved the Little Theatre's tearoom for its sumptuous cakes and errands to the *Little Review,* where Margaret Anderson entertained them while Caesar Zwaska got up a bundle of the current issue.

Being a late owl, Sandburg was often the final straggler. With a bit of additional income, he had rented a small apartment for himself. He was a confirmed floor-sitter at artists' and writers' parties, usually in deep conversation with one or two others, but with a guitar ready for a call to sing. He liked to entertain, and had different lyrics for different audiences. The more Rabelaisian words were for men only. He was rather a prude in mixed company, never playing the Freudian game, and he was a carper at Dreiser for sex frankness in print.

He was beginning also to travel a higher road, if not to the great mansions of the scions of the Builders, at least to the spacious homes of rising men where he was a welcome guest, even a weekend camper. If late at night the drooping-lidded host and hostess gave up and went to bed, Sandburg never took offense. When ready to retire, he consulted the ice box for a leisurely snack, and if fearful of waking up hungry, packed a "lump," as in the old days on the road. Hosts might take Sandburg the monolith or leave him alone. Most took him, for in addition to his folksongs and pleasant conversation, the eccentricities of a man hailed by the East as a man of genius were either amusing or to be forgiven.

At last Sandburg was confident of his power. He went on pecking out his verses on the typewriter or setting them down in his surprisingly neat hand. For the moment he was turning from the city to bucolic subjects for poems that would be gathered in his book, *Cornhuskers.*

21

Chicago's
"Great Unpublished Author"

ONE late April evening of 1915, Sherwood Anderson borrowed a copy of *The Spoon River Anthology* from a young musician named Max Wald, fellow tenant of a rooming house. Anderson was unacquainted with Masters, but to Wald he mentioned that Tennessee Mitchell, also a friend of Wald's, knew him well. All of Chicago's unknown literary hopefuls were excited by the attention being given to one of their recent number. Anderson climbed to his third-floor room, switched on the naked light bulb hanging from the ceiling, and stretched out on his narrow bed. It had been raised above the level of the high window sill in order that he might gaze down at the Loop, half a mile south. He began to read. When finished, the rudiments of a book of his own, eventually to be titled *Winesburg, Ohio,* was in his mind.

The rooming house, tall and narrow and shallow, with a mansard roof, was one of the Near North Side's old fashionable houses. The address was 735 Cass Street (later Wabash Avenue) at the corner of Superior Street. *Poetry*'s office was only two blocks south. Nearby was a Catholic school of the Little Children of Mercy. Anderson called the rooming house the Little Children of the Arts, since the partitioned-off rooms had mostly aspiring musicians, writers, actors, painters. He readily included himself among the Little Children—although now approaching thirty-nine. George Daugherty, a friend since the old days at Wittenberg Academy, had moved here with him last year from a South Side rooming house near Jackson Park.

They both worked in Anderson's old advertising agency, now Taylor-Critchfield-Clague. It boasted offices in New York and Detroit and Boston as well as in Chicago, but in fact was not very large. Most of the seventy to eighty accounts were of the "Kalamazoo Ranges direct to you" type, and the loss of one account spread consternation to everyone in the office—except Anderson. When news of a golf ball firm's defection reached his cubby-booth, his loud "Goody!" startled the dedicated. Obviously here was a flat-tired go-getter, cynical into the bargain. His salary, figured on accounts handled, was minor—usually between thirty and forty dollars a week. Everybody knew that he was kept on largely owing to a soft spot for him and his aspirations in the heart of the firm's president, Bayard Barton, a poet in the old days when they had been fellow copywriters in the agency.

Cornelia was teaching school in Indiana. The two boys—Robert, seven, and John, six—were at school in the town where she taught; the little girl, Miriam, was not yet four. Both partners of the marriage now agreed that it was finished, that Cornelia would go about arranging a divorce. Anderson from time to time sent a little money. He had turned his romantic interest from Margery Currey to Tennessee Mitchell. He was still, of course, a blessing to young ladies who yearned to be free in spirit and at the same time a sacrifice to male genius. He merely stood—or sat—and waited to be bagged. To those, like Fanny Butcher, who were not pulled to the male in him and hadn't the urge for self-sacrifice, his air of indifference came out as simple rudeness. The Ben Hecht type was utterly nonplussed that a cynical stance failed to get the same results. They did not understand that Anderson's eternal vocal yearning for the meaning of life seemed a kind of innocence that was extremely appealing to the self-sacrificer. Here was the male devoted artist—perhaps a genius—into whom female artistic yearnings might be fused to the advantage of both and of literature. On the other hand, for the strong woman he was a plastic substance to mold as well as to shelter.

Tennessee Mitchell, very strong, had, of course, always been drawn to men with artistic longings but inability to cope with the harsh world. Anderson had not coped well—and now didn't even want to. She was nearly forty-one, almost two years older than Anderson; both looked younger. Anderson seemed almost boyish when in casual dress, hair tousled loosely (not carefully swirled and terraced as in the posed photograph with the stick). Margery Currey had been right for picking up and encouraging him. Tennessee was physically the more attractive, the more worldly, positive, and creative (as her later sculpture would show). She earned a good living and at least knew fashionable society. Her underlying maternal instinct joined with these other qualities to create a perfect mixture for Anderson at this time of his life.

No group felt a deeper emotional shock of recognition upon reading *Spoon River* than refugees from villages of their youth. Out of the haze of memory stepped faintly understood characters, at last bathed in light. The more sensitive and hurt the refugee as a child, the more electrifying the voices from the grave. Few had been hurt more than Anderson. With all the "go-getter" layers melted in the heat of adult competition, he again saw the village through the sensitive eyes of the adolescent. To Dell he had professed, of course, to despise the grotesque and the lorn in fiction—only to learn from readers of *Windy* and *Marching Men* that these ingredients were indeed the striking portions. Now here was a book mostly about the small town grotesque and lorn, already celebrated, earning a good deal of money. Whether Anderson had seen Reedy's tribute to *Spoon River* as "marvelous in the art of exclusiveness," it wasn't needed to demonstrate that heavy structural lumber was useless or worse. True, poetry was better for making a quick image, and the first-person epitaph set the reader's mood for brevity.

Anderson was ready enough to include himself among the poets. An imitation of *Spoon River,* though, was out of the question. In prose the same force might be achieved in brief tales by distilling the essence of character in revealing incidents. Any parallel with *Spoon River* would end here. Anderson owned a horde of characters —or seeds of them—from his own experience. Moreover, his literary view of the human condition greatly differed from Masters'. He could be waspish in private comments on individuals, but his creative imagination was empty of villains. A bad deed was done because life had maimed the doer. In a society of cripples who could be guilty of bludgeoning another? To Anderson, *Spoon River* was the work of an angry man, even a hating man (evidently to be forgiven since he was crippled like everybody else). Whereas his own works flowed from love and compassion.

Anderson never declared that the impact of *Spoon River* had any influence on his concept of *Winesburg, Ohio.* He insisted, rather, that he invented a form—and in prose, both in the short story and in a book of interrelated tales, it has usually been conceded that he is entitled to share the credit. Yet a germ was in *Spoon River,* whether he was conscious of it or not. Nor was it a coincidence that Masters had been, and Anderson was being, subjected to Tennessee Mitchell's tough-minded outlook on life and art. Anderson confessed to being "in and of" adolescence, but able to look out. Tennessee's greater maturity helped to steady his gaze. Later he wondered irritably why so many got an impression that "I am a thing to be molded." Perhaps Tennessee did not mold or altogether guide him—but she was a good judge of the likely ends of the paths he contemplated or set out upon. He never granted, as Masters indirectly did, that Tennessee opened his eyes to many truths. But indirectly he admitted borrowing strength by reporting her exhortation not to "let them turn you aside."

He did not at once begin the Winesburg stories. For one thing, he was at work on a novel he usually called *Talbot Whittingham* but sometimes *Talbot the Actor* or *The Golden Circle.* A portion had been brought from Elyria, along with that of another titled *Mary Cochran.* In New York, Dell had been patiently moving *Windy* and *Marching Men* from publisher to publisher. He advised further work on *Marching Men.* Anderson bowed to the judgment but put off the task for the moment. (In time Dell would emerge in Anderson's mind as one of those who had seen him as "a thing to be molded" as well as his "literary father.") Each new or revised chapter of *Talbot* was being typed and sent to Dell. Anderson had laid part of the novel in a small town—in Winesburg, Ohio. In the manuscript (never published), Talbot's father, a doctor, is thought of as an eccentric—perhaps a grotesque—by townspeople because of his "Golden Circle," a study group tending to unorthodoxy on social questions. Talbot, wanting to be an actor, which meant yearning for the broader range of the city, was out of step with the Philistines, too. And so the general treatment of the town was similar to that of *Windy* and *Marching Men.* Dell found the novel promising enough but his hands were full trying to place the others.

That summer of 1915 Anderson took his vacation at Lake Chateaugay in New York's upper Adirondacks in the camp of Alys Bentley, who gave lessons in what she called "rhythmic dancing." Tennessee, a devotee, went there each summer; her presence drew him. Another Lake Chateaugay summer resident was Trigent Burrows, a psychoanalyst at Johns Hopkins University. A year earlier Burrows and his wife had made the acquaintance of Tennessee, an event which he later called "the best experience of our summer." Anderson was later to be called by some a "Freudian" writer, a description that he rejected while calling Burrows another who had tried to "mold" him. Burrows himself declared that any Freudian insights Anderson may have gained only deepened his own. Yet Anderson's knowledge of Freud, if not always precise, was considerable. Lucian Cary had, of course, introduced Freud's theories to the Dell group long before Anderson joined it, and in late August of 1913 the *Friday Literary Review* had devoted a long report to Freud's *Interpretation of Dreams*. Mrs. Brör Nordfeldt as a psychologist and Dell as a lay student had followed the new movements (long afterward she recalled Dell's warning that "Freud will swallow you"). Most others picked up the jargon secondhand.

The Freud game was on in Chicago's bohemia a decade before its popularity spread to bourgeois sophisticates. Everyone busily analyzed everyone else and a dream with recognizable symbols was a rich morsel if the dreamer shared it—which he usually did. Anderson was an enthusiastic player. (Under the heading "Sexology" the *Little Review* would soon be running classified advertisements for Freud's *Three Contributions to Sexual Theory* and *Selected Papers on Hysteria and Other Psychoneuroses;* Dr. E. Hitschmann's *Freud's Theories of the Neuroses;* Dr. August Foral's *The Sexual Question;* Margaret Sanger's *What Every Girl Should Know.*)

At the end of July, Anderson, back from his vacation, wrote Dell asking for the draft of *Marching Men,* since he was in a mood for "patient sustained work" on it. *Windy* still had not found a taker, but Dell thought he could get a sympathetic reading from the John Lane Company, publisher of Dreiser's *The Titan* and now bringing out his *The "Genius."* Dell, engaged by Jefferson Jones, the firm's U.S. editor, to cut the final draft, had found that Dreiser repeated himself at chapter ends, so that a portion could be sliced off. He hoped that his connection with the Lane editor would be favorable to *Windy,* and that in a close decision Dreiser might say a balance-tipping word.

Exactly when Anderson turned from, or interrupted, his "patient sustained work" on *Marching Men* to a group of related small town tales is not known, nor likely ever to be. He later gave differing versions—his normal procedure. In his *Memoirs,* for example, he misstated his departure from Elyria by some two years, giving it as 1910 rather than early 1913. Taken together, the major accounts of his beginning of *Winesburg* would place the season as late fall or early winter, since in one a late fall rain is coming down and in the other snow is falling. Neither identifies the year but other evidence places the time as late 1915, or perhaps early 1916. (Book publication was not until 1919.) The evidence further clearly shows a part of his method. From it his development of the whole book can be fairly surely established.

The tale which Anderson always spoke of as having been written first (the other evidence bears out his memory) was "Hands," which of course holds its place in the final sequence, although preceded by a prologue called "The Book of the Grotesque." Since this was his original title for the entire work, the likelihood is that he wrote it prior to "Hands"; and certainly he did about the same time, for he sent it to Dell and it was printed in the February 1916 issue of the *Masses.* For the reason that the "prologue" has little bearing on what follows, a logical assumption is that Anderson wrote it as a guideline for what he intended to do, and then partly turned aside. In it he tells—in barely more than a thousand words—of an old writer creeping into his bed, which had been raised to a high window so that he might look out into the trees. (The writer might have been himself except for the differences of age and Anderson's purpose of wanting to look out over the city.) Before the old writer's eyes, as he lies in the never-land between wakefulness and sleep, parade men and women known in his life—now grotesques, although some are amusing and others almost beautiful. After an hour of watching, the old man rises and begins to write about one of the flitting characters. Later he describes more of them.

A conceit of the old writer's is that he has known people more intimately and differently from anybody else (just as Anderson surely understood some facets of character better than most and had an overall view peculiar to himself.) Along with the conceit goes a theory that each person snatches up one or more of the truths lying about in the world—among them "the truth of virginity and the truth of passion, the truth of wealth and of poverty." And then, if a truth has been made his own and he has endeavored to live by it, he becomes a grotesque and the truth is a falsehood. The old man's book of grotesques has not been published, but the present author, Anderson, has read the manuscript, thereby deepening his own insights. By implication he will now proceed with tales of his own to show how the embracing of some truth turns it into falsehood and the embracer into a grotesque. This concern with "truths" —the endless search for the meaning of life—was pure Anderson, demonstrated already in his manuscripts.

The plan for a group of characters, each seizing a truth and striving to live by it, only to become a grotesque clutching a falsehood, was a marvelously ironic concept. Realization of it was quite another matter. Anderson was at sea in a realm of philosophy. After proclaiming, say, the "truth of virginity," he was at a loss to go on (if indeed a special truth is to be found in virginity). How to marshal proof that striving to live by a truth makes it false and the striver grotesque? Any one able to accomplish that feat (or the appearance, since as a generalization it is absurd) would need a gift of irony beyond Anderson's. In the end he settled, by forgetting the original concept, for what he could bring off. By deciding on grotesques for subjects—or anyhow the grotesque in his subjects—he found a true vessel for his talent. The circumstances of writing "Hands" returned to his memory in this fashion:

I walked along a city street in the snow. I was working at work I hated. Already I had written several long novels. They were not really mine. I was ill, discouraged, broke. I was living in a cheap rooming house. I remember that I went upstairs and into the room. It was very shabby. I had no relatives in the city and few enough friends. I remember how cold the room was. . . .

There was some paper on a small kitchen table I had bought and brought up into the room. I turned on a light and began to write. I wrote, without looking up—I never changed a word of it afterwards—a story called "Hands." It was and is a very beautiful story.

I wrote the story and then got up from the table at which I had been sitting, I do not know how long, and went down into the city street. I thought that the snow had suddenly made the city very beautiful. . . . It must have been several hours before I got the courage to return to my room and read the story.

It was all right. It was sound. It was real. I went to sit by my desk. A great many others have had such moments. I wonder what they did. For the moment I thought the world very wonderful, and I thought also that there was a great deal of wonder in me.

Of course, he also had a somewhat different memory of it.

> I had got into my bed in that rooming house. I was very tired. It was a late fall night and raining and I had not bothered to put on my pajamas. I was there naked in the bed and I sprang up. I went to my typewriter and began to write. It was there, under those circumstances, myself sitting near an open window, the rain occasionally blowing in on me and wetting my back ...

Discrepancies in the weather aside, he erred in the first account by declaring that he never changed a word, and in the second by putting himself at a typewriter. He did not know how to type. Otherwise the two versions and the other evidence add up to the same thing: the tale leaping into his mind and the rapid composition of it.

For writing material he had used a pencil and the backs of sheets from an old draft of *Talbot Whittingham*. Perhaps because of the manuscript he laid the story in its town, Winesburg, Ohio. The opening paragraph stood as first written, except for insertion of "half decayed" at the beginning:

> Upon the half decayed veranda of a small frame house that stood near the edge of a ravine near the town of Winesburg, Ohio, a fat little old man walked nervously up and down. Across a long field that had been seeded for clover but that had produced only a dense crop of yellow mustard weeds, he could see the public highway along which went a wagon filled with berry pickers returning from the fields. . . . Over the long field came a thin girlish voice. "Oh, you Wing Biddlebaum, comb your hair, it's falling into your eyes," commanded the voice to the man, who was bald and whose nervous little hands fiddled about the bare white forehead as though arranging a mass of tangled locks.

Wing Biddlebaum's grotesqueness has been established at once by making him an object of ridicule for even the youth of the town. And there is nothing subtle in the basic reason for it. Whether the people believe that he is a homosexual is never clear, but he knows that he must be extremely careful with his hands, for twenty years ago, then a young schoolteacher, he had been whipped in a distant town by men who misread his gentle caressing of boys. He had come to live—or hide from life—just outside Winesburg with an old aunt who raised chickens. She is dead now and he lives alone, earning a little money by berry-picking and other field work. His incredibly swift hands make him especially apt in it. The nickname

Wing is derived from the soft white hands "like unto the beating of the wings of an imprisoned bird."

The desolate little man, forty but looking sixty-five, is strikingly unworldly. He doesn't know precisely why he got into trouble, except that his hands were to blame. Yet for immediacy a current relationship with a boy or young man is almost essential. Anderson found a device for it without intruding on the mood. He invented a young reporter for the local paper, George Willard, the only person with whom Wing Biddlebaum has "formed something like a friendship," and had the old man hoping that the youth will come to spend the evening talking with him. George Willard never comes. Had the author brought him to the scene, the mood would have been broken by the mechanics of getting him in and out. By relating bits of past talks and describing Biddlebaum's gestures (leaving out Willard's), he tells what is needed while keeping the attention on his main, really his only, character. Although the ironic truth-into-falsehood-into-grotesque concept has been scuttled, a "truth"—not a very original one—has a place. One time Biddlebaum cried out to the boy that he was destroying himself because he had the inclination to dream but was afraid of dreams.

In the original version, the old man's hands "stole to George Willard's shoulders." But lest the reader expect the youth to show revulsion, or show it himself, the line was changed so that the hands "stole forth and laid on George Willard's shoulders." A moment later Biddlebaum "raised his hands to caress the boy and then a look of horror swept over his face." He leaped up, tears in his eyes, and hurried away.

George Willard's failure to appear during the evening becomes one more part of Biddlebaum's loneliness. (The original "he still hungered for the boy" was changed to "he still hungered for the presence of the boy.") He washes dishes, and seeing a few crumbs on the clean floor, kneels in the lamplight and begins carrying them rapidly to his mouth. "The kneeling figure looked like a priest engaged in some service of his church. The nervous expressive fingers, flashing in and out of the light, might well have been mistaken for the fingers of the devotee going swiftly through decade after decade of his rosary."

The final symbol was hardly needed to apprise the reader that Biddlebaum, already a victim of decades of loneliness, will pass through as many others. In a very short space—barely more than two thousand words—Anderson has taken the reader into the shivering, ghostly existence of the victim of a town. Since the perceptive reader knows that he, too, might regard the old man as a joke if meeting him in the flesh, the desolation is magnified a hundred times. Freud's dictum that in every person is an element of the opposite sex had been the subject of discussion among Anderson and his friends, but whether he expected the reader to feel that "but for the grace of God there go I" is not pertinent. Each man and woman contains seeds of the grotesque and being made to feel it (which can happen if the displayed grotesque is of a different kind) is a shattering experience.

The cause of the sudden emergence of Anderson's talent would later be the despair of those critics who, like judges and lawyers, search for precedents; and who, unlike patent authorities, refuse to believe that two or more persons may independently invent or improve a device. Some immediately thought of Chekhov, whose stories, often lacking the usual beginning-and-middle-and-end, depended for impact mainly on atmosphere and quick insights. When Anderson denied having read Chekhov, it was insinuated that he was lying or had unconsciously imbibed knowledge. Katherine Mansfield had used the form more recently. But in the light of Anderson's failure to credit her, the critics were thrown back on the unconscious theory. Some of the magniloquent rhythms were declared to stem from the Old Testament, and part of the manner from Mark Twain. At least Anderson confessed an admiration for *Tom Sawyer* and *Huckleberry Finn*, and never disclaimed having read the Bible.

The influence of Gertrude Stein was charged, and Anderson admitted to a minor debt. His brother Karl had looked into her *Tender Buttons* because it was being said that she was doing for language what the Postimpressionists and cubists had done for painting. Amused by the repetitious and seemingly jumbled march of words, Karl had passed the book on to Sherwood, who, after first ridiculing it, had gotten the earlier and more coherent *Three Lives* and found that repetitions of words and even the rigid monotony of simple ones could, together with flashes of imagery, bring about concreteness and a sense of immediacy. The imagery of Biddlebaum's hands, of course, runs all through "Hands" in different manifestations, the phrase "like unto the beating of the wings of an imprisoned bird" being perhaps the most telling. The "unto" and similar usages may have been responsible for the suggestion that he had drawn on the Bible. At any rate highly formal words strewn here and there provide a certain awesomeness of tone which is abetted by the unfailing use of full names, as "Out of the dream Wing Biddlebaum made a picture for George Willard." Gertrude Stein had used this device in a portion of *Three Lives*.

Aside from this admitted debt, there is no reason for believing that Anderson borrowed form or manner from any source. Nor was the plan for a book or interrelated small-town stories an imitation of *Spoon River*. Masters' book simply had lifted Anderson's horizons and quickened his pace on a way he was already traveling. After all, in the *Little Review* he had declared against the traditional story plot. And comments by readers of his novel manuscripts had taught him that scenes peopled by characters who came out grotesque were his best.

From the evidence, it seems that Anderson at first did not think of George Willard as a unifying character to go with the single-town locale. In the second and third stories, written after "Hands," the young reporter is absent, and in the fourth he appears briefly toward the end when the main character needs a listener. In the published book, No. 3 has moved all the way back to No. 15, and another dealing mostly with Willard has been put in its place; No. 4 has been moved to No. 21, and a tale in which he appears has been substituted; No. 8 in the writing has been moved up to No. 4. In this way the young reporter was made a figure in all but one, the shortest, of the first five stories. It is also probable that one or more early Willard-less stories were excluded from the final version.

In "Mother," the fifth story to be written, which became the third in the book, Anderson came to the Tom Willard family theme, which more than anything else was to unify the book. In vague outline, but clear enough, are his favorite subjects: young Sherwood (as George Willard), his father (as Tom Willard), his mother (as Elizabeth Willard). Tom, a village dude with a twirled black mustache and a military step, keeps Winesburg's run-down hotel but puts on airs as a big man. He has acquired the hotel by marrying Elizabeth, a stage-struck girl. Now, at forty-five, she is gaunt and listless. She hopes that her son will fulfill her dead dream of an artistic career, rather than being "smart and successful," as Tom wishes. After eavesdropping on what she takes to be an intimate father-son talk about the lad's dreaminess ("You're Tom Willard's son and you'll wake up"), she resolves to ward off "something threatening my son" by executing her husband.

A pair of long shears is chosen as the weapon. Rummaging out her old theatrical makeup box, she prepares for her role. "No ghostly worn-out figure would confront Tom Willard. . . . The figure would be silent—it would be swift and terrible. As a tigress whose cub . . ." Her will collapses, but of all the grotesques she is the one allowed to taste victory, when George Willard reveals that he distrusts his father's slick ideas and that he plans to go away in a year or two, presumably to be a serious writer. "She wanted to cry out with joy . . . , but the expression of joy had become impossible to her." Anderson was never to fully develop Tom Willard (after all, *Windy* was being offered to publishers), but no surrogate of The Major could be expected to win in his pages.

In providing young Willard with greater depth and awareness as a budding writer absorbing impressions of the town, Anderson freed himself from the narrow range of the dolefully crippled. Since the young reporter is not a grotesque he can experience common adventures and feelings of adolescence while standing in the twilight world between the grotesque and the normal inhabitants. In his role of normal adolescent, Willard becomes a central figure, as in "Nobody Knows," where he has a sexual experience with a loose girl and afterward nervously reassures himself that "She hasn't got anything on me" (nobody else knows of the incident); and in "Sophistication," when during a walk and a talk with the banker's daughter he suddenly feels grown up in a world where "he must live and die in uncertainty, a thing blown by the winds, a thing destined like corn to wilt in the sun." In other tales the reporter is a foil, as in "The Teacher," where he is the desired male object of frustrated Kate Swift; and in "An Awakening," when Belle Carpenter, a milliner, leads him into the bushes in order to inflame bartender Ed Handly, whom she wants as her lover. She believes Handly is lurking nearby and will knock the youth aside.

But usually Willard is the intermediary figure between the two worlds. In "Respectability," the incredibly gross telegraph operator, Wash Williams, relieves his pain by telling the boy how he came to be a misanthrope. Long ago in a city he had wildly loved his girl bride, until, finding her faithless with many men, he had sent her to her parental home. In a final devastating horror his mother-in-law, the most respectable of women on the surface, had invited him to the home in an effort to bring about a reconciliation and then had pushed the girl naked into the room where he waited. In "Queer," Willard is the one person to whom an ex-farm boy unable to adjust to the town believes he can explain himself. In "The Strength of God," the Reverend Curtis Hartman, after breaking a church window panel in order to peep at teacher Kate Swift in her bedroom, incoherently tries to explain himself to the reporter.

When feeling the need, Anderson simply dragged the youth into the story by the heels, as in "Adventure," where Alice Hindman, a dry-goods clerk, has waited so many years for a man, identified as having been employed, like George Willard, on the Winesburg *Eagle,* that her frustration causes her to run naked in the rain. And once the sequence of the tales had been rearranged, the reporter's absence from a few of them mattered little.

Anderson sent a number of the early Winesburg stories to Dell for possible use in the *Masses,* but only "Hands" was immediately chosen. It ran in the March 1916 issue. A few months later "The Strength of God" was accepted for the August number. Anderson blamed Dell for the magazine's failure to print more of the stories and in his *Memoirs* went so far as to charge that his "literary father" had sought to persuade him to quit writing them. (Anyone who became associated with "father" in Anderson's mind probably was in for trouble.) But decisions on the *Masses* content were arrived at by a vote of the editorial board, and a majority felt lukewarm toward this group of stories.

Dell admired them—and in due course reviewed *Winesburg* favorably—but he was critical of what he saw as Anderson's tendency to degrade most of his characters beyond reason. This, with some personal observation of the author at work, led him to a suspicion that Anderson was either incapable of portraying warmth and beauty or had a strong disinclination to do so. Once he had told Anderson a real-life incident which he believed held these qualities and had seen it turned into something he regarded as ugly. In Dell's story two mourners, a girl and a man, kept watch through the night beside the casket of the girl's dead lover. The man had been his good friend. To alleviate their pain they had crept into another room and made love. As it happened, they were anarchists and so not inhibited by bourgeois morals. To Dell their act was an honest reaching-out of grief-stricken people to each other, an affirmation of life amidst death. Anderson had requested permission to rework the incident as fiction if Dell had no plan to do so, and it had been given. (Margaret Anderson said that no one ever denied him the use of a told story because in his later version it was never recognizable.)

Anderson made over the death-watch episode into a tale he called "Vibrant Life." In it the dead man becomes a philanderer killed in an escapade with another man's wife. His coffin rests on trestles in the home of his well-to-do brother, a lawyer, who has become one of the two mourners. The other, the girl, has been turned into a nurse who had been in love with the philanderer and by him had been introduced into the household as an employee. As the night wears on, the lawyer becomes restless, paces about, drinks wine, is excited by the picture of a stallion on a magazine cover, and begins to pursue the nurse. She takes refuge near the coffin. The tale ends: "They struggled, and then as they stood breathless with hot startled faces, there was a crash, the sound of broken glass and the dead body of his brother with its staring eyes rolled from the fallen coffin out upon the floor."

The story appeared in the *Little Review* in the same month that "Hands" was in the *Masses*. Internal evidence suggests that it had been awkwardly forged into the one-town mold as part of the grotesque series. The lawyer has deserted his first wife in the town, has become a success elsewhere, and comes back with a new wife, who is a surgeon—to account for the presence of the nurse. In "Vibrant Life" Anderson had achieved the grotesque, but mostly through ugliness. By touching ugliness with compassion, as in "Hands," he achieved the mood of the tales which finally went into the book.

Dell still believed that the ugliness was too dominant, and wondered if a need to degrade characters was not the true Anderson, the compassion largely simulated. Yet he kept pushing, and at last his effort to win publication for *Windy* seemed on the verge of success. With the John Lane firm debating its possibilities, Anderson in early January 1916 had, following Dell's suggestion, written to Dreiser introducing himself and asking the older man to recommend *Windy* to the Lane editors if he could see his way to do it. Anderson had met Dreiser briefly in Margery Currey's studio the night that Margaret Anderson had announced the *Little Review,* but the unknown striver was not certain that the famous lion would remember him. As the eternal drum-beater for his Chicago friends and their friends, Dreiser urged the Lane editors to a favorable decision. The manuscript was accepted and scheduled for publication in the fall.

The marriage of Anderson and Tennessee Mitchell was in the new, emancipated spirit. Cornelia, who had gotten the friendly divorce as planned, remained friends with Tennessee. The children and Tennessee had grown fond of each other. Indeed, feelings were so good all around that Anderson and Tennessee arranged to spend a portion of their wedding journey with Cornelia and the children. The gossamer bonds were fastened at Lake Chateaugay in late August. It was understood that each partner would be self-supporting and, probably, separately domiciled. After returning to Chicago they would, true, establish a joint residence in the lower floor of a brick house on Division Street on the Near North Side. But it was to be a trial arrangement and they rather doubted that this bourgeois aspect of the married state would hold for very long. Jealousy was too far out of the question to merit discussion. (Later, when a woman presumably hot with "amour" thundered into Chicago bent on having her way with Anderson, he wrote to a friend describing Tennessee as "bully" in these situations.)

With the publication of *Windy,* Anderson, just turned forty and barely three and a half years after the grim exodus from his smashed business career, emerged as a contender for a place in serious American writing. True, it was no startling dash into the limelight. Not many critics bothered to notice him on the fringe, and sales were not impressive. But the book's extollers sounded a high note of delight which was bound to reverberate for some time. Hackett devoted a page and a half of the *New Republic* to the work, saying that "it has a freshness that fairly belongs to the springtime of creation. It is not merely a novel of personal fortunes. It is a novel of the meaning of life." Said the *Friday Literary Review*: "It is the rolling of drums. In its pages lie the promise of a new human comedy and a new, fresh, clean, and virile spirit in American literature." A reviewer in the *Bookman* declared that "its final effect is of a constructive realism, in contrast with the destructive naturalism of a Dostoevsky or a Dreiser."

"Emerging Greatness" was the heading put by *Seven Arts,* a new avant-garde magazine published in New York, over a long review. In a sense the magazine's young editors—Waldo Frank, Van Wyck Brooks, and James Oppenheim—had chosen to emblazon Anderson's name on their banner. In the next two numbers they would feature his "Queer" and "The Untold Lie" from the Winesburg stories, and they planned to follow with others. The tenor of the praise was far more important to Anderson than a flood of usual review adjectives would have been. Here was recognition that the torrent of words pouring from him in the Elyria attic had been literature (his revisions had never really changed anything). And even if *Windy* happened not to be quite of the top order, he was reinforced in the notion that the pouring-out, the semiautomatic method of composition, was valid for him. It was genius without the need for taking pains. The reverence of Waldo Frank, with whom he had started up an intimate correspondence, for the Winesburg stories, as well as the admiration of Van Wyck Brooks for them, contributed to the notion, since, after discovering the form, his revisions were slight.

The method worked for Anderson, when it did, because of his "sheer virtuosity, the fluency, the control over words," as an astute but far from all-admiring critic later noted. Thus when Anderson had something to say he said it quickly and almost perfectly. The method failed when he had nothing much to offer, but the flow of words was undiminished. When sitting down to "patient work" on revisions, as for *Marching Men*, he only poured out more of the same. The critic quoted above, although not exploring the "pouring" technique but rather indicating his suspicion of trickery, described the impression given by Anderson as a "dynamic man who sees all, feels all, understands all but is kept from telling what he knows by his insuperable inarticulateness." This impression may have affected those who hailed *Windy* early for its total performance. They would overlook the inanities of Sam McPherson's hunt for mysteries of life by assuming that his clear insights were muddled by the ineptness of a first novelist's prose. Anderson often expressed his belief that many wondrous truths were known only to him (as when in a letter to a friend he claimed to have led Tennessee to a secret door of life, put her hand upon the knob, and found her lacking the courage to go in—all without giving the slightest idea of what lay beyond the door or without awareness on his part that she was a bolder gambler in life than he).

The pouring-from-an-inner-spring mode of composition very nearly returned Anderson to oblivion, while, paradoxically, ushering him into the most satisfying period of his life. In early 1917 his confidence was soaring. Lane had accepted *Marching Men* on the strength of the *Windy* reviews. Wasn't it reasonable to suppose that Nos. 3 and 4 of the attic novels, *Talbot Whittingham* and *Mary Cochran,* would follow in their proper order? *Seven Arts* ran its third Winesburg story, "Mother," accepted "The Thinker." When the editors rejected "Loneliness" and "Drink," Anderson forgave them for lack of perception, which he ascribed in part to innocence. "There is something reeking and vulgar about life you haven't got at," he explained to Frank. Growing ever more expansive, he offered to advise other writers in articles which might be used anonymously if his name seemed to be ubiquitous in the pages.

Then suddenly he veered off to Whitmanesque poetry. He let it flow happily unabated all spring into a book-length manuscript which he titled *Mid-American Chants.* The editors of *Seven Arts* found them less fascinating than he had expected, but they printed two, and *Poetry* ran a few others. The response in Chicago included a good deal of hilarity, especially for the line, "See the corn. How it aches." The title "Poet of Chiropodists" awarded by the irreverent did not, however, bother him. He was having a grand time and who could say whether the tables would be turned?

For the first time in all his days he relaxed for an extended period —June through August of 1917—in an atmosphere without strain. He vacationed with Tennessee at Lake Chateaugay; nearby his former wife and their children tented. He loafed, danced in Miss Bentley's rhythmic classes, argued psychoanalysis with Trigent Burrows (holding that it was of little if any curative value), talked life and literature with pilgrim Waldo Frank, and wrote. Now he was engaged on a "big Ohio farm novel" called *Immortality,* and his state of exuberance was shown in a later report to Frank that it "will not be the book you expected. It has gone insane; a really delicious, garrulous, heavy, lame fellow with shaggy eyebrows is writing." In truth he looked a decade or so younger than he was— fresh, relaxed, and happy. The self-image of a delicious, shaggy-eyebrowed fellow showed at least that he was capable of having disguised himself for "The Book of the Grotesque." For the moment he was not much concerned with getting the Winesburg stories into book publication. He pressed Lane, instead, to bring out his *Mid-American Chants.*

Now his luck shifted. When *Marching Men* came out, the notices were mostly bad and the sales very poor. The faith of the Lane editors held to the point of issuing *Chants,* in 1918. Its fate was doleful. Fewer than two hundred copies were sold and such reviews as appeared were cruel. Since the editors had little faith in the new novel or the two old ones (none was ever published), Anderson's self-indulgence in the poems and the shaggy-eyebrow role might have been disastrous except that he was able to fall back on a prepared fortification: the Winesburg stories.

The ridicule that had greeted magazine excerpts of *Chants* may have pierced deeper than he admitted. Anyhow, Anderson mixed a portion of *Immortality* with two earlier short tales and made a long, four-part story called "Godliness," and with it expanded the Winesburg stories. At this time he may have rearranged the sequence, and perhaps dropped out a story or two. Earlier he had told Waldo Frank that the group included two or three stories which had been in the *Little Review;* yet only one, "Paper Pills," was selected. At the time he wrote to Frank, the *Little Review* had printed two others, "Vibrant Life" and "Sister," which further suggests that "Vibrant Life" had originally been intended as one of the series.

With the sudden darkness, Anderson extended a hand toward another maker of the Chicago Renaissance. He sent the Winesburg stories to Hackett, who recommended them to Ben Heubsch, a small but adventurous publisher. Heubsch accepted the manuscript, supplied *Winesburg, Ohio* for the title, and issued the book in April of 1919.

The impact was so enormous that a year later Anderson was able to casually drop into a letter the information that the *Mercure de France* had called *Winesburg* the most important book published in any country since the Armistice.

IV
Prophets in Their Rags

22

War Troubles and After

THE Chicago Renaissance, if defined as a movement of vigorous intellectual activity, reached its crest in 1915–1916 with Masters' *Spoon River* and Sandburg's *Chicago Poems* and the magazine appearances of Anderson's *Winesburg* stories. *Poetry* and the *Little Review* and the Little Theatre were in the moving stream, but the last was sinking, and Margaret Anderson would soon take her magazine and go elsewhere. By 1921, after Sandburg's *Cornhuskers* and *Smoke and Steel,* Anderson's *Poor White* and *The Triumph of the Egg,* and Dell's *Moon-Calf* (the last stretching the geographical but not the emotional borders), the stream was no longer vigorous.

Later generations would associate the Renaissance with the twenties, for understandable if mistaken reasons. For one thing, the term itself was not applied (nor its companion, the Chicago Group) until after enough time had gone by for the cumulative influence to be roughly assessed. For the same reason, no one could identify the contemporary roiling as mostly froth in the wake of the main current. H. L. Mencken's grand proclamation of 1920 naming Chicago "the literary capital of the world" was the single largest catalyst in the early glorification. His use of hyperbole stated as flat truth was well known, but the catch phrase was too wonderful for local pridefuls to examine with a cold eye. It behooves the newspapers of any literary capital, to say nothing of the whole world's, to give ample space to bookish matters, and there were plenty of bright young journalists ready to spread themselves. The city rooms were filled with editors and reporters who, straining for genius themselves, saw to it that literary events were given thorough coverage.

A number of press stars had fallen into the habit of lunching together at a restaurant called Schlogl's. A large round table was reserved for them and kindred spirits from other walks of life. Famous literary travelers were brought in as guests. Inevitably the doings and sayings at the Round Table got into the papers, then into magazines, topical books, and finally rosy-hued memoirs. It was not easy for readers to escape the impression that the Renaissance had been casually run up amidst brilliant *mots* at the Table. If not, then surely amidst the bacchic revels at the Dill Pickle Club, the Tooker's Alley speakeasy where pseudo-bohemians, including slummers from the Gold Coast, met for Al Capone's hootch, poetry readings, one-act drama shockers by Ben Hecht and Max Bodenheim with no extra charge for a sight of the authors, and sex "lectures." Chicago's mood shifted with America's during the war and its aftermath, and the disastrous impact on literary affairs was even more pronounced. The Renaissance had sprung from the freshness of hope and idealism and dedication which the war largely strangled, and the Era of Nonsense—sometimes called wonderful—was further dissipating.

The Little Theatre was in part a war casualty, and with it, of course, the tearoom salon. *The Trojan Women* was revived in 1915 and taken on the road as a peace play, which gave Browne a pacifist reputation that sat badly with the Theatre patrons. After the United States entered the war, his weakened position caused many to ignore their pledges.

Other adverse factors had been at work, not the least being the intransigent personality of Browne himself. His dictatorial manner caused a revolt in the cast and the withdrawal of several members. He quarreled with the management of the Fine Arts Building. Besides, his amorous exploits caused a strain with his best player, who was also his codirector and wife. (In his memoirs forty years later he could not help recalling a time when during one of their estrangements a "radiant" girl had left her honeymoon to dance naked for him in the snow; he had then been living over the stables at the Arthur Aldis estate.) Also, the stage fare may have been too esoteric for Chicago palates—or those of any city—taken as a steady diet over a period of years. The Abbey Players, after all, had given the Dubliners mostly native Irish plays. Browne did not care much for realistic portrayals of American life nor, for that matter, folk legends. Yet he discovered few American writers able to do the classical verse plays he wanted. Arthur Davison Ficke's *Mr. Faust* did not come off well. The single artistic success was Cloyd Head's *Grotesques,* which Harriet Monroe found worthy of a whole number of *Poetry.* A young native of suburban Oak Park, Head married Eunice Tietjens and remained in the Little Theatre as a manager, but he wrote no more plays. Browne, to satisfy his tastes, had to return to the ancient Greeks and the Europeans. Only Shaw's *Mrs. Warren's Profession,* with its theme of harlotry, drew profitable audiences.

An effort was made to take up the slack with puppetry. Nellie Browne had visited Germany before the war for a study of the art, and later, after much trial and error under the severe eye of her perfectionist husband, had mastered it. With the aid of Harriet Edgerton, Bettie Ross, Louise Mick, and puppet-makers Carroll French and Kathleen Wheeler, she developed shows that pleased adults as well as children. Meanwhile for the regular stage there was always fresh talent to respond to Browne's cries for art, art, art—among them John Martin, who was to become a leading New York dance critic; Danny Reed, who left the commercial stage for the Little Theatre's more dedicated art; Bernadine Szold, a vivacious girl whose husband formally charged the Little Theatre with having alienated her affections; and Helen Head Fivey, a tall, willowy girl with a striking voice.

In early December of 1917 the Little Theatre closed its doors, five years and a month after the opening. True, the quarters in the Fine Arts Building had earlier been padlocked for nonpayment of rent. The last unhappy days had been spent in the ramshackle Central Music Hall, where *Medea* and *Candida* played to nearly empty houses and the mails were empty of pledge checks. It was not enough that the venture had been, according to *Theatre Arts* magazine, "the most important chapter yet written in the history of the art theatre movement in this country," or that in a later time Shaw would hail the accomplishments of that "fourth floor back," and that Browne would be ranked with Gordon Craig of England and Max Reinhardt of Germany as major prophets of the new theater. At the time he merely set off, figuratively in rags, and certainly bankrupt, as a strolling player for ten years of wandering in California and Utah and New York. Nellie had left the marriage but remained always nearby, at least in spirit. After his return to London by cattle boat and his rise to be its most spectacular producer, she would help direct operations while trying to blunt his drive toward self-destruction.

Several other Renaissance-makers were in trouble owing to the wartime change of atmosphere. Because morals censors usually regard themselves as better patriots than others, it was little wonder that their power increased. The common note was struck by the *Tribune's* Mrs. Peattie in her review of Dreiser's *The "Genius."* Its heading, "Mr. Dreiser Chooses a Tom Cat for a Hero," was in her usual vein. But even though the United States was not yet in the war, she waved Old Glory and clapped a Kaiser's helmet upon Dreiser's head. In repudiating the book as an American prose epic, which Randolph Bourne, John Cowper Powys, and others had called it, she declared that "I have not yet lost my patriotism, and I will never admit such a thing until I am ready to see the American flag trailing in the dust dark with the stains of my sons, and the Germans completing their world rule by placing their Governor General in the White House."

The Society for the Prevention of Vice came down on *The "Genius,"* with the formidable head of its New York chapter, John S. Sumner, leading the battalions of the pure. In the story of the "tom cat" hero, by the name of Eugene Witla, a painter, but very much like the author, "instances" of lewdness and profanity were cited—"damns" and kisses on a girl's neck and, worst of all, young Witla's positive male reaction to a painting of a "great warm-tinted nude." Sumner's threats of prosecution frightened the John Lane Company into halting sales, and Dreiser was plunged into a decade of bitter struggle to lift the ban.

Meanwhile, as Dreiser's romance with Elaine Hyman-Kirah Markham was riddled during his search for fresh "understanding," the tigress in Elaine took over from the "darling." Once Monroe Wheeler, a young Chicago poet-publisher who was visiting New York, watched spellbound in Romany Marie's, a famous Greenwich Village hangout, as Elaine battled furiously to get into a phone booth occupied by Dreiser, who kicked backward like a bull elephant while still talking with the party at the other end of the line—presumably a rival of Elaine's. On another occasion Nellie Browne, visiting New York, was prevailed upon by Elaine—distressed by the constant fighting with Dreiser—to go with them to an event in Madison Square Garden. Nellie's actress-director's eye was drawn, as they sat in the audience, to the savage casts of Dreiser's face—he plainly didn't want to be with either woman—in contrast to the sensitive beauty of his hands resting on a stick. Finally the end to the romance came with the help of a tall, red-haired Villager named Howard Scott, to whom Elaine shifted her affections for a while. (He turned up in the Depression thirties as the leader of a movement called Technocracy.)

Dell was troubled more than the others by the leaden war climate, since the U.S. Government sought, presumably, to take his life for obstructing (in the opinion of the Department of Justice) the war effort as an editor of the *Masses*. Since its founding in 1911, and especially after Max Eastman had assumed the top editorship in 1913 and been joined by Dell and John Reed, the *Masses* had aways been more rambunctious than dialectically radical. The staff and contributors, especially the artists led by Art Young, seemed to have great fun, and many of the readers, among them Sherwood Anderson, were always to call it the freshest, most delightful magazine ever published in America. Contents ranged from Sandburg's assault on Billy Sunday to Anderson's somber grotesques, and from funny cartoons (Art Young's housewife pointing out to her husband his good fortune in working down in a cool sewer while she slaved over a hot stove) to satirical drawings of bloated and often unclothed society ladies. An anonymous versifier made fun of the fun-makers:

> They draw nude women for the *Masses*
> Thick, fat, ungainly lasses—
> How does that help the working classes?

But the editors remained firmly pacifist after the United States' declaration of war, and the Government suppressed the magazine and put Eastman, Dell, and others on trial for utterances declared to be seditious. The jury disagreed, and after the Armistice the case was dropped. Dell turned to a novel, *Moon-Calf*, the story of his boyhood, which appeared in 1920. Its sale was greater than any book of the other Renaissance-makers except *Spoon River*, and the critical reception was very good, but Dell was not put into a "new" category like Dreiser, Anderson, Lindsay, and Sandburg. Dell had with Eastman started a new magazine called *The Liberator*, and his name would for a long time be associated with Greenwich Village because of his articles and books about free love and bohemia. But Dell himself turned his back on these upon marrying B. Marie Gage, a strik-

ing blonde from Wisconsin, who, although in the ranks of the emancipated, had no compulsion to sacrifice to male genius. She kept her
job as an executive for a fund-raising organization and ran the
household with a firm hand. They planned a family.

Carl Sandburg changed to a pro-war stance, making him a different
sort of casualty. The resulting break with many old Socialist comrades was painful. The *Day-Book* folded due to a newsprint shortage,
but that was no hardship. He got a job as editorial writer for Hearst's
American at quadruple his old $27.50-a-week pay—and with it
another wrench. At first, owing to lack of space, he was given a desk
in the managing editor's office. After several days he was told to
move into less distinguished quarters, whereupon he slapped on his
hat, departed, and never came back. It was thought in the office that
he had gotten sore, but the removal order was only a coincidence.
He had been suspicious about the job all along. Some friends argued
that if he had been paid, say, thirty dollars a week, he would have
been content. They said he didn't realize that Hearst, knowing that
many journalists disliked the flamboyancy of his papers, always
offered high wages to those he wanted, and his Chicago editors believed that Sandburg's plain-people style would be valuable. To him,
the wage increase meant that higher-ups were scheming against his
integrity. He sat waiting for an overt move. It didn't come, but the
mounting suspicions became intolerable. Those friends who liked to
joke about his parsimony told each other in awed tones of his failure
to pick up the wages due him. They granted, however, that the
whole incident was Sandburg the monolith, sometimes willing to
change directions, but never if believing that somebody was trying
to haul or push him.

He found a reporter's job on the *Daily News* and was required to
sit in the courtroom while Big Bill Haywood and other pacifists were
convicted of sedition and marched off to prison. His former revered
leader, Eugene V. Debs, was put behind bars on a similar conviction.
(Years later Sandburg was visiting Debs's home when a dog plunged
at him. Debs, laughing, warded off the animal and explained that
"he only wanted to search you for your credentials," meaning evidence that Sandburg, too, had gone to prison. It was the only comment the gentle Debs ever made on the subject.) But Sandburg,
although never to be a Socialist again, had not given up his quest
for social justice. During postwar race riots he wrote powerful articles

demanding better treatment for Negroes. And he held fast to an almost mystic faith in "the people."

By 1920, Sandburg was making his way on the lecture trail, although restricted by his newspaper job. Being without the dramatic talent of Vachel Lindsay, he compensated with his guitar and folksongs. The young poet-lawyer Mitchell Dawson established a kind of Sandburg lecture bureau and got Midwestern dates for him. Sandburg let his now iron-gray hair grow unduly long on the back of his neck and parted it in bangs over his forehead, rumpled his clothing more than usual, and became the good gray poet of the plain people, much enjoyed by women's clubs and college societies—and much enjoying them. He remained, too, the in-city hobo party guest and weekend visitor in the homes of friends. Genuinely liked, he never changed toward intimates as his fame increased. But he was sometimes crotchety, which led to good-humored tales about him. Sometimes he read from his *Rootabaga Stories,* written first for his children and later published. Once he had fixed himself to read when distracted by the host's children, who, although anxious to hear the tales, were noisy in getting settled. He asked that the room be emptied of the young ones, thereby producing an anecdote happily bruited about. Again, he was at a theater in the company of Alfred MacArthur, an insurance broker, when a chattering woman nearby distracted him. He threw his program at her, whereupon her husband invited him outside. Sandburg went, thoughtfully taking along MacArthur, a very tall, large man. The fact that MacArthur, also a gracious man, won peace without fisticuffs led to raillery about program-throwers and bodyguards.

Margaret Anderson's departure may have been hastened by the war clouds which dimmed cultural affairs. But sooner or later she would have gone. It was Chicago's misfortune that she did not remain a few years longer—and in a way hers too. The local newspapers would have known better than New York's how to make a grand show of her trial on charges of having lowered the nation's morals, and this would have called from her an even more gleeful performance.

In the spring of 1916, Margaret's horizons changed when someone brought Jane Heap into her convivial office. The two had somehow missed each other in Jane's time as a member of the Little Theatre's original cast, and for several years Jane had been abroad, most of the time studying art in Germany. When she came in, Margaret was pretending to listen to a woman whom she afterward referred to in print simply as Nineteen Millions but whose name was Aline Barnsdale. Whether the number of the millions was accurate, the lady was indubitably rich. Therefore a display of attention was only good sense, for Nineteen Millions was about to make a sizable cash gift to the *Little Review*. Jane Heap listened for a while. Whatever was being said, she did not agree with it and made cutting remarks. Nineteen Millions stomped out. Margaret was enthralled, for now she could listen to Jane Heap. She listened for days and months and eventually years, which was remarkable since she had rarely listened to anyone. True, everybody liked to hear Jane Heap talk, excepting, of course, rival talkers like Ben Hecht, who was regarded by her as pretentious and whom she enjoyed slicing up. Her acerbity, though, was only a part of her gift. In time no less an authority than Gertrude Stein would publicly hail her conversation, while finding Margaret less interesting, thereby suggesting that Margaret had not widened her listening range to include the wit and wisdom of Miss Stein.

Jane Heap was thirty-one when she met Margaret, short, stoutish, with a full, clear face surmounted by dark hair worn in a pompadour. Margaret proposed almost at once to make her boss of the *Little Review*. Jane declined, but became coeditor (though not on the masthead). Nearly penniless, the two, along with Caesar Zwaska, acting as a kind of Sancho Panza to the female Don Quixotes, set off for California with the *Little Review* in a carpetbag, so to speak. Margaret hoped that Nineteen Millions, who had an estate there, would forgive Jane's impertinence and take them in. Clemency not being forthcoming, the three weary travelers moved into an empty farmhouse which later, when a little money came, they rented. What with the endless Jane-Margaret talk, and Margaret's practice on the Mason and Hamlin piano, and the shortage of cash, an issue of the *Little Review* containing mostly blank pages went forth to subscribers. Margaret declared with a straight editorial face that nothing worthy of print had shown up. The blank number received wide attention, including a letter from Ezra Pound deploring the waste of clean paper and tendering his services as European digger for literary jewels. The offer was accepted. Although still on fairly good terms with Harriet Monroe, "the London authority" felt that *Poetry* was growing overtimid.

Timidity was as far out of Jane's line as it was Margaret's, and she claimed an advantage over most people as she had been raised in an insane asylum. She proved the value of the background easily enough to most hearers, but when pressed had to confess to a limiting circumstance. She had never been certified and so was never a true member of the in-group. Her father was a civil engineer for the state asylum at Topeka, Kansas, and lived in it with his family. Jane had spent a good deal of time with the inmates, and she was precocious. After taking all the art and drama courses in the Topeka High School, she had graduated at sixteen and talked her parents into letting her go at once to the Chicago Art Institute. They had gained one point: she must live at first with an aunt. Later at Chicago's Lewis Institute she studied costume jewelry design and—of all things—domestic science. In the former she was very talented— just as her sense of color was remarkable—and for a while she had taught at the Institute. But Jane Heap was meant to be a critic— mainly a talking critic—of painting, the theater, music, literature, and humankind. And to be a smasher of old molds and a searcher for new.

After a few months in the West, the *Little Review* band had returned to Chicago, paused briefly, and gone on to Greenwich Village. They somehow kept the magazine going, and then, in 1918, received through Ezra Pound the manuscript of James Joyce's unpublished *Ulysses*. Reading it, they discovered the thing of blinding beauty, the superb penetration of the human condition, on which their existence was staked. Late in the year the *Little Review* began to serialize it and continued all through 1919 and into 1920, hounded by the morals-keepers. If unable to decipher Joyce's involved sentences, they could make out short words usually seen on back fences, which would surely, if brought from hiding, corrupt souls. Inevitably the editors (Jane was now on the masthead) were hauled into the dock, where they had a glorious time, especially when a juror, awakening as a disputed passage was being read, demanded cessation lest—pointing to the angelic-looking Margaret—an innocent girl be damaged beyond repair.

They were convicted, but somewhat to their disappointment only fined. A well-to-do Chicago friend, Joanna Fortune, who did not at all sympathize with the printing of the controversial material but who from time to time gave money to support the arts (for many years she anonymously subsidized a *Poetry* award) quietly supplied the money needed to make them free. Not long afterward, Margaret and Jane stowed the *Little Review* in its carpetbag and sailed for Paris, never to return to the U.S. for very long.

In the lives of Edgar Lee Masters and Vachel Lindsay the war caused no external upheavals. Masters was, of course, nearing fifty in 1917 and his age and dependents made conscription into the armed forces unlikely and eliminated inner and outer pressures to join the colors. Being single and under forty, Lindsay faced possible draft and the stern finger of Uncle Sam demanding YOU as a volunteer. Having thought of himself as a Socialist-pacifist, he was required to deal with inner turmoil. He resolved it in his poem "Abraham Lincoln Walks at Midnight" by coming down (bringing Lincoln for company) on the side of those who held an Allied victory to be essential to a free Europe and an end to wars. He neither enlisted nor was drafted, but as travel was restricted his poetry readings were curtailed and most of the war months were spent at the Springfield family home. His third major book, *The Chinese Nightingale and Other Poems* (the title poem was always to be his favorite among his works) appeared in 1917, followed in 1920 by his *The Golden Whales of California*. For the next half-dozen years he would be a towering figure on the plusher lecture circuits.

Masters was severely distressed by the war, as by all catastrophes which brought suffering to large numbers of people. And there were new personal causes for black depression, foremost being success. His editor at Macmillan's had warned him to expect jibes, that it was the nature of critics to lay for successful authors. Indeed, his *Songs and Satires* and *The Great Valley*, hurried into print in 1916 while *Spoon River* was a best seller, had been greeted as of lesser caliber. The fates of *Toward the Gulf* (1918) and *Starved Rock* (1920) had been no better. Worst of all, most critics pitted each new volume against *Spoon River,* until he believed they sought his ruin by making him out a one-book author. Ezra Pound, among others, warned that unless he found greater discipline he was lost. But had not *Spoon River* been written at white heat? For twenty years prior to it the critics had ignored him, until forced to sit up and take notice; and in his opinion they would be compelled to sit up again. Then he had turned to novels with *Mitch Miller* (1920), the first of a trilogy, laid in his native region with a Tom-Sawyer-like boy for hero. Critics noted the Mark Twain subject matter, to Masters' disadvantage. He only widened the break in the dam and let greater streams of prose and poetry rush out.

Any of the makers of the Renaissance, big or little, if offered a brief span of genius in exchange for a later heavy penalty, would have quickly accepted the terms. Such dedication had been in the air; without it there could have been no Renaissance. But Mephistopheles never walked openly up to a driven soul, at least in Chicago, and laid out an honest covenant. Had he done so, Masters probably would have been the quickest to sign (especially if, as in the ancient German legend of Faust, the award of a Helen of Troy, heroine of perhaps the favorite of his early verses, had gone with it). And he would have abided by the terms, wrestling only, as was his lawyer's right, over interpretation of the fine print. Instead, the Prince of Darkness had secretly imbedded in him a leaping dynamo of genius, and then, as it was diminishing in strength and thereby allowing him to breathe more easily, had with the acclaim for *Spoon River* increased the horsepower a thousandfold. The cleverest and cruelest twist had been the wait until his middle age when there was not the strength to either crush or harness it. Whatever the agony, his life was to be dominated by the vibrations of genius.

Masters did not for some years quit the law, despite the rushing stream of poetry and prose. When his practice dwindled he blamed his decision to throw off his pseudonym, holding, as before, that lucrative clients shied away from poet-attorneys. There was money from the books—mostly from the foreign editions and steady domestic sales of *Spoon River*—but taken all in all, his income was half that of the time of the Darrow partnership. His family naturally was bewildered by the change, but his wife, after all, had urged him to use his own name. And he was always willing to concede, even when his anger at her was the most scalding, her willingness to follow him no matter what the hardship. What Helen Masters would not do was to stand idly by while he went on his own; or, in more brutal terms, cast her aside. Dreiser had been right: she had a surprise for him. Masters in his memoirs was contradictory on this point, since if he had tried unsuccessfully to win release in order to marry Tennessee Mitchell, as he claimed, there ought to have been no surprise when later the same kind of trouble arose.

For two or three years after the publication of *Spoon River* the Masters' domestic affairs had gone more smoothly than usual because of his illness and emotional fatigue, plus a degree of fulfillment in the wash of acclaim, even of the lady poets shunted to tea with his wife. She handled them gracefully, which pleased him, for the truth was that he liked hardly anything better than talk of poetry, and he joined the company if time was available. At the family dinner table he had ceased reading his poetry aloud, since flattery enough was to be found in the wide world. Besides, the children had reached an age where holding them silent might have been difficult. Hardin was nineteen when the war ended; Madeline, rather the apple of his eye, was in her middle teens; Marcia was ten. The children still found him aloof, not from sparsity of devotion but because he was occupied with his thoughts, his reading and writing, and in adult conversations.

Or perhaps with the baby chickens, which in season he kept in the recessed dining room windows the better to keep an eye on them. He loved chickens, as he loved all of nature, and the fowls were of high importance at the Spring Lake, Michigan, summer home and farm bought in part with the income from *Spoon River*. The chickens had a lamentable habit of falling into a rain barrel, and then he would fish the inert bodies out and put them into a hot oven. To the children it was symptomatic that he would forget them, so that all were alert for the squawking of those which recovered in order to save them from a new disaster. His complex family attitude was shown by the results of a mistake of one of the children. He telephoned from his office, found only little Marcia home, and told her that he had been called to New Orleans and would leave from the Chicago station at such and such a time, adding a piece or two of information which Marcia did not catch exactly. After hanging up, she got the notion that he had instructed the family to be at the station ready to travel. (Much later she was of the opinion that, because she loved so much being with him, her mind had unconsciously misarranged the facts to fit her desire.) Helen Masters, receiving the addled account and used to obeying her husband's instructions, quickly packed and hurried with the children to the station. Although nonplussed, Masters did not turn them around and send them home, nor tell Marcia of her error. They all went to New Orleans, but it seemed to Marcia that her father took remarkably little notice of their presence.

Masters' reputation as a general companion grew more varied as the subjectivity of his moods increased. To those who barely knew him or had no more than heard him recite his poetry, he was a glum and dullish stick, while Margaret Anderson and Jane Heap found him a twinkle-eyed indulger in slapstick humor. Alfred MacArthur enjoyed taking him to a bon-ton restaurant for his sardonic comments on well-known fellow diners, but shoeshine boys and elevator operators found him a great card. A noted historian later going through *Poetry* correspondence was aghast at a letter from Masters seeming to invite Harriet Monroe to a rendezvous—not understanding that it was a joke and that often his humor was ribald (as Harriet knew very well and either appreciated or forgave). Eunice Tietjens remarked in her autobiography on what she called Masters' collection of erotica, which she thought might rival that of Goethe. Yet on visits to Masters' summer home she and Cloyd Head found his wide-ranging talk on large topics so brilliantly stimulating as to be in the end mentally exhausting. Cloyd Head perceptively analyzed Masters as thinking and behaving emotionally like a genius owing to the inner dynamo. This concept, if joined to Eunice Tietjens' remark about Goethe, may lead to a better understanding of Masters. Both he and Goethe were precocious and deep-sorrowing lovers. Both were trained in the law and hated it. Both were poets, dramatists, novelists, and if one was a giant and the other not, how was Masters to know that in time he would not be seen as a colossus? The machine of genius drove him with unabated fury, and the pain was hardly lessened by the failure of the gears to mesh in perfect rhythm.

One evening in 1919, Masters "wandered out of the iron-dark air of Chicago" into a ballroom, unknowing that soon he would be led "into meadows of larks, into gardens of robins, into happiness beyond anything I had ever known." And then, as he ought to have realized, hurled into an abyss where the nerves of his solar plexus would again writhe like serpents. A passionate love was, of course, responsible for these journeys. As he was to call Tennessee Mitchell Deirdre in his memoirs, the new object of his devotion was to be "Parmela" (and in the latter case there seems no valid cause for removing the disguise). At the ball, Parmela had been in a group including a friend of Masters, who introduced them. Maturely attractive, poised, more than well-to-do, she was an appreciator of verse and famous men. They were soon much together. For him, Parmela's gracious estate over the Indiana line was a sanctuary fit for a lord. For her, Masters was a celebrated author who needed, in order to realize his full genius, the inspiration of a cultured, understanding woman.

Whether marriage between them was ever her vaulting hope, it became his, and he sought his wife's agreement to a divorce.

Helen Masters was not by this time determined to hold him forever against his will. But there were the children to feed and clothe and school. Even though her husband and his Parmela might agree to take them, she had no intention of giving them up nor they of leaving her. Aiming to quit the law, Masters had put aside twenty thousand dollars for tiding him over to full-time writing. Nearly five years had gone by since his one commercial book success, which raised a natural doubt that his income would be either large or steady. To Helen Masters there was a difference between sacrificing for a cause in which she would participate and sacrificing for the contentment of her husband and his (to her mind at least) paramour.

So it came about that attorneys descended on Masters "like footpads from an alley" and wrecked his plans. "They crawled like pythons across my garden mashing down the blossoms." Worse, in the lead was Clarence Darrow. Masters fled the Kenmore Avenue home, but they tied up his assets. Parmela did not seize a club against the footpads and pythons. Rather, she married someone else and left the Chicago region. Masters sought peace of mind and escape from the ever-more-forbidding law and Chicago in a journey to Egypt and stays in New York, always writing. A new volume of poetry, *Domesday Book*, was issued in 1920, and another, *The Open Sea*, the following year. The trilogy of novels was interrupted by *Children of the Market Place* but resumed with *Skeeters Kirby* and *Mirage*. His fame increased—as the author of *Spoon River*. Besides outselling the others it was ever more highly praised as critics made it a heavy stick (as he saw it) for beating him when each new book came off the press.

The estrangement between Lee and Helen Masters was beyond repair; only the dispute over terms of a settlement was a barrier to divorce. He expected some time to marry again—he hoped to a woman much younger than himself, as if to make up for the stifling days when his emotions had been closed to Apollo's song. Meanwhile he luxuriated in the company of young ladies who enjoyed poetry— or better yet, also wrote it. A favorite with whom he pursued a bantering courtship was a tall, dark girl named Dorothy Dow, whose verse had been accepted by *Poetry*. She found him a jolly companion but noticed that he welcomed a touch of melancholy. When finding her blue for some reason, he would read sad poems aloud, often

Browning's, and if she wept he joined in, squeezing out a tear or two. Dorothy Dow was under the impression that in many things he was far more conventional than he pictured himself as being, and that above all he wanted to appear "respectable." Although admiring the wealthy class who seemed to him to be cultivated, he remained provincial, in looks the dressed-up small town banker, never knowing which clubs were the best, likely to be shocked by the unorthodox. The South Side jazz cabarets were being patronized by whites, and when she took him to one he thought it garish and somehow outrageous. She had a look at his bitter side after he had written an introduction to a book of her poems. Realizing that she would not be serious about his courtship, he withdrew the introduction. It was done playfully and they remained friends, but it stayed withdrawn.

In the spring of 1923, after three years of separation, the Masters couple were reported by the newspapers to have effected a reconciliation "for the sake of the children." It lasted a day. Soon afterward Helen Masters won a divorce, which, ironically, he had contested against the "footpads," who, in his opinion, won too much for their client. Now he shook the last of the Chicago dust from his feet and moved to New York, leaving a time bomb to explode in the autumn. It was made up of sonnets dealing with a man's emotions upon coming together with his wife after an estrangement. Her aura was "spider gray," as the golden aura of youth changed with the passage of long years. Altogether the verses were powerful in their boiling hatred. The editors of *Poetry*, accepting them for the September number, had been curiously obtuse about what was sure to be taken as their meaning. The newspapers ran long stories calling them tasteless blows at his wife of a quarter century. And so the angry fires burning in a part of him eclipsed the jolly man and the sympathizer with the woes of others.

When the United States entered the war in early April of 1917, Sherwood Anderson had been planning his summer's holiday at Lake Chateaugay. Past forty, married, and a man who in youth had responded to his country's call, he was subjected to no outer or inner pressures to take up arms. Nor were there bothersome old pacifist beliefs. The time coincided, besides, with his period of literary euphoria, so that the war upset him perhaps least of any of the Renaissance figures. He was content in the rhythm of his life with Tennessee, including, sometimes, the rhythmic dancing learned at Lake Chateaugay. A vignette of Anderson dancing happily by himself in a cold gymnasium would, in the later years of his fame, often come to the mind of Mark Turbyfill, the poet-dancer-painter. One winter's evening Tennessee picked up Turbyfill at his job in Marshall Field's book department and took him to her dance class in a high-school gymnasium. Anderson and John Palmer, a composer, were the only others to attend. Tennessee, wearing a large hat with cock's feathers, sat down at an upright piano. The others ran about to loosen up, and then, with the lights extinguished, danced as she played. It was believed that in the darkness they were better able to enjoy the rhythm of their movements. Turbyfill could not see Anderson, and due to the large space there was no bumping; but it was easy to picture Anderson finding peace in the dark cavern.

Anderson still worked for the Critchfield agency, but his ties with it, and with Chicago, were loosening. He spent a part of 1918 in New York doing movie publicity, and after his return set up a small office for himself, although his work was mainly on Critchfield accounts. After *Winesburg* was receiving wide acclaim (but not large sales) he began looking about for a way to devote all of his time to writing. His idea, he explained in a letter to Trigent Burrows, was to find a sponsor who would provide two or three thousand dollars a year. None appeared, but in the spring of 1920 he was able to break away to Mobile Bay at Fairhope, Alabama, for work on his novel *Poor White*. Tennessee joined him, and it was here, finding clay of red and yellow and blue, that she began to sculpt human figures. Anderson later said that he taught her, which he may very well have believed, since in this period he did some quick paintings afterward asserted to Chicago friends to be nonobjective marvels. However, the years of accepting him as a great unpublished author had been strain enough; the friends lacked patience for a stage in which he would be the great unrecognized painter. Indeed, those playing the Freudian game called attention to his heavy use of reds, wagged their heads knowingly, and spoke dolefully of blood.

To other advertising men Anderson was plainly on his way out of their line of work, and they watched in some amusement the transition to his version of a man of letters: heavy tweeds and gay-colored ties and scarves and socks, hair worn longer and more tousled (Tennessee did his barbering). He watched the change in himself with an equally amused and far more clinical eye. If he seemed aloof from the others it was only because, as his friend and colleague

Y. K. Smith remarked, they were not "low or miserable enough to interest him much." Yet at give and take he was an affable hand, and liberal with advice to anyone seeking to follow him into creative writing. An Irish fellow worker with a gift for anecdote was encouraged by him to transfer it to the printed page. The Irishman rented a room away from his family and undertook a novel. He labored mightily but got nowhere. Meanwhile, now in the ranks of the artists, he lost his taste and touch for advertising.

The struggle between the poles was watched by Anderson with fascination and seeming indifference. Of course he had meant the best, and had himself, after all, kept his head above water in the trade while writing fiction. But Smith, watching him coldly observe the Irishman flounder and sink, thought it an example of his clinical attitude toward the human race.

It was in Smith's home that Anderson in the fall of 1920 met Ernest Hemingway, boyish editor of a house organ, who wanted to be a poet and a short-story writer and a novelist. Anderson encouraged him, too—with, of course, different results. Smith was a few years younger than Anderson, a generous man with his feet on the ground in advertising but with a perceptive feeling for literature and a keen eye for unrealized talent. He had lived at Horton Bay, Michigan, where Hemingway's father had a summer home, and there he had known Ernest as a boy. He had recently sublet cheap a spacious apartment (the town home of Mary Aldis who was abroad) on the Near North Side, and was dividing his good fortune with others. Hemingway shared a room with William Horne, a young advertising man he had known in the war. Another one, Donald Wright, had a room to himself because, unemployed and laboring most of the night to become a writer, he slept late. Edith Foley and Smith's younger sister, Kate, who were collaborating on magazine articles, had a room together. (Kate later married John Dos Passos.) Smith's wife, like him, was fond of the best in old and new literature.

Anderson sometimes came into this congenial literary household for an evening, and then Smith noticed a change in Hemingway's manner. At twenty-one, big and full of animal spirits, he was given to horseplay and much talk of the fight gymnasium in which he hung out and sometimes boxed. For these reasons Smith's wife thought him too much a vulgarian and was perplexed by her husband's desire to have him around. Smith's reply was that Hemingway had genius; he didn't know what kind, but there it was, worn up front, and watching it develop would be interesting. When Anderson was there, Smith and the other advertising men baited him amiably about his garish attire, his painting, or some other foible; and he enjoyed parrying or thrusting deftly. Hemingway's manner was quietly respectful and he liked to turn the conversation to writing, especially its techniques. Anderson's *Poor White* had now appeared, and while its hero, another "Jobby," did not appeal to the critics, many had praised his picture of a once rural town becoming industrialized. And his post-*Winesburg* stories were receiving much attention, especially those in the *Dial*, which, after new owners had moved it from Chicago to New York, had been made into a showcase of avant-garde literature.

Anderson, like Smith, thought he saw genius in Hemingway. So far the younger man's work had been mostly journalism. For a few months after he had graduated from Oak Park High School, he worked as a reporter for the Kansas City *Star*. Then he joined the American Red Cross Ambulance Service. Invalided home, he had been for another few months on the Toronto *Star*. Now he was editor of a magazine nobly dedicated to a "cooperative commonwealth" but, unbeknownst to him, the organ of a shady promoter. By now Hemingway's stack of manuscripts of poems, stories, and sketches—all rejected by magazines—was high. These were not shown, however, to the visiting author, nor was Hemingway's journalism above the average. Anderson's belief in his genius came from intuitively feeling it in the young man himself.

If Hemingway was a disciple—and critics were almost unanimously to see evidences of Anderson's influence in his later work— he was not a humble or even an admitted one. He did not, for example, take Anderson's books and inquire of him why he had done thus and so. Doubtless Anderson would have obliged—in a frustrating way, elaborating his theory that creation of art is largely unconscious and not subject to being taken apart like a piece of machinery. When now and again Anderson read from one of his manuscripts, Hemingway always listened politely but afterward might express reservations. Smith felt seeds of aggression in Hemingway which he explained by a theory he had formed in observing him as boy and man. It appeared to Smith that Hemingway had organized a private club in his head, and that, having absolute power, he was constantly taking in new members and casting out those who failed to meet his standards at a given time. Anderson was needed by Hemingway and so had been taken into the club. But his sin—that of being larger than the founder—had accompanied him, and the mark for later slaughter was upon him.

In the following year Anderson's reputation grew larger and he further loosened his ties with Chicago. Although a regular sponsor had not been flushed, a New York admirer, Paul Rosenfeld, a critic with private means, took him and Tennessee on an expense-paid visit to Europe during the spring. In the Paris avant-garde set (the flood of expatriates was becoming a tide) Anderson discovered his fame to be greater than at home. To its matriarch, Gertrude Stein, he humbly confessed his debt and was awarded the palm of greatness. In the autumn, back home, he received a *Dial* award of two thousand dollars. And his new collection of stories, *The Triumph of the Egg*, was not only hailed as a worthy successor to *Winesburg* but went quickly into a new printing.

By this time Hemingway had married a St. Louis girl, Hadley Richardson, a gifted pianist he met while she was visiting her friend Kate Smith in Chicago. They were about to depart for Europe, where he would be a reporter while going on with his writing. Anderson generously provided warm letters of introduction to Gertrude Stein and others in Paris, and in return was showered with canned goods when the Hemingways broke up housekeeping. In Paris, Margaret Anderson and Jane Heap would publish in the *Little Review* Hemingway's first works in the vein for which he would become celebrated.

Anderson was as willing as ever to read to small groups, and he gladly played Socrates in dialogues with young writers. One of these conversations was preserved by Hi Simons, a slight, dark, intense young journalist who had served a prison term as a wartime conscientious objector. Simons had recently married vivacious, even more intense Bernardine Szold, who had been in the Little Theatre and was now a reporter for the *Evening Post*. They had converted a Near North Side carriage barn to a gaily-painted bohemian home and rendezvous for their friends in the various arts. Anderson, as a dedicated art-for-art's-sake writer, was for all of these an authentic hero, a genius who believed in himself, bravely eschewed all easy diversions, and had at last won through. Simons had given up his job and was working at home to set his genius free, with the understanding that, if results proved slow, he would get a job and allow Bernadine to stay home to summon *her* genius.

"The trouble is, we're not humble enough," Simons quoted Anderson as saying. "We don't simply let the story tell itself. We get in the way of it ourselves. We don't write for the sake of the story; we write for ourselves." Simons was then forced to admit that he was more interested in being a writer than in writing. Anderson continued: "I can't see why the hell anyone wants to be a writer. My God! there's nothing in it. The only reason for writing I can see is because you can't help it. And then it cleans you out. It's like emptying your bowels. A certain kind of evacuation takes place."

Simons quoted a chunk of talk about the suppression of literature.

Theodore Dreiser's the real hero of the whole thing. Mencken —all those fellows stem from Dreiser. Because he stuck. Norris, London, all the rest of that crowd flopped. Except Dreiser. He's stood for poverty all his life, and he's trying it now. But he's never flopped. That's why he's a really heroic figure.... But it's curious about him: it must have hurt him awfully in some way. Because he lacks something—he lacks tenderness.

Don't you think it's reverence he lacks?

Yes—I do. Think how reverent Dostoievsky must have been. And Dreiser has none of it. There's no wonder in him. I don't know whether I've got reverence or not. But I feel I'm full of questions. And there are no questions in Dreiser. And then he's a heavy man. He's got that great heavy body, and heavy thoughts, and heavy lusts. They say when he makes love he talks to a woman in the most vile sort of language—the worst kind of talk—and he gets a certain sensuous pleasure out of it.—Yeh.

Anderson did not give his source for the purported revelation of Dreiser's bed conversation, but he was appalled and worried enough to mention it to others at different times.

The topic changed to Sandburg, and the comments of Anderson were recorded:

Isn't it funny that Sandburg never writes any love poems. Think of it—a man, a lyric poet, *never* becoming lyrical about a woman. Yet it's true. There's not a real sex-poem in all his books. I mean it's some curious Swedish kind of puritanism. Because he's written them. The strangest, most curious kind of sensualness. Crapping-can poems things like that. I know, because I challenged him once, why he didn't publish them. And he said, "Do you think after I've been so long building up a little public that I'm going to lose it all?" You know, I feel different about it. I feel a man ought to stand for anything he writes. . . . Except, of course, anything he thinks is bad writing.

Anderson was now ready to leave Tennessee, along with Chicago. He was sorry for her and went about asking mutual friends to be "kind to Tennessee" because he knew that she would be devastated. Trying to analyze the causes for the marriage's end, some friends believed that Tennessee had made a mistake in going abroad with Anderson, that he had not wanted her to and that she had insisted. In a letter to a friend he called her hand "gloomy" and "heavy." There was her strain of melancholy, but the "gloomy" may have been inspired by her realistic but often satirical comments on some of his fantasies, as when he got a notion that he could work in the ironic vein of Pirandello. Others felt that Tennessee had erred in becoming a sculptor, that he could not abide the artistic rivalry. True, he had used photographs of her figures to illustrate *The Triumph of the Egg*. Proponents of the rivalry theory called his use of the figures a sop. A third school maintained that he felt a need for a different wife for each major stage of his life; that in the new one of great published author, Tennessee was out of date.

At the end of 1922, Anderson departed, first for New Orleans but on his way to New York. Tennessee was devastated, as he had expected, and would remain so for the rest of her life. Yet a bargain was a bargain, and the next year she gave him a divorce so that he might take another wife.

For Harriet Monroe, the war caused no special hardships. *Poetry*'s circulation was not large enough to be hurt by the paper famine. When patrons forgot their obligations in the stress of other matters, she had only to issue an appeal and the funds came in. The magazine was respectable, after all, and if few of the moneyed class actually read it, they knew that its cultural esteem in the world was a boost for Chicago. By and large, however, the great pioneering days were over.

T. S. Eliot's "The Love Song of J. Alfred Prufrock," the first of his major works, had run in *Poetry* back in 1915, secured by Ezra Pound while his ardor for the magazine was running high. Nothing by Eliot had been in the pages since 1916, and "The Waste Land" went into the *Dial* in 1922. Nor had the magazine a vital role in the career of another giant of modern poetry, Robert Frost. He had been in the pages in 1914, also by way of "the London authority," but his first book had already appeared (in England) and afterward he was little identified with *Poetry*. Nor did the magazine have a large part in the career of Robinson Jeffers or the resurgence of Edwin Arlington Robinson. Nevertheless, it had aided them and the others by lighting the way for a Renaissance in American poetry which stimulated new and old magazines to use verse with pride rather than as fillers, and the book publishers to increase the volumes of poetry on their lists.

Although Chicago produced no more famous poets, the dedicated spirit of the Renaissance held longest in the ranks of the verse-makers. Harriet listened to Lew Sarett, an Illinois University English instructor, give Indian chants learned as a youth in the Michigan-Wisconsin Chippewa country, and got him to put them into verse for *Poetry,* and later into books. Robert Morss Lovett, the Chicago University English professor who had heard Sherwood Anderson's initial "formal" reading of *Windy McPherson's Son,* invited her to his students' Poetry Club. During half a dozen years beginning in 1919 she found magazine space for or otherwise encouraged some of the members: Glenway Wescott, Yvor Winters, Jessica and Sterling North, Gladys Campbell, Elizabeth Madox Roberts, Janet Lewis, Vincent Sheehan, George Dillon, and a score of others. In Evanston young Monroe Wheeler published volumes by Wescott, Winters, and Mark Turbyfill. In Chicago Ralph Fletcher Seymour and Will Ransom and the firm of Covici-McGee issued an occasional book of verse.

23

End of the Twenties

SCHLOGL'S Round Table came too late for the actual days of the Renaissance, yet it reflected a great literary era of the Chicago newspapers, a match for those of any American city. It was a time when Henry Justin Smith, news editor of the *Daily News,* peered over the shoulders of his off-assignment reporters to get a peek at the titles of books they might be reading. If it was a good book, the reporter's stock went up. A man or woman trying to write was safe on the job, and apt to find assignments lighter. Sandburg at the *Daily News* was becoming competent at in-depth social reporting, poor at spot news, and a comfortable dozer in movie balconies as a reviewer.

Smith was middle-aged (he had been news editor since 1913), and rather ill at ease with people. In the early twenties he had written a novel, *Deadlines,* not an especially good one, but an honorary badge of merit. He sat regularly at the Round Table, not saying much, yet a literary bulwark due to his newspaper power. The *Daily News* itself was in a nearby ramshackle, crazy-floored building, or rather a throw-together of several. It had been a penny paper and, although not a people's advocate like the old *Day-Book,* sent its reporters dashing after the crime and sex news and sought the airy touch in feature stories.

The *Daily News* had been slow to have thorough book coverage. In a way, Chicago's literary upsurge corrected the lack. In the late teens a personable, somewhat brash young man named Henry Blackman Sell, an ex-furniture promoter, had talked the management into letting him edit a book section, predicated on whether he could sell enough advertising to support it. He had been well up to the challenge, and had taken out of the advertising department an attractive, dressy youth named John V. A. Weaver, who wrote poetry in the man-in-the-street vernacular, to be his assistant. They had run a sprightly, if not very deep, section—and hung out at the Table— until Sell went East to become editor of the fashionable *Harper's Bazaar* and Weaver followed to work at various journalistic enterprises and in the theater.

That left an opening for the Davenport friend of Floyd Dell's youth, Harry Hansen, who had been working for the *Daily News* for many years, some of them abroad. By now the book department was on a firm basis. As he was not compelled to sell space, Hansen was able to give more serious consideration to books. He raised the level, and was enough of a Schlogl's devotee to have written a book, *Midwest Portraits* (1923), which had to do almost exclusively with Table people.

Schlogl's had become an institution, trying for an atmosphere like the English coffeehouses of Samuel Johnson's time. The longish downstairs room was for males only. Women and their escorts had to climb the stairs to a dining room with a cracked ceiling, peeling wall paper, and a long-piped coal stove. The main room was in better repair, although caution was taken lest it become fresh or modish. The ornate tin ceiling and cut glass chandeliers and the huge pendulum clock and the wall paintings of monks in wine cellars had grown dim with dust and smoke. Tables and chairs were of black walnut, properly well worn. Prices for food (German pancakes, Wiener schnitzel, hassenpfeffer, etc.) were rather high, which meant that when the sardonic wit of Max Bodenheim was wanted, somebody edse had to pick up his tab. The high prices also kept Sandburg from being more of a regular than later memoir-accounts suggested.

The change in atmosphere was illustrated by the presence at the Table—and even more in the pages of the *Tribune*—of the usually embattled Burton Rasco, an avid fan of Dreiser's. As successor to Elia W. Peattie in 1918 he made a complete about-face, castigating the genteel in favor of the moderns. He was still under thirty when in 1922 he went to New York. His replacement was Fanny Butcher, the young girl reviewer for Hackett and Dell in the *Friday Literary Review*, who was a welcomer of the new in literature—although so fresh-faced and sweet that she gave writers the impression that they oughtn't to compose anything naughty. The only backward step was taken by the *Evening Post*, whose Llewellyn Jones, although an erudite wit at the Table, looked askance at the moderns, including Sherwood Anderson.

Anderson was usually on hand when in Chicago, and Masters occasionally sat in, although never completely at ease. At least Hansen described him in *Midwest Portraits* as being aloof—which of course he never had been around the *Little Review* or *Poetry* or *Reedy's Mirror*. Hackett and Dell were hardly more than memories. Neither got back to Chicago often enough to become a part of the group. Lindsay was a visiting celebrity when off the lecture circuit, and he was more likely to be found with the *Poetry* editors or at Mrs. Moody's salon. Dreiser and John Cowper Powys were occasional guests, to be entered, with the others, in the ceremonial book kept by Richard Schneider, the Round Table's waiter.

Among the regulars were the new breed of newspaper columnists. Richard Henry Little had succeeded B. L. T. as conductor of the *Tribune*'s "Line o' type." Keith Preston was the major wit on the *Daily News*. Rigarius Atwater was with the *Evening Post*. The Table's elder wit, and perhaps the best in conversation, was graying Ashton Stevens of the *American,* who was primarily a theatrical critic but discoursed on whatever came to mind. Among the other featured commentators were Charles Collins; James Weber Linn, who also taught at Chicago University; Howard Vincent O'Brien; and Vincent Starrett, like a young Old Roman, who knew more than the others about the European decadents. Best known of the newspaper artists was urbane Gene Markey, although Wallace Smith, a dashing reporter, was developing line drawings somewhat remindful of Aubrey Beardsley.

Many others whose names were well known in journalism or literature would be seen at the Table: Lloyd Lewis, who would later team with Henry Justin Smith for the engaging *Chicago: the History of Its Reputation,* and write Civil War books on his own; T. K. Hedrick, who had been an editor for Reedy; Samuel Putnam, later a translator in Paris; Robert J. Casey, Paul Scott Mowrer, Edgar Ansel Mowrer, Julian Mason, Charles MacArthur, John Gunther, Vincent Sheehan. A few regulars were from other fields: Pascal Covici and Billy McGee, who had a joint bookstore-publishing house; Morris Fishbein, physician and medical editor; and Alfred MacArthur, the insurance man.

Above all, there was Ben Hecht. In a way the Chicago of the twenties was the Age of Hecht. He wrote plays, sometimes with Bodenheim or a wealthy youth named Kenneth Goodman, sometimes by himself. Nearly always his aim was to alarm the staid citizenry if by no more than an obscenity. His novel *Erik Dorn* (1921) had been somewhat in the European decadent manner and therefore might be, for all anybody knew, great literature or a long step toward it. His feature stories in the *Daily News* had caught on and would add to his reputation when published as *1001 Afternoons in Chicago*. Hansen described him as "the most enigmatic figure in Chicago, if not in the nation," and called him "Pagliacci of the Fire Escape."

It would be inaccurate to say that Hecht absolutely needed the Dill Pickle Club, or, for that matter, that The Pickle, as intimates called it, relied totally on Hecht. But they did a great deal for each other. Impresario of The Pickle was an ex-Wobbly organizer named Jack Jones. Indeed the original club had been a radical, if somewhat raffish, hangout founded by Jones in 1916 in an old barn-garage at the foot of Pearson Street on the Near North Side. By now it had been moved west to Tooker's Alley off State Street, with a crooked, tunnel-like entrance for a titillating speakeasy atmosphere. The likes of Ben Reitman were still welcome as kind of atmospheric props, but the good money was in the slumming trade. Hecht's plays, with their daring subjects or dialogue, were customer-drawers. And the presence of Hecht himself was a guarantee of The Pickle's eminence in the new age of cynical glitter.

Finally Hecht made what seemed a gargantuan effort to combine his various talents, imitative and otherwise, with the peccadillos of the times into a mighty project that would make him the top enigmatic figure in the nation if not in the world. Burton Rasco declared later that Hecht believed that by writing a book which would be suppressed, and then suing the censors, he would make a financial killing. At any rate, his *Fantazius Mallare* came off the press in 1922, published by Covici-McGee. The style and the story were imitation Huysmans, having to do with the diseased-brained Mallare, his dwarf Negro servant, and a dull-witted gypsy girl. To follow the tale, if indeed there was one, seemed a pointless effort which few attempted. Wallace Smith had provided striking line drawings, one seeming to depict a man copulating with a tree vaguely resembling a woman, others which some took for phallic symbolism.

As if fearful that all this was not enough, Hecht had inserted an introduction which seemed two parts Mencken, one part Mallare, and three parts egomania. "This dark and wayward book is affectionately dedicated to my enemies—to the curious ones who take fanatic pride in disliking me . . . to the prim ones who fornicate apologetically (the Devil can-cans in their souls) . . . to the reformers—the Freudian dervishes who masturbate with Purity Leagues, who achieve involved orgasms denouncing the depravities of others . . . to the righteous who finger each other in the choir loft . . ." And so on and on and on.

If he had expected an exciting joust with the Purity Leagues, Hecht was disappointed. No less than the U.S. Government stepped forth and collared him, along with his illustrator and publishers. He was fired by the *Daily News*. Most readers observed less than genius in the book. Yet Hecht was not easily dashed. Clad in a martyr's robe, he vowed never, never to bow a knee to the Government's charges. And he launched a newspaper that, while aimed to back Covici-McGee books, was a parody of the serious days of the Renaissance. This was the *Chicago Literary Times*, a weekly which began March 1, 1923. The tone was quickly established with a blast at the city—"The jazz baby . . . reeking, cinder-ridden . . . bleating, slant-headed rendezvous of half-witted newspapers, sociopaths, and pants makers . . ." Usually it was only four pages (12x18 inches) of jumbled headings and badly-proofread type, but a certain razzle-dazzle was achieved by various loud colors of paper. The presence of Max Bodenheim as associate editor added to the air of raffish nihilism.

For the *Times*, Sherwood Anderson had become "a phlegmatic, practical-minded con-man" with the "mellow garrulity of a small town barber." Hecht and Anderson had always been of two minds about each other, of course, and Hecht especially resented the ease with which Anderson pulled his leg. In the *Times* he expressed annoyance at Anderson's suggestion that they drop the friendship part of their relationship and carry on strictly as enemies; it would be more fun. Sandburg also came in for lumps. "A certain manic megalomania characterizes nearly all his remarks. . . . The ten years that have witnessed his ascent have brought about a change in manner. . . . His sense of importance would embarrass the Pope of Rome. A formidable wariness lurks in his eyes. A sense of vast injury and vast defiance animate his simplest remarks."

The *Times* ran on for a little more than a year, until it went to an even smaller size and disappeared with the issue of June 1, 1924. Meanwhile Hecht had gone into public relations and continued with his plays. None of the dramas was successful, and by 1926 he dropped his martyr's robe, pleaded no contest in the *Fantazius Mallare* case, paid a thousand-dollar fine, and departed for New York.

As the twenties ebbed, the old Renaissance-makers were scattered over the world, some engaged in rich enterprises, others repining for better days and seeking new footholds. In London, Maurice Browne had produced R. C. Sherriff's *Journey's End* and after a smashing hit had carried it around the world. The Chicago engagement was a hero's return. From a suite in the Blackstone—where long ago the "professional little Englishman" had called abjectly on Arnold Bennett—he emerged for rounds of applause, much of it, he noted sardonically, from the rich patrons who had failed him in 1917. Arthur Aldis (not one of those who had failed him) gave a businessman's lunch for the ex-bankrupt, who had paid his Chicago debts now, and a reception was held in the restaurant which occupied the Little Theatre's old site. "When I was here before," the wizard of the London theater told a friend, "the stage moguls laughed at me, and now they come all the way to London to talk business."

Dreiser had struck it rich with his two-volume novel *An American Tragedy,* which sold to the movies, and he was living partly in Hollywood and partly at an upstate New York country place with another beautiful companion. Ben Hecht and Charles MacArthur were coining money with their play *Front Page.* Dell had turned to the stage with *Little Accident,* a money-maker created with the help of young writer-actor Thomas Mitchell. The Dells with their two sons were living at a country place while B. Marie watched over their adventures into the stock market.

Harriet Monroe traveled widely, still climbing mountains, and ever since 1924 Jig Cook had been buried on one, Mount Parnassus, after living for three years with Greek shepherds. Margaret Anderson and Jane Heap, still living in France, had become disciples of the philosopher Gurdjieff and were often sojourners at his Fontainebleau chateau. Francis Hackett published *Henry the Eighth,* which launched him on a series of highly praised and lucrative biographies. He went home to Ireland but was not satisfied and settled with his wife in her native Denmark.

Sherwood Anderson's life went in a different direction while late in his middle age, he unwound skeins of flannelly prose. In 1924 he married Elizabeth Prall, a New York book store manager, and lived with her much of the time in New Orleans or New York or wandering from place to place, including Chicago. His clothes became ever more colorful. While extolling a need to rub shoulders with the masses, he took ever greater joy in gatherings where he was a flattered figure. The marriage wasn't very happy from the start. His wife was, after all, set in her ways as a youngish spinster-business woman. When she insisted on working in the book store, he appreciated the additional income—despite his high reputation his books sold poorly—but he missed the coddling to which he had become accustomed.

By now Anderson had a reputation as a daring voice of the emancipated twenties. His novel *Many Marriages* (1924) had been taken as particularly advanced. Its businessman hero had discovered that sex between a man and a woman draws them closer together, whereupon he had deserted his cold, stodgy wife for a more exciting girl in the office. Endless talk between the hero, stark naked, and his almost adult, almost nude daughter was taken for symbolism of a kind. His *Dark Laughter* (1925) had seemed destined to hit the jackpot of cash as well as fame. The story was a culmination of his rapturous stay in New Orleans plus his enchantment with the works of James Joyce and D. H. Lawrence. Anderson's "dark laughter" stood for the uninhibited mood of Negroes as he imagined it to be, and he had gone about busily making a Lady Chatterley type and her lover into primitives, using Joyce's stream-of-consciousness method as a tool. The result (at least it came out prior to *Lady Chatterley's Lover*) was an even murkier atmosphere than usual in Anderson's novels. However, the subject and technique being extremely "modern," to read it was to win a cultural badge. The author was raised high in the avant-garde parade with Joyce, Lawrence, James Branch Cabell (whose *Jurgen* had been suppressed amidst wild and hilarious outcries), and even Freud.

How was Anderson to know that the "founder and president of the Ernest Hemingway Club" (Hemingway himself) would take such umbrage as to lash out? Hemingway was still living most of the time abroad, and besides his newspaper work, he had published three small books. One of them was *Three Stories and Ten Poems* (some of the latter had been in *Poetry*). Its sole review in the United States (publication was in Paris) was in the *Dial,* by young Edmund Wilson, who noted the influence of Anderson and Gertrude Stein.

Another book, *in our time,* had been issued in Paris from vignettes in the *Little Review.* With short stories added, it was published in the United States as *In Our Time.* Other critics noted Hemingway's dependence on Anderson as well as on Miss Stein. To cap it all, Anderson once more turned up in Paris, more celebrated than ever.

One afternoon Hemingway telephoned Bernardine Szold, who by now had divorced Hi Simons and was living in Paris. Her recollection of the incident follows:

> The phone rang one day and it was Hem, and he asked if I were free and I said yes and he said could I come at ONCE to the Closerie de Lilas, one of his favorite haunts. He said he had a terrific surprise for me. It was mid-afternoon, there were very few people there, and we sat vis-a-vis, and I saw that he had a manuscript on the table. He said he had just the very moment before he called me finished this—novelette it was really—about Sherwood, and because I knew Sherwood so well, he couldn't wait to try it out on me. He was very excited—took a slug from the drink he'd ordered before I got there and said, "Now, I'm going to *read* it to you. Every word. By God, THIS will show him up!" He began reading it aloud (I'm not fond of having some one read aloud to me, and between that, and the gloating that emanated from Hem, I was uncomfortable and, as it went on, indignant and unimpressed.) The writing seemed sloppy. The malice was inexcusable, and I was bewildered that any writer would take out so much time from his true métier to produce that little book of childish rancor. He was so immersed in his private glee that he never looked over at me, convinced I presume that my response was identical with his own gratification. When, after an eternity, he got to the end, he did not ask me what I thought of it (fortunately for me) but finished his drink, said the one thing he couldn't do but wished he could was to see Sherwood's face when he read it—and, chuckling away, off he bolted. I sat for a few minutes, stunned in a way, more bewildered than outraged, and as I well recall, amazed that what appeared to me to be such a very BAD book could give him such complacence. I felt so certain it would never be published that I quite controlled any apprehension as to how Sherwood would feel about it.

Bernardine had sided with her closer friend, Tennessee, in the marriage breakup, and her sometimes caustic remarks about Anderson may have led Hemingway to believe that she, too, was an implacable foe.

The novelette was issued in the United States as *The Torrents of Spring*. For the Negro primitives of *Dark Laughter* Hemingway had substituted American Indians, and made the leading characters cardboard-stiff but talkative as they mulled and moiled over vague profundities, just as characters in Anderson's novels often did. There were imitations of Anderson's asides: "He wondered." "She wondered." "The two Indians walked by his side. They were all bound in the same direction."

The parody caused Anderson no particular harm, for too many critics and readers had already discovered that in his longer tales he poured out words without much concern as to whether they made sense. The high sale (for him) of *Dark Laughter*—some 25,000 copies—had netted several thousand dollars, promptly used to build a mildly sumptuous fieldstone house in Virginia. Also, Horace Liveright, the publisher, was advancing him a hundred dollars a month, come what might. At last Anderson had all the time he wanted for his writing—and he wrote less than before. He tried to lose himself as editor-publisher of two weekly newspapers at Marion, near his Virginia home, after an admirer had lent him money to buy them. Tiring of this, he turned the papers over to his oldest son, Robert. His books still rolled off the presses: *Tar* (1926), a romanticized story of his boyhood; *Sherwood Anderson's Notebook* (1926), some jottings; *A New Testament* (1927), more jottings; *Hello Towns* (1929), clips from his newspapers.

During Christmas week of 1929 the dead body of Tennessee Mitchell lay undiscovered in her Chicago studio-apartment. Finally her part-time maid, having for several days been unable to get in, raised an alarm and the police smashed down the door. Her long, narrow, high-ceiling studio at 153 East Erie Street (only a few blocks from the rooming house in which Sherwood Anderson had written *Winesburg, Ohio*) was almost a salon, with its grand piano, two fireplaces side by side, brass candlesticks, antique furniture, original paintings, and sculptures. In bed, clad in nightclothes, Tennessee had suffered a hemorrhage of the lungs, perhaps owing, the police conjectured, to an overdose of sleeping pills. The newspapers carried pictures and stories, noting that gift packages for her ex-husband's children were ready for the mail. (Oddly for a "new woman," Tennessee had continued to use the name Anderson after the divorce.)

Anderson himself was described as spending the winter in Saint Petersburg, Florida.

The police handled the affair routinely, but a rumor sprang up that suicide had been the cause. In New York, Masters leapt to the suicide theory and concluded that what he considered the burning emotions aroused by him two decades ago had been responsible.

In Graceland Cemetery Chapel on the far North Side, Eunice Tietjens rose and to an audience of less than a dozen mourners said a few words of Tennyson's:

> And may there be no moaning of the bar,
> When I put out to sea.

Harriet Monroe was there, and Mark Turbyfill and Helen Dupee, who had a studio apartment in the same building. A string quartet costing a hundred and fifty dollars played soft music over Tennessee's ashes. The expensive music was out of character, yet ironically it was at her own expense, being the gift of her long-estranged sister—the one who had sided with their stepmother—who had come on from Arizona to claim her estate as sole relative and heir. It would be worth some nine thousand dollars (half in ready cash) and the hiring of the quartet was a proper gesture.

The presence of this sister, now Mrs. Joseph F. Deck, was logical evidence against the theory of suicide. That, and the nine-thousand-dollar assets. After all, Tennessee had been conducting her own affairs since girlhood. She would have known that a will scratched as a death note would have been valid. The sister was a dim, unpleasant memory. With contemplation of death, her thoughts would surely have gone to the three Anderson children; they were not only close but needed aid in starting their lives. Had there been a gun wound or cut wrists or other violence, it might be thought that a quick emotional storm had blacked out everything else. But with sleeping pills . . . her realistic disposition made self-destruction unlikely while loose ends dangled.

Yet it was known to many—and especially to Eunice Tietjens—that Tennessee had lately been much distressed. Anderson had been in Chicago and Tennessee had spent days trying to arrange a face-to-face meeting. Since his third marriage was on the rocks, some of her friends believed that she hoped for his return to her. He was well beyond fifty now, troubled about his writing, emotionally beaten in another marriage, altogether in need of help. Tennessee loved him more than ever, and if anything she was stronger than ever. A dream of once more becoming a sheltering harbor was natural enough.

For several years her reputation as a sculptor had been rising. Blanche Matthias had written in the *Evening Post:* "There is something about Tennessee Mitchell Anderson which suggests that new thing in art, life, clothes, which for want of a better term we call Movement." Many of her figures were satirical, some gently, as the furrow-browed club woman desperately seeking to comprehend a lecture by Bertrand Russell. Or outrageous, like the dignified but spindly shanked flapper wearing only a cloche hat, a strand of beads, gauntlet gloves, high-heel red shoes, and carrying a light swagger stick. Or savage, like the group of hefty naked females prudishly hiding their pubic regions with bunches of roses and carrots, a fan, an enlarged heart, and the bald false head of a man. She had told Blanche Matthias that "since childhood I have seen the strange pattern which faces and bodies assume, and when I began working I found I had a storehouse in my mind which was filled to overflowing with these remembered impressions and patterns, so I have never been at a loss for subjects." Her works had brought a part of her living and she had continued to teach both music and dancing. The *Tribune's* death story, besides carrying a photograph, called her "prominent in the Near North Side art colony." To younger men and women she was admired as a symbol of the sophisticated woman of the arts—just as nearly two decades earlier Floyd Dell had seen her as carrying the banner of the emancipated woman.

These very things would probably be against her with Anderson, since his own work was in disrepair and he sought the comfort of adulation rather than an urge to new boldness. Anyhow, she had a more direct matter to discuss with him. Eunice knew only that she had been making plans for a talk with him and was annoyed by his constant breaking of engagements. The subject to be considered had not been mentioned. Probably it had to do with Tennessee's autobiography, an answer to her letter inquiring whether he minded if she wrote of their life together. Already she had filled a composition book and other pages about her earlier life. It was too sketchy for publication, as she must have known. Many of the characters, Masters for one, would have to be named and better rounded with events and remembered conversations. In the first draft she had been ready to introduce Anderson. As Tennessee Mitchell Anderson it would have been very odd to have published an autobiography without mention of her celebrated ex-husband. She had not, of course, needed permission to write about him, yet in her letter had expressed a desire not to trade on his name. She had been aware that he disliked having certain myths exploded—like that of having been a successful manufacturer.

As the days passed, Tennessee had remarked to Eunice that she was taking more and more sedatives without getting proper rest. Finally the meeting with Anderson had taken place, at lunch, but he had brought along a friend as if for protection. Nothing was settled, Tennessee had reported to Eunice—adding that tonight she intended to take whatever number of pills were needed to get sleep. The tonight was Friday, December 20. Anderson had caught a train south. In an evening gown, Tennessee, who was always depressed during the festive holidays, had stopped at the studio of another tenant to check the time, and then had gone out with friends. Later, presumably, she had taken sleeping tablets, perhaps too many for her system to bear. Thus her death, in the opinion of authorities, was either from natural causes or from an accidental overdose of sedatives. Eunice's account of the heavy use of pills had been responsible, inadvertently, for the rise of the suicide theory among acquaintances.

Anderson when leaving Chicago had been in one of the most distraught moods of his life, next perhaps to that which had sent him stumbling down the railroad tracks from Elyria. Almost five years had passed since a novel of his had appeared. He had started some, but quit in despair. In mid-December he had written to Horace Liveright about a current project called *Beyond Desire:* "I have to have this book right, not only on account of its chances of success, but also because of myself. I want to whip out of this sense of defeat I have had." The book was going slowly and would not be ready for nearly three years. From being a writer's writer he had become a collector's writer, saving his hand-draft manuscripts for the advertising man who had financed his purchase of the Marion newspapers. Indeed he was passing into a state where he was a kind of institution, a famous writing man of the past on exhibit. Only in a rare story was he able to recapture a part of the man who in almost white heat had poured out *Winesburg, Ohio.*

The last fires of the Chicago Renaissance were going out as the Great Depression came to the world. Margaret Anderson and Jane

Heap in 1929 closed down the *Little Review* for good. Floyd Dell's savings had gone down the drain in the stock-market crash, a new play failed, and a year or two later he would disappear into the made-work Federal Writers' Project in Washington. Dreiser was never to undertake another "big" novel on the scale of *The Financier* or *An American Tragedy*. Masters settled into New York's old Hotel Chelsea on Twenty-third Street, a favorite of writers and artists, and rarely came out except for a swim in the YMCA pool across the street or a visit to The Players' clubrooms. Manuscripts were flowing from his pen as usual, with the usual published results of those after *Spoon River*. In 1924, *The New Spoon River* had been taken for a tired patch on the old. His debunking *Lincoln—the Man* (1931) would be called the work of a gone-sour writer moving in with the cranks.

It had seemed inevitable, somehow, that Vachel Lindsay, after winging through the skies, would crash to earth. After the war he had taken the lecture road again, more sought after than before. On a journey to England he was celebrated at Oxford. He had taken along his mother to prove to her that he was something of the genius she had prescribed, if in a different category. In the early twenties the path had grown harder. It was the age of T. S. Eliot, Sinclair Lewis, John Dos Passos, Hemingway. Audiences responded only to the old poems of Lindsay, mainly "General Booth" and "The Congo," and he was tired, very tired, of reciting them as if giving a vaudeville show. His temper unexpectedly was growing short. Once he departed from his routine and gave a diatribe against women's clubs, who, along with college groups, were his best-paying audiences. He was sick of lazy clubwomen who escaped their own housework, sick of their teas, and besides was of the opinion that they had "used" him. This was news coming from the Hobo Poet. The papers carried it far and wide, and the clubwomen belted him right back.

His mother died—Dr. Lindsay had already passed away—and, with the old home closed, he was lonely. Then, too, his sexual urge had been rising after his middle thirties. He talked more often of his deplorable virginity. At the same time his desire was for ever younger girls. He passionately courted teen-age Isadora Bennett, whose spirit was as flaming as her hair. She had grown up in Springfield, the daughter of stage people, and knew the Lindsay family. Then she had gone to the University of Chicago. He was enamored of her manner of reciting his poems—better, he said, than he could do them himself. She was made the heroine of his *The Golden Book of Springfield*, which was to have been his masterpiece but which came out badly confused. Isadora was extremely fond of him, but love for a man over twice her age—especially one lacking the strong male wallop—was out of the question.

Late in 1923 he came close to a nervous breakdown in Gulfport, Mississippi, and was forced to abandon his tour. For a year he taught at Gulfport Junior College for Girls, where he was, of course, in a delightful element. A young girl with whom he fell in love gave him a morsel of encouragement. Now he proclaimed himself Don Quixote rather than Ulysses; as his Dulcinea she had replaced Penelope. But in the end he was able to carry away only photographs of her. In 1925, he moved to Spokane, Washington, where he had many friends, and tried to send down firm roots. His hope was to be a kind of city poet, sponsored, even partly subsidized. The old love of hotels sapped his finances; he lived in one of the best. Yet here he found a girl, blonde, blue-eyed Elizabeth Conner, twenty-three, ready to go all the way to marriage. She was a Latin and English teacher in the high school, the unworldly daughter of an unworldly Presbyterian minister, enraptured by poetry and poets.

Briefly he hesitated, debating whether to cast off a dozen years and take to the vagabond road again. Perhaps it was too late; perhaps it was too late for marriage. In May of 1925 he came down on the side of marriage. The ceremony was performed in his hotel room, after someone hastily swept the Dulcinea photographs from the bureau top into a drawer.

Now the earthly world was very much with the poet. A daughter was born and then a son. Book royalties were low. He had to drive himself on the lecture trail, in a falling market. By 1929, desperate, he thought the answer was a return to Springfield. They renovated the home place, going far into debt. He found, of course, that going home again to his youth was not possible. His nerves went on deteriorating until he was in and out of reality, not helped when at home by the presence of his lank, dour minister father-in-law, who had taken up Springfield residence to watch over his daughter—and in Lindsay's opinion, as reported later by his wife, to murder him.

One night in early December of 1931, in more agony than usual, he told his wife that he must go tramping again, that he must be free to dream the old dreams, to write the old songs. Late, after she and the children were in bed, he got out his old albums, leafed through them, propped up the pictures of his children, and made for himself a death pallet on the bathroom floor. Downstairs he drained a bottle of Lysol but was in too much pain to find the pallet. On hands and knees he mounted the stairs, collapsed, and soon afterward died.

The suicide was not revealed until Edgar Lee Masters published a biography of him two years later. Springfield, the long-ago war now forgotten, named a bridge for him and put up a bust at one end.

Even Sandburg was encroached upon when the *Daily News* felt that it could no longer afford its good gray poet. His salary was not very high, but his work was not essential, and it was believed that separation would be less a hardship for him than for others. By now his *Abraham Lincoln: The Prairie Years* had provided a nest egg larger than modest. The dismissal only pushed him harder on *Lincoln: The War Years* and millionaire status. The firing naturally caused a trauma in so penurious a man, and as usual it brought his friends considerable mirth.

It happened that a very high *Daily News* executive and a lady editor were much taken with one another, at least to the degree of spending comfortable evenings in her apartment. When the lady invited Sandburg to drop by with his guitar for songs, he was happy to oblige. It was all pleasantly informal, just the three of them, the executive perhaps with his necktie loosened, the hostess perhaps in lounging pajamas. Sandburg performed admirably and was given a warm reception. Quite by coincidence, lesser executives had been going over the payroll to decide who might be spared, and among those to be pruned—unknown to the higher executive—was Sandburg.

The wounded monolith was furious when news of his dismissal was given to him. He saw a connection: it was like Nero ordering a fiddler-slave executed. He telephoned his friend Lloyd Lewis, *News* manager editor, thundering like a prophet of old: "Get out, Lloyd, get out of that whorehouse before it's too late!"

Lewis didn't get out, but the Sandburgs moved up into Michigan, leaving in Chicago only Harriet Monroe of the major Renaissance-makers—and she there only when she was not traveling.

24

An Upsurge in the Thirties

A NEW generation of Chicago novelists sprang up in the late twenties and early thirties, influenced to some degree by the Renaissance-makers, but their heritage and the times made a wide difference. They were city-nurtured rather than products of small towns or intellectuals from abroad, and they tended to portray the ethnic groups from which they had emerged. James T. Farrell wrote of the Irish, Meyer Levin of the Jews, Richard Wright of the Negroes. Nelson Algren, half Swede and half Jew, chose the Poles for subject matter. Albert Halper, a Jew, depicted the mixed elements he had been thrown with on manual labor jobs. All were hurled, before going far, into the grinding maw of Depression. Most were poor boys. Inevitably they turned, like their Renaissance forebears, into political radicals searching for a better world. The sense of commitment steadied their purpose, so that, reflecting their times, they were a fresh wave flowing over the brackish eddies of the twenties.

Farrell, although not the first to publish, was the earliest to make his mark large. He had grown up in an Irish neighborhood on the South Side, where he attended parochial schools and hung around with his comrades on the streets and in the pool halls. It was through Sherwood Anderson that he gained self-discovery. Working in a filling station, reading *Winesburg, Ohio* and other stories, he saw that Anderson had taken the little people of his environment and fashioned them into literature. Why, then, couldn't he do the same with the little people he knew? When it came to the actual writing, though, his bent was more in the naturalistic plodding vein of Dreiser. In the late twenties, far from a rah-rah student of the age, he was a kind of college bohemian, spending part of his time in the Jackson Park colony where Anderson had begun his public reading career.

Farrell did little reading from his manuscripts; the sight of their vast bulk would have driven away prospective listeners. But, as had Anderson, he won a reputation as an "unpublished author." Acquaintances with unlocked doors were never surprised to come upon Farrell, short, owlish behind his spectacles, disheveled, pounding on their typewriters. Sometimes he hauled his manuscripts around in a laundry bag. Yet recognition arrived early, compared with the time spent in the struggles of Dreiser, Anderson, Sandburg, and Masters. In 1932 the first of his *Studs Lonigan* trilogy appeared; when the last came out in 1935 he was a top-ranking name in U.S. letters.

Albert Halper was born on Chicago's West Side, son of a shopkeeper who had emigrated from Lithuania. He grew up on the West Side, drifting in his youth from job to job: order picker in a mail-order house, factory machine operator, postal sorter. After beginning to write, he, too, found a medium in the naturalistic form, weaving his experiences and observations into stories and novels. A measure of success came early to him, also. His novel *Union Square* in 1933 drew wide attention as interest grew in the hard lives of plain people. Critics, noting Halper's and Farrell's roughly similar works, began to speak of a new "Chicago school."

Meyer Levin's father was a tailor in a West Side ghetto which changed, as the boy grew up, to become Little Italy, sometimes called the Bloody Nineteenth Ward. The Levins stayed on because they owned a building. Yet Meyer remained all Jew, in fact obsessed with being a Jew in a mostly Christian world. He did well at Chicago University, especially in his English courses, and landed a job on the *Daily News* under the kindly eye of Henry Justin Smith. Of the new Chicago group he was the first to publish a book, a novel entitled *The Reporter*, which came out in 1929. It wasn't until 1937, however, that he arrived in the "Chicago school" with *The Old Bunch*, dealing with his youthful Jewish associates as Farrell had done with the Irish.

Richard Wright was the first of the group who was not Chicago-born. He did not arrive in the city until 1934, but it was into a Negro ghetto not very different from those he had known in the South. His father, a farm and mill worker, had deserted the family when the boy was five. His mother, a schoolteacher near Natchez, Mississippi, became an invalid when he was ten. That had meant orphan homes. At fifteen he had struck out on his own in Memphis. He was working in Chicago's post office when in a curious way he was pulled into a literary set. A group called the John Reed Club had been formed. It was guided mostly by Communists, whose program was to involve all the Negroes possible. There had been very little participation by Chicago Negroes in white cultural affairs. The club's leader one night issued an ultimatum: Some Negro artists and writers must be recruited. A member announced that a young Negro working beside him in the post office was, he believed, trying to be an author; he would invite him. This young man was Wright, and he came. Handsome, personable, talented—and of a coveted minority besides—he was soon a favorite. Other members on the WPA Writers' Project helped land a job for him. By 1938 he had won a prize with a book of stories, *Uncle Tom's Children,* which was a critical success. Two years later his best-selling *Native Son* would rocket him to fame.

Nelson Algren, youngest of the five, was a native of Detroit, but the family moved to Chicago when he was a boy, to the South Side into a mostly Irish neighborhood. Therefore he had no close relationship with his father's people, the Swedes, or his mother's, the German Jews. He worked his way through the University of Illinois, emerging into the Depression, and bummed his way to the Southwest. Out of his experiences he got material for a novel, *Somebody in Boots,* published in 1935. After returning to Chicago he was in the John Reed Club—there to welcome Wright—and also on the WPA Writers' Project. He married a Polish girl and lived on the Northwest side among the Poles, finding material for short stories and a novel, *Never Come Morning.* It would not be until 1949, however, that his *The Man With the Golden Arm* (Carl Sandburg had helped land him a grant to aid in the writing) would establish him as one of the nation's leading novelists.

Algren alone stayed in Chicago. As young men all the others had gone on, with New York the major destination. After catching briefly the old spirit of the Chicago Renaissance, they had hastily followed the majority of their predecessors to what they took for a more stimulating world. Yet they, too, had done their best work either in Chicago or out of their Chicago experiences.

Time had run out for most of the Renaissance-makers. After Vachel Lindsay, the first to go was Harriet Monroe. She had been, after all, past fifty when beginning the major work of her life. As the 1930's opened she had gone calmly into her seventies, editing

Poetry as before, worrying over her poets, and traveling the world. The Depression made fund-raising harder, but she managed. Chicago would never let down its grand old lady and her famous gem of a magazine, reflecting glory as it did on the city of its birth.

In the autumn of 1936 she went to South America for a convention of P.E.N. (International Association of Poets, Playwrights, Editors, Essayists, and Novelists). The journey had another purpose: she would have a chance to go up mountains, up to the ancient Inca ruins. Doctors warned her that she was too old and frail for such heights, but at seventy-six she was quite as brave as ever. The doctors were right. She died of a brain hemorrhage on September 26, in Arequipa, Peru.

The final dozen years of Sherwood Anderson's life were almost constant frustration, except for a domestic peace in his fourth marriage. The novel *Beyond Desire,* which he had explained to Liveright must be labored over endlessly to get right, did not come out right. By the time it was ready for publication in 1932 he had become greatly worried, like the rest of the nation, over the Depression, and was involving himself in the distress of Southern factory workers. He had made his hero into another confused Sam McPherson or Beaut McGregor—except that in the changed times he was dispatched to a martyr's death in a strike rather than to success and maundering philosophy. The side moods had lost the freshness of his earlier works.

It had been Anderson's good fortune soon after the breakup of his third marriage to meet pert, youngish Eleanor Copenhaver. Her home town was Marion, where his newspapers were located, but she had been away much of the time as an organizer of Southern factory women. Her interests deepened his social concern, but her main value to him was as a sympathetic admirer (without Tennessee Mitchell's often caustic criticism, which now might have been more than he could stand). After their marriage in 1932 she became a sort of curator, harboring him as befitted a national literary shrine while creating an atmosphere in which both hoped he would recover his powers.

At Ripshon, his fieldstone home near Marion, Anderson received the pampering he loved and needed. If a croquet game ran over into mealtime, Eleanor waited contentedly until he and his guests were ready to eat. Each morning he retired to a stone cabin where he "warmed up" for serious composition by writing letters. This was mostly an escape. He started novels and quit, or tried again on one discarded long ago. Sometimes he moved about the country, seeking the "feel" of the times. Out of these journeys came magazine pieces collected under the title *Puzzled America* (1935). They were not very satisfactory. He was able to depict characters and events only in the impressionistic manner of his fiction.

At the same time he was mellowing. This was shown in his amazingly changed view of that villain of old, his father. For a *Reader's Digest* "unforgettable character" series The Major came out a warm, knowing man long misunderstood by his son. Nostalgia was responsible for a vague, strange concept of modern life. The machines, he felt, were not only destroying civilization but, as a step in that direction, masculinity. The women were taking command. His last novel, *Kit Brandon,* published in 1936, was the story of a girl rumrunner among defeated males in a Southern rural country fallen on the evils of an encroaching machine society. It had little impact. The giant of the twenties was an aging, declining figure in the world of letters. He reworked old material—including a *Winesburg* play—and labored intermittently on his *Memoirs.*

In late February of 1941 Anderson and his wife embarked for South America, where he was to be an unofficial goodwill ambassador for the State Department and try to work up usable impressions for the *Reader's Digest.* On the way he fell ill of an intestinal obstruction. At Colon, Panama, he was taken from the ship to a hospital, where he died a few days later, on March 8, 1941. He was sixty-four.

Dreiser was next. His reputation, too, had gone down, and most of his books were out of print. To many, however, he was the old titan who had never been given his proper due, as Sinclair Lewis bowed to him when receiving a Nobel Prize. Either his power had diminished following *An American Tragedy* or other affairs had drawn off part of his creative force. Except for *Jennie Gerhardt, The Financier, The Titan,* and *The "Genius,"* bunched in the first half of the teens, a decade had elapsed between novels. By the thirties he was engrossed with political and economic and philosophical matters. Always a sympathizer with the poor, he had nevertheless rather openly admired the powerful who got the better of the weak, like his Cowperwood. Now he turned to a greater faith in the ability of the common people to redress their wrongs. Like Anderson, he tried to depict the Depression suffering in magazine articles and his book *Tragic America*. And he involved himself deeply in getting up social protests and acting on reform committees.

As always, Dreiser's relations with women were stormy. The affair he had begun long ago with Helen Richardson, a secretary with ambitions to be an actress, had persisted through countless explosions. She was twenty-three years his junior, stunning enough to retain his pride, yet with a devotion and fierce spirit enabling her to survive their quarrels. As he had tried to make a place for Elaine Hyman-Kirah Markham in the New York theater, he worked, with a degree of success, to land roles for Helen in the movies. Eventually they were living most of the time in Hollywood. After the death of his wife in 1942 freed him of the bond of more than four decades, they were married.

Then, approaching his middle seventies, Dreiser experienced a creative surge. *The Stoic*, final book of his Cowperwood trilogy, partly written, was much in his thoughts. He put ahead of it, though, another earlier project, *The Bulwark*, the story of a Quaker banker. Dictating slowly, he finished both, although by the standard of his earlier novels they lacked vigor and force. On December 27, 1945, he was still revising *The Stoic*. Next day he went to bed with a severe kidney attack, and the day after that he died. He was seventy-four.

Masters was in his seventy-fifth year when, just before Christmas of 1943, the newspapers told of his being found ill and starving in the two rooms where he lived alone in New York's Chelsea Hotel. The report was less than fully accurate. True, he had been rushed to a hospital and found suffering from pneumonia and malnutrition. The latter was not due, however, to lack of funds. His teeth and appetite were poor and he was apt to nibble on cheese or fruit rather than go to a restaurant for a meal. The startling news stories caused the Author's League to raise a purse for him. The Academy of American Poets awarded him a five-thousand-dollar fellowship.

Conceivably Masters took wry pleasure from the false reports after his health improved. In his biography of Vachel Lindsay he had indicted the nation for shoddy treatment of its great poets. The starving tale might at least have been a shock to the public conscience. Besides, the error had only been one of detail. For thirty years, ever since opening his ears fully to the song of Apollo, each new work had, he felt, been insulted if not ignored. People bought the old *Spoon River* (it accounted for half his income) but *The New Spoon River,* in his opinion a deeper work, had caused no more of a ripple than his other later books of verse. His novels were forgotten, his books on Lincoln and Mark Twain and Walt Whitman and Chicago rarely consulted. Yet whatever the agony, he had played out his adopted role to the end. His family begged him not to publish *Across Spoon River,* his autobiography, for the working over of old love affairs had made them tawdry. He replied that it was the duty of a literary man to tell all.

Now he was too old to live alone. His second wife took him in with her and their teen-age son. She had been Ellen Coyne, one of the poetry group at the University of Chicago, when he had courted her. They had been married in 1926—she thirty-one years his junior—and afterward she had taught English in colleges, usually spending only the summers with him. Now as the years passed he became increasingly enfeebled, strong of mind and spirit but writing to friends that he was a "basket case." At the age of eighty-one he died in a Philadelphia convalescent home on March 5, 1950.

Two others of the ten major Renaissance figures died in the fifties. Maurice Browne had fallen from the heights of a London stage tycoon, mostly due to quarrels with associates. In 1949 he was for a while artist-in-residence at the University of California, then returned to England, where he lived out his days on a pension from his ex-wife, Nellie Van Volkenburg of the old Chicago Little Theatre adventure. He died on January 21, 1955, aged seventy-four.

Francis Hackett's residence in Denmark was interrupted by the German occupation during World War II, and with his wife he returned to the United States for the duration. By now his reputation as a critic was overshadowed by his biographical works—*Henry the Eighth, Francis the First, Queen Anne Boleyn.* He died in 1962.

In 1966, half a century after the best work of the Renaissance was done, three of the major figures were still alive.

Floyd Dell had not published for a long time. It was as though he had paid with later silence for the extraordinary bloom of his youth. In the midst of the Depression, with a wife and two boys to support, he had taken a job on the WPA Writers' Project in Washington. His admirers had waited for new books or plays, but even his magazine writings diminished until new generations, reading his books or literary accounts about him, thought of him as a legendary figure long since dead. After his retirement—he had continued to do government work—he maintained his home in Washington, reading widely as always, exchanging long letters with friends, graciously aiding scholars seeking to recapture the events of which he had been a part.

Margaret Anderson wrote to an acquaintance not long ago from Chalet Rose, her home in Le Cannet, France: "I'm living as a *very* happy recluse, seeing almost no one, and I shall stay on in this loved country until I die." This was not to say that she was idle. At that moment she was engaged on two books, one called *The Entirely Beautiful*, a protest against modern ugliness, and *For Art's Sake*, an extension of her old crusades. She expected only French and perhaps British publication. In 1961, though, her *The Unknowable Gurdjieff* was issued in the United States. A small book aimed at explaining and advancing the ideas of Gurdjieff, who had died in 1949, it was at the same time a personal document with no loss of the verve that had gone into the *Little Review* and her autobiographical *My Thirty Years War* and *The Fiery Fountains*. Jane Heap also had remained loyal to the Gurdjieff creed, working with study groups until her death in London in 1964.

Carl Sandburg, of course, has grown into a kind of U.S. monument. His *Lincoln: The War Years* (1938), added to his earlier Lincoln books, has made him in the popular mind the true biographer-singer of the national hero. His newer poetry has gained somewhat lesser attention. He wrote a very long novel called *Remembrance Rock*, which he felt told the story of much of America, and part of his autobiography, *Always the Young Strangers*, along with lesser works. Meanwhile he continued to lecture, usually with his guitar at hand for intervals of folk songs. He was still, in a way, the hobo. He enjoyed being put up in a wealthy home, where he would raid the refrigerator at his leisure, get up late in the afternoon, organize the household around himself. His attitude was simple: The hosts seemed to want him for his fame, so let them pay a price for it. (With old friends, though, he was quick to pick up the check.) From Chicago he moved to Michigan, and then to a stately house at Flat Rock, North Carolina. When he visited the President of the United States, the event was handled by the newspapers as a mutual honor.

In late years the Renaissance-makers have been making a comeback, both with critics and general readers. For a long time Dreiser had been put down as too awkward, too gauche, not sensitive enough to be a true artist. Now there is a reappraisal. Many of his works are in paperbacks; most reprinted of all is *Sister Carrie*, which is the more pertinent owing to its place as a catalyst of the Chicago Renaissance. As if he were living again, Dreiser not long ago was personally lambasted in a massive biography reminiscent of Elia W. Peattie. The attention was at least a sign that he is once more influencing the reading and writing of the times.

Modern poets and critics as a rule downgrade the main poets of the Renaissance. The tunes of Vachel Lindsay are out of fashion. Doubt is again expressed that Sandburg is a poet at all. Masters is called verbose and often derivative, and even the techniques of *Spoon River* are decried. Yet Lindsay still has a substantial body of appreciators. And it seems that Sandburg's famous-poet-national-hero stance has distracted readers from the earthy vigor of his early poetry. In many areas Masters' *Spoon River* is being rediscovered. Readers of a new paperback edition find the old shock of recognition. A Broadway production of readings interspersed with songs ran for many weeks; another was put on in London, still another in Chicago. Harriet Monroe's *Poetry* is, after more than half a century, the most firmly established magazine of verse in the world.

Sherwood Anderson's reputation is rising again. Hemingway never acknowledged a debt to him, but others did: William Faulkner and Thomas Wolfe. The plotless story that he pioneered has become a standard form. For young readers there is nothing quite like the drench of icy water from the reading of his *Winesburg, Ohio*. A volume of his letters has been published, scholars have pored over his scrawled manuscripts, getting up theses and books. Floyd Dell's *Moon-Calf* is in reprint for study in the colleges, Margaret Anderson's *Little Review* is being awarded a hallowed place in literature, and the little theater movement, rising from Maurice Browne's experiment, has spread over the nation.

Appreciations and Notes on Sources

FIRST of all I want to thank the Louis M. Rabinowitz Foundation, Inc., for a grant of money which supported more thorough research than otherwise would have been possible. In the dedication I have already thanked Angus Cameron for suggesting the book, but here I would like to pay further tribute for his guidance of the project through the Foundation. Let me especially thank, too, Larry Goldberg for his aid in research and unflagging support. Naturally various libraries have been helpful. Much original material was available in the Newberry Library, Chicago, which extended to me its splendid facilities. I am particularly indebted to Amy Nyholm, who is more familiar than anybody else with the Sherwood Anderson, Floyd Dell, Eunice Tietjens, and other collections, and to James M. Wells, curator of the Rare Book Room. The library of the Chicago Historical Society provided much useful material. The New York Public Library is, I think, underestimated as a rich source of information to be found nowhere else, and I pay my respects to that valuable institution. I heartily thank Julia Bartling, reference librarian, and others of the staff of the University of Iowa Library who were patient with me as I hauled wheelbarrow loads of books and bound magazines from the stacks and consulted material in the Special Collections division.

The bibliography is selected, as noted, and I apologize to scholars for not being more detailed with notes. Still, having read hundreds of dropped-note books, essays, and theses, I am in doubt as to whether extensive notes are an asset or a pedantic mask for errors or failure of penetration.

The most helpful source person, over all, was Floyd Dell. After all, he had been at the center of the early Renaissance, and his memories were rich and clear. Of the other chief Renaissance-makers, only Margaret Anderson and Carl Sandburg are alive. Margaret Anderson aided greatly with correspondence from her home near Paris. Carl Sandburg has ignored my communications to him. Fortunately his amusing tale of his early years when he was "Charlie" in *Only the Young Strangers* was available, along with much other printed material and, above all, live sources. In view of the godlike stance of the old poet-biographer in his later years, it may be just as well. Another, if minor, figure who rebuffed me was the late Ben Hecht. Again I was content, for no one had more personal and, to me, false views of the Renaissance.

I can best define the personal-source contributions by relating them to the individuals whom I consider the ten chief Renaissance-makers, and I will set them down according to their appearance in the book.

FLOYD DELL. Himself, of course, and his collection in the Newberry Library. Others interviewed: his wife, B. Marie; Lucian Cary, a book figure, of course, in his own right; critic Harry Hansen; Otto McFeeley, Chicago newspaperman and fellow Socialist, who was also on intimate terms with Carl Sandburg; Elaine Hyman-Kyra (formerly Kirah) Markham, who is herself a major character—this by letter; Ellen Van Volkenburg Browne; Margaret (Mrs. Brör) Nordfeldt. Dell's first wife, Margery Currey, was, in my view, of great worth to the Renaissance. She was known by most of the above and I was in correspondence with her sister, Mrs. Paul Day, and her sister-in-law, Mrs. Harold Currey. I spoke with her niece, Mrs. Philip Tobin and her friend Mary Dougherty, and had a reminiscence from a girlhood chum, Ruth Raymond.

THEODORE DREISER. His flood of autobiographical works provide a wealth of information about his early life. I had the benefit of the memories of William Lengel, his secretary, companion in Chicago, and friend for the rest of his life. Homer Croy told me, among other things, of the threats to Dreiser of mayhem or worse and the chair-arm scene with Thelma Cudlipp. Dell related his various experiences with Dreiser. Elaine Hyman-Kyra Markham wrote me of her original boredom with the hero-monster and their subsequent friendship. I am indebted to Ellen Van Volkenburg and Margaret Nordfeldt for passing on their keen observations of

Dreiser, the one from the vantage point of skilled actress-director, the other from that of trained psychologist. Vincent Starrett recalled Dreiser's presence at Margery Currey's studio when Margaret Anderson raised the flag for her *Little Review*. W. W. Swanberg kindly exchanged information with me while engaged on his massive biography of Dreiser.

SHERWOOD ANDERSON. Floyd Dell knew him at the most critical point of his writing life. The one person who knows most about his first marriage is, of course, his first wife, Cornelia Anderson, who lives with their daughter, Miriam. But Cornelia will not talk about her ex-husband, nor will Miriam. I did speak with one of the Anderson sons, John, artist and art teacher in Chicago (the other, Robert, is dead). But John, if able to throw light on those dark days in Elyria, was reluctant to do so. The best research done on Anderson for that period is by William Sutton, who, for a thesis written more than twenty years ago, was able to find much original information. Sutton's contribution has not been properly appreciated or even consulted by most critics who write about Anderson. I talked with Sutton and made careful use of his work. Another thesis of great value was that of William L. Phillips, who by close study of the *Winesburg, Ohio* manuscript (in the Newberry Library) went a long way toward establishing the sequence in which the tales were written. The notes of conversations with Anderson made by Hi Simon were furnished to me by his ex-wife, Bernadine Szold, who also gave me the word picture of Ernest Hemingway reading his *Torrents of Spring*. She knew Anderson well. Y. K. Smith told me of the Anderson-Hemingway incidents in Chicago. Ernestine Evans gave me her memories of Anderson reading from *Windy*. Others who provided first-hand information were Eleanor (Mrs. Sherwood) Anderson, Fanny Butcher, Netta Cooper, Sue DeLorenzi, Christopher Sergel, Mrs. Vernon Lake, and Mrs. Mitchell Dawson.

The reader will have noted that I consider Tennessee Mitchell to be one of the more fascinating characters of the book. Bernadine Szold, who aided me tirelessly by letters, was even a closer friend of Tennessee than of Anderson. Other friends of Tennessee with whom I spoke were Lucile Swan, former wife of Jerome Blum, the artist, and Rudolph Weisenborn, the artist, and his wife. Blanche Matthias wrote me of Tennessee and her sculpture. Mark Turbyfill described Tennessee's funeral and gave me other information. Jack Daball of the Jackson, Michigan, public library discovered facts about the Mitchell family and other early information about Tennessee. The facts about Tennessee's will, the inheritance by her sister, and the like, I discovered in Chicago court records. My strenuous efforts to trace the sister were unrewarding. However, Mitchell Dawson, who had acted for the sister at the time of Tennessee's death, had secured from her the fragment of Tennessee's autobiography and had subsequently placed it in the Newberry Library, where I consulted it.

CARL SANDBURG. Dell knew him slightly, as described. Otto McFeeley was his friend from the early Chicago years. Mary Dougherty knew him on Hearst's *American*. Mary's sister, Kathryn Lewis, wife of the late Lloyd Lewis, a Civil War author, was a friend of many years. Insurance executive Alfred MacArthur, the brother of the literary Charles, was a host to Sandburg on his in-city tramp outings in the early days. Jerry Nedwick, longtime proprietor of Chicago secondhand book stores, furnished at little expense many of the old magazines largely from which Sandburg wrote his Lincoln books. Jack Ryan, an old Wobbly, knew Sandburg from far back. Ralph Newman, proprietor of the Lincoln Book Store in Chicago, is a collector of Sandburgiana, which he kindly allowed me to see, and is a longtime friend. So is Paul Angle, the noted Chicago historian. For half a century Sandburg has been an occasional guest in the home of Mary Hastings Bradley, the author and big game hunter. Geraldine Udell knew Sandburg first when he hung out in her parents' Radical Book Store. Harry Hansen sat with the graying poet at Schlogl's. Mrs. Mitchell Dawson first knew Sandburg when her husband was getting up lectures for him. I talked with all the people mentioned above. I see no point in attributing the various Sandburg anecdotes to individuals, especially as they were told by many.

EDGAR LEE MASTERS. The person I talked with who knew Masters best in his time of glory was Cloyd Head. In those days a poet-playwright, Head was married to Eunice Tietjens. She, as an associate of Harriet Monroe on *Poetry*, was a special friend of Masters. Often the Heads visited Masters at his summer home for long weekends filled with conversation. To them he was so brilliant and varied as to be sometimes exhausting. Head fully understood that Masters felt like a genius, acted like a genius, and—who could tell?—maybe was a genius. In my view Masters is the most interesting character of the book—perhaps because at first, judged on his published photographs and autobiographical writings, he appeared so monumentally dull. One of Masters' daughters, Marcia Schmid, was an excellent source for her father's early married background, especially because she well understood the problems her mother had faced. I talked with Dexter Masters, novelist and consumer expert, who had known his uncle in New York, and with Alice Davis Tibbetts, who had served as Masters' secretary and, as a near-worshipper, had kept notes of his conversations. Unhappily, Masters' second wife, Ellen, was abroad most of the period during which I was writing the book and we were limited to correspondence. Others who gave me reminiscences were Dorothy Dow (Mrs. James Fitzgerald), August Derleth, Mrs. Chester Hart (daughter of Eunice Tietjens), Isadora Bennett, and Danny Reed. The first actor readings of *Spoon River* were given by Mr. Reed in the Chicago Little Theatre.

VACHEL LINDSAY. The best direct insight into him was provided by Isadora Bennett, who had known him while she was a little girl, had later been courted by him, and in whose home in New York (she is the wife of Danny Reed) he was often a guest until the end of his days. The biographies by Edgar Lee Masters and Eleanor Ruggles were valuable, and obviously much was gained by study of Lindsay's privately issued publications. Dell, of course, knew Lindsay in the sad-sweet time prior to his ascent to fame. Ralph A. Schroeder, a Lindsay collector, put valuable material at my disposal.

FRANCIS HACKETT. Since he was more of a layer of the groundwork than a full participant in the Renaissance, I was not compelled to treat him at as much length as the others. Dell, of course, knew him intimately on the job at the start, and his autobiography provided sufficient background on his earlier life. George Soule generously wrote for me the account of Hackett's explosion in the New York publisher's office.

MAURICE BROWNE. His wife and co-founder of the Chicago Little Theatre, Ellen Van Volkenburg Browne was obviously the very best living source. She was gracious in the time given for interviews, and a better observer of events and people could not have been desired. Another member of the original cast, Alice Gerstenberg, later a playwright, speculated that of the two Brownes, Ellen was the stronger, and may even have made the larger contribution to the Little Theatre. Miss Gerstenberg was an indefatigable and charming informant. Much, too, was gained from a talk with the gracious Helen Head Hunter, an early cast member (who knew also Sherwood Anderson well and indeed lived for a while at the same time as he in the rooming house where he wrote *Winesburg*). Raymond Jonson, Danny Reed, and Bernadine Szold were other cast members who gave me their recollections. Margery H. Drake of the Rare Book division of the University of Michigan Library was extremely helpful by searching out material from the Little Theatre collection stored there.

HARRIET MONROE. I relied mostly on her autobiography and the memoirs of associates for the facts of her life and career. However, excellent word portraits of her were drawn for me by Ralph Fletcher Seymour, Cloyd Head, Geraldine Udell, who for many years was business manager of *Poetry*, and Mrs. Chester Hart, who as a little girl was often at the *Poetry* office with her mother, Eunice Tietjens.

MARGARET ANDERSON. Oddly, a question about her in the reference room of the Chicago Public Library brought only a blank stare. Perhaps she has been gone too long from both Chicago and the country. I was able to find only two Chicagoans who knew Margaret: Ralph Fletcher Seymour, who remembered her from the days she walked, a blonde goddess, in the Annex's Peacock Alley, and Mark Turbyfill, who had visited her in France and was still in touch. Dell was, as usual, an excellent source for the old days. I talked, too, with Joanna Fortune, a former backer (although not agreeing with many of her aims), and with Monroe Wheeler, who still sees her now and again in France. George Soule wrote the brief memoir for me. Mrs. Donald Culross Peattie, daughter-in-law of Elia W. Peattie, confirmed that Elia was indeed "Sadie Iverson" (although disagreeing with my allegation that Elia was a "genteel" critic). After a long search I found Charles (Caesar) Zwaska—in the Ozark mountains of all places—and had a long visit with him. He has kept up with Margaret over the years—more than fifty of them now—and indeed sat with her and Jane Heap at the feet of Gurdjieff in France.

Margaret, although nowadays a recluse, was gracious with correspondence. Her *My Thirty Years War* still makes exciting reading. Jane Heap died in London in 1964. Her sister, Mrs. H. L. Clark, sent me valuable background information about her.

Others who assisted me in one manner or another include Harry T. Moore, Nelson Algren, James T. Farrell, John Drury, Adolph A. Kroch, John S. Mayfield, M. O. Penn, Franklin Meine, Henry Sell, Janice Cole, Janet Flanner, Lois Kramer Bayles, Jackson Bryher, Alice Hamilton, Edmund Randolph Biddle, Kathryn Krug Stevens, Peter Rubin, Ija Adler, Dan Levin, Frank Walsh, and John and Dell Bobbitt.

Selected Bibliography

Anderson, Margaret, *My Thirty Years War;* Covici-Friede, New York; 1930.

Anderson, Sherwood, *Marching Men;* John Lane Company, New York; 1917.

———— *Memoirs;* Harcourt, Brace & Company, New York; 1942.

———— *No Swank;* Centaur Press, Philadelphia; 1934.

———— *Windy McPherson's Son;* John Lane Company, New York; 1916.

———— *Winesburg, Ohio;* B. W. Huebsch & Company, New York; 1919.

Anderson, Tennessee Mitchell, manuscript autobiography, in Newberry Library, Chicago.

Browne, Maurice, *Too Late to Lament;* Indiana University Press, Bloomington, Ind.; 1956.

Chase, Cleveland B., *Sherwood Anderson;* Robert M. McBride & Company, New York; 1927.

Cook, George Cram, *Greek Coins,* with memorabilia by Floyd Dell, Edna Kenton, Susan Glaspell; George H. Doran Company, New York; 1926.

Currey, Margery, to Floyd Dell, undated and unsigned letter in Dell collection, Newberry Library, Chicago; identified by author through handwriting and confirmed by Dell.

Dell, Floyd, *Homecoming;* Farrar & Rinehart; 1933.

———— *Women As World Builders;* Forbest & Company, Chicago; 1913.

Dreiser, Helen, *My Life with Dreiser;* The World Publishing Co., Cleveland and New York; 1951.

Dreiser, Theodore, *Dawn;* Horace Liveright, Inc., New York; 1931.

———— *Hoosier Holiday;* John Lane Company, New York; 1916.

———— *Jennie Gerhardt;* Harper & Brothers, New York; 1911.

———— *Sister Carrie;* Doubleday, Page & Co., New York; 1900.

———— *The Titan;* John Lane Company, New York; 1914.

Dudley, Dorothy, *Dreiser and the Land of the Free;* Beechcroft Press, New York; 1932.

Duffey, Bernard, *The Chicago Renaissance in American Letters;* Michigan State University Press, Ann Arbor; 1954.

Elias, Robert H., editor, *Letters of Theodore Dreiser;* University of Pennsylvania Press, Philadelphia; 1959.

———— *Theodore Dreiser, Apostle of Nature;* Alfred A. Knopf, Inc., New York; 1949.

Friday Literary Review of the Chicago *Evening Post,* 1909 through 1912. Bound copies in Newberry Library, Chicago.

Fuller, Henry B., *Under the Skylights;* D. Appleton and Company, New York; 1901.

Glaspell, Susan, *The Road to the Temple;* Frederick A. Stokes Company, New York; 1927.

Goldman, Emma, *Living My Life;* Alfred A. Knopf, Inc., 1931.

Griffin, Constance M., *Fuller, Henry Blake,* dissertation for Ph.D.; University of Pennsylvania, Philadelphia; 1929.

Hackett, Francis, *I Chose Denmark;* Doubleday, Doran & Company, New York; 1940.

Howe, Irving, *Sherwood Anderson;* William Sloane Associates, New York; 1951.

Jones, Howard Mumford, editor, with Walter B. Rideout, *Letters of Sherwood Anderson;* Little, Brown & Company, Boston; 1953.

Lindsay, Vachel, *Adventures While Preaching the Gospel of Beauty;* Michael Kennerley Co., New York; 1913.

———— *Collected Poems;* The Macmillan Company, New York; 1952.

———— *Rhymes to Be Traded for Bread;* published by himself; 1912. Consulted in Special Collections, University of Iowa Library, Iowa City.

Little Review, Margaret C. Anderson, editor. Files consulted in Newberry Library, Chicago.

Masters, Edgar Lee, *Across Spoon River* (autobiography); Farrar & Rinehart, New York; 1936.

——— *The Spoon River Anthology;* The Macmillan Company, New York; 1915.

Mencken, H. L., "The Literary Capital of the United States," in the London *Nation;* supplement edited by Francis Hackett; April 1920.

Monroe, Harriet, *A Poet's Life;* The Macmillan Company, New York; 1938.

Norman, Charles, *Ezra Pound;* The Macmillan Company, New York; 1960.

Phelps, William Louis, *Sherwood Anderson's Winesburg, Ohio,* dissertation for Ph.D.; University of Chicago; 1949.

Powys, John Cowper, *Autobiography;* New Directions, New York; 1960.

Putzel, Max, *William Marion Reedy;* Harvard University Press, Cambridge, Mass.; 1963.

Ruggles, Eleanor, *The West-Going Heart* (biography of Vachel Lindsay); W. W. Norton & Company, Inc., New York; 1959.

Sandburg, Carl, *Always the Young Strangers;* Harcourt, Brace & Company, New York; 1953.

——— articles and poems in *Tomorrow,* a magazine; October 1905 and July 1906. Copies in New York Public Library, New York.

——— *Chicago Poems;* Henry Holt & Company, New York; 1916.

Sandburg, Charles A. (Carl), *In Reckless Ecstacy;* Asgard Press, Galesburg, Ill.; 1904.

Seymour, Ralph Fletcher, *Some Went That Way;* published by himself; Chicago; 1945.

Simon, Hi, Notes on Sherwood Anderson, made following interviews, and made available to the author by Bernadine Szold, former wife of Simon.

Social Evil in Chicago, published by the Vice Commission of Chicago, Inc., for distribution by the American Vigilance Association; 4th edition, July 1, 1912. Consulted in Newberry Library, Chicago.

Sutton, William Alfred, *Sherwood Anderson's Formative Years,* dissertation for Ph.D.; Ohio State University, Columbus, Ohio; 1943.

Tanselle, George Thomas, *Faun at the Barricades: The Life and Works of Floyd Dell,* dissertation for Ph.D.; Northwestern University, Evanston, Ill.; 1959.

Index